THE LANGUAGE LIBRARY

THE WORDS WE USE

First published May 1954 by
ANDRE DEUTSCH LIMITED
12 Thayer Street Manchester Square
London W1

Second impression December 1954

Printed in Great Britain by
TONBRIDGE PRINTERS LTD
Tonbridge Kent

CONTENTS

written for English-speaking people, to pay a great deal of attention
to the freakish, the idiosyncratic, the bizarre, the obscure, the provincial, and the vestigial. All these things are interesting and illuminating and worth attending to and, in a sense, important; but what is more
important than any of them is the normal and the general, and, just
because native speakers of any variety of English are so familiar with
what is for them normal and general, and unconsciously so sequacious
of its unceasing movement, they are likely to be as imperfectly aware
of its essential qualities and tendencies as of those of the air they breathe'.[1]

Critics concerned particularly with the present-day language may
also feel that too much emphasis is placed upon the period before 1450,
though this is more apparent than real. It has, however, been done
deliberately, in order to emphasize how much of our everyday vocabulary was firmly established in the language some five hundred years
ago, and to show that, although this hard core of language is overshadowed in the dictionary by a multitude of newer adoptions and
formations, most of the words which form the bulk of our modern
working-vocabulary were in use in the language by the end of the
fifteenth century. Sixty years ago Emerson made the same point when
he said: 'It will be noted that the author has emphasized throughout the
development of the native element in English. This has been done
because many studies of the English language seem to give undue
prominence to the foreign element, and to leave an incorrect impression
as to what would have been the development of our mother tongue if
there had been no such contact with foreign nations as has taken place
in the history of the English people'.[2] The treatment here is somewhat
broader, for there is detailed treatment of the earlier loan-words which
were established in the language so early that they seem now to be as
natural as our native words, but no apology is necessary for repeating
and re-emphasizing this point, for it is one that can be too easily overlooked if English vocabulary is studied from the dictionary and not
from the words as we actually use them in everyday speech and writing.

Other aspects of the study of vocabulary might well have been
expected: the change in the meanings of words through the centuries
is a fascinating topic; the range of vocabulary could well have been
extended to include words peculiar to regional dialects, which are as
much the living English language as the literary language and Standard
English; a list might have been compiled of writers to whom credit is
given for the first use of a particular word in literature, and a discussion
of Place-names and Personal-names would not have been out of place.
The treatment was, however, restricted by the permitted length of the
book, which had to be kept within reasonable bounds if it was to serve

CONTENTS

FOR BETTY

PREFACE

This account of the development of our English vocabulary had its origin in a series of lectures designed for first-year students taking Honours in English Language and Literature who would perhaps not specialize later on the linguistic side of the syllabus. In the present work the scope has been extended, some explanatory material added, and the number of illustrations increased, in the hope that it would appeal to a wider class of people interested in their language in a more general way. It is not intended for the specialist, who will quickly realise that there is little fresh material here, though the treatment may present a new aspect of the subject, but rather to the amateurs interested in their language, to students not specializing in the linguistic side of English, and perhaps to those who are, since here they will find a good deal of the available material collected in an easily-accessible form. In this attempt to be all things to all men there is a distinct risk of falling between two stools, for the student, even the non-specialist, requires much that is not necessary for the general reader, and the latter needs guidance which the student finds unnecessary. Perhaps a word of advice may be useful here for the reader who knows little of mediæval English. Such a reader may, in Chapter Four, safely ignore the lengthy word-lists illustrative of the Old English poetic vocabulary, and the examination of the vocabulary of the prose passage from Ælfric, so long as the main lessons of the chapter are learnt, namely, the inherent richness of the vocabulary of Old English, its capacity to meet all the demands of the people using it, its importance for the everyday language of our own time, its great capacity to extend itself almost indefinitely by derivation and compounding, and its independence, its preference for native material rather than loan-words when the need arose to express new ideas.

Some justification is perhaps needed for the choice of material, which has been strictly limited by the title. It would have been easy to confine attention to the later period, to the freak formations of some modern writers, and to list, if not explain, the host of fantastic and specialized terms of the present century, but all this has been rejected, and attention directed to words which have established themselves firmly in the language, and stood the test of time, rather than to creations which may be merely ephemeral. As J. W. Clark has well said: 'Just because of the variety of forms of discourse called English, and because of the human faculty of wonder, it is tempting, in any book on the subject

7

written for English-speaking people, to pay a great deal of attention to the freakish, the idiosyncratic, the bizarre, the obscure, the provincial, and the vestigial. All these things are interesting and illuminating and worth attending to and, in a sense, important; but what is more important than any of them is the normal and the general, and, just because native speakers of any variety of English are so familiar with what is for them normal and general, and unconsciously so sequacious of its unceasing movement, they are likely to be as imperfectly aware of its essential qualities and tendencies as of those of the air they breathe'.[1]

Critics concerned particularly with the present-day language may also feel that too much emphasis is placed upon the period before 1450, though this is more apparent than real. It has, however, been done deliberately, in order to emphasize how much of our everyday vocabulary was firmly established in the language some five hundred years ago, and to show that, although this hard core of language is overshadowed in the dictionary by a multitude of newer adoptions and formations, most of the words which form the bulk of our modern working-vocabulary were in use in the language by the end of the fifteenth century. Sixty years ago Emerson made the same point when he said: 'It will be noted that the author has emphasized throughout the development of the native element in English. This has been done because many studies of the English language seem to give undue prominence to the foreign element, and to leave an incorrect impression as to what would have been the development of our mother tongue if there had been no such contact with foreign nations as has taken place in the history of the English people'.[2] The treatment here is somewhat broader, for there is detailed treatment of the earlier loan-words which were established in the language so early that they seem now to be as natural as our native words, but no apology is necessary for repeating and re-emphasizing this point, for it is one that can be too easily overlooked if English vocabulary is studied from the dictionary and not from the words as we actually use them in everyday speech and writing.

Other aspects of the study of vocabulary might well have been expected: the change in the meanings of words through the centuries is a fascinating topic; the range of vocabulary could well have been extended to include words peculiar to regional dialects, which are as much the living English language as the literary language and Standard English; a list might have been compiled of writers to whom credit is given for the first use of a particular word in literature, and a discussion of Place-names and Personal-names would not have been out of place. The treatment was, however, restricted by the permitted length of the book, which had to be kept within reasonable bounds if it was to serve its original purpose and be within the means of the student and the general reader.

The debt to the *New English Dictionary*, without which a book such as this would be impossible, is obvious, but even then the survey is necessarily incomplete, for much work still remains to be done on the influence of individual languages. Moreover, our knowledge of the vocabulary of earlier periods is also incomplete, great as is the N.E.D., and until the great period-dictionaries promised by the Americans are completed we shall not achieve finality either in placing accurately the first appearance of a word, or indicating the author who first used it.

No writer on the English language today can escape obligations to the many workers who have gone before, and this work, from the way in which it has grown, necessarily owes much to earlier scholars. Acknowledgement is made where these obligations are recognized or remembered, but many a turn of phrase, many a point of argument, many a particularly well-chosen example will have been unconsciously incorporated. It seems best, therefore, to make a general acknowledgement of indebtedness, in particular to the works listed in Section A of the bibliography, and in general to the many other works which have treated the question of English vocabulary, and to express regret for the use of any material borrowed or adapted and not specifically acknowledged because of the difficulty of identifying the source so long after a particular work has been read.

Several of my colleagues have read the work, in manuscript or in proof, and have placed additional material at my disposal. One in particular, who insists in remaining anonymous, has read through the whole book while it was still in the proof stage, and his diligence and scholarly attitude have enabled me to avoid numerous slips. For such errors as remain the responsibility is mine. A pupil, Mr D. H. Shaw, has kindly revised and enlarged the index.

TABLE OF CONTRACTIONS

IE	Indo-European
ME	Middle English
NE	New English
NHG	New High German
OE	Old English
O Fr.	Old French
O Fris.	Old Frisian
OHG	Old High German
ON	Old Norse
OS	Old Saxon
PG	Primitive Germanic

CHAPTER ONE

*

INTRODUCTION

This book is, as its title implies, concerned only with the vocabulary of English. It is not a history of the English Language, but merely a study of one aspect of that large subject, and we shall, therefore, not be concerned in the following chapters with the sounds of English words, the syntax of English, that is, the arrangement of the words in sentences, nor what is loosely referred to as grammar, by which those who thus use the term mean the inflexion of words and their function in the sentence, except when these three aspects of the study of the English language have some influence upon either the formation or development of words themselves. But the history of the words cannot be ignored in a study of vocabulary, and so we shall concern ourselves with the origins of our words, the ways in which they have been formed, and the ways in which they have developed and changed through the centuries.

The scope of the work has been deliberately limited to include only words which have been accepted in standard dictionaries, or which, if not yet accepted, have so wide a currency that they merit attention. Few dictionaries manage to keep up with the constant increase in words; indeed, the larger and more authoritative the dictionary, the less will it be possible to produce new and revised editions sufficiently frequently to include new words as they become accepted in normal speech. On the other hand, there are a great number of these new words, especially those occurring in the writings of what we may call the slick columnists, which are purely nonce-words, and which must, by their very nature and the purpose for which they have been used, be ephemeral, and unlikely to become part of our standard vocabulary, and, interesting as these words often are from the point of view of word-formation and the psychology of word-coinage, they have had to be omitted from the scope of the present work in order to keep it within reasonable bounds. Individual studies have been made, from time to time, of some classes of these words, and reference will be made to these in the bibliography and notes.

Let us begin by asking ourselves what we mean by vocabulary. The word has different meanings: in its widest sense it refers not only to all the words in an authoritative dictionary, but also to those which have not yet found acceptance, yet are in common use in polite circles. But some division is possible: it can be shown that there are regional vocabularies, occupational vocabularies, and even others, such as class vocabularies, some confined to relatively small groups. People may even be recognized by their vocabularies; not only the man who uses words understood only in particular areas or in different trades, but even the practised writer: often we feel we can recognize the author of even a short passage merely from the words used in it. This leads us to the final sub-division, for each individual has his own vocabulary, distinct in some way or other from that of other people in the circle in which he moves, and often quite as characteristic of him as his style of writing, or the actual sounds and intonation of his speech. Phoneticians tell us that no two people, even of the same family, speak exactly alike, so far as sounds are concerned, and in the same way no two people use exactly the same words, or use them in the same way.

We shall see, in the chapters which follow, how the national vocabulary has been developed gradually, but there are stages of development in the individual vocabulary also. We start with the early words – baby words – learnt by word of mouth, then pass on to simple words learnt from the printed page, and after that there is further development along these lines in proportion to the amount of reading done in later life. We may even see, in the case of the individual vocabulary as in that of the national vocabulary, not only additions to the stock, but also loss of words, and rejection of words once in common use. The child soon discards the earliest baby words in favour of those used by older children, and pet words for *dog, horse, train* and other objects attractive to the youngest children are replaced by the standard word. Later, words of schoolboy slang are discarded when the boy or girl goes into the outside world, and later still the particular – and peculiar – vocabulary of the teenager is also rejected. Alongside this loss of words we have also, of course, a much more rapid increase in vocabulary as the child is brought into contact with new objects, experiences, and ideas. Thus we see that no vocabulary is ever stable, but is constantly changing, constantly growing and constantly decaying. The individual vocabulary is, of course, often very much restricted, and it has been shown that even Shakespeare used only some fifteen thousand words – though that was naturally a bigger proportion then than now – and Milton about eight thousand. Figures such as these, however, may be deceptive, for while the nature of their writings – particularly in the case of Milton – made it impossible for them to use all the words with which they were familiar, they also made much use of poetic licence in the coining of new words and compounds and in using words with a meaning not commonly accepted. According to the *Encyclopædia Britannica* it has been estimated that a 'normally educated person' has a vocabulary of twenty to twenty-five thousand words, though most of us find some four to five thousand sufficient for our daily needs, and the originators of Basic English think that eight hundred and fifty, with the addition of a few specialized words, are enough for all ordinary purposes!

Such a discrepancy naturally leads us to the consideration of two aspects of individual vocabulary – the words a person uses, and those he understands. The first will comprise his ordinary colloquial vocabulary, the vocabulary peculiar to his occupation, and the more extended vocabulary he uses when writing, and this last shades imperceptibly into the second type – words he understands, but does not himself use. There is also what we may call the vocabulary of special occasions, perhaps a mixture of the two last-mentioned types; we all know the difference between our ordinary colloquial speech and that used on special occasions, between the language, even, of the playground and the classroom. Chaucer called this last type of language 'Heigh style, as whan that men to kynges wryte'. We see, therefore, that vocabulary may even differ with the strata of society in which it is used; to use the technical term – we have levels of language. It is the second type – what we may call the literary vocabulary – which is most general and uniform; individual, occupational, regional, and class vocabularies all differ greatly, even to the extent of being unintelligible – or partly so – outside their own spheres, but within limits the literary vocabulary remains fairly uniform. The qualifying phrase 'within limits' is very necessary, for the language of poetry may differ greatly from that of everyday prose, being often archaic, using words confined to poetic usage, and employing more figurative expressions, and unusual compounds quite unsuitable for prose.

The vocabulary we are to consider, then, will vary with every reader, but it will all lie between the few hundred words first deemed essential for Basic English and the half-million words to be found in the last edition of the great American *Century Dictionary*, larger than our own *New English Dictionary* chiefly because it has admitted far more compounds. But these two, like all large dictionaries, contain many academic and technical terms, which can hardly be considered part of the English language in common use, and they also list many obsolete words. Two hundred years ago Johnson's *Dictionary* had contained less than fifty thousand words, but, despite his industry, this dictionary was far from exhaustive, and certainly failed to reflect fully the language spoken at the time. For one thing, unlike our great present-day lexicographers, Johnson had not an army of skilled staff at his disposal, and, moreover, he refused to recognize as good English many words which were current in his time, though even then he was blamed by some critics for admitting 'low' or dialect words.

This huge total of words available to us today invites us to consider the ways in which vocabulary develops. A living language is never stationary; words are always being both acquired and lost, and words also develop new meanings, generally expanding the idea which they express, often to such an extent that there seems no similarity or connection between the first meaning and the final development. *Glamour*, originally Scots, is a corrupt form of *grammar*, in the sense of 'profound or occult learning'. Through the sense of 'enchantment, spell, magic illusion' it has developed to its common meaning today, of mysterious charm, some elusive magical feeling, later weakening to a vaguer sense of charm or delight, but one can be sure no schoolboy sees any connection between grammar and glamour, particularly as the meaning of the latter word for him has been largely coloured by associations with Hollywood. Or we may consider the word *expire;* its original sense was to breathe out, but by extension it came to be connected with the last occasion on which one breathes out, and so became synonymous with *to die.* From a purely materialistic point of view, dying is connected closely with coming to an end, and so today the lease of one's house *expires.* Finally, for an even more metaphorical usage, let us take *pluck;* originally it was the name given to what was plucked forth or drawn from a dead animal or bird – we still speak of a *pluck of lights*, meaning the lungs and other offal of a beast sold for catsmeat. The most important organ in this *pluck* was the heart, which in mediæval times was held to be the seat of courage, and so eventually, by transference, the word came to have its present-day meaning. We can see exactly the same process at work in the word *guts*, but this is still only a slang or colloquial expression, whereas its predecessor *pluck* is now fully established.

But the most obvious fact in connection with the development of English vocabulary has been its enormous growth. The vocabulary of Old English, as it survives for us today, contains some thirty thousand words, and although this may by no means represent the whole of the words then used, for not only have comparatively few works come down to us, but even those are largely confined to a type which would be preserved by monks, and many words would, by their very nature, not be recorded in such works, we can at least take this number as a basis, as, if dictionaries of Old English do not record all words then in use, neither do our great dictionaries record our colloquial vocabulary completely. It would seem, therefore, that the vocabulary of English may have increased as much as tenfold in a thousand years. This is all due, of course, to the new objects and ideas which have been introduced during that period, as a result of the development of science and extension of trade, and changes in the methods of government, the legal system, changes in social conditions, and the widespread effects of the general increase in culture as education has become available to an ever-increasing number of people.

But do we not take all this 'wordy matter' – the skeleton of Basic, our own individual vocabulary, the huge, but even then incomplete, bulk of the *New English Dictionary* – do we not take all this rather too much for granted? The English language has the richest and most extensive vocabulary of any language in the world, due partly to historical factors, partly to what we may call the 'genius of the language', for English has always been ready to absorb foreign words, and coin new words for ideas for which the existing foreign terms were not for some reason acceptable, but do we ever stop to consider in detail how this great wealth of vocabulary came about, how all these words came to be part of our English vocabulary, who first used them, when, and why, whether they were at once accepted as filling a long-felt want, or rejected as totally unnecessary? Or have we ever considered the great number of words which have found only a temporary place in our language, and then have been lost, at any rate so far as our modern vocabulary is concerned? This is most important, for example, for the 'inkhorn controversy' of the sixteenth century, and even for another two hundred years or so, for the battle over purity of language was still going on in the eighteenth century, and during those centuries many words appeared which have since become obsolete. This obviously leads us to consider why some words have lived through the centuries – we still say *sing*, just as King Alfred did twelve hundred years ago, and as his ancestors did hundreds of years before that – while others have died, or have maintained themselves only by changing their meanings. When we consider this we are led to enquire into the struggle between the 'residents', as it were, the native words, and the invaders. This line of thought will, perhaps, tempt us to explore the whole psychology of borrowing, which languages borrow freely, and which do not, and whether the tendency to borrow, so noticeable in our own language, is a sign of health or weakness in a language. Finally, as all these problems present themselves for consideration, we shall be struck by the extremely mixed character of our vocabulary, and perhaps be inclined to ask how all these foreign words came into our language, why they were adopted, what words, in some cases, they displaced, and what they reveal to us of the history of our people. We do not often, perhaps, connect historical events, such as conquests and attempts at colonization, and trends of thought at particular periods, with the words which we use every day, yet the connection is obvious enough if only we take the trouble to look for it. After all, we shall hardly expect such events as the conversion of the heathen Angles and Saxons to Christianity, the Scandinavian and Norman Conquests, with first their enmity between invaded and invader, and their later fusion, the influence of French, and Italian, literature, the Renaissance, with its new interest in Humanism and the old classical literature, the rapid increase in scientific knowledge from the middle of the seventeenth century, and the equally rapid increase in knowledge of other lands and other peoples, as a result of either colonization or commerce, or both, for as knowledge grows, language grows with it, owing to the need to express new ideas, new perceptions, new shades of meaning, or to give names to new inventions, new discoveries – we shall, then, hardly expect all these to have taken place without in some way affecting our thought, and therefore in turn the words needed to express this thought. Thanks to the labours of the editors and readers of the *New English Dictionary*, in which every word has been traced back to its origin, and all the changes in form and meaning recorded, we are now able to examine the history of our words, and often discover what it was that brought them forth. Words can be separated according to their age, starting with the original vocabulary, and adding layer after layer in successive periods. In these layers we find enshrined the life and thought of the English people, and all the conditions and events which have affected our nation are recorded as clearly in these words as the history of the earth is recorded in its fossils and geological formations. Just as we are able to discover the extent of a writer's knowledge by reference to a word he uses, the method of 'internal evidence', so we are able, by examining the vocabulary of a nation at a particular time, to see what has been affecting that nation at that time or in an earlier period, what knowledge the nation has so far gained, and what contacts it has made.

Even a study of vocabulary such as this, on the broadest and most general lines, will prove interesting, but we may extend our study to examine in detail periods and writers, and by so doing we shall often see how vocabulary reflects a particular attitude of mind, or changing psychological values, or a changing sense of social values. For example, the significance attached to *politician* and *enthusiasm* in the sixteenth and seventeenth centuries, to *polite* in the eighteenth, and *gentleman* in the nineteenth tells us a great deal about the outlook and mentality of those periods. A future generation may judge us on our use of *bourgeois*, *middle-class*, *public school* and *Victorian*, once terms of solid respectability, but now used more often in a disparaging sense. Or we may see how the writers of one period reflect the thought of that period by a tendency to use abstract rather than concrete nouns. As this shows stages in the development of a people, so it may, on a smaller scale, show the development of an individual. How would this fondness for concrete or abstract expressions apply, for example, to the language of Marlowe and the young Shakespeare, and what should we learn by a comparison of both of these with the language of the mature Shakespeare? Or we may think of the words we ourselves used when young – almost entirely names of concrete objects – and then compare them with the more abstract terms we acquire as we grow older and our ideas change. An examination of vocabulary on these lines will often help us to understand what people were doing and thinking in particular periods, and as all literature is itself a reflection of what people were doing and thinking at the time at which it was written, such a detailed study of vocabulary may help us to understand great literary works more fully, to attain to a full understanding of texts by our own efforts, rather than those of commentators. But perhaps a word of warning is necessary here: we should not try to run before we can walk, and notes and introductions are not to be lightly discarded by the beginner. A little knowledge, particularly in the realms of etymology and semantics, can be a very dangerous thing, but anyone who is prepared to work at the vocabulary of texts of particular periods or authors in order to reach a full understanding of the thought contained in them is assured of both a fruitful and a fascinating pastime.

Before going on to examine the development of our vocabulary under particular headings, we may first pause to consider in a general way the scope of the enquiry, which can conveniently be allowed to fall under two headings – methods of development, and a chronological examination. The study of methods of development must of necessity include an examination of the treatment of the native material itself, and also of extension of this by the addition of foreign material. The discussion of foreign loan-words will lead us to examine the ways in which foreign words may be introduced into a language, and to consider the philosophical and psychological aspects of borrowing, and, which is perhaps more important, whether or not a language is improved by extensive borrowing, whether it is better, stronger, and more efficient if it confines itself to its own words, and is satisfied to produce new compounds of its own words as new objects and ideas are introduced.

Let us first consider, but briefly and merely by way of introduction to a fuller study later, our first heading – methods of development. In the earliest times vocabulary was extended largely by derivation, the adding of affixes to root-forms, and some scholars still believe that this is the way by which almost all our words were formed. It may be that, as some scholars think, these affixes were originally independent words, so that derivation was merely one form of the process known as compounding, but we cannot be sure of this, for as yet we know little of some of the affixes used. By this process new words could be formed and the function extended or changed, so that a word which was originally the simple name of a concrete object might in time yield also an adjective, an adverb, an abstract noun, and a verb, all containing some aspect of the idea expressed by the original simple noun. There was also, again in the earliest periods, the process known as *ablaut*, or gradation, whereby new words were formed merely by the variation of the vowel of a root within a fixed series; the result of such a method of formation is still to be seen in Modern English in such groups as *ride*, *rode*, *ridden*, *road*, and *sing*, *sang*, *sung*, *song*. Development could also occur by *umlaut*, or mutation. By this process one root could be made to form words different in form and function, and often slightly different in meaning, thus extending the vocabulary. Mutation was operative only in the Old English period, but many pairs of words, one with a mutated vowel and the other with the original unmutated vowel, with some distinction in meaning, are still to be found in our language; for example, the noun and verb *deal* (OE *dǣl* and *dǣlan*, with mutated vowel) and *dole* (OE *dāl*, with unmutated vowel) have an obvious semantic connection; *heal* (OE *hǣlan*) and *whole* (OE *hāl*) are a similar pair. There is also the process of compounding, once so characteristic a feature of the Germanic languages, and also, often still within the native material, particularly in the early period, a process sometimes, but not always, allied to compounding – the coining of new words.

All the above are examples of word formation, but vocabulary could also be extended by other means. For example, the function of a word could be changed without changing its form, particularly after the decay of inflexions had resulted in the loss of characteristic suffixes. Vocabulary may also be developed by change or extension of meaning; *cnapa* and *cniht* were almost synonymous in Old English, but such has been the development of the two words that *knave* and *knight* are now almost antonyms.

Change of meaning may also be effected, though not so obviously, by means of figurative language, the use of metaphors, or, which is a similar process, the use of a concrete term for an abstract conception, or the abstract for the concrete. Such a process is to be seen in the concrete *lunatic* [< Lat. *lūnāticus* (adj.) – affected by the moon, temporarily insane], where the reference is to the influence of the *moon* (Lat. *lūnā*) on a person's actions; or we find words denoting characteristics such as *courage, melancholy,* or the temperaments early described as *phlegmatic* or *choleric,* all based on physical attributes supposed to be reflected in these characteristics.

Another process of development within the native material, though almost equivalent to borrowing from a dead language such as Latin or Greek, is the deliberate revival of archaisms, or words which have become completely obsolete, from older stages of our own language. This process, adopted by Spenser in the sixteenth century, and by Scott in the nineteenth, to mention only two well-known exponents, is a purely artificial process, and does not often spread widely.

But the most important means of development in the historical period, so far as English is concerned, has been direct borrowing from another language, the result of contact either with the people of another country, or with their literature.

All these methods of development and extension, and in particular the last, with the implications which lie behind the adoption of words from other languages, and – which is a parallel process – the way in which contact with foreign peoples or literatures may stimulate the native element of the vocabulary, will be considered in detail in later chapters.

A chronological investigation must obviously begin with the native tongue, that brought to these islands in the fifth century by the Germanic tribes who eventually overran the native Britons. The importance of this purely Germanic basis is often overlooked, largely because of the great number of foreign words incorporated in our present-day vocabulary. But an examination of actual usage, as opposed to mere presence in a dictionary, shows how important the native words are. The next step will be to discuss the foreign words which have found a way into our language from those early days, and see not only which words they have displaced, when the object or idea was already known, but also what effect they have had on the native element.

Our method, then, will be to take the old Germanic element as the basis, and regard everything else as foreign. But it is not easy at first to grasp what this means. Many of the words we shall have to class as 'foreigners' will seem at first sight 'true-born Englishmen', for they have been part of our vocabulary for centuries, but they have only a 'certificate of naturalization', not a right by birth. When, under this heading, such familiar words as *candle, face, inch, mile, ounce, rose, school, street,* and *wine* are mentioned, it will be realised that we shall need to classify under foreign borrowings, or loan-words, to use the technical term, many more words than the ordinary reader has been accustomed to consider under that heading, and some, at least, which are usually looked upon as native words. And yet, for all general purposes, though not for our special purpose, they might be considered natives: it all depends on the point of view and the strictness with which distinctions are made. There is, in East Anglia, an area very small in both size and population, forming a pocket between a river and a road; all those living beyond these two boundaries are 'other folk', foreigners, to the natives of the area. Narrow and insular as such a view may seem to us, it must be our attitude when considering the origin of words; length of domicile is not a modifying factor in an accurate and scientific study of the sources of vocabulary.

The need for this accurate knowledge of the origin of our words will be obvious enough, upon mature consideration, but another aspect of the study of vocabulary may not be so obvious. A chronological investigation is a historical study of the development of vocabulary, and this historical aspect entails consideration not only of the words we use today, but also of the words which *have been used*, either native words which have been discarded, or words which have entered our language from foreign sources and have not found a permanent place. We might take as our basis the material of the *Shorter Oxford Dictionary*, as described in the Preface: 'The vocabulary is designed to include all words in regular literary and colloquial use, together with a selection of those which belong to the terminology of the arts and sciences and those which are current only in archaic and dialectical use, as well as of words now obsolete but of importance during some period of our literature'.

At the same time, however, we shall in the main confine our attention to what may be called the literary language. Many of our regional dialects, particularly in the remoter districts, contain both native words, once in common use but no longer found in the standard language, and also loan-words, especially Scandinavian words, which have not found a place in the standard language. These are extremely interesting, and will be touched upon in the discussion of regional and occupational vocabularies, but the study of that aspect of our living speech will not form an important part of this present treatment of vocabulary.

Let us now conclude this general outline of the scope of this investigation by considering generally, and only briefly, in preparation for a detailed study later, when these words were adopted into our language, and whence they came. It has already been made clear that a chronological investigation must begin with the language as brought to this country in the fifth century, but we must really go back a little further, for these tribes had been in some sort of contact with the Romans for some centuries before that, and had already acquired some Latin words, which they brought with them to this country. Latin is, of course, related to Germanic, and both languages will therefore contain words from the common Indo-European vocabulary, but we can tell, by phonological tests, for example, by Grimm's Law, what words were borrowed later from Latin, as the two languages had developed differently, and even approximately at what date they were borrowed. To take an example: Latin *piscis* and English *fish* (OE *fisc*) are cognates; the common root was **pisk-*, but we know that every IE *p* developed to *f* in Germanic. This change did not take place in Latin, and so we are able to explain the difference in initial consonants in the Latin and Old English forms. But, from the initial consonant, we can tell that our adjective *piscatorial* must have been borrowed from Latin at a later period, after the sound changes known as Grimm's Law had ceased to operate in the Germanic language. As we shall see, other Germanic tribes allied to the Angles and Saxons also have these early words, which points to a borrowing at a period prior to the migrations of the Germanic peoples. When the Germanic invaders came into contact with the natives of this island another opportunity would arise for acquiring loan-words. There has been much controversy about the language spoken by the Britons in the fifth century, and later we must consider the problem in detail, but it may suffice here to say that there was at least an opportunity for the influx of more Latin words, from Britons who had learnt Latin from the Roman occupying forces, and also of Celtic words, from that part of the population which still used its native language. The next important factor affecting our language was the introduction of Christianity in the sixth century by Roman missionaries, and the subsequent contacts with Roman civilization and scholarship. This introduced many objects and ideas new to the English, and we shall have to consider how their vocabulary was adapted to express these ideas, not only by way of borrowing Latin words directly, but also by forming hybrids and by adapting native words, for it must be stressed that we are concerned here not only with the borrowing of foreign words, but with the development of the vocabulary of English in general, and if the introduction of new ideas from abroad has resulted in new meanings being attached to native words, or to new combinations being formed from existing words, then obviously that will be our concern. The next important event affecting the English language was the invasion of the country by some of the Scandinavian races, in particular the Danes and Norwegians. There was a close affinity between Old English and Old Scandinavian, for both languages developed from the parent Germanic language, and many words in our language today have been ascribed to Scandinavian influence which may have been part of the vocabulary of Old English. We need to remember, as has been pointed out already, that probably only a very small part of Old English literature has survived, and that the literature as a whole probably did not record all the words used by the English at that time, so it is fairly certain that only part of the Old English vocabulary has been preserved. If, therefore, a word is found in one of the Old Scandinavian languages and also in Middle English, but not in Old English, we must be careful that we do not accept it as the result of Scandinavian influence without further test, for the word may have been common in spoken Old English but may not have been recorded in the literature which has survived. Later we shall consider additional tests which may be applied, but in the meantime it will suffice to point out that these Scandinavians, in their lengthy stay in this country, must have introduced new ideas, new objects, and new customs, and possibly new names for them too. This will conclude the study of the language of the Old English period, and indeed much of the evidence for Scandinavian influence is found only in Middle English writings, though the influence must have been exerted several centuries earlier.

We may say, speaking in the most general terms, that the Norman Conquest is the dividing line between Old and Middle English. Various scholars may have their own opinions on the precise effect of the Conquest on the English language, but most will agree in putting the end of the Old English period just after the Conquest had been completed and implemented. The influx of a conquering race who spoke an entirely different language was obviously a factor likely to lead to some changes in the language spoken in this country. When the English overcame the Celtic inhabitants, much the same conditions had been operative, and the result had been the extinction of the Celtic language throughout most of the country, and this is what we might expect to have occurred then. Such, however, was not the case, and although French was the language of the Court, the Church, and the Law Courts, many of the English, particularly away from the centres of French influence, continued to speak their own language. This state of affairs continued for some two or three centuries, until finally English once more became the language of the whole country. But during this time, in addition to the influence of the ruling classes, another influence had been at work, that of French literature; not only was there access to the rich literature of the continent, but for about two centuries much of English literature consisted of translations from French works, chiefly romances, and English poetry was also strongly influenced by French models. But this literary influence was not confined to the immediate neighbourhood of the Court, as we see from the vocabulary of *Piers Plowman*, and the result was that when English once more became the dominant language it had greatly changed, and in the process of change had acquired a vast number of French words. Many of these words have now become part and parcel of our everyday speech, and we might have difficulty in recognizing them as loan-words, but foreigners they were, and as such we must consider them.

This ruling French class had another influence on the English language which is not so well known, because it was not so widespread. Most of the chief positions in Church and State were occupied by Frenchmen, and their literary culture was higher than that of the native English. Not only did they extend the use of Latin for original theological and historical works, but they also caused many Latin books of devotion and Latin chronicles to be translated into English, and very often Latin words were introduced into these translations when an English equivalent either did not exist or was unknown to the translator. Thus we get another period of Latin borrowings.

The next important event affecting our language was the Renaissance. The revival of Greek learning in Western Europe opened up a new source for loan-words in English. There had been borrowings from the Greek language at an earlier period in English, but they had come in through Latin, either direct or through French. Latin was still at this time the language generally employed throughout Europe for science, philosophy, and, to a lesser extent, religion, and so most of these new Greek terms were first used in Latin works, and as a result the convention was established that the Greek words were treated as if they had first been adopted in Latin, and then passed to the various European languages.

Another result of the spread of classical learning was the crop of new formations direct from the Latin, as against the form which had been borrowed earlier through French. Scholars became aware of the etymology of words, and, perhaps pedantically, went back to the original Latin form of the word, so that M.E. *perfet, parfet*, from French *perfait, parfait*, was replaced by *perfect*, Chaucer's *peynture* gave way to *picture*, and his *aventure* was replaced by a form *adventure*, with the full Latin prefix. Other examples of pairs of words, originally from the same source, one showing evidence of phonological decay in French, the other the form nearer to the Latin original, are *blame, blaspheme; chance, cadence; count, compute; dainty, dignity; dungeon, dominion; sure, secure.*

But at this period it seemed that everyone with even a smattering of Latin or Greek felt himself licensed to add to the vocabulary by coining new words based upon forms from the classical languages, and so we shall have to take notice of something which has not so far been apparent, at least in an active form, a deliberate effort to prevent borrowing from other languages, and it is possible to collect, from essays of the sixteenth and seventeenth centuries, evidence of a movement to control English vocabulary, beginning with the objection to 'inkhorn' terms and culminating finally in a serious effort by competent critics to establish an Academy in England which would function on the lines of the French Academy as a guardian of the purity of the language. This opposition movement was active over a period of more than two centuries, and serious efforts were made in Dr Johnson's time to establish an Academy. The idea is still popular even today among a certain group of scholars.

The next important period of development is again concerned with the classical languages. By the middle of the seventeenth century, science was already beginning to expand rapidly, and the enormous increase in our knowledge of the physical sciences over the last three hundred years has had its effect on our vocabulary. One of the requirements of the scientist is a precise vocabulary, terms which shall be capable of bearing one meaning, and one meaning only. Over the course of centuries words in everyday use tend to become less and less precise as they attach to themselves more and more shades of meaning – we may take as an example a word just used, and note how, from the limited sense of *shadow* the sense has been expanded, in the related word *shade*, which now has much wider significance – and so it is obvious that the vocabulary of everyday speech is not nearly precise enough for the scientist. Greek is peculiarly well fitted for a scientific language, for it possesses an almost unlimited capacity to form derivatives and compounds. Moreover, the capacity of the language to express accurately the most minute distinctions in meaning had been developed as a result of its use by a long succession of philosophers, so that in Greek there was a lucid yet precise language at the disposal of the scientists. The result was that they went to the Greek language for the multitude of new terms which they needed, and a tremendous number of words derived from Greek have been added to our vocabulary since the late seventeenth century, and more are continually being added. Professor

Hogben in *Interglossa* (Penguin) suggested that, since Greek derivatives are international, a common language might be evolved by forming words from Greek roots and affixes which are familiar to most nations through the vocabulary of science.

Another influence, important, if not so extensive, was also at work in the middle of the seventeenth century. During the reign of Charles II there was a close connection between the English and French Courts, and a knowledge of French language and literature was fashionable in Court circles. All this, of course, was partly the result of the Civil War and the residence abroad of the Court during the Commonwealth period, another instance of how the history of our language is tied up with the history of the country itself. But this was not the only effect of the Civil War; the Puritans themselves were steeped in the Bible, and in religious works whose style was based on that of the Bible, and although the literature which they produced added little by way of loan-words it did serve to popularize and retain in the language words and expressions which perhaps would otherwise have become obsolete, and if, in the course of years, some of them have since disappeared, yet they do deserve attention in any examination of the development of our language. But the first-named influence was greater, and many new words passed into our language from French during that period.

Since the sixteenth century communication between the remoter parts of the earth has progressively increased, not only through improved means of transport, but also through colonial development and trade expansion; in addition, the literature of some of the lesser-known countries has become increasingly available, and all this has led to borrowing from countries whose languages had had no effect on ours before this time. As we shall see, it is a great mistake to think of our loan-words as being only from Latin, Greek, French, and Scandinavian, or that the period of borrowing ended centuries ago. Admittedly ninety per cent of our vocabulary comes from native sources or these four languages, but the other ten per cent contains important words, and many in very common use, and although a great part of our ordinary vocabulary was established by the seventeenth century, a very great number of words have been added since then. Nevertheless, in treating foreign loan-words, most attention has been devoted to Scandinavian, Latin, French and Greek, for these are the most important sources.

This short summary completes our introductory study of periods of borrowing, but this is not the only approach to the study of foreign words in English. Borrowings might be considered from a national point of view, and by examining the type of words borrowed from a particular language we could discover how a particular country has influenced the life and thought of our own people, and also what part various countries have played in the expansion of knowledge. For example, we find that many of the expressions we use in art and music have come from Italian, suggesting that the Italians were our teachers in these subjects. We all know how the Elizabethans felt about the 'Italianate Englishman', but there is no doubt that Italian taste in literature and dress, and also Italian social customs, did for a time set the fashion in Court circles in England, and thus affected our language by introducing terms for new objects and ideas. Many of our nautical terms, and quite a number of terms connected with some of our trades, are found to be of Dutch origin, thus showing the influence of the Dutch in these fields. We also find words from Low German in these classes, dating from the period of the commercial and nautical supremacy of the Hanseatic cities. Spanish influence can also be traced in our language, and we shall find that the German aptitude for philosophy and science had its effect on our vocabulary in the nineteenth century. Many recent borrowings from French are names of objects or processes connected with women's clothes, cosmetics, and certain types of luxury goods. A subtle difference between the German and French character is to be seen in some of the recently-imported words of German origin, connected with what we may term the coarser articles of food, such as *frankfurter*, *hamburger*, *lager*, *pretzel*, and *sauerkraut*, as against the more refined delicacies of French origin.

Since, then, these foreign loan-words are so important for the development of our English vocabulary, it may well be worth while to consider how such loan-words may be introduced into a language. Windisch, discussing mixed languages and the adoption of loan-words, has pointed out that it is not the foreign language exerting the influence which is contaminated, but that the native language becomes mixed as a result of contact of one kind or another. Jespersen has made the same point in another way by pointing out that when we speak a foreign language we use words from our own only in cases of dire necessity, whereas we tend to interlard our own speech with words and phrases from a foreign language. He adds: 'One of Windisch's illustrations is taken from Germany in the eighteenth century. It was then the height of fashion to imitate everything French, and Frederick the Great prided himself on speaking and writing good French. In his French writings one finds not a single German word, but whenever he wrote German, French words and phrases in the middle of German sentences abounded, for French was considered more refined, more *distingué*'.[1] The acquisition of loan-words from another language usually shows that the borrower feels that there is something superior in the foreign language, or in the people who speak it, for we may suppose that no reasonable being would deliberately make use of foreign words if he felt that his own language possessed words which did the job better; 'reasonable being' is used here advisedly, in order to exclude such types as the 'Italianate Englishman' and other victims of affectation.

The adoption of any considerable number of foreign words in a language implies bilingualism. The first steps occur when a bilingual speaker uses foreign words in speaking his own language, the reason often being necessity, when he wishes to express some concept for which his language has no word. At first there is no intention to introduce a new word into the vocabulary. Such words gain an entrance gradually, being first used among a small group of people with similar tastes, and from them the words spread to other related groups, and finally to the whole community, by which time they are no longer felt to be aliens.

The influence of a foreign language may be exerted in two ways, through the spoken word, by personal contact between the two peoples, or through the written word, by indirect contact, not between the peoples themselves but through their literatures. The former way was more productive in the earlier stages, but the latter has become increasingly important in more recent times. Direct contact may take place naturally in border regions, or by the transference of considerable numbers of people from one area to another, either by peaceful immigration, settlement, or colonization, or through invasion and conquest. It may also take place, though to a more limited extent, through travel in foreign countries and through residence abroad, for trade or other purposes, of relatively small numbers of people.

The type of word borrowed by personal contact would undoubtedly at first be names of objects unfamiliar to the borrowers, or products and commodities exchanged by way of trade. If the contact were maintained over a long period, then ideas concerned with government, law, religion, and customs might be absorbed, and perhaps the names of these would be adopted. Only in the case of nations in relatively advanced stages of civilization would there be much influence exerted through the written word; concrete objects would come first, then abstract ideas learnt from what might actually be seen from their effects in everyday life, and abstract ideas through the indirect contact achieved by books would come much later.

The most obvious way in which loan-words may be introduced is by compulsion, through conquest, or perhaps colonization, when a conquering race imposes its language upon a conquered people. This is what we may call one-sided borrowing, with an 'upper' or dominant language, spoken by the privileged group, and a 'lower' or submerged language, spoken by the subject race. Not always, of course, will the conquerors be able to impose their own language. Except in the case of mass migration the conquerors will be in the minority, and, unless they remain in close contact with their original home and are constantly reinforced by new arrivals, and, more important, bring their own womenfolk, thus avoiding the weakening effect of mixed marriages, it is probable that the native language will survive, though it will no doubt acquire some words, chiefly concerned with government and law, from the language of the conquerors. This, as we shall see, happened when the Normans overcame the English, and there are other examples, such as that of the Franks in Latin-speaking Gaul, and the early Scandinavian settlers on the northern shores of France.

But if the conquerors retain close contact with their original home, and receive regular reinforcements, it is probable that in the course of time they will establish their own language, as the Romans did in several of their provinces, but it is likely that this language will gradually be changed in pronunciation, as was the case with vulgar Latin in its gradual differentiation into French, Spanish, Portuguese, and Rumanian, and that it will also acquire many words from the language of the conquered people, for many on both sides will be bilingual, though once the dominant race sink to being bilingual their language is likely to die out, unless it receives constant reinforcement from outside; this was very apparent in England after, in the thirteenth century, the Normans in England lost their lands in France.

In both cases, whichever language may ultimately prevail, it is likely that the conquerors will introduce new objects and new ideas, and may possibly introduce also their own names for these, particularly if the language of the conquered people is not of the type which strongly resists the influx of foreign words. On the other hand, the invaders will probably acquire some of the native names of objects with which they were not before familiar, and these words may eventually find their way back to the home of the conquerors, and become part of their standard language. It is, however, usually the submerged language which borrows predominantly from the language of the conquerors; for example, the Romance languages have only a few words adopted from the languages previously spoken in the territories they conquered, English has very few words borrowed from the Celtic peoples, but on the other hand the native Germanic and Celtic tribes on the Continent probably borrowed freely from Latin where they were in contact with Roman armies or traders, as did the Celtic peoples here from Old

English where the two races were in touch with each other, and as English itself did freely from French when the Normans made French the dominant language. But English, as the upper language, has adopted relatively few words from native sources in Australia, India, New Zealand, and South Africa, and American English but few from the languages of the North American Indians.

So far we have considered cases where the conquerors were in the minority, but it is a different matter when the conquest is part of a plan for colonization, extension of empire, or migration from unsatisfactory lands. In such cases the conquerors may be more numerous than the original inhabitants of the country. Then the language of the conquerors will be more important from the very outset, and psychological factors will make it unlikely that the conquerors will take the trouble to learn the language of the conquered people. As a result, it is probable that the native language will disappear, or at any rate survive only where the natives are allowed to congregate. This was the case when the Angles and Saxons conquered Britain; they acquired very little of the language of the Britons, and that language survived only in the kingdoms which the Britons were able to retain in the barren, mountainous areas of the west. A similar thing has happened in America, where the Amerindian languages have survived only in the reservations, and in Australia, where the language of the aborigines is restricted to similar relatively small areas. But even where the language of the conquerors prevails it will not do so entirely unaltered. There will of necessity be many new things encountered, animals, trees, plants, even perhaps occupations, trades, manufactured articles, and, unless the conquerors are either imaginative enough to coin new words or skilled in forming new compounds in their own language, most of the native words for these new objects will be adopted into the language of the conquerors. This happened, to a limited extent, in the case of the Angles and Saxons, and, as we shall see later, has resulted in many native words being added even in comparatively recent years to the languages of the civilized peoples, as their explorers have penetrated further and further into hitherto unknown lands.

Sometimes, comparatively rarely in early times, but more frequently later, we find a kind of mass immigration, achieved sometimes by conquest, sometimes by peaceful means, in which a large number of people, driven from their own land for one reason or another, settle in a foreign land which has the capacity to absorb them, and live side by side with the original inhabitants. If the two races are reasonably alike in temperament the result of their being compelled, while retaining their own languages, to live alongside each other, and through necessity

B

to be able to understand and deal with each other, will eventually be a fusion of the two races, and, provided the languages are related, the people will soon reach the stage of being bilingual, the people of both races tending to introduce into their speech words from the language of the other, and after that the two languages will probably tend to fuse, each language losing its peculiar characteristics of accidence and syntax; when complete bilingualism is reached it is probable that one language will begin to die out, rather than that a new dual or mixed language will emerge, and social and intellectual conditions, quite as much as linguistic considerations, will decide which language shall survive; but the final language will in any case almost certainly have a very mixed vocabulary, and the language which disappears will leave traces of its existence in pronunciation, vocabulary, and idiom. This is what we may call complete absorption, the greatest influence one language may have on another.

If the two languages were not at all related then presumably one or the other would eventually predominate, though in a greatly altered form, but as there would be comparatively few common features we could not expect any large degree of fusion.

An example of this type of complete fusion is perhaps to be seen in the effects of the Scandinavian settlement of England in the ninth and tenth centuries, effected at first by conquest, though the two peoples soon settled down to live amicably together. Englishmen in the north acquired a good deal of the Danish and Norwegian languages, and the Scandinavians became equally bilingual. In the interim period it is probable that both languages became simplified, so far as accidence and syntax were concerned, these being the chief points of difference, and that each borrowed words freely from the other. The final result was that by the time Danish and Norwegian had died out as independent languages in this country very many Scandinavian words remained in use, and in some cases replaced the English words, and many influences of the Scandinavian languages can still be traced in northern dialects.

When the immigrants are not sufficiently numerous to compete with the original inhabitants they will, for a time, retain their own language, particularly where they are able to establish strong communities, but eventually, largely because serious social and commercial disadvantages may result from their inability to use freely the language of their adopted country, they will acquire this language, though again words of their own may be added to its vocabulary as a result of their influence. We have seen this process at work during the last century in the United States, where communities of settlers from Scandinavian and Central, East and Southern European countries have gradually been absorbed. As a result, American English contains loan-words from many of these languages that have not been adopted in what we may call, using for convenience the American term, British English.

All the cases we have considered so far have been those where foreigners have, by one means or another, established themselves permanently in a new country, but a language may be affected by less permanent contacts. As a result of colonization, men and women of our own country have spent more or less lengthy periods abroad, and, although in the main retaining their own language, they have acquired new words for everyday objects and actions from the natives with whom they have been in contact. In many cases such words have established themselves firmly in our language. Phonological changes may be seen in such words, and different pronunciations may arise. The people who have acquired the words by residence or travel in the foreign country will also have adopted to some extent the native pronunciation, as the words will have been learnt by word of mouth. But the words will also become known to another group at home, though only through the written word, from private or commercial correspondence, or books, magazines, and newspapers, and they will tend to produce spelling pronunciations, giving to the letters or combinations of letters in the foreign word the ordinary English values.

Again, where contact between peoples has been restricted to trade or literature, words have still managed to make their way from one language to another. A language whose literature is widely studied because of the art, philosophy, or culture enshrined in it is likely to be a strong influence. Latin was such an influence throughout the Middle Ages, because of the old literature of Rome, and the spread of Roman Christianity, Greek became increasingly important after the Renaissance, and French has exerted great influence through its literature and culture in the last six hundred years or so. There is, however, a difference to be noted in this class of words. In many cases they belong only to certain aspects of life, and they do not really become part of our everyday vocabulary. Examples of such words are to be found as early as the late Old English period, when many Latin words appeared in translations almost without change, often keeping their original inflexions, or at least not acquiring the native inflexions. Many of these were learned words, unfamiliar to the ordinary people and indeed not needed by them, and they have in many cases failed to maintain their place in the language. Similar learned words have become part of the vocabulary of science in the last three hundred years; these again often retain their foreign forms and inflexions unchanged, but they are again chiefly 'book' words, though some, such as *telephone* and *gramophone*,

and the names of some of the commonest diseases, have found a way
into our everyday speech.

Trade was one of the chief factors in the introduction of early Latin
loan-words into the common Germanic language on the continent,
as we shall see later in studying the types of word borrowed, and
Modern English also contains many words, names of natural or manufactured products, occupations, and so on of foreign lands which have
come in through trade. In this class of word again there is a tendency
to establish spelling pronunciations, for in most cases the word is merely
seen, not heard.

In some cases, even, words may be adopted when there seems to be
little or no contact. As we have seen, words were adopted early from
Greek, with which people and language the English had practically no
dealings in that period, but the words came through Latin, or French,
where there was direct contact. At a later period words were borrowed
from Greek, and from Latin, in what we may call a purely abstract
manner, for there was then no contact with the peoples, and, in the
particular case we have now in mind, the coining of scientific words,
there was little, if any, connection with literature, the sole pre-requisite
in this case being a knowledge of the elements making up the words in
the language. The lack of real contact with either people or literature,
and the purely arbitrary method of formation from parts of words
rather than writings, is shown by the fact that compound words have
been coined which never existed in the original languages.

Words may not always be adopted directly from one language into
another. We have already noticed that some Greek words have come
into English through Latin, and there are other examples. In the early
Middle Ages many eastern words made their way into Europe along
the great caravan routes, and some of these words have come into
English through Latin, and indeed some had passed through Greek
even earlier, and had later been adopted into Latin. So complicated
was the pattern of trade in Western Asia and Eastern Europe, and
around the Mediterranean, that these words travelled in all directions
throughout the area as trade flowed and ebbed, and often changed
their form or pronunciation in the process. Dr Serjeantson says: 'Even
in the early centuries of this era, before communication became as
simple and rapid as it is today, words travelled thousands of miles,
westwards from Asia to Europe, across Europe from east to west and
from south to north, all round the shores of the Mediterranean, from
nation to nation and from generation to generation. Most of these
much-travelled words are objects of trade or culture. The word *pepper*,
for instance, came first from some eastern language into Greek, thence

into Latin, and thence into English; *elephant* was first Egyptian, then Greek, Latin, French, and finally English; *camel* was originally Semitic, and this too passed through Greek and Latin before reaching our language. *Albatross* is based ultimately on a Phœnician word which drifted successively into Greek, Arabic, and Portuguese, and then into English. *Apricot* began a long history in Latin, from which it passed in succession to Greek, Arabic, Spanish, French, and English. *Silk* has been Chinese, Greek, Latin, and finally English. *Carat* comes through Greek, Arabic, Italian, and French'.[2] As we study the particular sources of foreign loan-words in later chapters we shall often see examples of words passing through one or more languages before being adopted into English.

In conclusion, we may perhaps consider very briefly the treatment of these foreign words once they have been adopted into English. We find that in general they undergo all the changes affecting native words, so that, for example, Latin words adopted into Old English sufficiently early will undergo such sound changes as fronting of *a* to *æ*, breaking, diphthongization by initial front consonants, and i-mutation. Similarly French words adopted during the Middle English period have been affected by changes which took place later, as the change from ME *ā* to [ɛ:] and finally [eɪ], as in *blame*, or from *ī* to [aɪ], as in *fine*. It follows, therefore, that the longer a word has been in English, the more it is likely to differ in form and pronunciation from its foreign source word, especially as the latter may have also developed on different lines in its own country. For example, *carriage* and *savage* have been completely anglicized, and the original French pronunciation of the final syllable has been completely lost, so that no one now pronounces anything but [kærɪdʒ] and [sævɪdʒ] in English. *Garage*, however, is a much more recent importation, and as a result more people are aware of its origin, so that, according to class dialect, we may hear a close approximation to the French pronunciation, as [gərɑʒ], with stress on the final syllable, or a more anglicized form, with the stress thrown forward according to the Germanic pattern, as [gærɑʒ], or even the completely anglicised form [gærɪdʒ].

We have already noticed that some Greek words adopted as a result of the Renaissance have been given the form they would have had if they had been borrowed through Latin. In the same way, in the case of modern borrowings it is not always easy to see if a word has been borrowed direct from the classical languages, or adopted from another language which borrowed it earlier. Of some of the later borrowings, and coinages from the classical languages, Professor Bloomfield has written: 'Since the Romans borrowed words from the Greek, we can do the same, altering the Greek word in accordance with the Roman's habit of latinization, plus the Frenchman's habit of gallicizing Latin book-words, plus the English habit of anglicizing French learned words'.[3]

Differences in inflexion are not so important, because English has largely lost characteristic inflexional suffixes, particularly in the case of nouns. Although many of the more uncommon words tended to keep their original foreign inflexions in Old English, words in common use soon became hybrids, the Old English inflexion being added to the foreign stem, as in *ceastre*, where the usual Old English dative singular inflection appears. In Modern English we also have examples of both forms, with this difference, that quite a number of foreign plurals are in common use; we say *crocuses* and *irises*, using the native suffix, but *gladioli*, with the foreign suffix, is equally common, and although we use *irises* few people would say *crisises*, the foreign *crises* being common even in popular speech. In some cases double forms have arisen, and often there has been differentiation of meaning, as in *indexes* and *indices*.

This concludes the introductory view of the subject as a whole, and we pass now to a detailed examination of individual aspects of the study.

CHAPTER TWO

★

WORD-FORMATION AND EXTENSION
OF VOCABULARY

Any account of how our own words are formed in English should surely begin with an account of how words had their origin in the earliest stages. We must bear in mind that any discussion of words and word-formation in the earliest period of our language is hampered first of all by the fact that we have no raw material immediately available, for we have no written records of the language; further, we do not know with any certainty who the people were who spoke the language, where they lived, their state of culture, or the time at which they were speaking the language. As a result, we cannot be sure, apart from comparative investigation of the later languages, what concrete objects they had to speak about, or how far they were developed mentally so as to be able to think about and make statements connected with the objects they saw. With such scanty material available, any conclusions on the form and development of words in the earliest period must be based purely upon hypothesis and the results of comparative study, and it is not surprising that scholars are not agreed upon this subject.

First of all we may ask with what type of language we have to deal, from a morphological point of view. We may perhaps start with an attempt to define components of our words, separating them into free forms, which may occur in isolation, and bound forms, which never occur alone. For example, *blackberry* consists of two free forms compounded, as both *black* and *berry* are found in isolation. If we examine *raspberry* we may at first think it is the same type, for we undoubtedly do have a word *rasp*, but although the forms are identical phonetically they are not identical in meaning, and *rasp*, in the sense in which it is used in *raspberry*, is not found in isolation, except in the shortened form of *raspberry*, for *rasp* is often used colloquially for both the bush and the fruit. In the case of *bilberry* we are on even safer ground, for the element *bil-* is not found in isolation in English, and is therefore quite definitely a bound form.

From this definition of free and bound forms we may arrive at one classification of languages, into the analytic type, which consists in the main of free or independent forms, and synthetic languages, which are composed of synthesized forms, made up of one or more forms, either free or bound. Modern Chinese is a purely analytic language, whereas Esquimo is an extreme form of a synthetic language. Few languages fall entirely within one or other of these classifications, but we may speak of a language as being analytic or synthetic in character when its main features fall within one type or the other; for example, English today is largely analytic, Old English was a synthetic language, depending to a much greater extent on inflexions, Latin and Greek were even more synthetic, and we may conclude that the parent IE language was highly synthetic.

Or languages may be divided, by a different analysis, into four types, isolating, agglutinative, polysynthetic, and inflecting. The isolating type is the best example of the purely analytic type mentioned above, consisting entirely of independent forms, which are never combined, and never modified by affixes or inflexions. Chinese is an example of such a language. Agglutinative languages are those in which the elements of a word are, as it were, 'glued' together, as the name itself implies. Turkish is a good example of this type. Polysynthetic languages, as we gather from the name, combine semantically-important elements into one fused word. Esquimo is an example of a polysynthetic language. Inflecting languages attach inflexional affixes to roots or stems in order to indicate aspect, tense, person, number, mood, or other grammatical features. Latin and Greek are examples of this type, and the parent IE language was, so far as we can see, an even more extreme example of an inflected language.

The origin of language, as distinct from languages, has not so far been satisfactorily explained, and we have no records early enough to provide specific information on words or word-formation in the earliest period. But by the process of comparative philology we can, by noting similarities in related languages, arrive at some sort of idea, however hazy, of grammatical and lexicographical features of a parent language. Moreover, by taking the material now available to us, the language of the present day, and noting carefully the linguistic processes now operative, and comparing our conclusions with what we are able to discover of the development of language within the historical period, for which chronologically-accurate records are available, we may perhaps discover something of the way in which language developed in earlier times.

A comparison of one of our longer words with shorter forms containing a part or whole of its meaning, and with words in languages which are known to be related, or from which it is certain that our own language has borrowed, immediately suggests that the longer word has been developed from a number of elements which are found elsewhere, either alone or in different combinations. For example, *hopefully* contains three such elements, *hope-*, *-ful-* and *-ly*, all of which may be found elsewhere. It can be proved that these three elements were originally independent words, which could be combined with each other, or with other elements, to yield new words, as *hopeful*, *fully*, or, with other elements, *hopeless*, *fulsome*, *useful*, *aptly*, and so on, and the two formatives have also remained as independent words, as *full*, and *like*, of which *-ly* is merely an unstressed form. If, on the analogy of chemical analysis into elements, we take the analysis of these formative elements to the ultimate point, we arrive at forms which have been called roots, and which have been considered as the primitive raw material of language. This, surely, is our starting-point in word-formation.

There is as yet no complete agreement about these roots, or their function in language or the development of language. Bopp, following Sanskrit grammarians, thought they were all monosyllabic, but some later scholars have postulated disyllabic roots also. It has been suggested that the vowels of roots were always short, and that all roots began with a vowel, but other scholars consider that the root was rather a consonantal framework which expressed the essential meaning, and that different vowels were inserted into the framework to indicate various grammatical features. This is the case, for example, in the Semitic family of languages, to which our own Indo-European family may be ultimately related. It is, moreover, by no means certain that vowels so inserted were always short; the stretch-grade vowels of quantitative ablaut would seem to prove the occurrence of long vowels in primitive roots, and there is also evidence for the use of diphthongs in roots, a diphthong being quantitatively the equivalent of a long vowel, and even for long and short diphthongs. These roots were probably not at first numerous, when language was really primitive, and perhaps were all real, independent words, each capable of expressing a thought, if the language at that time was a real language. That such a language, consisting only of simple, unmodified roots, is possible is proved by modern Chinese, which does today function on those lines, whatever its earlier character may have been. The meanings first attached to these roots, again perhaps as a result of the influence of Sanskrit grammarians, were chiefly verbal in character, indicating actions, states, qualities, but others apparently indicated other less definite conceptions, as of time, place, direction, and so on. It has been suggested that there was a period in the development of our language when root-formation was operative, and language consisted entirely of roots, and that later this form of activity came to an end. But Jespersen has argued against this, maintaining that new roots have been formed in recent times and contending also that primitive roots could have been formed in different periods.[1]

So far we have mentioned two types of root, the verbal type and the type much less definite in meaning, sometimes called the pronominal type, since many are found in pronouns. It seems likely that roots of the second type were later attached to those of the first type, so as to provide some aspect of relation, and the second type apparently became eventually mere formatives. This is the process we find in the agglutinative languages, and some scholars have argued that after an initial period in which language consisted of roots only, and linguistic development was confined to the creation of roots, there followed another period, the agglutinative period, in which roots of various types were fused, resulting in the formation of stems. These stems, being limited and given particular meaning by the effect of the added root, were naturally clearer and more definite than the original simple root, but they were not yet words as we understand the term, that is, they were capable of expressing some thought, as, indeed, to a lesser extent, the original root had been, but they were not yet nouns, verbs, adjectives; a further process was required before this stage could be reached. Jespersen considers that this agglutination theory 'contains a good deal of truth; but we can only accept it with three important provisos, namely, first, that there has never been one definite period in which those languages which are now flexional were wholly agglutinative, the process of fusion being liable to occur at any time; second, that the component parts which became formatives were not at first roots, but real words; and third, that this process is not the only one by which formatives may develop; it may be called the rectilinear process, but by the side of that we have also more circuitous courses, which are no less important in the life of languages for being less obvious'.[2]

These formatives, originally pronominal roots in most cases, and perhaps at first even independent words, gradually weakened until they became mere derivative formatives, that is, affixes which were capable of being used in the process known as derivation, and there can be no doubt that some, if not all, of our inflexional endings go back to this type of word, or formative element, as the case may be.

As civilization advanced and the need grew for finer discrimination in expressing thought, these stems would be further limited by the addition of another formative, and it was this which gave us the process of derivation, and supplied us with the early forms of so many of the derivational affixes we use today.

And so we come to the final stage, that of inflexion, which is to transform these complex stems into words as we know them. In this process we find that suffixes are added to stems so that the stems are limited in various ways, with the result that they are made capable of combining syntactically with other members of a sentence, and expressing various aspects of time, place, manner, gender, person, number, mood, voice, and case, so transforming what were mere stems into what we know as parts of speech, and eventually producing in the parent language eight or nine cases, three genders, three numbers, three persons, three voices, five moods, and seven tenses, although not all of these are found recorded in any one language.

There can be no doubt that some at least of these inflexional suffixes were originally independent words. Some scholars go so far as to say that all were originally independent, but there is as yet no agreement on this point. In Old Norse, and the present Scandinavian languages, there is evidence that the passive has been constructed by adding the reflexive pronoun *sik* to the active form, the original construction having had both a passive and a reflexive force. However, the number of inflexional suffixes which can be proved to have been independent words is very small, and that of derivational suffixes not much larger, and it is more than probable that, while the addition of independent words to a stem in the processes of derivation and inflexion is a demonstrable fact, there were also other, perhaps more productive, methods of effecting the two processes. Jespersen notes that 'in the list of English suffixes enumerated in Sweet's *Grammar*, only eleven can be traced back to independent words, while seventy-four are not thus explicable'.[3]

The difficulty facing us here is that we have no information about the IE language, or any later development of it, at a period prior to the establishment of inflexions. The earliest records of IE languages, in Sanskrit, Persian, Pr. Greek and Pr. Latin, all show highly inflected types, but, although we have in most cases no specific information about the process itself or the elements employed, we can be reasonably certain of the general nature of the process, and indeed in some cases we can see, in the historical period itself, originally independent words becoming attached to stems. In the earliest OE records the inflexional ending of the second personal singular is -*es;* this was often followed by its pronoun, *þu*, and later we find that this pronoun has become attached to the verb, the initial consonant has been changed to *t*, and the vowel dropped, so that a new inflexional ending -*est* appears in later OE, and persists in the later periods of the language, and its origin was so far forgotten that the pronoun *þu* was again used with the new form.

As we have seen, the older languages were highly inflected, and the story since then has been of a gradual loss of inflexions, so that in present-day English we have very few surviving, the most important being -s or -es as the sign of the genitive or the plural, a few plurals in -en, -(e)s, -(e)d, -t in verbs, -ing, -ed, -(e)n in participles, and a few inflexions in pronominal forms. A comparison of a paradigm of a verb in Gothic – a language related to OE, and with records some four hundred years earlier – with one in OE, ME, and modern English would show how much has been lost in the way of inflexion.

This seems to be a rather unusual state of affairs, with a first period of adding affixes and a later period in which they are dropped, and, as might be expected from such a paradox, we are still far from complete agreement on the subject. Jespersen has put the orthodox view very concisely, although only in order to criticize it; he says 'an originally isolating language, consisting of nothing but formless roots, passed through an agglutinating stage, in which formal elements had been developed, although these and the roots were mutually independent, to the third and highest stage found in flexional languages, in which formal elements penetrated the roots and made inseparable unities with them'.[4] If we attempt to argue from the known to the unknown, we see that modern English is but slightly inflected, ME and OE were more highly inflected, Gothic even more so, yet these were simple compared with the highly-inflected Sanskrit language, which itself had, in all probability, already simplified some of the complexities of the parent language. What we have then, apparently, is a language beginning with simple, non-inflected roots, gradually developing through composition, or coalescence, by agglutination, derivation, and inflexion, until a highly complicated system has been built up, so complicated and unwieldy perhaps that it ceased to be convenient, and the expression of thought became difficult. At that point the reverse process began to take effect, and gradually the inconvenient grammatical accretions were dropped, and language made easier to handle. But it should be noted that the loss of all this grammatical apparatus has in no way impaired the efficiency of English as a vehicle of expression. Rather we see that, with fewer forms, and those much shorter, we are able to accomplish all that our ancestors could with their complicated forms. It is, therefore, not a question of decay in language, but of progress, a movement towards economy of effort, and therefore greater convenience in use, and this latter should surely be the goal in the development of language.

We may now, after this brief consideration of word-formation in the early period of the language, go on to consider in more detail the processes which have resulted in the form of the words we use today. The processes already considered are all really of one type, composition, in that words or elements have been compounded to form longer, complex

words. But there are in English a great number of simple words, consisting of a root only, and we ought therefore, before examining
complex words, to examine these simple forms.

We may perhaps deal first with ONOMATOPŒIA,[5] which has been
suggested as one of the chief origins of our vocabulary. It is perhaps the
oldest, certainly the simplest, of methods of word-creation, and, though
it can account for only a small proportion of our present-day vocabulary, it is an important source of language. It is by no means certain,
however, that we are here employing the best definition, for but few
names accurately reproduce the noises, human, animal, or whatever it
may be, with which they are connected, and it may therefore be more
accurate, and certainly easier for the ordinary person who knows no
Greek, if we adopt the term preferred by Sir James Murray – echoism –
for the process which produces these imitative words.

Many words in our vocabulary today are purely imitative, e.g. *buzz*,
click, *hiss*, *pop*. *Cuckoo*, which is not recorded until the ME period, the
OE being *ʒēac*, surviving in ME dialects as *yeke*, is an example coming
very close to onomatopoeia. The NED notes a tendency in other
languages also to replace the traditional name of this bird by a form
reflecting the sound more closely. Northern dialects have, however,
retained *gowk*, developed from ON *gaukr*, the cognate of OE *ʒēac*. All
these imitative words explain themselves; we need no dictionary for
meaning or etymology. *Fuss* and *flimsy* date from the eighteenth
century, *pom-pom*, as the name of an automatic weapon, from the South
African war. *Burp* is fairly recent, and is extremely expressive of the
slightly inelegant belch. *Barbarian*, from Greek through the Latin
barbarus, is generally considered to have been developed in Greek by
the rather scornful verbal imitation of the speech of the neighbouring
foreign tribes, which was, apparently, to the Greeks, uncouth, unintelligible babbling.

To people of every nation their own echoic words may seem the
natural ones, the only ones. Yet there is but little sign of agreement in
such words; for example, English *cock-a-doodle-do*, German *kikeriki* and
French *coquelico* have little in common. English *whisper*, German
flüstern, French *chuchoter* are not very much alike, but all contain the
voiceless fricative which suggests the sound of whispering.

Such words, closely imitating the actual sound, are obvious, but
another factor, a kind of sound symbolism, is also found alongside
echoism in some words. For example, the very sound of *slither* suggests
slipperiness – yet it is not the sound made when slipping – and the
sound of *awful*, *awe*, and *oh* – even the facial expression as the words
are pronounced – suggests wonder and amazement. With such words

we move from pure and simple onomatopœia and echoism to sound-symbolism.

As Jespersen points out – 'The idea that there is a natural corres-pondence between sound and sense, and that words acquire their contents and value through a certain sound symbolism, has at all times been a favourite one with linguistic dilettanti, the best-known examples being found in Plato's *Kratylos*. Greek and Latin grammarians indulge in the wildest hypotheses to explain the natural origin of such and such a word, as when Nigidius Figulus (the Roman scholar and grammarian of the first century B.C.) said that in pronouncing *vos* one puts forward one's lips and sends out breath in the direction of the other person, while this is not the case with *nos*. With these early writers, to make guesses at sound symbolism was the only way to etymologize; no wonder, therefore, that we with our historical methods and our wider range of knowledge find most of their explanations ridiculous and absurd. But this does not justify us in rejecting any idea of sound symbolism: *abusus non tollit usum!*'[6]

There is indeed much to be said for the theory: *me, we* by the position of the speech organs, particularly the lips, suggest a withdrawing towards the speaker, *thou*, especially in its original form *þu*, and *you* in turn, by the same means, suggest a projection of energy towards the person addressed, and there is more than a suggestion of oblique reference in the position for pronouncing *they*. Yet what are we to make of *he* – with some repetition of the sounds of *me*, yet with the oblique reference of *they*? Such an example shows the difficulties inherent in this theory, difficulties which will be touched upon from time to time in the examples which follow.

An obvious example would seem to be the use of [ɪ] or [i] in words expressing smallness, lightness, or daintiness, e.g. *bit, child* (originally [tʃild]), *chink, chit, kid, little, pigmy, slit, tip, wee*. Yet what are we to make of *big*, or, better still, of the different vowel in *tiny*, of unknown origin, which suggests something smaller than *little*. But even here the theory holds, for the variant *teeny* in turn suggests something smaller than *tiny*, and *teeny-weeny* something smaller still. The use of this vowel with such a meaning seems to be natural, for it is not confined to English; French has *petit*, Latin has *minimus*, German has *kind*, to mention only one example each from but three languages. Probably every language would show numerous examples. The diminutive suffix -*y*, or -*ie*, shows a similar tendency, and there is perhaps some suggestion in the mere sound that *baby* refers to a smaller infant than does *babe*.

On the other hand the vowels *a, o*, and *u* are found in words of opposite meaning, giving an impression of bulk, solidity, or heaviness.

We may compare *hit* with *bang* – yet *tap* has the same vowel as *bang*, and is perhaps more indicative of lightness or daintiness than is *hit*, and *tot* is used to indicate something very small. The second member of each of the following pairs seems to suggest heaviness and solidity, as against the lightness and daintiness suggested by the first member: *ding-dong, clink-clank, chip-chop, snip-snap*. Even the onomatopœic *tick-tock* of an old grandfather clock gives the same impression, almost of lifting and dropping. Or we may compare *flip* with *flop* or *flap*, *creak* with *crack*, *squeak* with *squawk*, and *squeal* with *squall*.

The effect can be more easily illustrated with consonants. The clearest example is perhaps to be found in the repetition of consonants, which suggests a repetition of movement, quick with short vowels, slow with long vowels, as in *bubble* and *murmur*. *P, t, k* are frequently found in words connected with quick action, e.g. *clutch, kick, pitch, tap*, and the explosive consonant at the end of a word, especially mono-syllabic words having a short vowel – for a long vowel almost always suggests long-drawn-out movement – gives the impression of an action brought to a sudden stop, as in *clip, clap, knock, pop, rap, slap, snap, snip, stop*, while a fricative consonant gives the impression of a slow ending. On this ending the NED comments, in a note on *clash:* 'The initial element is that of *clap, clack*, etc.; the final that of *dash, splash, smash, swash*, etc., or perhaps a direct imitation of the element of sound common to these. *Clash* thus suggests an action produced in the same way as a *clap* or a *clack*, which, instead of ending abruptly like these, is broken down as it were into, and results in, a mingled mass of smashing or rustling sounds. A parallel relation exists in *crack, crash*, perhaps in *smack, smash*, and in the dialect *swack, swash*. . . . There is no *phonetic* relation between *clack* and *clash;* i.e. no way by which -*ash* could have been developed (in English) out of -*ack* by the mere operation of phonetic processes'. But care is needed in this distinction between final stop and spirant. *Twitch* and *itch*, both sharp movements, now with final spirant, had -*k* in the earlier language. Again, a liquid at the end of a word suggests an even more dragged-out ending, as in *rumble, murmur*. A different ending – dull and heavy – is suggested by -*mp*, as in *bump, slump*. *Bl-* suggests inflation, possibly from its connection with the inflation of the cheeks in pronunciation, as in *bladder, blast, bloated, blow, bubble*. *Fl-* occurs in words suggesting hurry, or speed of move-ment, as in *flash, flee, fling, fly, flicker, flounce, flurry*, and often a clumsy movement, though even then there may be a suggestion of short, sharp movements also, as *flop* and *flounder;* -*ump* also suggests a clumsy, awkward movement, as in *bump, clump, stump, dump, lump, slump, thump;* *kw-* often occurs in words associated with shaking or trembling, as in *quagmire, quake, quaver, quiver,* while *st-* is found in words denoting stability, as in *stable, stand, staunch, steadfast,* and *still;* yet here we may note *stammer, stumble,* and *stutter,* all expressing the reverse idea. There seems to be an identity of idea also in words beginning with *gr-,* as *groan, grouse, growl, grudge, grumble, grunt.* Words beginning with *skr-* often have a sense of loud outcry, as in *scream* and *screech* – and *shriek* had originally the same initial consonant combination; indeed, it still has this initial sound in some northern dialects. *Wh-* occurs in words denoting secrecy, or something subdued, as in *whisper* and *whist,* yet *whistle* has the opposite sense, being the reverse of subdued, and intended to attract attention. It is perhaps a question of using some kind of voiceless fricative, thus producing the effect of whisper. We have already noticed English *whisper,* French *chuchoter,* and German *flüstern;* to these we may add Danish *hviske,* ON *kvisa,* and Spanish *susurar.* The sound of a whisper is closely paralleled by the light rustling of leaves, for which the learned term is *susurration,* from the perfect stem of Latin *susurrare,* with which we may compare *susurrus* – a whisper, the Spanish development of which is noted above. Here the same process has been at work. The *wh-* is not common to all these forms, but all have some kind of voiceless fricative or affricate.

A word of caution is necessary, as may be seen from the examples of *child* and *shriek;* moreover, in considering sound-symbolism one needs to consider the sound at the earliest period for which we have records, nearest to the time when the word was formed. Jespersen points out that *crow* is not nearly so good an example of echoism as is the older form, OE *crawe.*

From the exceptions which have been mentioned above, and from the obvious fact that many examples of all the types mentioned could perhaps be quoted, with contrary meaning, e.g. *thick,* and *thin,* which vary in only one consonant, yet are opposites, it seems to be dangerous to pursue this line too far. It is also not easy to see the connection sometimes, as in the case of *st-* words quoted above; there seems to be no connection between the sound of this consonant combination and the idea of stability and firm security, yet some of these words are certainly very old, and are found in all the Indo-European languages, suggesting that the idea was present in the Indo-European period itself. In spite of the exceptions and the apparent lack of connection between sound and idea, and statements such as that of Whitney – 'Inner and essential connexion between idea and word . . . there is none, in any language upon earth' – there is ample evidence in favour of the view that echoism and sound-symbolism are important formative factors in language. There seems to be a close connection between the two, and so easily does one shade into the other that it is sometimes difficult to differentiate. One of the objections against echoism as the origin of language has been that it can include but a very small part of our vocabulary, yet, though no one today would maintain the theory that in echoism alone we have the explanation of the origin of speech, this method of word-formation, with the closely-related sound-symbolism, can be made to account for a very large number of words in use today, and, as Jespersen has said, 'it would be an interesting task to examine in detail and systematically what ideas lend themselves to symbolic presentation, and what sounds are chosen for them in different languages'.

There is also another process of word-formation within the root itself, the process of ABLAUT, or GRADATION, by means of which our ancestors were able so to modify roots as to indicate different grammatical features. This is, of course, not the place to enter into a long discussion of the intricacies of Ablaut, about which, indeed, scholars are not yet – and probably never will be – in complete agreement, but a simple explanation of the facts themselves will not be out of place, more especially as, although the process is not now used in word formation, it was extremely productive in the early stages of our language.

Ablaut is the term used, first by Grimm, to describe variations, in both quality and quantity, of the vowel element of cognate words, or even of different forms of the same word. These variations go back to Indo-European, for examples are to be found in all the IE dialects, but it would be a mistake to think that Ablaut is peculiar to the IE languages. The Semitic languages, for example, possess Ablaut systems much more highly developed than any we find in the IE languages, and there are traces of Ablaut, too, in Finno-Ugrian. Ablaut may be found in any part of a word, in stressed or unstressed syllables, but as a factor in word-formation we shall consider Ablaut only as it affects the root vowel of a word. The phenomena of Ablaut, as we find it in the recorded IE dialects, are to be traced back to the parent language itself, and depend upon factors which no longer operate in the present-day languages to any appreciable extent, so that any explanations of the process must be sought, through the medium of comparative philology, in the parent-language. Many views have been put forward in explanation, some of which conflict with others, and indeed it is likely that we shall never arrive at a complete and accurate understanding of Ablaut, for its workings are buried so deep in the earliest strata of our language.

The most recent and most generally accepted views agree that Ablaut arose as a result of the two IE types of accentuation, pitch and stress. These are the two essential aspects of accent, variations of intonation,

resulting in pitch, or musical accent, and variations of intensity, resulting in stress, or dynamic accent. The former depends upon the rate of
vibration of the vocal chords, the latter upon the force of expiration.
Among present-day languages we find a tendency towards one or other
of the types, the Germanic languages, for example, being of the stress
type and the Romance languages of the pitch type, but neither type is
found absolutely alone in a language.

In the earliest period to which our knowledge extends accent was
free, being able to fall on prefix, root, or suffix, but the accent system
was developed and regulated in different ways in the various IE dialects
in the course of time. In Germanic, the language with which we are
primarily concerned, the accent tended to be fixed on the first syllable
in very early times, though there are exceptions to that rule in Germanic,
just as there are in Modern English, which tends to place the main stress
on the first syllable, but does not do so invariably.

Pitch accent apparently resulted in an alternation between front and
back vowels, the front vowels tending to be used for the present tense,
and back vowels for past tense, though perhaps the original idea was
not one of tense, but rather of nearness, either of time or space. In
general, front vowels are distinguished from back vowels by pitch and
oral resonance. Experiments with apparatus designed to test larynx
vibrations have suggested that front vowels have a higher pitch than
back vowels. The difference in oral resonance is one of high oral
resonance for front vowels, and low oral resonance for back vowels.
The former requires greater muscle-tension, which is perhaps to be
expected when the speaker is concerned with actions very close to him
in time or space, and therefore of great interest, whereas low oral
resonance implies relaxed muscle-tension, and a corresponding slackening of interest in more remote events. This type is generally known as
qualitative Ablaut, as the effect is a change in the *quality* of the vowel. In
IE *i* and *u* were not original full vowels, but occurred only as the result
of reduction of diphthongs, and therefore the alternation in pitch, as
regards full-grade vowels, is limited to *a*, *e*, and *o*. The variation in the
Germanic languages is usually between *e* and *o*, though *a* may also occur.
It should be noted that the alternation is apparently between vowels of
equal importance, for there is no evidence that the back vowel was
secondary to the front one.

Stress accent resulted in the weakening or disappearance of unstressed
vowels, or the lengthening of vowels in particular circumstances. Vowels
which, under normal conditions, are short may be weakened or disappear altogether in an unstressed position, or may be lengthened in
circumstances of particular emphasis. Vowels which are normally long

may be reduced when unstressed; they rarely disappear completely, and there is no certain evidence for the Germanic languages of further lengthening of long vowels corresponding to the lengthened grade of short vowels. As an example in Modern English of this type of variation brought about by change of stress we may note the vowel *o* in the following related group: in *histórical* it bears the full stress, and is a full or strong-grade vowel; in *hístory* it bears reduced stress, and is a reduced or weak-grade vowel; in *híst'ry* it has disappeared completely, and this is called the zero or vanishing grade. The lengthened grade, the result in this case of overstress, is heard in one line of a popular song, where we are told that Rudolph, the red-nosed reindeer, will '*go down in histőry*' [hɪstɔrɪ], according to most of our singers. The same kind of lengthening is found often in feminine intonation, where, for example, [æ] may be lengthened to [ɛ:], as in '*Where's my băg* [bɛ:g]?' or '*What a băd* [bɛ:d] *boy!*' At first there were possibly as many grades of vowel as there were syllables in the word, but for practical purposes only four are recognized, full grade, reduced grade, zero grade, and lengthened grade. One final point remains to be stressed: in this type of Ablaut we are concerned with the normal type of vowel as the basis, between normally-long vowels and their variations, and normally-short vowels and their variations, so that an alternation between a normally-long and a short vowel of the same quality, where the latter is the result of reduction, is possible, but an alternation between a normally-long and a normally-short vowel of the same quality is not acceptable as a result of Ablaut.

The variations, as we have them in the Germanic languages, are found in several series, usually developed by the effect of both types of accent, and there are generally four grades of vowels for each. In theory, all related words should show one or other vowel of a particular series, for it seems that when a new word was coined in the parent language it was done by varying the vowel within the series to which the word belonged; to put this in another way, we may say that, if the original limitations were still in force, and we wanted to coin a new word related in any way to the idea of riding, we should be limited to a 'framework' of *r – d*, the sense-form, as it were, and our choice of root-vowel would be confined to [aɪ], [ov] or [eɪ], or [ɪ], for those are the vowels of that particular series, as in, for example, *ride, rode, road, raid,* and *ridden.*

As a result of the effect of both types of Ablaut, there developed in Indo-European a series of Ablaut-rows. These can be illustrated in the various Indo-European dialects, but our concern is with English, and the examples will therefore be confined to Germanic Ablaut, and the particular development of it in Old English. The working of Ablaut produced the original vowel-variations, of which the chief is the so-called 'e – o – x – stretch-grade' series, where e and o are the vowels varied qualitatively, and x is the reduced or zero-grade vowel by quantitative Ablaut, and the stretch grade the lengthened vowel, also by quantitative Ablaut. There are others, but they are less important, and their proof not so certain. The original vowel-variations were then further modified in the different dialects, particularly by the influence of neighbouring sounds. We have no space here to enter into a long account of the phonological changes which thus took place before the period of recorded Old English; that is a very specialized study, and beyond the scope of the present work, even if, which is much to be doubted, it would arouse the interest of the ordinary reader. It is sufficient to say that, as a result of all this, Ablaut-rows existed in Old English which can be most clearly seen in the principal parts of the strong verbs, though they are to be found in all parts of speech. These Ablaut-rows are set forth in Old English in seven groups, according to neighbouring sounds, and the groups form the basis of the seven classes of Old English strong verbs. Examples will now be given of these Ablaut-rows, group by group, with illustrations from various parts of speech. Considerations of space must limit the number of illustrations from each class, but even an elementary acquaintance with Old English soon shows how widespread the process was in the early language.

The four variants in each Ablaut-row provide the four principal parts of the Old English strong verb. The first two are the present and pre-terite singular stems, with, at least for Classes I–V, variation between e and o by qualitative Ablaut. The third and fourth stems arise by quanti-tative Ablaut, and are those of the preterite plural and past participle. Opinions vary on the exact development of these stems within the various groups, and it will be sufficient to say here that in some cases at least the main stress did not fall on the root syllable, as it did in the case of the present and preterite singular, but on the inflexional ending, so that the original vowel of the root-syllable was reduced or lost, because of lack of stress. In some cases we have evidence for the stretch-grade vowel in the preterite plural stem.

In Old English Class I strong verbs the vowel-variation is ī, ā, i, i; we may take as an example the verb stīgan – to ascend, which had the following principal parts: stīgan, stāh, stigon, stigen. In words semanti-cally connected the variation of vowel is always within this series. For example, the first stem shows stīgend – a sty (or swelling, rising) on the eye; the second stem is found in the adjective stægel – steep, and stæger – stair, in both cases the original ā having been modified by a following sound. The third and fourth stems, identical in this class, are found in *stig-rāp* – stirrup (lit. a mounting-rope), *stige* – a going up or down, *stignes* – descent, and *stigol* – a place of climbing a fence, a stile. Or we may take *witan* – to know, formed originally from a verb with stem *wīt-*, and therefore a form with unstressed vowel; we find also *wāt* – (pret. pres.) he knows, *wītig* – wise, *wītega* – wise man, prophet, *wita* – wise man (also *witness* – one who knows because he has seen), *wit* – understanding, *wit-lēas* – foolish, mad (lit. *witless*), and, *witena-ʒemot* – parliament – lit. meeting of wise men.

We may perhaps further illustrate this class, in order to show at the outset the possibilities of the process, and then confine illustrations of the other classes to one or two examples. Of the alternation of the first and second stems we may note the following, using now Modern English examples: *abide, abode; drive, drove* (verb and noun in both cases); *ride, road, rode, raid* (the last three all from OE *rād*); *shrive, Shrove* (in *Shrove Tuesday*, for example); *strike, stroke; writhe, wroth*. As examples of the third and fourth stems we may compare the following: *bite*, with *bit, bitten, bitter* (lit. that which *bites*); *drift* (compared with *drive*); *slit* (cf. OE *slītan* – to tear); *written*, and *writ* (something written), compared with *write*; and *shrift, shriven*, compared with *shrive* and *Shrove* above.

The Old English vowel-variation for Class II verbs was ēo (also ū), ēa, u, o. As an example we may take the verb *bēodan* – to offer; its principal parts are *bēodan, bēad, budon, boden*. In *bēod* – a table or bowl (on which something is offered) we see a formation from the first stem; *bydel* – a herald, beadle (< **budil*) is derived from the third stem, and *bod* – command, message, *boda* – messenger, *bodian* – to announce, preach, *bodere* – teacher, and *bodigend* – preacher, are from the fourth stem. We may note here that the vowels of the third and fourth stems were originally identical, so that it is not always possible to know from which of these stems a form is derived. As an example of the second stem we may note *sheaf* (OE *scēaf* – pret. of *scūfan* – to push, hence, something pushed together), from the third stem we have *suds* (cf. OE *sēoðan* – to boil, NE *seethe*), and *tug* (cf. OE *tēon* – to pull), and from the fourth stem *bow* (OE *boʒa*, cf. OE *būʒan* – to bend), *frost* (OE *frost, forst*, cf. *frēosan* – to freeze), and *sodden* (OE *soden*, pp. of *sēoðan*).

Class III shows much variation, because of sound changes effective after the Ablaut-row had been established, chiefly because of following consonants. The original series was e, a, u, u; in Old English *e* may appear as *e, i,* or *eo; a* may appear as *a* or *ea,* and *u* of the fourth stem appears also as *o*. OE *drincan* – to drink, provides illustrative examples; its principal parts were *drincan, dranc, druncon, druncen,* and from one or other of these parts are derived in Old English *ȝedrinc* – carousal, *drinca* – a drink, *drenc* – a drink, what is drunk, *drencan* (< **drankjan*) – to give to drink (here the medial consonant was fronted, and so we have the development to *drench*, still used in its original sense, for it has the meaning 'to give a dose of medicine to cattle'), *druncen* – intoxicated, *druncnian* – to be drowned, give to drink, become intoxicated, and *drync* (< **drunci*) – drink, potion.

An interesting example of Ablaut-formation in different languages may be seen here. In the strong-grade first stem of a formation in this series we have Latin *dent-* (cf. *dens, dentis*), found in *dental, dentist*, etc. The second stem yielded **dont;* by Grimm's Law the *-t* became *þ*, and in the period just before the settlement of the Angles and Saxons in these islands a nasal was absorbed before *þ*, with compensatory lengthening, to give OE *tōþ* – tooth. This change did not take place in Old High German, which has *zand*, with *z < t* by the Second Sound Shift. Another Germanic language, Gothic, developed from the third or fourth stem, and has *tunþus*.

As an example of semantic development we may note OE *wyrd* – fate. OE *weorþan* – to become, to come to pass, had preterite plural *wurdon;* from this stem *wurd-*, with an i-suffix causing mutation of u > y, we have *wyrd* – what is to come to pass, the Anglo-Saxon 'fate'.

In Class IV verbs in Old English the Ablaut-row was e, æ (or a), ǣ (or ō), o (or u). OE *beran* – to bear, provides sufficient examples; its principal parts were *beran, bær, bǣron, boren*. From one or other of the stems of these words are derived *barn, bearn* – child (cf. Northern *bairn*), something *born*(e), *bærwe, bearwe* – barrow, *bær* – bier, *byre* (< **buri*) – son, youth, *byrd* (< **burdi*) – birth, *byrðen* (< **burðeni*) – burden, *bora* – one who bears.

A wide range of examples may be drawn from the IE series *kel-*, *kol-*, *kl̥-*, which appears in Old English as *helan* – to conceal, with principal parts *helan, hæl, hǣlon, holen*. Derived from this root we have OE *helm* – helmet (lit. a covering), *heall* – hall, shelter, *hell* (by j-mutation, cf. Gothic *halja*) – hell, *hol* – cave, hollow, *hulu* – hull, outer shell or husk; *holster* owes its meaning to Dutch influence, but OE had *heolstor* – hiding-place. From the Latin *cella* we have *cell*, from the Latin verb Middle English has derived *conceal*, and from Latin, through French, *occult*.

In Class V the vowel-variation is between e, æ, ǣ, e. OE *cweþan* – to speak, has as its principal parts *cweþan, cwæþ, cwǣdon, cweden*. From these forms are derived *ȝecwed* – a declaration, *cwedol* – eloquent, *cwiddian* – to speak, *cwiddung* – report, and *cwide* – statement, etc.

From *weȝan* – to carry, weigh, we have *wǣȝe* – weight, scales, which has given us *weiʒ* – a weight, as in a *wey* of cheese, for example. From the second stem of this verb we have OE *wæʒn* – wain, wagon. *Wagon* is not derived directly from Old English, being borrowed from Dutch, but Dutch *wagen* is cognate with OE *wæʒn*, which early lost the spirant before the nasal, with compensatory lengthening, to give ME *wain*.

From the stem which gave OE *licʒan* – to lie, originally *leʒjan*, has been derived OE *leʒer* – a lying, couch, bed, lair. *Trade* meant originally the path we tread, therefore our manner of life, and meant in Middle English a path in general. In its present sense it is probably a Low German loan, perhaps picked up from traders or seamen from the Hanseatic cities, meaning perhaps originally the course of a ship, and derives from *trad* – one of the stems of the W. Germanic Ablaut series which has given us OE *tredan* – to tread. From the meaning of 'path' it came to mean 'one's path or manner of life', then easily from that was developed 'employment', and so 'occupation'.

These are the clearly-established series of Ablaut-rows for Old English, Classes VI and VII presenting more difficulties in explanation. Examples of word-formation in these last two series exist also, but sufficient examples have already been quoted to show how productive was this method of word-formation in the early stages of our language.

We may perhaps conclude our examination of formation by means of Ablaut-variation by noting how often members of Ablaut-rows appear in compound formations, some of them colloquial, as in *riff-raff*, *pit-a-pat*, and *pitter-patter*, *snip-snap*, *knick-knack*, *zig-zag*, *chit-chat*, *tittle-tattle*, *shilly-shally*, *dilly-dally*, *ding-dong*, *sing-song*, *slip-slop*, *wishy-washy*, *ping-pong*, *see-saw* and *hee-haw*. Some of these may be onomatopœic, and it may be that sound-symbolism enters into the formation, for all seem to show alternation between front and back vowels, but this, on the other hand, may be merely the principle of using a front vowel for near objects and ideas, whether of place or time, and back vowels for remote objects and ideas, as was suggested in the discussion of qualitative Ablaut, and which survives in such expressions as *this and that*, *here and there*, and many others.

Here we leave formation of simple stems and pass to composite forms, compounded from either roots and formative affixes, or from two or more independent words.

DERIVATION[7] is one of the commonest methods of word-formation, and also one of the oldest, being found in almost all languages, certainly in all IE languages, and we may therefore assume the process was used in the parent language. The term is applied to the process by which new words are formed by adding prefixes or suffixes, or both, to a root-form already in existence. Many of these affixes were no doubt originally independent words; indeed, some scholars go so far as to say that they were all independent in the earliest period. If we admit the original independence of these affixes, then the process is, in a sense, a type of compounding; however, many of these affixes soon ceased to be considered as independent words, and became rather indicative of general ideas, added to modify the meaning of the existing word, and so the process is used more freely than compounding. It is difficult, if not impossible, to draw a clear line between derivation and inflexion, for the case-endings of nouns, pronouns, and adjectives, and the endings used to indicate person, number, tense, mood, and voice in verbs, are usually affixes added to a root. So far as English is concerned the process is to some extent connected also with borrowing from foreign languages, for many of the affixes are not native words. Although the process is ancient, it has lost little of its force, and it has been perhaps the most fruitful method of word-formation in the modern period. As a result of this process we see families of words arising, and the process thus helps to preserve a word in the language, for, while one solitary word may eventually be lost, it has more chance of survival as a member of a group. As extreme examples of this process we may note *advert, convert, controvert, divert, extrovert, invert, introvert, pervert, revert, retrovert, subvert,* and the various related words, for only one of each type is here listed, or, from Latin *scribere,* and its p.p. stem, we have the nouns *conscript, conscription, description, inscription, prescription, proscription, scribe, script, subscription, superscription,* the adjectives *descriptive, prescriptive, proscriptive,* and *scribal,* and the verbs *describe, circumscribe, escribe, inscribe, prescribe, subscribe,* and *scribble,* and these by no means exhaust the list of formations from this root.

The process was a common one in the earliest stages of our language, and such modern words as *freedom, kingdom, friendship, lordship, length, strength* are all developed from early formations. Indeed, many Old English types are still in use, as the following examples prove; the words are here given in their modern form: *-en* to form adjectives, as *brazen, golden, wheaten; -er* to form agent-nouns from verbs, as *binder, learner,* the archaic *fisher,* still common as a surname, *singer,* and *weaver;* (in one case here the wheel has come full circle. OE had *godspellere*–the preacher of the gospel. This was later replaced by the loan-word *evangelist.* The old word has now been revived in the American [*hot*] *gospeller*); *-ung* [later *-ing*) to form the verbal noun, as *greeting, reading; -less,* as in *careless, homeless, speechless; -ness,* forming abstract nouns from adjectives, as *bitterness, blindness, cleanness; -y,* forming adjectives from nouns, as *hungry, stony; -isc* (later *-ish*) to form adjectives from nouns, as *childish, English;* also, though perhaps from Dutch rather than a native type, the original diminutive suffix, found in ME and NE as *-kin, -ikin,* as *manikin, napkin.* An obvious development was the attachment of this suffix to a name, perhaps first as a term of endearment, or a nickname, and already in ME such forms are recorded as surnames. Modern forms include *Simkin(s), Tomkin(s), Wilkin(s),* and, by a double formation, the latter becomes *Wilkinson.* The sense seems to have changed to one of contempt in *bumpkin,* which is perhaps to be derived from Dutch *boomkin* – a little tree, or log. In OE *-ing* was used to form patronymics, as *æpeling* – son of a noble or prince (< *æpele* – noble). This sense is still found in such names as *Browning, Fielding, Manning,* and is also preserved in place-names such as *Reading* and *Worthing.* In the north, however, the Scandinavian form *-son* is more frequent, as *Atkinson, Richardson, Tomlinson.* The only common adverbial suffix to survive is *-ly.* Some of the examples quoted above were not felt to be independent words in the OE period. Examples of independent words so used, really a type of compounding, therefore, in Old English, but not recognised as such today, are *-hood,* as in *childhood, maidenhood, priest-hood, -dom,* as in *Christendom, freedom, kingdom, martyrdom, -kind,* as in *mankind,* and *-scipe,* as in *lordship, worship.* Another example, OE *-lāc,* survives now only in *wedlock.*

An interesting position arises in the case of nouns of agency. The common form *-er* has already been noticed. OE also had a suffix *-estre,* used to form feminine nouns, e.g. *bæcestre, tæppestre,* and this survives in *-ster,* in *spinster,* and such personal names as *Brewster* and *Webster.* The NED quotes OE *bæcestre* as one of the few examples of the use of this suffix to form a masculine noun; the normal masculine type is, of course, *baker* (OE *bæcere*), with the feminine form surviving in the surname *Baxter.* The suffix is frequently found in ME in feminine forms, where, for example, we have *webbe* (masc.) and *webbestre* (fem.), but the significance of gender has been so far lost today that we generally add a second feminine suffix to make the gender clear, and alongside the original *spinster* type we have *seamstress* – cf. OE *sēamestre* – and *song-stress.* The feminine significance is completely lost in later forms such as *maltster* and *teamster;* recent formations such as *gangster, trickster, youngster* seem to be analogical types; they are certainly not directly descended from the OE *-estre* form.

Among the prefixes we may note *be-,* frequently used to make intransitive verbs transitive, as in *speak, bespeak* (cf. *bespoke* tailoring). *Be-* had also a strong form *bī-;* both were originally independent words, and so in the first place new formations were really compounds, but the meanings of the independent word and the prefix later diverged so much that we now no longer look upon these forms as compounds. We also find *mis-*, as in *mistake, misunderstand; with-* (against), as in *withstand; mid-* (with), as in *midwife; for-*, as in *forbear, forsake; un-* is still in common use as a negative and reversing prefix. Of these, though examples recorded in the early period still survive, some are no longer formative elements, for example, *mid-*, *with-*, and *for-;* the last-named was very fruitful in the earlier period, and was quite distinct from the preposition, being used to express loss or destruction, or in a privative sense, or, later, as a mere intensive, and we may note in these senses *forbid, forget, forgive, forgo, forlorn, forswear*, but it is not now used for new formations. Prefixes are much more commonly used now than suffixes, and are chiefly foreign.

In some cases the affix may be obscured, as a result of later phonological changes, changes of stress, syncope, and assimilation. For example, the PG suffix *-iþō*, used to form feminine abstract nouns from adjectives, survives only as *-th*, which might be taken as part of the stem, as in *length*, but the nature of the original suffix, the vowel of which caused i-mutation in OE before it underwent syncope, can be seen by comparing the unmutated stem-vowel of the adjective with the mutated stem-vowel of the abstract noun, as in *broad* and *breadth*, *strong* and *strength*, *whole* and *health*.

Not all the affixes are native forms; Greek, Latin, and French forms are common. Many native affixes are still productive, and will probably continue so, but the language has apparently felt the need of greater powers in derivation, and has called upon the resources of other languages to remedy its own deficiency. Some of these foreign affixes, such as *ante-*, *anti-*, *contra-*, *post-*, and *pre-*, retain their original forms, but others show assimilation, as, for example, *dis-* in *difference*, *in-* in *illegal* or *improbable*, or *ad-* in *assimilation*. These foreign affixes may be used with English roots to form hybrids, probably because we are comparatively poor in productive native affixes today, and of these hybrids Bradley has said: 'When such pairs of words as derive and derivation, esteem and estimation, laud and laudation, condemn and condemnation, had found their way into the English vocabulary, it was natural the suffix *-ation* should be recognised by English speakers as an allowable means of forming "nouns of action" out of verbs'.[8] Perhaps we may here illustrate this by one example only; one of the earliest hybrids formed with *-ment* is perhaps Wiclif's *one-ment* (the state of being at one with God), which obviously anticipates *atonement*. Later, in the sixteenth century, are recorded *acknowledgement, amazement, betterment, merriment, wonderment*, all of which have survived, and Spenser's *dreariment*, an expressive word which failed to establish itself permanently, and since then there has been a long succession of such forms.

As an example of the formation of hybrids, and also at the same time of the productiveness of some foreign affixes, we may note the French -é. *Employee* and *nominee* are both fairly early. The original sense of the French past-participle termination, with its passive force, is not always kept in English. Among examples may be noted *evacuee*, *examinee*, *internee*, *referee*, *refugee*, and such business terms as *consignee*, *drawee*, and *payee*.

Foreign affixes are frequently used in English to make entirely new types, unknown in the language from which they are adopted. *Nōn* was used in compounds in Latin, as *nōn-nulli*, but was not apparently an element used in derivation, but it has been freely used as a prefix in English, and is still very productive, especially in scientific and learned vocabulary. Among examples we may note *nonage*, *nonconformist*, *nondescript*, *nonentity*, *nonjuror*, *nonsense*, and many others, apart from hyphenated forms such as *non-combatant*, *non-user*, and others, which seem to suggest an earlier compounded type. The Latin suffix -*bilis* yielded -*ble*, appearing in English as -*able*, -*ible*, and was originally used only to form adjectives from verbs of Romance origin, but it was soon added to native words, as in *breakable*, *lovable*. It occurs as early as the fourteenth century, its adoption being perhaps helped by the presence of the independent form *able*. Among early forms we may note *unknowable*, *understandable*, *answerable*, and *laughable*. In Latin it has both active and passive force, but it is chiefly passive in English, as *admirable*, *legible*, *navigable*, *soluble*, though active forms are also found, as *durable* and *sensible*. It is still productive, and can be used almost anywhere where an adjective is needed. It may even be used as a formation from verbs normally requiring a preposition; Shakespeare used *laughable*, and this form was criticized in the nineteenth century, it being held that the correct form should be *laugh-at-able*, but, apart from the authority of the earlier use of the form, and the ugly form of the proposed alternative, we do find this the accepted form today, with the meaning 'fit to be laughed at'. Similarly we use *rely upon*, but *reliable*. But this type is naturally not invariable; for example, although there is the authority of the dictionary for the form, do we normally say that a house is *livable*, in the sense of 'fit to be lived in'? One may feel that *livable in* is not a happy expression.

The French suffix -*ous* (< Lat. -*osus*) is added to forms where it did not belong originally, but this is not purely an English characteristic, for we find that there are similar adjectives in French where apparently Latin had no corresponding form in -*osus*. *Famous* and *copious* have Latin equivalents; not so *joyous*. English has added *-ous* to any Latin stem whatsoever, regardless of whether or not Latin had a form in *-osus*, for example, *capricious*, *sonorous*, *stupendous*, and then extended the practice to native words, as in *murderous* and *wondrous*, and this suffix is still extremely productive. Here we may note that the types developed consciously and deliberately from Latin forms in *-osus*, for example, *grandiose*, *morose*, *otiose*, *verbose*, tend to be on a more dignified level.

A similar state of affairs is found in the case of *-al;* it is found in adjectives and nouns which had a similar formation in Latin, as *animal*, *equal*, *mortal*, in French loan-words which did not have the form in Latin, as *arrival*, *national*, and also with native stems, as *bestowal*, *betrothal*. So also with *-age*, which is found in original Latin types, as *voyage* (Lat. *viaticum*), and was then used to form derivatives from any source, as in *bandage*, *luggage*, *poundage*, or to form nouns from verbs, as *marriage*, *usage*, and is still very productive. Also we may note *-ery*, added to native roots in such forms as *bakery* and *brewery*.

Although Latin provides no precedent for our modern use of *pro-*, which seems to date only from the early nineteenth century, one cannot but feel that forms with the prefixes *pro-* and *anti-* are happier than those developed with the suffixes *-phile* and *-phobe*. It is interesting also to note that forms with the prefix are hyphenated, but those with the suffix are fully compounded, to make one word.

These foreign affixes are now so much a part of the language that the utmost freedom is possible in their use. Words are found containing two foreign suffixes, as *monstrosity* and *pomposity;* with such we may compare a type having two native suffixes, as *hopefulness*, *hopefully*, *thoughtlessness*, *thoughtlessly*. In *comically* we have Greek *-ic*, Latin *-al*, and English *-ly*. Hybrids are therefore extremely common, as *witticism*, with a native root and two Greek affixes, *unjust*, which is English prefix + French root, or *hemidemisemiquaver*, where the three prefixes are Greek, French, and Latin respectively. Robertson quotes an interesting example; speaking of *re-macadamized* he says: 'Here is a word that will not strike most of its users as in any way objectionable or eccentric. But re- is Latin, mac is Celtic, adam is Hebrew, -ize is French, originally Greek, and -d is English'.[9] An extreme example, though the word is in common use, is *incomprehensible*, with, as Professor Potter has pointed out, 'its root hen and eight affixes and infixes'.[10]

Mention has already been made of the paucity of native affixes. A study of the way in which some of these have remained productive through the ages and others have ceased to be so is interesting. We have already noticed the suffix *-th*, used to form abstract nouns from adjectives. OE had a great number of these words, but few have been formed recently: *growth*, probably coined in the late sixteenth century, has remained, but Bacon's *lowth*, Walpole's *greenth* and Ruskin's *illth*, on the analogy of *wealth*, have never become part of our vocabulary. We may pause to wonder why *wealth* is accepted and *illth* rejected. A recent form, H. G. Wells' *coolth*, is either deliberate or unconscious revival, for NED cites it from 1594. In new formations -*th* seems to have been replaced by -*ness*. The decay in the use of *for*- has already been noted, and other affixes, extremely productive in the earlier period, such as, for example, -*dōm*, are now rarely used for new forms. Of old native forms still productive in recent times we may note the use of -*ful*, -*ish*, -*less*, and -*y* to form adjectives, and -*ly* to form adverbs, which became much more common when the other OE adverbial suffix, -*e*, lost its significance because final -*e* ceased to be pronounced. Also in use today is -*ness*, used to form abstract nouns, and this is one of the most productive of English suffixes, having apparently replaced at least four older forms, -*th*, -*hood*, -*dom*, and -*ship*, and being now added commonly to foreign nouns, especially from French and Latin, to form abstract nouns, as, for example, *graciousness*. In OE -*en* was used, generally to denote material, in forming adjectives from nouns, e.g. *gylden, wyllen;* the mutated vowel in the OE adjective as against the unmutated vowel in the noun shows the nature of the original suffix, but NE has generally restored the unmutated form, by analogy with the noun, as *golden, woollen,* and often the simple noun is used, almost as a compound form, as in *gold watch, wool fibre.* This is very common in some regional dialects, where we hear, for example, of a *wood door*. There has been a remarkable extension of the use of the suffix -*isc* (later -*ish*). Its chief use in Old English was to form adjectives of nationality, and, more rarely, of quality, as *folcisc, cildisc.* Later, in the fifteenth century, it was used in a rather vague, indefinite way with adjectives of colour, and from that has sprung our common colloquial use of the suffix in that sense, where it is added to almost any adjective, as *oldish, smallish, sweetish, youngish,* and even to phrases, as *I'll meet you for tea at four-ish,* or even *See you for lunch at one o'clock-ish.* In some cases it seems to have acquired a rather derogatory sense; for example, *mannish* and *womanish* are very different in sense from *manly* and *womanly.* We may also note that, with the intrusion of women into male spheres, the feminine suffix is falling into disuse. *Poetess, authoress* are now usually replaced by *poet, author. Doctor* is the common form for both sexes, but not *actor,* for *actress* remains. We even have *chairman,* when the chair is occupied by a woman, although the form *Madam Chairman* may be used in addressing the Chair.

Many new formations by derivation are of an academic or technical nature. Greek affixes have proved extremely useful for the close definitions needed for the expression of our abstract thought today. Forms with *-ic*, *-ism*, *-ist*, *-ize*, *-cracy*, and *hyper-*, *pseudo-*, and *neo-* are in common use for new formations, and the special use made of Greek affixes in scientific nomenclature is obvious to all. Some of these apparently exceptional and unnatural types may become a permanent part of language. For example, *democracy* is a term of great value, and was soon on everybody's lips. Thus the suffix *-ocracy*, unnatural as it may seem in English, was on the way to being generally established. *Mobocracy* is so far only colloquial and vulgar, but it may one day win its place. The un-English *bureaucracy* has found a permanent place in the language, much as some may regret it; perhaps we can only be thankful that we have that form, which has at any rate a not unpleasant sound, for the monstrosity *officeocracy* might have developed instead!

The process of derivation, in so far as formations at the present time are concerned, is used more perhaps for the learned than the common vocabulary, the words being created by scholars for specific purposes. Sometimes they are ugly and cumbersome words which can add little to the convenience of everyday language; a recent example, *miniaturization* – a technical term in the radio industry for the process developed during the war, of making miniature components, is hardly likely to become generally accepted, but some do filter down into everyday speech. Very frequently these formations throw light on the character of an age: for example, comparatively little of an original nature resulted from the nineteenth century, but, being largely dominated by Idealism, it did delight in the worship and imitation of the great and magnificent, whether men, styles, institutions, or whatever it might be, and one result of this was the large number of formations with *-esque*, an adjectival suffix expressing style or manner, as *picturesque*, *Romanesque*, *statuesque*. Ruskin used such forms freely. Perhaps our own preoccupation with theories and doctrines is reflected in our frequent use of *-ism* and *-ist*. The suffix *-ism* is not new: it was adopted from the French in the thirteenth century – *baptism* is an early example; it was a living element by the sixteenth century, after which its use developed rapidly, and it was probably the most fruitful suffix in the nineteenth century. In the same way the widening of horizons, the narrowing of natural divisions and boundaries, and the consequent increase in communication between distant parts of the world may be reflected in the use of *inter-* in such forms as *international* and *inter-racial*, and a similar movement in the realm of religious thought perhaps in such forms as *inter-denominational*. The further development of the process can be seen in the demand, frequently expressed in many quarters now, for *international* to be replaced by *supra-national*.

One type peculiar to English must be noted. The usual method of formation from Latin verb-stems is to make use of the present stem, but English has very frequently based new formations on the past participle stem. This perhaps arose in the first place from the common use of the past participle as an adjective, as in 'devil incarnate,' and the natural feeling, which developed later, that this adjective was based upon a verb with a similar stem, and as a result we have such forms as *dedicate*, *frustrate*, *accumulate*, *associate*, *create*, *liberate*, *radiate*, *translate*, and others, including some based on non-Latin forms, as *dehydrate*, from a Greek root, *facilitate* and *tolerate* from French roots, and even *titivate*, from *tidy*.

No account of the process of derivation can be complete without a discussion of the question of hybrids. The general rule seems to be that, when the foreign affix is simpler and more convenient than its English counterpart, or there is no English equivalent for a foreign affix, the latter is fully naturalized – e.g. *re-* is used equally with native and foreign words, being one of our commonest prefixes, for although the English equivalent does exist, the alternative would be to use it as a clumsy prefix, as *to againmodel* – an impossible form we may think, though ME had *agen-bien* – to buy back, redeem, and *agenclepe* – to recall – or else be content to retain it as an adverb – *to model again*. Then again, although purists are always ready to maintain the original source of words, some foreign loans become so common in use that they are felt to be almost English, and one feels no discord when an English affix is added, and only when the loans have remained recognizably alien need we concern ourselves with linguistic harmony. Old hybrids such as *frailness* and *gayness* have been replaced by homogeneous forms, and *simpleness* has given way to *simplicity*, yet some which have been so altered seem to have roots completely naturalized; for example, Wyclif's hybrid *unglorious* has been replaced by *inglorious*, and the *unpossible* of the 1611 Bible by *impossible*. Admittedly, to our ears *unglorious* and *unpossible* sound strange, hardly acceptable, yet *glorious* and *possible* are so regularly used as to be regarded as naturalized. Examples of other hybrids, common in ME, which have been recast are *unexperienced*, *unfirm*, and *unpatient*. Yet *un-* does frequently remain before a foreign loan, as in *unpleasant*, and many others. Here we may also note both native and foreign affixes attached to the same root. It would seem that in *unjust* beside *injustice*, *unequal* beside *inequality*, and *ungrateful* beside *ingratitude* there may be some distinction arising because of the length of the word, yet we have *unconquerable*, with *un-* prefixed to a still longer form! Both *class* and *cry* are French loans, but so firmly are they established in the language that few people would object to the hybrids *outclass* and *outcry*. Some foreign affixes have been similarly naturalized, and only a pedant would take exception to such hybrids as *dishearten*, *goddess*, and *recall*. In *The King's English* we find the authors taking exception to *racial* on the grounds that, 'the termination *-al* has no business at the end of a word that is not obviously Latin', yet they acknowledge, 'it is too well established to be now uprooted'.[11] Would they also object to such a common form as *postal*, and many others in regular use? They do indeed refer to 'coastal' as an ugly word for the same reason.[12]

A further extension of the purist attitude is seen in the objection to purely foreign hybrids, as, for example, a Latin root and a Greek affix. As we have seen, the Latin *-al* is very productive, but in recent times Greek *-ist* has become even more productive, particularly in certain fields of knowledge, and the Greek suffix has been added to many Latin (or Latin through French) roots. No one will presumably object to *socialist* today; *scientist* was long regarded as an objectionable Americanism, though, as L. P. Smith has pointed out, it was first used by Wm. Whewell in 1840.

An interesting position arises, however, when meanings are differentiated by choice of affix; for example, *distrust* and *mistrust* are not synonymous, and there is a good deal of difference between *disinterested* and *uninterested*. Another type of distinction is found in the variant pronunciation of *re-*. The regular form is [rɪ], as in *repeat*, *reveal*, alongside an emphatic form [ri], as in *re-enter*. This latter seems to be common in new formations, and is usually distinguished by a hyphen, as in *recover* and *re-cover*.

The attitude of the purist is, of course, native roots, native affixes, and foreign roots, foreign affixes. There has been in recent years, perhaps as a result of a wider knowledge of languages among a greater number of people, a strong movement against forming new hybrids; we still see many letters in the correspondence columns of our newspapers on this subject, and indeed there is something to be said for it. Today our linguistic sensibility would be shocked by *fishic* or *fishous*, but it is really only a question of what we become used to. There is nothing contrary to the spirit or genius of the English language in *fishous* – *officious* has merely one unstressed syllable more, and the latter is so frequently used that it seems almost English now. There are hybrids in almost all languages: the Romans used Greek elements, the French have made use of German elements. Many of our loveliest words are hybrids, for example, *atonement*, *beautiful*, *forbearance*, *graceful*, and *merciful*, and while the sentimentalist may regret the decay of native affixes, with foreign affixes spreading in our language like weeds in a garden in a rainy summer, and may claim that many of the native words are more expressive, more imaginative, and contain within themselves more of our history and spirit, yet the only test, for purposes of ordinary speech, can be the merit of the word, not sentiment or abstract linguistic principles, and, if it come to a struggle between reason on the one hand and imagination or sentiment on the other, reason must win, for, regret it as we may, modern language is concerned more with efficiency than with beauty, and dull as our *-ations*, *-isms*, *-ities*, and *-izes* may be, they are essential for the clear thinking and expression of science, politics, and economics, with which our present age is so much concerned. Moreover, apart from the undeniable beauty of some of these hybrids, it has long been our custom to form such types, and our greatest writers, including Shakespeare and Milton, have coined or used them. The English language itself is far too much of a hybrid growth for the purists to take exception to hybrid formations in either compounding or derivation.

We pass now to a process in which *independent* words are joined. WORD-COMPOUNDING[13] is a process similar to, but not the same as telescoping and the formation of portmanteau words, or blends, both of which are discussed below; two words are joined, but compounding differs in that no part of either word is lost, e.g. *blackbird, bookcase, earthquake, goldfish, highway, housewife, overcoat, pocketbook, railway, rainbow, waterproof, workman*. In the examples just quoted the elements have been fused, making one word, but in some cases the elements may be joined by a hyphen, e.g. *air-raid, dug-out, lamp-shade, lean-to*. It is probably a question of degree of establishment: we have two distinct words, joined in thought by some connection in meaning; after the first stage of two distinct words, when the words came to be regularly connected in thought and writing the hyphen was used, to signify a closer connection, and the third stage, that of one fused word, followed when the two ideas had finally become one, with no conscious analysis into elements to arrive at the meaning. The main point to be noticed in a compound is that we have not only one word, but one conception, not the sum of the two conceptions expressed by the two elements. For example, the 'high way' was originally a way raised above the surrounding countryside for better drainage and ease of travel; later it became *high-way*, and now we use *highway* without any idea of the original sense of the first element, and without splitting the word into its component parts. (It is interesting to note that the fused word appears, as *heiȝwai*, as early as the Romance of *William of Palerne*, c. 1350). The proof of the fusing of the two ideas into one may be seen in *blackbird;* admittedly a *blackbird* is a black bird, so long as we refer to the cock bird, but the fusing of two distinct ideas into a whole which is quite

C

different from the sum of the parts is seen when the same word is used for the hen-bird, which is actually brown! Nowhere do we find a clearer expression of the way language is modified by thought than we do in the formation of compounds, for they are the result of the condensation of a mental image, two originally distinct images having been fused. Compounds should, therefore, clarify and simplify the original conception, though this is perhaps not always the case.

The most frequent type of compound is apparently that which the language has inherited from the parent IE language, one in which the general meaning of the final element is made more specific by the limiting qualities of the first element. The commonest type is probably *noun + noun*, as in *railway, apple-tree, weekend*, but there are many other ways in which English may form compounds; for example, we have *adjective + noun*, where the limiting effect of the first element is obvious from the part of speech employed, as in *greenhouse, sweetmeat;* compounds of *adverb + noun* occur, as in *downfall, outcome, overhead, upkeep;* of *noun + adjective*, an unusual type in native formations, since the word-order is un-English; many of these accordingly occur in poetical or figurative language; examples are *coal-black, sky-blue, penny-wise*. We also find *two adjectives* compounded, as in *light-green, south-east*, or an adjective as the second element qualified by an adverb, as in *fully-grown:* in this construction we frequently find an adverb qualifying a participle used as an adjective, as in *happily-married*. We may also see *noun* or *adjective + verb*, as in *wire-draw, whitewash, wisecrack*. Combinations of *adverb + verb* are common, but are usually old, for although this was a very common method of compounding in OE, it is not a very productive type today; examples are *overcome, understand, outweigh, overturn*. In the true English-type compound the adverb precedes the verb.

One element of the compound may be a derivative instead of there being merely a union of two simple members. From the noun *hair* we make an adjective *hairy*, almost never *haired*, but the form of the compound is *black-haired, curly-haired, short-haired*, in which the new form *haired* has the sense of 'provided with hair'; similarly we use *leafy*, but *four-leaved* clover. Here perhaps belong such forms as *open-handed, close-fisted, single-minded, foul-mouthed*, and *open-eyed*.

Another type of compound involving verbs must also be mentioned, that where the verb and its object are combined to form a new noun or adjective, as *breakfast, breakneck, killjoy, makeshift, dreadnought, daredevil, scarecrow, telltale*, and many others. The formation goes back at least to ME times, where *bere-bag, cutte-pors*, and others are recorded.

In ME we frequently find prepositions, articles, adverbs, and even pronouns combined with other parts of speech, but many of the old forms have been lost, or are regarded as archaic. Such forms as *anon* (an on = in one), *everichon* – everyone, *noon* (ne oon) – no one, *namore* – no more, are common in the older language, but few have survived into the modern period. Only *another* survives as an example of the compounding of the article, and a few forms in which the negative has survived are also found, as *nobody, none, nothing*.

It will be noticed that compounds so far examined have all been composed of two elements, but three-element forms were found already in OE, as in *burʒ-ʒeat-setl, deofol-ʒyld-hus, ea-stream-yþ, niht-buttor-fleoʒe, wulf-heafod-treo;* there are some, but not as many, in ME.

Another type is the group-compound. Here some care must be exercised, as the division between group-compounds and groups merely in regular syntactical relation is not always clear, and indeed Sweet refers to group-compounds as 'really intermediate between true compounds and word-groups'.[14] Bradley classes *father-in-law, man-of-war, jews' harp*[15] as improper compounds for this reason. Genitive compounds, even when the genitive appears by inflection, and not with the preposition 'of', are likewise not to be considered as pure compounds. Group-compounds can be distinguished from mere word-groups in that there is no freedom of word-order, they are joined by a special connecting-word, and usually have one element predominantly stressed. The lack of distinction between group-compounds and syntactical groups may be illustrated by comparing the words quoted above, which Bradley rejects as improper compounds, that is, 'a phrase consisting of words in regular syntactical relation', with those quoted by Sweet as group-compounds, among which he includes *son-in-law* and *man-of-war*. Of these group-compounds Sweet says, 'no such variations (of word-order) are possible, the order of the elements of these groups being as rigidly fixed as in a compound word', and, 'The essential difference between the two kinds of compounds (full compounds such as blackbird, and group compounds) is seen in the plurals sons-in-law, etc., where the first element is independent enough to take an inflection of its own'.[16]

Among other group-compounds quoted by Sweet we find *cup of tea;* prevalent usage here gives us some guide as to the way in which this is taken as a unit of thought, completely fused, and not as two distinct elements, *cup* and *tea*, from the fact that the adjective used to qualify the tea in the cup is regularly placed before the group; *a nice cup of tea* has no reference to the beauty of the cup, but to the quality of the beverage inside. Other examples of group-compounds listed by Sweet include *matter-of-fact, mother-of-pearl, commander-in-chief, head-over-heels*.

It is worthy of notice that group-compounds do not occur in OE. The process there was either a full compound or a genitive group, and

not until French influence had made itself felt in ME did the group
linked by a preposition come into being. Such groups were probably
not common even in ME, and the group-compound is a characteristic
of the modern period.

We may note the extremely wide function of the first element. In
homeland, *headache* it expresses place, in *daydream*, *nightmare* it expresses
time, in *godsend* we have the idea of origin, *churchgoer* seems to suggest
destination, *steelworks* the product, and *seasickness* the cause, though the
identical construction *homesickness* is far from suggesting the cause, but
rather is it the thing which will cure the sickness. In all these there is an
obvious economy of effort, and the first element performs the function
of a longer word or clause.

The process is an extremely old one. It belongs to the primitive stages
of language, or rather, we should say the primal stages, where the
purpose is to appeal to the emotions, rather than to reason. It is not
surprising, therefore, to find such words formed when passions run
high, and some of the best and most vivid examples are terms of abuse;
similarly we find such words fused in the intense heat of poetic creation,
not, admittedly, before the influence of the Renaissance is felt, for
Chaucer has none, but Shakespeare has *young-eyed Cherubims*, Milton
has *gray-hooded even*, *coral-paven floor*, and they are very numerous in
later poets, particularly in Keats.

Compounding was a characteristic of the Germanic languages, and
it almost certainly goes back, through PG, to the very parent speech
itself, IE. It is a feature of the vocabulary of OE, especially of OE poetry.
In OE poetry we find several types of compound, as *noun + noun*, as
in *mappumȝyfa*, *eorþscræf*, *adjective + noun*, as in *haliȝ-dæȝ*, *dreoriȝ-hleor*,
noun + adjective, as in *win-sæd*, or *adjective + adjective*, as in *wīd-cuþ*. In
all these, the second element is the controlling factor as to part of
speech, the first two groups being nouns, and the last two examples
adjectives, but conversion-types are also found, where *noun + noun* or
adjective + noun types become adjectival; the first may be termed double-
conversion, the second single-conversion. Sweet points out that IE must
have had these conversion types, citing Greek *rhodo-daktulos* in support.[17]
Bradley has pointed out that the first element in IE compounds was not
really a word, as such, but an uninflected word stem, and OE, being an
inflected language, shows this clearly, for in compounds where the first
element is adjectival there is no agreement, as in *gōddǣda*, as against
gōde dǣda, with the elements separate. Bradley goes on to note that
accordingly the first element 'admits of great variety of form', and adds
'the former of the two words may occur in it in any case or in either
number; and the meaning of the compound varies accordingly. A tree-

frog is a frog that lives in trees; a tree-fern is a fern that is a tree; a tree-fruit is the fruit produced by a tree'.[18] In OE prose, which developed later than the poetry, we find a tendency to combine two native words to express a new idea rather than to borrow the foreign words, as in *sundor-halga* – Pharisee, though many OE compounds have since been replaced by loans; examples are *ceasterwara*, replaced by *citizen*, *lǣcedōm*, replaced by *medicine*. Sometimes the compound has been lost because one of the elements was no longer used, as in *blōdȝyte*, where the second element fell out of use, or *eȝesful*, because the first element, OE *eȝe* – terror, was replaced by the Scandinavian word, though in the latter case we now have an identical formation, with the same suffix added to the cognate ON word. An interesting example of loss of the compound when both elements have survived is *ēaȝþ ȳrel* – lit. eye-hole. The second element may still be recognised in the final syllable of *nostril*, OE *nos(u)þ ȳrel* lit. nose-hole. Yet the OE word gave way to the ON loan-word *vindauga*, lit. wind-eye, which has yielded NE *window*. The IE languages seem to have no common word for *window*, perhaps an interesting sidelight on living conditions among the people who spoke the parent language. The loss of OE compounds is to be seen most clearly in terms for abstract conceptions. Such terms would probably be in use only among the upper and educated classes, and these were practically wiped out by the Normans, who used French or Latin, languages which did not favour compounding, and the decline in the formation of compounds in English dates from that period, the richness of OE in compounds having been modified by the influence of Latin and French. From this we see that languages vary greatly in their use of compounding. It is a feature of Germanic languages; OE employed it freely, as does modern German; it was common in Greek, but rare in classical Latin and rare in French. Of this aspect of the influence of French on the English language Earle wrote: 'There is perhaps no greater evidence of the profound influence of the Romanic element upon English than that it led us off to phraseology in lieu of making compounds which was our natural heritage'.

There may, however, be another reason for the comparative disuse of the process in NE, as compared with its prolific use in the earlier period. English is now an analytic language, and the process of compounding is one of synthesis, the exact opposite. In some cases compounding seems to go right against the analytic type, a verbal phrase being reduced to a single word, as in *fishing-rod* – a rod for fishing, *waiting-room* – a room for waiting, *walking-stick* – a stick for walking, and *seating-accommodation* – accommodation for sitting. Here we may compare *windmill* with *moulin à vent*, *warship* with *vaisseau de guerre*, *fishing-rod* with *canne à pêcher* and the recent *flame-thrower* with *projecteur des flammes.* We may note here the distinction between *waiting-room,* not a room which waits, and a doubtful form such as *rocking horse,* which, with the hyphen, is presumably a horse for rocking, and perhaps a horse which rocks; the latter meaning is certain if the hyphen is omitted, but then we have no compound, and 'rocking' is purely adjectival.

It is, however, still an active process in English, but chiefly today in the vocabulary of poets, or of a few authors who seek for effect in that kind of language, and in scientific terms. The revival, after the decline in the ME period, began with the Elizabethans, who were extremely free in their treatment of language, and among the liberties which they took, a most adventurous spirit in compounding is to be noticed. Ben Jonson, writing of compounded forms, says 'In which kind of composition our English tongue is above all other very hardy and happy, joining together after a most eloquent manner, sundry words of every kind of speech'. Compounding became more frequent in the nineteenth century. Some have seen in this the influence of German, but that influence would be strong only in particular fields, as in, for example, science and philosophy. Some of Carlyle's compounds were probably due to German influence, but very few of his coinings have proved acceptable, and they were no more popular in his own day if we are to accept Thackeray's opinion. The following criticism of Carlyle's style appeared in a newspaper review on the appearance of the *French Revolution:* 'it abounds with Germanisms and Latinisms, strange epithets, and choking double words, astonishing to the admirers of simple Addisonian English . . .' Jespersen,[19] quoting from E. A. Morris, *Austral English – A Dictionary of Australasian Words, Phrases, and Usages,* cites many new compounds of recent date.

Two disadvantages arise from the use of compounds, a loss of the flexibility found in purely analytic languages, and a tendency, through the very economy inherent in the process, to overload the thought-content of the sentence. We may note that, perhaps as a result of this latter disadvantage, compounds tend to drop out of use more quickly than simple words, and some scholars have also seen in the practice of abbreviation a revolt against the inclusion of too many ideas in a sentence. The use of *diner* and *sleeper* for *dining-car* and *sleeping-coach, motor* for *motor-car,* and *tram* for *tram-car,* may be cited as examples of this latter tendency, but surely, no matter how we may deal with the words themselves, we do have the two ideas in mind when using the abbreviated *motor.*

The normal English type of compound is a final determinative, that is, it has as its second element a word conveying the main idea, and the first element is a qualifying word, or determinant, as in Coverdale's *loving-kindness* (1535), or *steamship, short-lived, high-sounding,* thus following the usual English word-order, with a qualifier preceding the word it qualifies. Some foreign types, initial determinants, are found, as *court-martial, knight-errant,* which show the influence of French word-order, with the adjective following its noun, but such types are comparatively rare in all periods of English. However, several forms, all of recent origin, are found among scientific terms, such as *gum tragacanth, sal ammoniac,* and similar forms. *Gum arabic* is recorded from the end of the fourteenth century, and its order is probably due to French influence.

Exceptions to the normal English type of compound grow fewer and fewer, and most recent examples are best explained by analogy. For example, *inroad* is contrary to modern usage, but is perhaps due to analogy with other members of the large group of words beginning with *in-,* for we do not use *outroad;* yet Carlyle did coin *outcome,* presumably influenced by the construction of the Latin loan-word *event,* though the meanings later diverged. Similarly, on the analogy of the verbal construction *to light up,* we say *lighting-up time,* not *uplighting time.*

The mention of the last-named verb, *to light up,* leads us to an English construction which is becoming more and more popular. Strictly speaking, we should not include it in a discussion of compounding, for the words are always kept separate, yet, although the adverb is separated from the verb, it is in very close association with it, and there can be no doubt that the speaker has in mind one process only, not the separate ideas of an action modified by the conditions denoted by the adverb, and the expression of the thought in two words is merely a matter of convenience, to avoid an ugly construction, to *uplight,* the true English type, with the adverb preceding the verb, but one contrary to present-day usage. For example, *hang on* seems perfectly natural, but most people with an ear for language would boggle at *onhang.* Similarly with *give up, boil down, own up, run across.* These phrasal verbs are very important in Basic English. We may note, too, that fusion into one word, with the necessary change in word order, would often alter the meaning, as in *break out,* as against *outbreak;* indeed, so necessary is it to keep two distinct meanings separate that we speak of a 'break-out' when prisoners escape from gaol, in order to avoid confusion with the usually-accepted meaning of the noun *outbreak,* and in one case, of verbal forms, *upset* and *set up* are actually antonyms. Similar examples include *go under,* different in meaning from *undergo,* and *take over,* differing from *overtake.* *Look over* differs in meaning from *overlook,* though Shakespeare uses *overlook* in the sense of 'peruse' in *Hamlet*, and the modern *overlooker* also retains the same sense. Corresponding to these verbal constructions, we also have the related noun forms, again with double forms and perhaps with variation of meaning. Some examples have already been given, to which may be added the following: *income* now has the sense of 'money received', but in the earlier language it was the equivalent of 'entry' (i.e. *come in*), and Shakespeare uses *comings-in* where we should use *income*. Bradley quotes *upkeep* and *uptake* as being due to Scottish influence, the type being more frequent in the Scottish dialects. Often we find a native type in the noun-form corresponding to a phrasal verb, as in *outlook* and *look out*, *intake* – perhaps a technical word – and *take in*, *outfit* and *fit out*. Although some of these expressions are still colloquial, they do enable us to achieve finer distinctions of thought and meaning, and must therefore be mentioned in a discussion of word-formation and enlargement of vocabulary.

Once a compound has been formed it is subject to all the phonological changes affecting English polysyllabic words, and the approximate age of a compound may sometimes be told by its form, or by the stress given to the components, though without historical records of actual forms we can do little more than say whether a form is old, or recent. For example, *fret* was already a compound in OE, the form being originally *fra-etan*, and later *fretan*, with *fra-* modifying the sense of the verb *etan*. Perhaps because it was inconvenient to keep the two neighbouring vowels separate in pronunciation in quick speech, the word eventually became monosyllabic and all trace of the original first element was lost, so that now only a student of the history of our language would recognise it as an obscured compound, as would undoubtedly be the case also with *lord* (OE *hlāf-weard > hlāford* – guardian of the bread), *lady* (OE *hlǣfdiȝe* – bread-kneader) or *barn* (OE *bere-ærn* – barley-house). Even more obvious examples may not be recognized. Few now recognize *holiday* as *holyday*, or a *bonfire* as a *bone-fire*, or the *Sheriff* as the *Shire-reeve*. Words which have undergone such phonological changes can hardly be recent formations; they show not only compounding but also some obscuring of the original elements.

A more obvious test of form arises from the actual method of formation of a compound. As we have already seen, compounds must originally have consisted of two distinct words, and only in the course of time would the later developments, first to a hyphenated form, and later to a single word, take place. But English has never shown much consistency in the use of hyphens. The hyphen is not found in OE, and there is often a lack of consistency in the writing of compounds as distinct units or fully-synthesized forms. The hyphen is found in ME, though it is completely wanting in many MSS, and in those in which it does appear it is not used consistently. Its use becomes more frequent in the modern period, but it is not possible to trace any rules. We find the same compound written as two words by one reputed author, as a hyphenated form by another, and as a single word by a third. The writing of many of these words seems to depend upon the personal taste of the author, and the degree of fusion which he sees in the compound. Nor is there agreement among what may be called the standard dictionaries. Fowler has discussed the question at some length, and his opinion is that 'the chaos prevailing among writers or printers or both regarding the use of hyphens is discreditable to English education'.[20] The SOED agrees with Fowler in printing *court martial* as two words, yet uses *court-martial* in a subsidiary note in the same entry.

Stress may also give us an idea of the age of a compound.[21] In its earliest form, as two words, we should have a spondee, there being naturally, apart from any question of sentence-stress, equal stress on two independent words. But, as the two elements came to be considered as one unit, the normal English rules of stress would apply, and the first element would retain its stress, but the stress on the second element would gradually be reduced. For example, if we say, 'Here is a black bird,' the stress is equally placed on *black* and *bird*, but in 'Here is a blackbird' we have a trochaic form, with the stress reduced on the second element. On the other hand, although an old compound such as *husband* shows greater reduction of stress on its second element than does a more recent formation, such as *hothouse*, it is by no means certain that the degree of reduction of stress is an accurate indication of the age of a compound. All that we can say is that the mere fact of reduction of stress having taken place is some indication of age.

Compounds, as we have seen, usually keep the full form of both elements, but in some cases a part of one or both words may be lost, as in PORTMANTEAU WORDS, or 'BLENDED' WORDS,[22] as they are sometimes called. Lewis Carroll had a particular aptitude for composing such words, so we may perhaps accept his definition of the circumstances which call forth such creation. In the Preface to *The Hunting of the Snark* he says: 'This also seems a fitting occasion to notice the other hard words in that poem, Humpty-Dumpty's theory, of two meanings packed into one word like a portmanteau, seems to me the right explanation for all. For instance, take the two words "fuming" and "furious". Make up your mind that you will say both words, but leave it unsettled which you will say first. Now open your mouth and speak. If your thoughts incline ever so little towards "fuming", you will say "fuming-furious"; if they turn, by even a hair's breadth, towards "furious", you will say "furious-fuming", but if you have that rarest of gifts, a perfectly balanced mind, you will say "frumious".

   'Supposing that, when Pistol uttered the well-known words –

      "Under which king, Bezonian? Speak or die!"

Justice Shallow had felt certain that it was either William or Richard, but had not been able to settle which, so that he could not possibly say either name before the other, can it be doubted that, rather than die, he would have gasped out "Rilchiam!" ' [23]

Of these formations Jespersen says: 'Blendings of synonyms play a much greater rôle in the development of language than is generally recognized. Many instances may be heard in everyday life, most of them being immediately corrected by the speaker, but these momentary lapses cannot be separated from other instances which are of more permanent value because they are so natural that they will occur over and over again until speakers will hardly feel the blend as anything else than an ordinary word. M. Bloomfield says that he has been many years conscious of an irrepressible desire to assimilate the two verbs *quench* and *squelch* in both directions by forming *squench* and *quelch*, and he has found the former word in a negro story by Page'. [24]

In this formation we really have part of one word intentionally or unintentionally combined with part of another, the words being usually, though not always, of similar meaning, resulting in the formation of a new word which, at least for a time, retains something of the meaning of both words, a sort of double abbreviation. A well-known example is Carlyle's *gigmanity:* he used the word to describe the smug, satisfied society of his time, and he probably obtained the idea from the report of the trial of John Thurtell for the murder of William Weare in 1823. According to one witness, Weare was, in his opinion, a respectable man, because 'he kept a gig'. Carlyle seized upon this standard of prosperity and respectability, the means to 'run a gig' – as we now assess the same standard by the possession of a car, or, more recently still, a television set – and, with typical sardonic humour, coined *gigmanity* – the section of humanity rich enough to own a gig. Lewis Carroll's *galumphing* (*gallop* + *triumphing*) is another well-known example. Neither of these can really be said to be accepted today – the first was put out of date when the gig disappeared, and the second was perhaps not meant as a serious contribution to vocabulary, though it *is* a good word, but there are many examples in common use today, among which is Carroll's *chortle* (*chuckle* + *snort*). We may note that *chortle* and *galumphing* have found their way into the NED, *chortle* and *snark* (*snake* + *shark*) are in the *Century Dictionary*, and *galumphing* is in the Webster *New International Dictionary*. The process itself is probably very early, and the first examples must have been unintentional, the result of confusion in the mind of a speaker who, endeavouring to express his thought, begins to use one word and, before it is completed, switches to the latter part of another of related meaning. Deliberately-formed examples must be much later, for they could be evolved only by people highly skilled in the manipulation of both words and meanings. Although all periods provide examples – Wentworth quotes, as the earliest example known to him – *euripidaristophanizein* (*Euripides* + *Aristophanes* + suffix *-izein*) from 403 B.C. – it is in the later periods, and particularly in contemporary speech and writings, that we find most evidence for the process. Many recent examples of this formation, both serious words and nonce-words, are to be found in the collections of Bergstrom and Pound. Harold Wentworth, (*Blend Words in English*, Ithaca 1933, abstract of thesis presented at Cornell), mentions three thousand six hundred examples collected in the thesis, in a list extending from Wiclif to James Joyce. Examples are to be found in literary works, as of Lear and Carroll, where the process is carried out deliberately, in folk-speech, where the blending is often unintentional and the result of ignorance, in scientific terms, commercial terms, and trade names, but the best-known examples are the common portmanteau words.

In spite of the work done on the subject by Jespersen, Pound, and Bergstrom, the process has not yet been fully investigated, the periods of formation have not been ascertained, the part played in the development of vocabulary has not yet been made clear, and we know little of the proportion of forms which have managed to survive and have become accepted in the standard language. This state of affairs arises largely from the difficulty inherent in the investigation of these blended forms. They can be traced most easily in the modern period, where we have the evidence, in the form of the original components, before us, and the process can be seen at work. But, because a blend is really a contaminated form, we are up against the same difficulty as we saw in the case of obscured compounds. Indeed, the difficulty is greater, for in obscured compounds the evidence is clearer to the philologist, for the formations are straightforward, whereas blends are often of a capricious nature. The words naturally do not circulate widely at first, and only when they have become comparatively well-established do they appear in print and attract the attention of the lexicographer, and by then real certainty as to their origin may have been lost. Because it is so difficult, then, to identify older examples with any certainty, it is also impossible to know just how many blends have become standard English, and again, because many never became widely current, it is not possible, without very extensive investigation, to estimate the proportion which became standard. For the same reasons it is difficult to establish the chronology of most of the forms, but, as has been said above, as a type of unconscious contamination it was probably very early. One of the earliest authenticated blends in English is Wiclif's *austerne* (*austere* + *stern*).

Perhaps the most familiar to Londoners is *Bakerloo* (the name of the Underground Railway from *Baker Street* to *Waterloo*), and the composite dish *brunch* (surely *breakfast* + *lunch*) served in the Lyons' cafés is almost as well known: this may be American in origin, as it is, I understand, used there for the meal taken about noon on Sunday, after a late rising. It is interesting to note here the probable blending with *lunch*, for *lunch* is itself probably a blend, for, as a short form of *luncheon*, it apparently goes back to a blend of *lunch*, a dialect word meaning *lump* (of food), and *nuncheon*. We have also *flaunt* (probably *flout* + *vaunt*, though it may be a provincial word of Scandinavian origin), *twirl* (perhaps *twist* + *whirl*, though there is an OE *þweran* – to stir, churn, with which it may be connected), and one would be tempted to derive *slide* from *slip* + *glide*, were it not for the OE *slīdan*. Yet, even allowing for the possibility of this process being very early, one must be on guard against what at first sight seem obvious examples; *flush* (*flash* + *blush*), *squash* (*squeeze* + *crash*), and *squawk* (*squall* + *squeak*) have been suggested as examples, but there are possible etymologies for the first two, and the last may be merely imitative. *Melodrama* (*melody* + *drama*) is another example, used originally of a play interspersed with songs, but there is in French the same term, *mélodrame* (Greek *melo*[*s*] – song, music), from which our own word may be derived, though that does not rule out the use of the process of word-formation we are now discussing, which is, of course, too obvious a one for it to be confined to one language. *Tragi-comedy*, in the same sphere, is perhaps no more than a mere convenient shortening of the adjective tragic, though admittedly we do get a retention of two apparently contradictory ideas. Among common words we may note *blotch* (*blot* + *botch*), *chump* (*chunk* + *lump*), *dumbfound* (*dumb* + *confound*), *electrolier* (*electric* + *chandelier*), *grumble* (*growl* + *rumble*), and *splutter* (*splash* + *sputter*). *Radiogram*, *electrocute* (*electro* + *execute*), and *comintern* (*communist* + *international*) are more recent examples, as are also the wartime *macon* (*mutton* + *bacon*) and *navicert* (*navigation* + *certificate*), a permit granted to avoid search for contraband.

American columnists have a flair for this type of formation, and from this source we have the fairly recent *socialite* (? *social* + *light* or *social* + *registerite*). Some of their examples are both witty and trenchant, as *reno-vated*, to describe a wife who has been legally divorced and somehow refreshed – in spirits if not spiritually – in the now famous Nevada town. But perhaps this last example should be looked upon as a freak-formation rather than a portmanteau word. Some of the more fantastic types have been collected by Robert Withington in his article 'Some Neologisms from Recent Magazines',[25] but all such words hardly fall to be considered as part of the normal vocabulary, for, while some are neat and seem likely to be useful additions to our stock of words, others are merely examples of cheap, slick humour, and are therefore unlikely to find a permanent place in the language. On the other hand some of Burbank's coinings for the names of hybrid fruit may be accepted eventually, as, for example, *pomato* (*potato* + *tomato*, helped by the American pronunciation of the second element), and *plumcot* (*plum* + *apricot*).

TELESCOPING[26] of words is also an old process in word-formation. There is a tendency to drop syllables, thereby making the process a kind of syncopation, and two words are made into one. *Don* (< *do on*) and *doff* (< *do off*), common in northern dialects with the sense of to put on or take off clothes, are also used occasionally in the standard language, and were formerly in regular use. The dialects even have an adjectival past participle *doffed*, meaning 'undressed', and a person is *donned up* when wearing his or her best clothes. A similar construction, *dout* (< *do out*) – to put out a fire, is also common in northern dialects, but does not appear in the standard language.

Atone (< *at one*), recorded as two words, with adverbial function, from 1300 in the NED, had been telescoped to one word by 1557, but was still adverbial. Shakespeare, in *Richard II*, apparently shows the first verbal use in 'Since we cannot atone you.' It will be noticed that the verb is transitive in Shakespeare; the intransitive use developed later.

Hussy (< OE *hūs* + *wīf*) is an example of telescoping which is not so apparent, except to the philologist, but the soldier's *hussif* is a little more recognizable. *Lord* (< OE *hlāfweard* – the guardian of the loaf) and *lady* (< OE *hlǣfdiʒe* – the kneader of the loaf) are not easily traced except by the expert, nor is *barn* (< OE *bere-ærn* – lit. barley-house). *Nostril*, which has already been mentioned, has changed considerably from even Chaucer's *nosethirle*, and OE *nosþyrel* is still further removed. *Petticoat* shows the English pronunciation of French *petit*, the earlier form being *petty coat*. *Dismal* is far removed from its original, the Latin *dies malus* – evil day, and *holiday* is only a little nearer its native source *holy day* (OE *hāliʒ dæʒ*). *Gospel* has really no connection with God linguistically, the OE form being *gōdspell* – the good tidings, and only the process of shortening before a consonant group has produced the confusion. *Daisy* is a survival of an old genitival construction, the OE form being *dæʒes ēaʒe* – day's eye. All these were originally compounds, then lack of stress caused syncopation of the unstressed elements. We may call them fused or obscured compounds, and some have already been mentioned as compounds.

The process is also obviously very similar to that by which blends, or portmanteau words are formed, especially such examples as *chortle* and *galumph*. Indeed the three processes, syncopation, telescoping, and the formation of portmanteau words are really almost indistinguishable, and some words seem to be derived from a use of all three methods in one word. Moreover, these processes are themselves only a particular aspect of both compounding and abbreviation, the two words being first compounded, and then, unlike true compounds, in which the full form of both words is kept, abbreviated in some way, and finally run together to form a fused compound, the word being no longer separable into its original elements. The tendency to shorten words, by removing initial, medial, and final syllables, or merely by dropping a consonant, has been noticeable in all periods of English. Even by the time of King Alfred the OE *cyning* has been shortened to *cyng*, and the gradual disappearance of inflexional endings is a characteristic of Late Old English and Early Middle English, one of the most obvious examples being the gradual loss in pronunciation, during the Middle English period, of the so-called silent final -*e*. An example showing successive stages is to be seen in the OE *ælmesse*, shortened from Latin *eleemosyna*, borrowed from Greek, and, through ME *almesse*, *almes*, becoming NE *alms*. The process is noticeable also in place-names, as may be seen from the present-day pronunciation of, for example, *Leicester* and *Worcester*.

ABBREVIATION is still a very popular method of forming new words, but it is by no means a recent process – Weekley notes *quack* (from *quacksalver*) in the sixteenth century and *gent* still earlier, from the time of the Wars of the Roses – and has always encountered opposition, especially from purists. Swift, in the *Tatler* for 28th September, 1710 (No. 230) refers to the practice – 'the next refinement, which consists in pronouncing the first syllable in a word that has many, and dismissing the rest; such as *phizz*, *hipps* [for *hypochondriacs*], *mobb*, *pozz* [for *positive*], *rep* [for *reputation*] and many more, when we are already overloaded with monosyllables, which are the disgrace of our language'. Of Swift's list only two have survived, *phizz*, alongside *physog*, in slangy colloquial language, for *face*, and *mob* < *mobile vulgus*, which is now standard English, and was indeed apparently well-established in his day, for in the same essay he writes: 'I have done my utmost for some years past to stop the progress of *mobb* and *banter*, but have been plainly borne down by numbers, and betrayed by those who promised to assist me'. Other eighteenth-century purists also had much to say against this practice of abbreviating words.

This process, which differs from those just discussed in that only one word is shortened, is still an active one, and there are today many words generally accepted in the standard language which are shortened forms of the words they have displaced. Few people, apart from a certain type, would use *pianoforte* rather than *piano; curio*, with a restricted meaning, is more popular than *curiosity;* an unmarried lady is *miss*, not *mistress*, and one asks for *gin*, never for *Geneva* or *Genièvre;* indeed, many names of drinks are abbreviations, an obvious convenience when long words have to be used frequently: examples are *brandy* (for *brandy wine*), *grog* (for *grogram*), *hock* (for *hockamore, Hochheimer*), *port* (for *Oporto*), *rum* (for *rumbullion*), and *whisky* (for *usquebaugh*).

It is not easy to be certain when the shortened form is fully accepted in the standard language – possibly it is when only pedants use the full form; e.g. *exam., lab., maths., matric., pub.* are not yet standard, but hardly anyone talks of going to the *Zoological Gardens*, though why *zoo* should have met with general approval, yet one always says *botanical gardens*, and never *bot.*, is not clear. Both words are equally convenient, and it may be that *zoo* has a better sound than *bot*, and is also in more frequent use, thereby popularizing the abbreviation. *Bus* is now accepted – hardly anyone says *omnibus*, and the apostrophe which used to be common at the beginning of the word has almost disappeared – and *bike, photo*, and *pram* are becoming accepted, at any rate in conversation. *Trike* – a common term before the tricycle gave way to the bicycle – is still frequently used in families where there are young children, though it is today little used elsewhere. A more recent formation is *Prom*, or *the Proms*, for the Promenade Concerts now so popular in London.

All these relatively late forms are recognized as abbreviations, even if the full-stop is omitted, as indeed it was – deliberately – in some of the examples in the preceding paragraph, but some are not so obvious, and are rarely recognized as shortenings; for example, *sport* (for *disport*), *cab* (for *cabriolet*), *consols* (for *Consolidated Annuities*), *chap* (colloquially, from *chapman*), *hack* (for *hackney*), *mob*, already mentioned, *taxi* (for *taxi-cab < taximeter-cabriolet*, a cab with a meter to register the 'tax', or fare, as distinct from a bus or tram, where one takes a ticket in advance), *wig* (for *periwig*), and even the recent *fan*, all that now remains of *fanatic*. Perhaps very few people now use *bicycle* rather than *cycle* as a verb, though it is equally common as a noun, and certainly *cycling* is almost unchallenged. The shortened form has the backing, too, of the C.T.C.

A different type arises from the shortening of a long phrase or clause, especially in official or legal language, as in *quorum* – the old genitive plural (= *of whom*), originally the initial word of the instructions to J.P's specifying the minimum number required for the proceedings to be valid, and now applied far more generally to committees, councils, and other bodies. *Affidavit* (= *he swears*) was the usual opening word of a sworn statement, *subpoena* (= *under penalty*) arises from the first word of the charge to a witness to attend under penalty for failure, *veto* (= *I forbid*) from the opening word of the Latin formula by which a sovereign forbids an act by a minister or a legislative body. *Decree nisi* is an example all too familiar these days, and *Ave Maria*, *Magnificat*, *Nunc Dimittis*, and *Paternoster* are all terms, common in religious circles, taken from the opening word or words of the prayer or canticle.

Abbreviations may vary with classes, groups, or occupations, certain ones being peculiar to and rarely heard outside their own groups. The sportsman has *pro.*, *ref.*, *rugger*, *soccer;* the young lady has her hair *permed*, or 'has a *perm*', her mother *vacs* the carpet – I believe the American housewife even *percs* her coffee – film stars are *mobbed* by their *fans*, and our young men are *demobbed* from the Services. Doctors and scientists have their own abbreviations, as does the schoolboy with his *hols.*, *matric.*, *prep.*, *school certif.*, and *trig.*, and the university student with his *vac.*, and in the entertainment world the theatre provides *rep.*, and radio has given us *mike* and racing has *tote*, a much more convenient and pronounceable form than *totalizator*. These will probably remain class-types, and are hardly to be considered as standard English, though certain forms, e.g. *rugger* and *soccer*, are widespread and may eventually find a place in the language; both are eminently suitable for adoption, and if *soccer* were to be adopted as a far more convenient form than *Association Football* – a term which is rarely heard now except as the introduction to a B.B.C. sports commentary – *rugger* would soon follow as a related analogous term.

Jespersen[27] has called this type 'stump words'. He considers that one may differentiate between shortenings by children and by adults, as children tend to keep the final part of the word and drop the beginning, since they 'echo the conclusion of what is said to them and forget the beginning or fail altogether to apprehend it'. He quotes examples of Christian names, later adopted by adults as pet-names, as *Bella* (for *Arabella*), *Bert* (for *Herbert*), *Bess*, *Bet*, or *Betty* (for *Elizabeth*), and illustrates the universal nature of the process by reference to other languages. Older people, he says, 'clip words which they know perfectly well: they will naturally keep the beginning and stop before they are half through the word, as soon as they are sure that their hearers understand what is alluded to'. An early example of this construction is *chap*, a shortened form of *chapman*, a trader. The sense of the original form before shortening may be seen by comparing two modern idioms of similar meaning, 'an awkward chap' and 'an awkward customer'. Even Dr Johnson suffered from this habit of so mutilating the names of his friends, and examples are quoted also from Thackeray. Jespersen quotes as adult shortenings *mob*, *brig* (for *brigantine*), *fad* (for *fadaise*), *cab* (for *cabriolet*), *navvy* (for *navigator*), all of which have ousted the original long words, and others, such as *photo*, *pub*, and *spec*, which he says are still felt to be abbreviations. Modern shortenings include *rail* (for *railway*) – we go by *rail*, yet buy a *railway ticket* – and *cinema* for *cinematograph*. Jespersen sees in the fact that family names – which children rarely use – are not shortened by dropping the beginning a confirmation of his theory, but admits the rule 'is not laid down as absolute, but only as holding in the main'. Certainly many examples, such as *cheat* (for *escheat*), *cute* (for *acute*), *drawing-room* (for *withdrawing-room*), *mend* (for *amend*), *sample* (for *example*), *spice* (for *espice*), *spite* (for *despite*), *sport* (for *disport*), *stain* (from O Fr. *disteindre*), *ticket* (O Fr. *etiquet*), *wig* (for *periwig*) are not children's terms. All the examples just quoted seem to be governed rather by stress, for in each case it is an initial unstressed syllable that has been dropped, and stress is frequently a determining factor in the formation of such abbreviations, the tendency being to retain the syllable with main stress, but there are notable exceptions, such as *ad.* (for *advertisement*), *bus* (for *omnibus*), *Dizzy* (for *Disraeli*), *exam.* (for *examination*), and the popular shortening of many Scottish names to *Mac*, used of Scotsmen in general.

Sometimes both forms, the original long word and its abbreviation, may continue to exist, but in this case there is usually some differentiation of meaning, as in *acute* and *cute*, *alone* and *lone*, *amend* and *mend*, *attend* and *tend*, *defence* and *fence*, *defender* and *fender*, *example* and *sample*. Perhaps the most interesting pair are *assize* and *size*. In olden times the standard length, weight, etc., had to be determined by a meeting of a specially constituted authority. This meeting was called an *assize*, or, in its shortened form, *size* – the dialects still refer to 'the Sizes' not 'the Assizes' – and the shortened form, by differentiation of meaning, came to be used for the authorized standard.

Sometimes it is merely a question of a very cumbersome word being changed to a more convenient form, as when *withdrawing-room* became *drawing-room*, or *line-of-battle-ship* became *battleship*, the latter, surprisingly enough, dating only from the end of the nineteenth century. *Phone*, the common term today as noun and verb, is just as clear as *telephone*, and more convenient. *Gram*, for *telegram*, does not quite fit the bill, and so a new type arose here, the form *wire* being used for verb and noun. Perhaps on the analogy of this form, *phone* is now giving way to *ring*, again as noun and verb. Yet *gram* has survived, with a different sense, not usually in the simple form, but regularly in *radiogram*.

A special type of shortening has given rise to double forms. Many Latin words with initial *s-* had *es-* in Old French, and the tendency in the early period was to take over the complete French form, but in the later period, either because of this tendency to shorten for convenience, or perhaps because of the influence of the Latin word, re-introduced, we find the shorter form without the initial syllable used alongside the older full form, the latter often tending to be archaic. Examples are *espy, spy; espouse, spouse; esquire, squire; estate, state.*

The process is a common one also in regional dialects, and among many which could be quoted are the following: *liver* (for *deliver*), *list* (for *enlist*), *divvy* (for *Co-op dividend*), *loony* (for *lunatic*). The question of class dialects may also arise: formerly the word *cit* (for *citizen*) was used, always in a contemptuous sense, and mainly by the upper classes. *Gent* was originally used among the same class without any derogatory suggestion, but was later dropped, and came to be used contemptuously for social climbers, or pretenders to gentility, and it is still used among a class of people corresponding to that type.

Although purists have always felt that this method of word-formation is a sign of degeneracy in language, their efforts have not so far stopped what can, properly used, be a convenience, and is indeed in full accord with the spirit of the English language, with its preference for brevity in words.

SYNCOPATION is another type of word-formation similar to abbreviation, but with at least two words involved. In this case we usually have the beginning and end of the word retained, but syllables are lost and consonants run together. An example is *pram* (for *perambulator*), and it would seem that here two processes may have been at work: *perambulator > prambulator* (syncope) *> pram* (abbreviation). This order seems the more likely one, rather than abbreviation followed by syncope.

There are many forms in Modern English which have arisen from a longer Middle English form by this process: for example, *once* was *ēnes, ǣnes* in the earlier language, *else* has developed from *elles*, and *hence* from *hennes*.

We may note also, as another example of this type, the frequent loss of the unstressed vowel in the final syllable (*-en*) of the old past participle of strong verbs, e.g. *born, forlorn, shorn, torn, worn*, as against the type where the syllable remains, as in *forgiven, forgotten*.

The next type of word-formation may perhaps be considered an extreme type of abbreviation, the initial letters only of words being used to form a new word. The use of initials is not new. Swift has such forms in the 'little language' he used when writing to Stella – MD, my dears; Pdfr – poor dear foolish rogue (Swift himself), ppt – poppet, or poor pretty thing. We speak of L.S.D. (Latin *librae, solidi, denarii*), an I.O.U., a J.P., a K.C., an M.A., or an M.P., and very rarely use the full form; similarly with B.B.C., C.I.D., F.B.I., I.L.P., L.C.C., M.C.C., and many others, including the wartime A.R.P. and V.I.P.; hardly anyone would think of using the full forms for any of these, and everybody is familiar with the meaning. The Services, particularly, make much use of this type of formation, and, perhaps by contact with them, we came to use many such forms in the last war, e.g. A.R.P., N.F.S., W.V.S. Many of the above probably arose from the written form, e.g. J.P. and M.P., commonly abbreviated in titles, but this does not hold for all the examples.

However, the examples quoted above, although they are used absolutely, performing the function of nouns, can hardly be said to be real words, but some combinations of initials lend themselves to forming a word closely conforming to a normal type, and some of these may really be regarded as words, and therefore an extension of vocabulary. In other words, they are not mere recitals of names of letters, but may be said to have become words. Service examples may perhaps be quoted first: one of the earliest is *Anzac*, formed from the initials of the composite name given to the Australian and New Zealand contingents in the 1914–18 war. More recent examples, from the last war, are ENSA, FIDO, PLUTO, and SHAEF. NAAFI has by now probably become too well established ever to be removed from Service language, but is of little use elsewhere, as there is no occasion to express the idea outside the Services. Similarly, *Wren*, from WRNS, seems established now, and is used outside the Services. The first two have become commonly accepted, and form part of our vocabulary in a limited sense – for example, we have *Anzac Day* – the next two were popular at the time, but will almost certainly disappear for good unless the idea for which they stood should have to be revived, and SHAEF – an ugly-looking word which achieved a more pleasing pronunciation – has also disappeared, apart from its use in war records, but its successor – SHAPE – is now with us. A more recent example, NATO, is ugly and hardly sounds like an English word, but is nevertheless frequently used.

Perhaps the best-known example in our historical records is *Cabal*, now used to describe a small party united for some secret design. The word is one of the few Hebrew words which have found a place in our language, but its use was no doubt strengthened by the combination of the initials of Clifford, Arlington, Buckingham, Ashley, and Lauderdale, ministers who intrigued against Charles II.

Basic English provides a recent example, BASIC deriving from British (and) American Scientific International Commercial (English).

DORA is another example from the 1914–18 war, a lady who is still, unfortunately, with us in spirit if not in name, and two others, equally well known and even more unpleasant, are *Gestapo* (*Geheime Staats-Polizei*) and *Ogpu*.

This 'acrostic' method is little used in English outside Service language, in spite of our liking for short forms, but it has obvious advantages in German or Russian, for by this means time-wasting poly-syllabic inflexions may be dropped. Professor Slauch[28] notes several interesting foreign types where the saving is obvious. English words have, to a great extent, lost these inflexions already, and the saving is not so obvious when short words are used.

METANALYSIS[29] – a term used by Jespersen – a re-analysis, or different analysis at a later period – is merely the learned term for faulty division of words, whereby the consonant at the end of one word becomes attached to the next one, or the initial consonant of a word is transferred to the end of the previous word. In some cases no division has been retained, and two words have been run into one. This is particularly noticeable in the case of article and following noun. In quick speech it is not always easy for a person unfamiliar with a language to know where one word ends and another begins – cf. the common pronunciation of 'at home' as 'a tome'; it is therefore likely to occur among people who know only the spoken form. Some misunderstand-ing is always implicit in such a process of word formation. Jespersen ascribes it to the influence of children. He says: 'Each child has to find out for himself, in hearing the connected speech of other people, where one word ends and the next one begins, or what belongs to the kernel and what to the ending of a word, etc. In most cases he will arrive at the same analysis as the former generation, but now and then he will put the boundaries in another place than formerly, and the new analysis may become general'.

The method is not new, for at the very beginning of the OE period we find that initial *t-*, assimilated from the initial consonant of the personal pronoun *þu*, following its verb, has become attached to the second person singular ending of the verb, to give the termination *-est*, which we still use, though it is archaic. In this case the remainder of the pronoun is lost, but in true cases of metanalysis there is no loss, merely a redistribution of the elements of the two words to give two new words somewhat different in form. The majority of examples arise from a faulty division between the article, definite or indefinite, and a following noun. A clear example may be seen in the archaic *nonce*, now used only in the phrase *for the nonce;* this was originally *for then ones*, where *then* goes back to the OE dative of the demonstrative adjective *þǣm*, the phrase really meaning *for that one (time.)*

A *nickname* (< *an ickname* – preserved until the fifteenth century) is merely an additional name, an also name, *ick* having developed from ME *eke*, OE *ēac* – also, in addition. A *newt* is recorded from about 1420, the earlier form having been *an ewt* (< OE *efete*); with this latter form we may compare the dialectal variant *an eft*. A *nugget* may be from *an ingot*, but the etymology is not certain. *Ninny* has probably developed from *a ninny*, a wrongly-divided form of *an inny*, a shortened form of *an innocent*. A *notch* is perhaps from *an otch*, ME *oche* < O Fr. *osche*, verb *oschier* – to notch or nick. *Tawdry* (< *St Audrey*) is recorded from 1548.

The process may work in the opposite direction; *an auger*, recorded quite early, develops from *a nauger; an umpire*, from 1480, was before then *a numpire* (< O Fr. *non pair* – not equal, hence supreme, unequalled); *an adder* is recorded from 1377, Late ME having *addre* (cf. Wyclif – Matt. iii, 7, *eddris*), the earlier form having been *a nadder*, ME *a naddre* < OE *nǣdre* (cf. OS *nādra*, Go. *nadrs*, for the initial consonant. OHG *nātara*, *nātr* gives NHG *Natter*); *an apron* dates from 1535, earlier *a naperon* (< Fr. *napperon*, the first element meaning cloth, cf. napkin). An *aitchbone* develops from *a nachebone*, ME *nache*, *nage* < O Fr. *nache*, *nage*, probably from a Low Latin variant of Lat. *natis* – buttock. An *orange* appeared before the thirteenth century as *a norange;* O Fr. has *orenge*, and the metanalysis may therefore have occurred before the adoption of the word in English; the word was originally Arabic *naranj* – cf. Persian *narang*, Sanskrit *naranga* – and in some languages the initial *n-* is preserved, as in Spanish *naranja*. The Yorkshire *Ridings* go back to *Thriding* (< ON *þriðjungr* – a third part), and *East Thriding, North Thriding*, and *West Thriding* show metanalysis and assimilation of [θ] to [t], and later disappearance of the consonant, in their modern forms *East Riding, North Riding* and *West Riding*.

A curious extension of this process is to be seen in *Whitsun*. It was originally *Whit* (= *white*) Sunday. The form appears to have become later *Whitsun* Day: from that *Whitsuntide* and *Whitsun* weekend followed naturally. The rarer, and later, forms *Whitsun* Sunday and *Whitsun* Monday are malformations, the former containing a redundancy, and the latter being a contradiction in terms, as opposed to the correct *Whit* Monday.

Jespersen places under this heading the formation of a new singular form from a type having a singular ending in -s; this -s was felt to be a plural inflection, and so a new form, without -s, was developed for the singular: examples are *cherry*, from ME singular *cherris* < Fr. *cerise*, *pea*, earlier singular *peas(e)*, *sherry*, earlier *sherris* wine (< *Xeres*). He compares here also the colloquial forms *Chinee*, *Portugee*, etc.

Metanalysis is a common process in all languages, and Partridge cites examples of articled nouns from Spanish, French, Italian, Dutch and Arabic. We are concerned here only with words which have become established in English, and the following may be noted, it being remembered that in these cases the faulty division has not arisen in English.

Eldorado is a mere joining of *el dorado* – the gilded, or golden; *alligator* arises from Spanish *el lagarto* – the lizard, and *lariat* from *la reata* – the rope.

French has given us *lacrosse* (< *la crosse*), and the stick is still called in English a *crosse*, O Fr. *croce* – a hook (cf. *crotchet*, and *crochet*, from the hook used). *Lisle*, really *lisle thread*, arises from an old spelling of *Lille*, the town where it was made, the earlier form being *l'isle*, modern French *l'île*, from the geographical position of the town.

From Italian, through French, we have *alarm*. ME *alarme* was borrowed from French, which had earlier adopted It. *all' arme* (= fem. pl. *alle arme* – to the arms). Similarly *alert* arose, through French *à l'erte*, later *alerte*, from It. *all' erta* – on the watch, lit. on the watch-tower.

From the German expression, used in drinking, *gar aus* – quite out, empty, we have, through French, our word *carouse*, and its derivative *carousal*.

Two examples have come from Dutch. *Decoy* is developed from the Dutch article *de* and the noun *koit* – a cage, and *daffodil* is *de affodil*, the Dutch noun being apparently derived, through French, from Latin *asphodelus*.

Examples with the Arabic article are so numerous that it is possible here to mention only a few of the commonest. *Apricot* has developed from Fr. *abricot*, borrowed from Port. *albricoque*, from Arabic *al-burquq*, the noun being connected with Lat. *praecox* – early ripe (cf. *precocity*). *Artichoke* has been borrowed from It. *articoccio*, itself a borrowing from Arabic *al-khurshūf*, a word which has been adopted in several European languages. *Elixir*, adopted through Med. Latin, derives from *al-iksīr* – the medicinal powder.

The influence of Arabic on the vocabulary of Architecture, Astronomy, Mathematics, Medicine, and Science is dealt with in detail elsewhere, but the following examples of articled nouns may be noted here.

Among names of stars we may note *Aldebaran*, Arabic *al-dabaran* – the follower; *Algebar*, Arabic *al-jabbūr* – the giant; *Algol*, Arabic *al-ghūl;* *Alnath*, in the horn of Aries, from Arabic *al-nath* – the act of butting; *Altair*, Arabic *al-ta'ir* – the flier, and many others. *Azimuth*, through Fr. *azimut*, derives from Arabic *al-sumūt*.

In mathematics *algebra* at once springs to mind. It derives, through It. *algèbra*, from Arabic *al-jabr*, the union of parts in a whole.

In science we have the old term *alchemy*, Med. Lat. *alchimicus*, and *alchemist*, from Arabic *al-kīmiya*. Our modern term *chemistry* contains the original root, from L. Gr. *khēmeia*, which had been adopted in Arabic. *Alcohol*, adopted from the mediaeval Latin of the alchemists, is derived from Arabic *al-kohl;* the noun-element is preserved in the present-day cosmetic term *kohl*, used for darkening the eyelids. *Alembic*, probably adopted through Old French, derives from Arabic *al-ambīq* – the still; the archaic form *limbeck* may be a mere shortening, or even an example of the reversal of the process which originally gave us the word, *alimbeck* having become *a limbeck*. *Alkali* derives from Arabic *al-qili* – the ashes of the salt-wort. *Amalgam* has been adopted from Fr. *amalgame*, a development of Med. Lat. *amalgama*, from Arabic *al-malgham* – the kneading or softening.

In architecture the commonest example is *alcove*, derived, through French, from Arabic *al-qubbah* – the arch, dome.

Almanac, ME *almenak*, is derived, through mediaeval Latin, from Arabic *al-manakh* – the weather, climate.

Anil, more frequent in its adjectival form *aniline*, is an obscured type. It is derived from Arabic *al-nīl* – the indigo plant.

Finally may be mentioned *admiral*, adopted from French in the ME period. The word had developed, through Latin, from Arabic *amīr-al* – commander of the – a clipped form of *amīr-al-bahr* – commander of the sea. The noun itself is preserved in the loan-word *amir*, later *emir*.

Of the process of metanalysis in these Arabic loans Partridge points out 'Within Arabic, there is only one instance (Allah) of the fusion of the article *al* with the ensuing noun. But certain European languages – most notably (and probably the earliest) Spanish – have incorporated *al* with a noun'.[30]

BACK-FORMATION is a fruitful source of new forms. Some of these are deliberate, though many were originally the result of ignorance; often it has happened that a word has been thought to be formed from a primary stem by the addition of a suffix when this has not been the case, and so a new 'root-form' has been unconsciously coined. Jespersen writes: 'I used the word subtraction to denote the phenomenon that a new word or form was equal to an older form *minus* something which had been (mistakenly) apprehended as an inflectional or derivational element and had therefore been discarded, thus the same phenomenon which is now generally called *back formation* with a happy term invented by Dr (later Sir James) Murray. In later books I have treated the phenomenon as a subdivision of the more general term "metanalysis".... '[31]

In the sixteenth century *grovelling* was an adverb, with the meaning 'on the ground, in an abject manner'. Because the adverbial ending -*ling* was confused with the ending -*ing* it was thought to be a present participle, for such a word could be used in many contexts where a present participle might be expected, and so a new verb *to grovel* was formed. *Sidling*, originally an adverb, yielded the new verb *to sidle*, and the old adverb *darkling* was thought to be the present participle, and so a new verb, *to darkle*, arose, but this has not survived. *Husht*, probably originally onomatopoeic, like *whist*, seems to have been considered as a weak past participle, and so gave the verb *to hush*.

By this process verbs may be formed from nouns. Jespersen comments: 'As is well known, English cannot originally form verbal compounds the first element of which is the object (or an adverbial qualification) of the second part. Where we do find such verbs, they generally have taken their origin in the circuitous way through a verbal substantive (action-noun or agent-noun)'. Included in the list he gives are *backbite*, *eavesdrop*, *globe-trot*, *sleep-walk* (not NED), *spring-clean*, all of which are now generally accepted, but, in spite of the authority of the NED, which he quotes in all the examples which follow, one cannot be quite so happy about the use of *to bootlick*, *to fortune-hunt*, *to handshake*, *to horror-strike*, *to tongue-tie*. Indeed, to use the context cited for one example in the NED Supplement (1898), the use of an expression such as 'he handshook his way from store to store' *horror-strikes* one!

As an example of verbs formed from nouns we may note *butcher*, from Fr. *boucher;* the -*er* has no connection with the English suffix -*er* to denote an agent, yet the verb *to butch* appears in some dialects. In the standard language *editor* gives *to edit*, though -*or* is an integral part of the word, and not a mere suffix added to a verbal stem (Latin *editor* – one who gives out from *edere* – to give out);[32] and similarly *to audit*, *to hawk*, *to peddle*, *to swindle*, developed from *auditor*, *hawker*, *pedlar*, and *swindler*. If the origin of *beggar* is Fr. *Beghard*, the name of a mendicant order, then *to beg* is another example: the verb occurs early and so the process is not a recent one. *To burgle* is quite a recent formation, but *burglar* goes back to Middle English, and *cobbler* is probably older than *to cobble*. This is a reversal of the usual process, for most names of agents are formed from a verb by the addition of a suffix, but in all these cases the noun is recorded earlier than the verb.

Nouns have been formed from adjectives by this process, as *greed* from *greedy*. *To diddle* is perhaps a back formation with a literary flavour; the noun *diddler* may have arisen from *Jeremy Diddler*, a notorious cheat in the nineteenth-century farce *Raising the Wind*, by James Kenney, though one may suspect that a slang or dialectal form may have been used by the author, to coin a name indicating character.

At least one example has been derived from a place-name; as a result of the joyful, if noisy, demonstration which followed the relief of Mafeking, a new verb *to maffick* was formed, but it has not so far been generally accepted. It is found in some dictionaries.

Some forms considered by Jespersen to be examples of metanalysis may really belong here; *pease* ME *pese*, plural *pesen* < OE *pise*, Lat. *pisum*, was felt to be a plural, though it was really singular – cf. the form *pease-pudding*, still in use – and so the back-formation *pea* arose in the late sixteenth century, although *pease* and *peasen* continued in use during the seventeenth century; similarly with *burial* (OE *byrgels*), *cherry*, *riddle* (OE *rǣdels*), *sherry*, and *skate* (Du. *schaatz*[en]) all now found in the singular only without the final -*s*, though I think the last-named is very rarely used in the singular, the usual expression being 'a pair of skates', but the new singular form has given the verb *to skate*. *Shay* is a seventeenth-century form, generally regarded as vulgar, which arose because *chaise* was thought to be a plural form.

Resurrection is a noun formed from the past participle stem, *resurrectus*, of the Latin verb *resurgere*: this noun yields a new verbal formation *to resurrect*, instead of *to resurge*. Similarly, we have a new verb, *to conscript*, not *to conscribe*, formed from *conscription*, yet this type of formation is sporadic, for the doctor, in giving us a *prescription*, *prescribes*, and does not *prescript*, and we do use *describe*, *inscribe*, *subscribe*, not *descript*, *inscript*, or *subscript*, though the related nouns are *description*, *inscription*, and *subscription*.

The verb *to donate*, developed from the noun *donation*, is perhaps hardly yet standard English, yet it is becoming more and more frequent, although the NED doubly damns it as 'chiefly U.S.' and, in the sense of 'grant, give', also 'vulgar'. Another recent example has developed from *television;* the second element of this word is from the Latin past participle *visus*, and from this, not from the Latin infinitive *videre*, we have developed a new verb, *to televise*. The Americanism *to enthuse*, developed from *enthusiast*, *enthusiasm*, is very recent, but has already gained a footing on this side of the Atlantic. *To vamp* seems to be well on the way to being established, and *to reminisce* seems to be used more frequently also, but other American examples such as *to emote*, *to orate*, *to peeve*, and *to frivol* have so far found little favour here.

This type of formation is found more frequently in colloquial speech, and has also been put to humorous use; G. K. Chesterton writes: 'The wicked grocer groces', the parodist J. K. Stephen has:

> *The Rudyards cease from kipling*
> *And the Haggards ride no more.*

and W. S. Gilbert in *The Pirates of Penzance* has 'When the enterprising burglar isn't burgling'. Only the last of these is acceptable yet in standard English, yet they do show a tendency, and indeed there is much good sense in such formations; if an *actor acts*, and a *painter paints*, why may not a *butler buttle*, or a *sculptor sculpt?* This last example is humorously illustrated by reference to a headline in an American newspaper, referring to the visit of Mrs Clare Sheridan to Russia – 'Trotsky described by Woman Who Sculped Him'.[33]

WORDS FROM PROPER NOUNS:[34] Many proper nouns have themselves been formed from common nouns, e.g. *Chapman*, *Sadler*, *Taylor*, *Turner*, *Walker*, *Webster*, and very many others. But the process has also worked in reverse, and not only nouns, but also verbs and other parts of speech, have been formed from the names of individuals. One of the earliest from names of people is perhaps *doily*, from the name of a man who, in the seventeenth century, sold fine material suitable for the table napkins, and so gave his name to the table mat made from such material. These formations are of all kinds, some merely slang or nicknames, others perpetuating the achievements of famous men, and they come from all sources, including history, science, trade, and literature. These words probably retained the capital letter at first, but many have now reached the final stage of acceptance in the language, as common nouns, with a small letter.

The names of many scientists have been used in the particular fields of study in which they were eminent: this is seen perhaps most clearly in the use of such names to indicate units of one kind or another, as in *ampere*, *farad* (< *Faraday*), *joule*, *ohm*, *volt*, and *watt*. These examples show also the international character of such usage, for these names are French, English, English, German, Italian and Scottish respectively. Recently *curie*, the origin of which is obvious, has been adopted as the name for the unit of radio-activity. Other examples are *Fahrenheit*, the name of the Prussian inventor of the thermometer, and *bunsen*, from Professor Bunsen of Heidelberg, the *Davy* lamp, and the *Maxim* gun. From science also we get such forms as *dahlia* (< Dahl), *fuchsia*) < Fuchs), ot saleet—do

Wistaria (< Wistar), and *cinchona* (< Countess of Chinchon, who introduced the Peruvian bark to Europe).

We may see examples also in names of garments, as *bloomers, bowler* (first advertised by Mr Bowler of St. Swithun's Lane in the *Daily News*, 8th August, 1868 – a family reunion was held recently. NED says from *bowl*), *cardigan, mackintosh, spencer* (once a short coat, but now a woman's garment), *wellingtons*, and one which is perhaps now almost a noun, though its main use is adjectival – *raglan*. *Pants*, a shortened form of *pantaloons*, derives its origin from the character in the pantomime. A *bowler* is also known as a *billycock*, said to be a corruption of *Billy Coke*, as the hat was first made for William Coke, later Lord Leicester. Among other garment names are *Dolly Vardon, Derby* and *Stetson* hats, *tam o'shanter, jemimas, Mae West* (life-belt), *plimsolls, Sam Browne* belt, *belcher* (a kerchief), *burberry, Gladstone, Vandyke* and *Byron* collars, *Dolman* jersey, and *joseph* (a multicoloured coat), and perhaps we may include, as ornament, *albert* – a watch-chain.

Other examples are *sandwich*, explained as the device adopted by the Fourth Earl of Sandwich, whose only refreshment during an uninterrupted spell of twenty-four hours at the gaming-tables is said to have been slices of cold beef laid between slices of toast – *brougham, daguerreotype, davenport, derrick* – a rather gruesome example as a method of hoisting, as it was the name of a famous hangman – *hansom, pinchbeck, pullman, shrapnel, silhouette, victoria* (a horse-drawn vehicle, named after the Queen), and *zeppelin*. *Namby-pamby* was adapted, as a term of ridicule, from the name of Ambrose Phillips, an eighteenth-century composer of pastoral poems of no great merit, by a fellow-poet, Henry Carey. Among more recent examples are *bakelite*, from its inventor, L. H. Baekeland, *pelmanism*, a system invented by a German, Poehlmann, *belisha* (beacon), *anderson* and *morrison* – shelters used in the last war – and *quisling*.

Christian names are also used, but less frequently: the best-known examples are perhaps *guy*, from *Guy Fawkes*, and *bobby*, from Sir Robert Peel, who reorganized the London police force; the form *peelers*, from his surname, is now rarely heard. *Dandy* may be a form of Andrew, as in Dandie Dinmont. It is found combined with Jack, as in *jack-a-dandy* in Congreve's *The Confederacy* (1705). Its origin is doubtful, but it is probably Scottish at source. Weekley dates it from the late eighteenth century on the Scottish border, but this is obviously too late, as the example from Congreve proves. *Tawdry* is another example derived from a Christian name, this time by aphesis. The word derives from St Audrey, OE Æþelþryþ, the patron saint of Ely. On her day, 17th October, a fair was held, at which gay finery, cheap jewellery, and knick-knacks were sold. Hence cheap and flashy finery and jewellery came to be associated with St Audrey, and then by aphesis came our adjective *tawdry*.

Personal names come also to be used as verbs, for example, *boycott* (from the persecution of Capt. Boycott, of Lough Mask House, Co. Mayo, by the Irish Land League in 1880), which has proved so popular – and it is indeed a most useful word – that it has passed from English into several European languages, for it is found in Dutch, French, German, and Russian. We find also to *lynch*, from the name of the American Judge Lynch, so far unidentified with certainty, but who is supposed to have started, or sanctioned, the practice, hence 'Lynch's Law', and another gruesome example in *to burke*, which carries us back to the Hare and Burke murders in Edinburgh in the last century. A further development of this verbal use is the addition of the suffix *-ize*, as in *bowdlerize, mercerize, mesmerize, macadamize, pasteurize*, and *tantalize*, from Tantalus. John Loudon Macadam died in 1836, and even before his death the verb was generally accepted. Southey writes in one of his letters 'macadamising the streets of London is likely to prove quackadamising'. On the other hand, the name may be shortened. From Dr Banting, who introduced a new method of weight control by rigid attention to diet, a noun *banting* was formed, to describe the regimen, and from this noun there developed a verb to *bant*.

An interesting development is the use of a particular word of this kind as a general term, particularly in colloquial language, where *hoover* is frequently used for any kind of electric vacuum-cleaner, with no regard for patent law, and the modern wife has further adapted the word, for she *hoovers* the carpet, no matter what make of cleaner she possesses.

Spoonerism, enshrining the memory of the Rev. W. A. Spooner, has become generally accepted as the term for a humorous, though unintentional confusion of words or syllables, and *malapropism*, from Mrs Malaprop's 'nice derangement of epitaphs' in Sheridan's *The Rivals*, is equally well known. This last example leads us to examples derived from literature, such as the adjectives *gargantuan, lilliputian, quixotic*, and *utopian*, and *gamp*, from the name of the character in *Martin Chuzzlewit*. *Pander*, from Pandarus, Criseyde's uncle, who acts as the go-between for the two lovers in Chaucer's 'Troilus and Criseyde', has also passed into general use, both as noun and, with a somewhat different meaning, as verb. Other examples from the classics include the verb *to hector; Adonis* needs no explanation; *mentor*, a wise counsellor, derives from Telemachus' adviser in the *Odyssey;* also the adjectives *epicurean* (Epicurus), *stentorian* (Stentor – herald of Greeks before Troy), *panic* and *platonic*.

Some of the names of our days and months go back to the gods of Germanic or classical mythology. *Tuesday* is the day of the Germanic deity Tiw, *Wednesday* of Woden, *Thursday* of Thor, and *Friday* of Friʒa. *Saturday*, however, has a classical origin, being the day of Saturn. *January* has its origin in the Roman god Janus, *March* celebrates Mars, *May* has developed from the name of the goddess Maia, and *June* from Juno. Two famous Romans are celebrated in *July* (Julius Caesar) and *August* (Caesar Augustus).

Also from mythology we get, through Italian, *volcano*, from the name of the blacksmith of the gods, *Vulcan*, and *vulcanite* is a later formation from the same name.

From Shakespeare we get a *Shylock* and a *Benedict*, and from the Bible a *judas*. The underhand idea behind this last may perhaps explain an unusual transference of meaning, for it is used of a peep-hole in a gate or door. One not easily recognized is *dunce*, from Duns Scotus, a celebrated philosopher, the term being first applied contemptuously to the schoolmen who opposed the new humanistic learning. *Don Juan* was a Spanish libertine, but literature has popularized his name. We owe *Mrs Grundy* to Morton's 'Speed the Plough'.

Some, however, of these common nouns derived from names of individuals still remain a mystery; the incident to which they refer was interesting enough at the time to connect it with a proper name, but not interesting enough to keep the record alive, and so the origin is now obscure. Shall we ever know who *Sweet William* was, or *Jack Robinson*, or who was the first *nosey-parker*, or which Jerry was the first *jerry-builder* (though it is by no means certain that here we have a personal name, for two Northern dialect words, *jerrymander* and *jerryburying*, both have a somewhat unsavoury meaning attached to them; the words are not recent in the dialect, and it may be that we have here a common first element, not so far identified)?

Apart from names of individuals, names denoting nationality have in the same way become part of our common stock. Some of these are obvious, such as *philistine*, *vandal*, and *hun*. We remember how the last-named was attached to the German people in the 1914–18 war – queerly enough it did not become popular in the last war – yet there is, of course, no racial connection, for the Huns were a Mongolian race. *Turk* and *tartar* are used for a ferocious person, a tough customer. An example from classical literature is the use of *amazon*. *Morris* dance, derived from the Spanish *morisco* – Moorish, is not so easily recognizable.

Place-names have similarly provided us with common nouns, often the names of products associated with the place, as *calico* (Calicut), *cambric* (Cambrai), *cashmere*, *currant* ('corinthes or currans,' says a seventeenth-century writer), *millinery* (Milan), *damask* (Damascus), *morocco*, *Muslin* (< *mussolina* < *Mussolo*, the Italian form of Mosul, in Iraq), *sherry* (Xeres), *tweed*. The latest is probably *bikini*, the swimsuit named after the atoll on which an atomic explosion was recently staged. The connection here is not immediately obvious. The connection does not always follow, or has perhaps not been maintained: *brussels sprouts* are now grown in other places than Brussels, and it is to the West Riding of Yorkshire, not to Worstead, in Norfolk, that we now go for *worsted*, a word used by Chaucer. The method of naval recruitment employed in Shanghai has given us the verb *to shanghai*, and the easy, ambling pace of the pilgrimage to Canterbury has yielded *canter*, for *Canterbury gallop*, the easy gallop suited to the pilgrimage. In 1653 there is a reference to 'smooth ambles and canterbury paces': the use of the word as a verb is later than its use as a noun. *Babel* derives from the Tower of Babel, and *Mecca*, as a place of pilgrimage, or the goal of one's ambitions, from the Mohammedan religion. From the Channel Islands we have *guernsey* and *jersey*, both originally fishermen's garments, and in the same class we may include *fair isle*, a particular type of jumper or sweater, which is now often used as a noun, as against the earlier adjectival form.

In some cases, however, the obvious connection proves to be the incorrect one. Popular belief connects *tram*, *tramway*, and *tramcar* with a certain Mr Outram, the reputed inventor, perhaps because of its occurrence in Smiles' *Life of George Stephenson:* it was also included in Worcester's *Dictionary* (1859). The word is probably Scandinavian, and seems to derive from a word meaning 'log', perhaps from the form of primitive carriages, or from the use of logs for the earliest wooden tracks on which the vehicles ran. However, the word is certainly older, particularly as a mining term, and in that industry we still have a *tram*, a *tramway*, and *trammers*.

New forms of words may arise through CORRUPTION, which is the result of misunderstanding, generally of foreign words and expressions. It is particularly common, therefore, among members of the Services who have been abroad. Most Service examples remain slang, and therefore do not penetrate into the standard vocabulary, but some have found a permanent place there. *San Fairy Ann* (*ça ne fait rien*) and *na poo*, both from the 1914–18 war, have almost disappeared even from slang now.

With this process is closely connected the production of new forms as a result of POPULAR or FOLK ETYMOLOGY, when speakers try to associate some foreign or unfamiliar term with one known to them, e.g. *sparrowgrass* has no connection whatsoever with the sparrow, but the learned word *asparagus* was unfamiliar, sounded something like *sparrow-grass*, two terms which were understood, and so the form came into being, and, though now considered vulgar, was accepted in polite circles in the eighteenth century. *Jews' harp* probably belongs to this class; there is almost certainly no connection with the Hebrew race, but its origin is obscure. If we had a record of the history of the word we could probably trace the corruption. Perhaps the likeliest source is the root which gave the OE *ceafl* and *cēowan* – cf. the Midland term *pigs' chauls* for pigs' cheeks, and the reference is to the manner of playing the instrument.

Sand-blind, used by Shakespeare, was originally *sam-blind*, half blind, the first element being OE *sam* – half. When this first element was no longer understood, the form was corrupted, and may have reached its present form because sand in the eyes could cause symptoms of blindness.

The word *cockroach* has no connection whatsoever with *cock*, the word being a corruption of the Spanish *cucuracha*, and the almost familiar form of the first syllable of the Spanish word provided the link.

Many inn names have been so confused, and a discussion of these forms would occupy many pages. One interesting example may, however, be quoted; in *Clouds of Witness*, by Dorothy Sayers, mention is made of an inn whose name, 'The Bridge Embattled', is corrupted to 'The Bridge and Bottle'.

Some of these forms are by no means new, especially those arising from foreign sources. French *jeu parti* – a game the result of which is in the balance – is found in Chaucer as *jupartie*, and by further modification has become the abstract noun *jeopardy*. The French *quelquechose* is found in Shakespeare as *kickshaws* – with a new plural in Toby Belch's

'*Art thou good at those kickshawses, knight?*'

Although in this particular context Shakespeare may have used the word with the deliberate intention of punning with *kick*, there is, of course, no etymological connection whatsoever.

Island is another example arising from ignorance, corruption, and popular etymology. The OE form was *īʒland* – the first element is connected with OE *ēa*, cognate with Latin *aqua*, and the meaning is simply 'water-land'. Medial -*s*-, not found before 1546, is a pedantic intrusion from the Latin *insula*, influenced by *isle*, the latter being perhaps thought to be a diminutive of *insula*. *Posthumous* was originally found without -*h*, being derived from the Latin adverb *postumus* – coming later in time. The second element was wrongly derived from the Latin *humus*, and so the word came to be identified with burial, and eventually with death.

Shamefaced should really be *shamefast*, the earlier form, with the sense 'fast, rooted in shame', but the modern corruption is this time much more expressive.

In Genesis ii, 18 we find 'And the Lord said: "It is not good that man should be alone: I will make him a help meet for him".' *Meet* here is obviously the adjective, meaning suitable, but woman was thought to be created to be *man's mate*, and presumably was intended to help him, hence the word *helpmate*, which is now good English.

Saler – O Fr. *salier*, a salt-box, Latin *salarium* – was a vessel to hold salt. The connection with salt seems not to have been evident, and so we have the redundant addition giving *salt-saler*, which yields our present form *salt-cellar*, with no connection whatsoever with *cellar*.

To explain *sirloin* the invention of a legend was apparently necessary. The first element is merely *sur* – above. This made no sense to those familiar only with English and it was confused with *sir*, and so we have the delightful story of the English king who was so pleased with this particular joint that he conferred upon it the honour of knighthood.

The first element of *cray-fish*, as a term defining fish, has no significance. The word derives from O Fr. *crévice*, French *écrevisse*, and so is merely a corruption of the French term, itself derived from OHG *krebiz*, modern German *Krebs*, cognate with our own word *crab*.

Wormwood is another example; here we have a double error, for there is no connection with either *worm* or *wood*. The OE word was *wēr-mōd*, but the first element was early misunderstood, and the word pronounced as if the elements were *worm* + *wood*. This pronunciation is at least as early as the fifteenth century. Perhaps the original meaning was 'mind-defender, mind-preserver', a reflection of a belief in the curative properties of the plant. Perhaps the Anglo-Saxons, like our grandmothers, thought medicine the more efficacious the more unpleasant it was!

Buttery has no connection with butter, but with bottles, being derived from ME *botery, botelrye* < O Fr. *boteillerie*.

Sometimes the mere form of a word may be affected by this process. the OE preterite *cūþe* gave ME *coude*; later -*l*- was added, probably by mistaken analogy with *would, should* (< OE *wolde, scolde*), where it was regular. This unhistoric consonant was even introduced into pronunciation in the sixteenth and seventeenth centuries, and was heard until fairly recently in some regional dialects.

What may be called FREAK FORMATIONS have also contributed to the vocabulary of English.

The word *tank*, as the name of a weapon of war, arose, it is said, through the operation of rules for security, the workmen who prepared the armour-plates for the prototypes being told that they were for special tanks for army use. On the other hand, one may perhaps prefer the simpler explanation, from the general appearance of the contraption.

Teetotal is said to have developed from *t-total*, the effort of a certain advocate, who stammered, to pronounce *total* (*abstainer*). Greenough and Kittredge, however, consider this word 'a reduplicated form of total', but do not explain the reason for reduplication.

Tandem is said to be a University witticism, from the Latin adverb *tandem* – at length. It was first applied to horses harnessed in that position, as the horses were at length, i.e. lengthwise, and was then extended to refer to cyclists in that position.

Funnybone is an obvious pun on the anatomical name – *humerus*.

Publican, for older *inkeeper*, may be a jest on the Biblical name for Roman tax-gatherers, and there may possibly be an implied suggestion of connection with what usually followed in the New Testament – 'and sinners'. The statement in Greenough and Kittredge[35] that the term has 'never become serious' in connection with the sense of 'keeper of a public house' is open to question. This was possibly true in the United States at the time the book was written, but it is hardly true in England today; indeed it is probably the only commonly-accepted meaning of the word, although the publicans, who, in common with members of many other trades and professions, have followed the tendency to adopt high-sounding names, now call themselves licensed victuallers, and their trade-protection association bears that name.

Some of these freak formations meet a need, and so survive and pass into the language, but most are nonce-words, coined for the occasion and then dropped. Professor Schlauch[36] quotes such an example from the United States: 'One ingenious business firm apparently conceives of the termination '-lier', in the word 'chandelier', as a usable suffix, and with its help has created the monstrous form 'lightolier'. We have now also the analogical formations *gasolier* and *electrolier*. [37]

CHAPTER THREE

★

THE COMMON HERITAGE

Mention has already been made, in the chapter on word-formation, of the existence in English of elements from other languages. The effect of the influence exerted by one language upon another is clearly seen, the foreign elements standing out in sharp distinction against the background of the native element, and the existence of two such words as *fishy* and *piscatorial* in English, one native, the other a loan word, but both arising from a common root and sharing the same basic idea, though their actual meanings vary, illustrates the differences in various languages. But, widely different as so many languages are today, it is possible to find also so many resemblances that we are able to group languages into what we may call families. Just as the individual members of a family are all different, yet all possess to some degree the family likeness and characteristics, so also related languages, though differing appreciably from each other today, possess sufficient characteristics in common for us to be sure that they have sprung from the same parent language. An examination of the languages spoken over large areas proves the existence of these family characteristics, and enables us to speak of families of languages. As we shall, in the chapters which follow, need to mention many other languages which have influenced English at one time or another, it will be worth while at the outset to consider these languages, their relationship one with another, and particularly their relationship with English, and also how these relationships may be established.

Only comparatively few of the languages spoken today have been scientifically examined, analysed, and compared. We have very scanty information about some, quite inadequate for a scientific investigation, and of many languages we know nothing, or practically nothing. We have written records of the earlier forms of many of the languages spoken today, and of some not now spoken, but these records have naturally preserved but a small part of those languages as they once existed. Of some old languages only a few personal-names or place-names have survived, of some we have no record other than the mere name of the people who spoke the language, and it is almost certain that many languages must have disappeared, leaving no trace whatsoever. In spite of the work that is being done in the field by many investigators today it is likely that some of the languages now being spoken in the more inaccessible parts of Central Africa and Central America will so disappear before they can be recorded. Hampered as we are by these gaps in our knowledge, it is indeed almost impossible to establish completely the relationship between various languages. By relationship we understand here resemblances in morphology, accidence, syntax, and vocabulary which can be explained only by the assumption of a common origin, that the languages as we now have them are divergent forms developed from the same parent language.

As long ago as 1822 Humboldt expressed the opinion that languages are so varied in form that it is impossible to classify them accurately and comprehensively, dividing them into groups which will include them all, and this opinion is still held by some modern scholars. Yet we do possess sufficient information to be able to classify, with some degree of accuracy, many of the most important languages. Examination shows that there are some striking resemblances to be noted in different languages, and in some cases these are far too numerous to be accidental. We must note, however, that very rarely shall we find absolutely identical forms in two languages arising from a common form; there is no common source for German *viel* and English *feel*, though they are almost identical phonetically. Languages have developed differently over the course of centuries, and two languages are therefore unlikely to have retained an original form unchanged, or both to have changed it in the same way. Yet English *calf, father, man, milk, mother, son,* and *sister* are too close to German *Kalb, Vater, Mann, Milch, Mutter, Sohn,* and *Schwester* for the resemblances to be merely accidental over such a range of sounds and forms, and indeed these pairs do go back to common forms in a parent language, Common or Primitive Germanic. This, in brief, is the comparative method of linguistic study, and if we are able by this method to establish sufficient points of similarity in vocabulary, accidence, and syntax, we may reasonably conclude that there is some historical connection between the two languages. Not all resemblances will be acceptable, however. There are, particularly in the case of English, which has borrowed words from so many other languages, resemblances due to common origin and resemblances due to borrowing. For example, English *veritable, human,* are close to Latin *veritas, humanus,* but this is because English has borrowed these Latin words.

A word of warning is necessary, however, before we proceed further. The term 'parent language' has been used, and it is a useful general term, but it may give a wrong impression. One language does not actually give birth to another, nor does one language cease to exist and another take its place in the line of succession, as we may be inclined

to think when we see the intricate 'family trees' so carefully compiled by some writers on language. We can say no more than that
certain languages are derived from, have developed from, other earlier
languages. For example, English may be quoted as a descendant of
parent Germanic, but in saying this we mean no more than that English
is the form which this parent Germanic has assumed under particular
conditions of isolation. We can not talk of the birth-date of English, or,
to continue the metaphor, say that at a certain time English was 'formed'
from parent Germanic, with the parent language continuing more or
less unchanged after English had been born. It would be quite wrong to
say that at some particular time Germanic suddenly yielded Old English,
that Old English suddenly yielded Middle English, or that Middle
English suddenly yielded Modern English. Just as the geographical
boundaries of our modern dialects are not sharp, so chronological
boundaries are not sharp. The Ouse, and, further north and west, its
tributaries the Wharfe and the Aire are generally regarded as a boundary
between Northern and Midland English, Northern English being spoken
to the north and east, Midland English to the south and west. In the
case of a town situated on one of these rivers, we do not expect to find
the people in the two parts of the town speaking different dialects,
sharply divided by the river. Rather we shall find here a buffer-area of
mixed dialect, and the further we get away from the river in either
direction so will the forms of the other area become less frequent. Just
as one regional dialect will, therefore, merge into the next, so did the
various chronological divisions gradually shade off one into the other.

We have already noted resemblances between English and German;
we could also include in this group Dutch, Danish, Norwegian,
Icelandic, Swedish, Frisian, and the now extinct Gothic language, all
of which possess so many common features as to enable us to say with
some certainty that they have sprung from a common ancestor, so that
common Germanic gave rise not only to English and German, but also
to all those other languages, all of which differ appreciably today, but
which are still known as the Germanic group of languages. We may
ask how these divergences from a parent language have taken place.
Unfortunately for us, in our study of English, we cannot see the
changes taking place in the period of recorded languages, for we have
no written records from the period when these changes were taking
place. But we are a good deal more fortunate in another group of
languages, for we can actually see the process at work in historical times
in the case of the Romance languages. French as we have it today is
merely a particular phase or development of the Vulgar Latin as it was
spoken in Gaul, Portuguese and Spanish of the Vulgar Latin spoken

in the Iberian Peninsula, Italian of the Vulgar Latin spoken in Rome itself, and the remainder of Italy, and the Vulgar Latin spoken in the Danubian provinces eventually gave us Rumanian. This Vulgar Latin, in its various forms, is merely a development, in special circumstances, of Latin, a language well known to us from written records. And so, thanks to a knowledge of the history, both social and political, of the Romance countries, we are able to watch what we might call a 'parent language' diverging under different conditions into different languages. In the Vulgar Latin spoken in Gaul, the Iberian Peninsula, Italy, and the Danubian provinces we have the clue to the problem, these variants being merely the form which Latin took in the mouths of the ordinary people of those areas. The divergence is easily explained by the phenomenon known as linguistic isolation, for we know that, within a large area, a language once spoken in a uniform manner will, particularly where there is little communication between the several parts of the area, become sub-divided into a number of dialects, and the difference between the dialects will differ with the degree of inter-communication, and the length of separation. If the separation is slight the differences will not be great, and we shall find merely local dialects, as in the dales of Yorkshire, or, with perhaps greater differences, though with the languages mutually intelligible, British and American English, but the separation may be sufficient to render one dialect unintelligible to speakers of the others, and thus we get separate languages arising, as happened in the case of the Germanic and Romance languages. Yet, even where the separation has gone so far, the various new languages will preserve sufficient common features of the original language to enable us to show that they are related, that they belong to the same family. If we examine such a group, say the Romance languages, we shall find certain features common to all, and some of these features discernible in Latin itself; we may therefore regard these features as survivals of the Vulgar Latin stage, a stage lying between classical Latin and our group of Romance language. Thus, by comparing and classifying these resemblances, we are able to make a comparative grammar of the Romance languages, work out essential features almost certain to have been in the intermediate stage, and so establish the link between them and Latin. But, owing to the fact that we have no written records earlier than Latin, our positive demonstration of relationship on historical and linguistic grounds comes to a halt there. But even then we are luckier than we are in the case of our own Germanic group, because we cannot check on our Primitive Germanic, through an earlier recorded form, as the Romance philologist can check his conclusions by reference to classical Latin.

Another method, the historical method, is also open to us. It is obvious that language is always changing; Shakespeare sometimes seems a little strange to us, Chaucer is only just readable for the present-day Englishman, and Old English is a closed book. We may investigate by examining the written records available to us from the earliest period from which such records exist, and see how the language has changed. In our own group of languages we shall find that English, German, Dutch, and the various Scandinavian languages have all changed independently in the historical period, so that any differences noticeable in the earliest records will have been increased and magnified by this independent development. As a result, comparison of related languages is much more difficult if we take modern forms than if we take earlier forms; we shall find that Old English is much closer to Old High German than modern English is to modern German. It will, then, save us a good deal of time and trouble if we make use first of the historical method, tracing our languages as far back as possible by this method, and then, having got as near as we can with certainty to the language at the point of divergence, we can start on the comparative method.

Having seen an actual example in the historical period of how languages diverge and form a family, let us see how we can extend the knowledge so gained to broaden our survey. We shall make use of this same comparative method, but now we shall be extending the method to a study of the languages of a period still more remote, languages of which we have no written records at all. We have seen how it is possible to arrive at a hypothetical reconstruction of the language from which the Romance languages have sprung by preparing a comparative grammar of those languages. We may infer that other groups of related languages, showing similar resemblances, have arisen in the same way, and it is only an unfortunate chance which has deprived us of written records of the language which was spoken before the members of the family diverged, to form the languages we know today. But we may overcome this difficulty. We may with certainty postulate a Germanic group of languages when we note resemblances such as OE *hand*, ON *hond*, Go *handus*, OS *hand*, OHG *hant*, or OE *horn*, OS *horn*, OHG *horn*, Go *haúrn* (with identical pronunciation), or OE *fæder*, Go *fadar*, OS *fadar*, ON *faðer*, OHG *vater*. We can have little doubt that we have a common ancestor for each of these sets of cognates. Comparative grammars of the modern Germanic and Slavonic languages, for example, based upon resemblances within the two groups, would enable us to reconstruct the essential features of the languages of Primitive Germanic and Primitive Slavonic. By this same method, of comparison of resemblances, it can be shown that these languages have some features in common with the Latin, at which point our Romance investigation ended, and that all three have features in common with the primitive forms of Greek, Celtic, Persian, Sanskrit, and other languages spread over a large part of Europe and Asia.

We may, for example, easily show the connection of English, a Germanic language, with Latin, a non-Germanic language, but both members of the Indo-European family. There are several differences distinguishing Germanic from the other Indo-European languages, but the most important is what is known as the First Sound Shift, a complete shifting of Indo-European explosive consonants in the transition from the parent-language to Germanic. The phenomena of this shift, and its later continuation and extension, are also known as Grimm's Law and Verner's Law, after the philologists who first classified the changes, though the details had been noticed earlier. Latin, being a non-Germanic language, will not show the shift.

First let us take the cycle of changes classified under Grimm's Law. This may be sub-divided into three series, the relative chronology of which is not yet firmly established. By these changes the IE voiceless stops p, t, k became the Germanic voiceless spirants f, $[\theta]$, $[x]$, the voiced stops b, d, g became the voiceless stops p, t, k, and bh, dh, gh, about the pronunciation of which in Indo-European times there is not yet complete agreement, became eventually the voiced stops b, d, and the voiced spirant $\mathfrak{z}$, which later developed into the voiced stop g under certain conditions. As examples of the first series we may compare Latin *pater*, *pes*, *piscis*, English *father*, *foot*, *fish;* Latin *tres*, *tenuis*, *tu*, English *three*, *thin*, *thou;* Latin *centum*, *cornu*, *caput*, English *hundred*, *horn*, *head*. In the second series we may note Latin *labium*, *lubricus*, English *lip*, *slippery;* Latin *duo*, *dens*, *edere*, English *two*, *tooth*, *eat;* Latin *granum*, *genus*, *ager*, English *corn*, *kin*, *acre*. The third series is not so easily illustrated, as divergences are to be noted in other languages, but we may compare Latin *fero*, *frater* with English *bear*, *brother;* Latin *hortus*, *hostis* with Old English *ʒeard*, *ʒiest*.

Comparison may also be made of consonants unaffected by Grimm's Law. For example, in the case of the nasals we have Latin *nepos*, *cornu*, English *nephew*, *horn;* Latin *vermis*, *mare*, English *worm*, *mere;* examples of unshifted liquids include Latin *mulgere*, *velle*, English (OE *meolcian*), *will*, and Latin *fero*, *frater*, English *bear*, *brother;* the semi-vowels are also not affected, as Latin *jugum*, *juvencus*, English *yoke*, *young*, and Latin *videre*, *velle*, English (OE *witan*), *will*.

In the case of examples covered by Verner's Law another factor must be taken into account. In some cases in Germanic it appeared that where a voiceless spirant might be expected by Grimm's Law we had a voiced spirant, or its development. Verner formulated the reasons for this, and his conclusions may be briefly summarized as follows: if the syllable preceding the voiceless spirant did not bear the chief accent in Indo-European, then the spirant became voiced. There were many opportunities for the operation of this law, for, as we have already seen, accent was free in Indo-European, and could occur on any syllable. For example, although Latin *pater*, English *father* apparently follows the rule, this is not really so, for OE had *fæder*, and the spirant sound medially in the Modern English word did not develop until the fifteenth century. In this word Indo-European had the accent on the suffix, and so the original voiceless spirant was voiced, and later developed to the voiced stop. Similarly Latin *dux*, connected with *ducere* – to lead – has a parallel in Old English *here-toga;* the last element is from the reduced grade stem of OE *tēon* – to lead, where the medial [x] was lost, as we may see by comparison with Go *tiuhan*. In Indo-European the preterite plural and past participle had the accent on the suffix, and so [x] was voiced to [g], giving OE pret. pl. *tugon* and p.p. *togen*, and *toga* is from this form.

Similar correspondences may be noted in vowels, and in cases where there is variation this is regular for Germanic. As examples of unchanged vowels we may note Latin *ad*, *pater*, *ager*, English *at*, *father*, *acre;* Latin *edo*, *fero*, *pellis*, English *eat* (OE *etan*), *bear* (OE *beran*), *fell;* Latin *piscis*, English *fish;* Latin *suīnus*, English *swine* (OE *swīn); Latin *flos*, English *bloom* (OE *blōma* with sense influenced by ON); Latin *mūs*, English *mouse* (OE *mūs*). Of the divergences, Latin regularly has the IE *o* against an English development of Germanic *a*, and *ā* against Germanic *ō*, as Latin *frāter māter*, English *brother* (OE *brōþor*), *mother* (OE *mōdor*).

Such resemblances are far too numerous and systematic to be merely accidental, and we can have no reasonable doubt that these pairs of words in Latin and English had common ancestors. Similar resemblances are to be seen in words from other IE languages, but the above examples are clear, and further illustration is unnecessary here.

It should now be obvious that if we continue our method of investigation still further, taking all these reconstructed primitive languages and treating them as we did the languages of the historical period, by assembling the features common to all, we shall be able to prepare a comparative grammar of the primitive Indo-European languages, which will lead us to Indo-European itself, just as the comparative grammars of the Romance languages led us to Vulgar Latin.

A word of warning is necessary about the term 'Indo-European'; it is a purely linguistic term, and has nothing to do with races. It is generally impossible, particularly in the early period, to establish a connection between language and race. As a result we are not helped much in the linguistic field by the work of anthropologists and archæologists. Philologists have been able to reconstruct the essentials of the language spoken by the ancestors of the Hindus, Persians, Greeks, Romans, Celts, Slavs, and Germans, but they have little or no knowledge of the people who spoke that language.

This comparative method, based upon resemblances, is reliable, but it can never be absolutely certain in the absence of accurate historical knowledge of the races themselves. In the human field not all doubles are related, and the same is true in language. But in the case of the important family of languages with which we are primarily concerned we have much of the necessary material, and as a result relationships have been established which are well-nigh incontrovertible on general grounds, even if there is not complete agreement on all the minor details.

Having established that relationships among languages may be demonstrated, we may now look at some of the great families so classified. We shall be chiefly concerned with one, the Indo-European, but mention may be made briefly of the other great families, first to make clear that Indo-European is only one amongst a great many,[1] and secondly because languages belonging to some of these families have affected our own, and provided us with loan-words.

In the far east we have the great Sino-Tibetan, or Indo-Chinese family, sometimes called the Monosyllabic group, from the fact that the languages now consist chiefly of one-syllable words which may not be inflected. Chinese is the most important member of the group, the other important languages of this family being Tai and Tibetan.

Stretching from China across north and central Asia as far as Europe are the Ural-Altaic group of languages. They are divided into groups, of which the most important is Turkish. Some scholars believe that this Turco-Tartar group is related to the Mongol and Manchu languages, the Altaic group, and also to Finno-Ugrian and Samoyede, spoken from the Altai Range to the arctic shore of Asia, but this has not so far been definitely established. The Finno-Ugrian group lies to the east of the Indo-European area; its original home was probably on the foothills of the Urals. Of the six groups, the Baltic-Finnish-Lappish group extends furthest north. Another branch, Hungarian, or Magyar, was brought into Europe by ninth-century invaders, and is now a flourishing language spoken in Hungary and the neighbouring areas. It has been suggested that Japanese and Korean belonged originally to this group, but no definite proof has been so far forthcoming.

The Caucasian group, as its name implies, is found between the Caspian Sea and the Black Sea. It seems to be an independent group, not belonging to the Indo-European, Ural-Altaic, or Semitic families. The chief members are Georgian and Circassian.

The Dravidian group belongs to Southern India, and is the language of the people who inhabited this great sub-continent before the Indo-European invasion from the north-west. The most important languages of the group are Tamil, Malayalam, Canarese, and Telugu.

Stretching eastwards across the Pacific is the Malay-Polynesian group, subdivided into Malayan, or Indonesian, Melanesian, Micronesian, and Polynesian. Javanese, a language of the Indonesian group, goes back some eleven centuries. Malagasy, the language of Madagascar, is a distant offshoot of Malayan, and the Maori language probably also belongs to the Polynesian group. There is little doubt that all these languages are related, but we possess such scanty information about some of them that it has not yet been possible to establish the relationships completely.

Two other apparently independent groups are found in this area, Papuan, spoken in New Guinea, and the Australian aborigine languages, but comparatively little is known of them.

In Africa we find the Bantu languages stretching over practically the whole continent south of the Equator: there are many languages in this group, including Swahili, Zulu, and Kaffir. In the south-west are two independent languages, those of the Bushmen and Hottentots. In Central Africa, between the Bantu group in the south and the Arab and Berber languages in the north, are a great mass of dialects, of which some hundreds have been distinguished, though very few are written. Various opinions are held as to the relationship of these dialects one with another, and with the neighbouring groups, but sufficient is not yet known for the problem to be solved. To the north of these groups is the Hamitic group, named after Ham, the second son of Noah. Egyptian, recorded from about 4000 B.C., is the most important language of this group. Another branch of this family is the Berber group of languages, spoken in North Africa, which are remarkable for having withstood the encroachment of Arabic. Some scholars would place the Ethiopian languages in this group, but others consider them to be a Semitic language. There are, indeed, resemblances between Hamitic and Semitic, pointing to a common ancestor, and some scholars prefer to speak of a larger Hamitic-Semitic family. This larger group has affinities also with Indo-European, and there is a theory that all three may really be divergent forms of a very early parent language, but definite proof of this has not so far been forthcoming.

The Semitic peoples are those mentioned in the Bible as being descended from Shem, son of Noah. The linguistic group is divided into eastern and western sections, of which the eastern section, Babylonian-Assyrian, is now extinct, having given place to Aramaic before the Christian era. The western group may be further subdivided into northern and southern groups. The former group includes Canaanite, Moabite, and Hebrew. This latter language gave way to Aramaic shortly after the beginning of the Christian era, but was preserved as a written language, and efforts have been made recently to revive it as a spoken language. It should not be confused with Yiddish, which is a mixed language that has developed in Central Europe. The other member of the northern group is Aramaic, which spread over Syria and a large part of Western Asia, and for about a thousand years competed with Greek as the chief official language of the Near East, but later gave way to Arabic. The southern group consists of South Arabic, spoken along the south coast of Arabia, and Arabic itself, the official, literary, and sacred language of Islam, which owes its wide expansion to the conquests of the Mohammedan Arabs.

In the New World are the Amerindian, or Red Indian, dialects of North America. These dialects are clearly differentiated, and there are a great number of them, perhaps more than fifty. A good deal of work is now being done on these languages, and some scholars think that a relationship may eventually be established between these languages and one or more of the other large families. There are also a large number of independent languages in Central and South America, some of which, such as the Mayan and Aztec groups, were the languages of important ancient civilizations.

There remains now only the one with which we are primarily concerned, the Indo-European family. Other names have also been used at various times. Aryan was formerly popular, but is now generally used to describe the eastern group, Indian and Persian. Indo-Germanic is another term, still widely used; it does indicate the geographical extremes of the group, but perhaps lays too much stress on the Germanic element and ignores such important languages as Greek and Latin. Indo-European is now commonly accepted, and with its linking of two continents, or at least a continent and a sub-continent, it indicates well the geographical location of the languages without putting undue stress on any one language. In this group are to be found practically all the modern European languages, and, in addition, Celtic, Sanskrit, Persian, Russian, Armenian, and Albanian. We have no records of the parent language, for it had already split up into a number of dialects by the period for which our earliest records are available, but it was apparently not a primitive language at the time of the split, but, as we see from a comparative study of the material now extant, a complicated, well-developed, and highly-inflected language. The comparative study of the Indo-European languages presents less difficulty than that of any other family, for they are the languages of peoples who have, for many centuries and throughout almost the whole historical period, been the leaders in culture and civilization, with very full literary records, lending themselves to a complete study of the development of the various languages. It is not surprising, then, that we know more about the development of the languages of this group than we do of any other.

But even then we have little knowledge of the people who spoke the language, when they spoke it, or where they spoke it. 'Indo-European' is a linguistic term, and we have no evidence as yet for the existence of a pure race speaking the language. Indeed, judging from the characteristics of peoples now speaking the Indo-European languages, from the tall fair Scandinavians in the north to the short dark Mediterranean peoples, and the inhabitants of Persia and India, we may assume considerable racial mixture at a very early stage. On the other hand, as the Indo-European peoples spread east and west, many conquered peoples may have given up their own languages, and adopted that of their conquerors. Similarly we cannot be sure of the period when the language was spoken, but we seem to have evidence of a social and cultural unit, and it is therefore reasonable to assume that these peoples, whoever they were, must have spent many centuries together, leading a communal life which eventually resulted in a common culture and a common language. Generally-accepted opinions place the end of this common existence and the beginning of the great migration period somewhere between 3000 B.C. and 2000 B.C. Of the antiquity of the records there is less uncertainty, the oldest, the Vedic Hymns, going back to 1500–2000 B.C., and these are in a language which already differed appreciably from the parent language.

There is also no exact knowledge, and little agreement of opinions, of the original home of these peoples. It is reasonable to assume, however, that it lay somewhere within the boundaries of the modern languages. From what we learn from primitive history, and the remains of non-Indo-European languages, the islands and peninsulas of the Mediterranean may be excluded, and also our own islands. Earlier, because of the Biblical tradition linking the Garden of Eden with Mesopotamia, Asia was favoured as the original home, largely because Sanskrit and Persian seemed to preserve the most archaic forms, and it was believed that a language which moved least from its original home would show the least change. But most of the languages have been in Europe throughout the historical period, and eventually the idea of Asia as the original home was abandoned, as it was felt that it was more reasonable to assume that the minority had moved a considerable distance east and south rather than that the majority had moved equally far west and north-west. As we shall see later in this chapter, the common vocabulary was also studied, and this confirmed opinions supporting a more westerly area. Moreover, all the languages may be divided into two groups, the 'satem' and 'centum' groups, based upon the development of the consonants found initially in those words. The dividing line runs roughly from Scandinavia to Greece, leaving on the one side the western or 'centum' group, consisting of Greek, Latin, Celtic, and Germanic, and on the other the eastern, or 'satem' group, consisting of Indian, Iranian, Armenian, Albanian, Slavonic, and Baltic. It seems reasonable to assume that the original home must have lain somewhere near this line, and that expansion took place eastwards and westwards. Prokosch[2] has postulated the existence of a 'Prairie' and 'Parkland' group, the former inhabiting the steppes of Southern Russia, and migrating, perhaps in distinct waves, partly to the south-east, to Persia and India, partly north-west, eventually forming the Balto-Slavonic group, and the latter inhabiting the forests and meadows of Central Europe, from which they migrated in two streams, an eastern group who moved south-east and settled around what is now Greece, and a western group who moved west from the Middle Danube, and later split again, one party, the Italic and Celtic groups, continuing west, the other, the Germanic peoples, turning north through the forests of Germany. There are, as we have seen, not only geographical but also linguistic differences between the two groups, but on the other hand it is not improbable that these two were once a much closer unit, occupying an area lying between Southern Russia and Central Europe, and that an earlier split, with migration east and west, or possibly of one group only, east or west, had already taken place.

The oldest records of the Indo-European languages are to be found in the sacred books of the Hindus, which date at least from 1500 B.C. After these come the Persian scriptures, going back to about 1100 B.C. Then come the earliest Greek records, from about 750 B.C., and the Latin records dating from about the fifth century B.C. Then, after a long break, come the Germanic records, with Scandinavian runic inscriptions of the third century A.D., and the Gothic translations of the Bible by Bishop Ulfilas in the fourth century. In all these languages we can trace the historical development from these early records almost without a break to our own times, though in some cases, as, for example, in Sanskrit and Latin, the classical languages may be broken down and replaced by the vernacular languages.

Perhaps the most important discovery relating to the Indo-European family was that of the affinity of Sanskrit with the languages of Europe, first suggested in the late eighteenth century and fully confirmed in the following century. Sanskrit preserves more of the original features of the parent-language than do Greek, Latin or Germanic, and, moreover, a great deal of information was available on the structure of classical Sanskrit of a very early date, thanks to the labours of grammarians such as Panini, their investigations dating from the fourth century B.C. Sanskrit, originally a religious language, was extended to secular use, and from it later developed the modern colloquial languages of India.

The other important member of the Aryan group is Iranian. It is spoken on the plateau of Iran, and its oldest records are rock inscriptions dating from about the sixth century B.C. The sacred books of the Parsees probably go back in their original form to about 1000 B.C., being in a language almost as archaic as that of the Vedic books, though the manuscripts themselves are comparatively recent. From this primitive language has developed modern Persian, and a few languages from the outlying parts of the original empire, including Afghan in the east, and the Caspian languages and Kurdish in the west.

The other members of the eastern group have records of a much more recent date. Armenian is spoken at the eastern end of the Black Sea, at the southern edge of the Caucasus Mountains, the original tribes having probably penetrated eastwards from the Balkans. In its modern form it is much contaminated, having been influenced by Persian, Greek, Turkish, and the Semitic languages.

Another minor branch, Albanian, is found north-west of Greece, on the eastern shore of the Adriatic. Like Armenian, it is also an individual language, and it also shows much contamination, particularly from Greek.

Greek itself is a much more important member of the family, and was probably carried into its present home about 2000 B.C., the area until then having been inhabited by non-Indo-European peoples, as very ancient remains prove. Of its four chief dialects, Attic, the dialect of Athens, became supreme, because of the cultural, political, and commercial domination of that city, and from it developed the language which was for several centuries the chief official language of the Mediterranean, and from which modern Greek is derived. We shall hear much more of Greek when we come to examine the growth of the English vocabulary.

The chief languages of southern Europe are the Romance languages all of them developments of Latin. Latin was only one member of the Italic group, but it was the dialect of the city of Rome, and, just as in the case of Attic in Greek, it became the dominant language because of the superiority of Rome itself over the other cities of Italy. This language, as the official language of the Roman Empire, spread to all parts of Italy, and then, as the empire grew, to many parts of Europe, including Spain, Gaul, the Danubian provinces, to our own islands, and as far as Asia Minor and the northern coast of Africa. Being spoken over such a wide area, it naturally tended to split up into sub-dialects, especially after the co-ordinating influence was lost after the fall of Rome, and these variants have remained as the languages of France, Spain, Portugal, and Rumania, and have also been carried to many parts of the world, including India and North and South America, by trade and colonization. It should be remembered that these languages, although derived from Latin, are not developed directly from Classical Latin, but, as in the case of the Indian languages, from the colloquial language of the people, which differed much from the classical language in both accidence and vocabulary. For example, French *cheval*, with closely-related forms in Spanish and Italian, is obviously not derived from Classical Latin *equus*, but from a variant Vulgar Latin form, *caballus*. These Romance languages, particularly Latin and French, have exerted great influence on the English vocabulary.

Next we may consider the Celtic group, at one time much more important than it is today, for the Celts were spread over most of Western Europe at the beginning of the Christian era, but the Celtic languages have been replaced, except in a few areas, by the Germanic and Romance languages. Celtic tribes carried their language to these islands, but were later driven further and further west by the Angles and Saxons, and today their languages survive only in Ireland, in Scotland, and the Isle of Man as one group, Gaelic, while Cymric, the other group, survives in Wales and Brittany, a third member, Cornish, having apparently died out almost within living memory. It can be shown that Breton is not a development of a language spoken on the Continent, but of the Cymric spoken in these islands, and it was probably carried back to the continent when fugitives from the Saxons fled across the Channel. Efforts, largely of a nationalist nature, have been made recently to revive these languages, and nationalist feeling may for a time halt the decline, but it may well be that within the next century what was formerly one of the chief languages of Europe and one of the most important members of the Indo-European family may disappear, borne down by the weight of English.

The Balto-Slavonic group consists of languages carried north, through Central Europe, by people who probably for a time formed a community, for there are sufficient resemblances between the Baltic and Slavonic languages to justify our speaking of a common parent language, and the two groups separated comparatively recently, a common language being spoken until perhaps as late as the beginning of the Christian era. Baltic survives today in only two languages, Lettish and Lithuanian, the latter a language retaining many archaic features. A third member, Old Prussian, died out in the seventeenth century. Slavic may be divided into three groups, West, East, and South Slavic. The two important West Slavic languages are Polish and Bohemian, the latter subdivided into Czech and Slovak. East Slavic consists of the Russian languages, probably a common language as late as the twelfth century, but now divided into Great Russian, the official and literary language, spoken in the north, east, and central areas, White Russian, spoken in the west, and Little Russian, or Ukrainian. South Slavic is separated from the other members of the group by Hungarian, a non-Indo-European language and a reminder of invasions from the east. South Slavic consists of Bulgarian, Serbo-Croatian, and Slovenian. It has the oldest Slavic records, in the ninth-century transla- tions of the gospels, the language of these texts being also called Old Church Slavonic, or Old Bulgarian.

Fairly recent discoveries have widened our knowledge of the Indo- European family. Early this century the ancient Hittite capital in Asia Minor was excavated, and the royal archives discovered, some written in Babylonian, but most in an unknown language, that of the Hittite people, and work so far done on them suggests a distinct, if distant, relationship with Indo-European, though it may be a mixed language, that of Indo-European conquerors imposed upon the original language. On the other hand, it may prove the link between Indo-European and the Hamitic-Semitic group, and pave the way for the establishment of a still larger family group, with an original home centred somewhere near the Euphrates, and split by subsequent migrations. At about the same time some remains were found, far to the east, in Chinese Turkestan. The language of these remains, Tocharian, is dated by reference to a king who, according to Chinese evidence, reigned in the seventh century A.D.

There remains now only the group which concerns us most closely, Primitive Germanic, or merely Germanic, the language spoken by the Germanic peoples before the emigrations to the Black Sea, these islands, and Scandinavia. The oldest records, as we have already seen, are third- century runic inscriptions in Old Norse, and the fourth-century Biblical translations in Gothic. From the eighth century we have literary records in Old English, Old High German, Old Saxon, and Old Frisian which lead without a break to the modern languages, and we have records of the Scandinavian languages from the tenth century. The common home of these people was probably the area between the Elbe and the Oder, and both shores of the Baltic, where they probably lived as a community, though not necessarily as a political unit, in the centuries immediately preceding the Christian era. The area was not fertile, and this, along with the threat from inundations, brought about movement and later migration, the result apparently being that northern, central, and southern groups eventually resolved themselves into northern, eastern, and western groups, as the central groups, driven out of their homes around the Kattegat area by inundation, moved east, and later south-east, settling first around the mouth of the Vistula, and then moving south-east to the Black Sea.

This later rearrangement also provides us with our linguistic subdivision of Germanic into the later East, North, and West Germanic. Because of the central position it formerly occupied between the northern and southern groups, East Germanic has affinities with both, but naturally developed along different lines when the peoples moved away from the Germanic homeland. There were originally several tribes speaking this group of languages, but of their languages all have either completely or almost completely disappeared except Gothic, the language of the tribes who moved first to the Black Sea area, where they settled and later divided into two groups, the Ostrogoths, east of the Dnieper, and the Visigoths, west of the Dnieper. The Ostrogothic kingdom was overrun by the Huns, but later they conquered Italy, where their king Theoderic ruled for a time, but later still they were defeated by Belisarius, and eventually absorbed into the Roman Empire. The Visigoths established empires in Spain and Gaul, but finally succumbed to the Moors. Their language has survived in fourth-century translations of the Bible, and, as it is some centuries earlier than Old English, and has not undergone certain changes which occurred in that language, it is extremely useful for comparative purposes. Some of the Goths settled in the Crimea, and a number of the words they used were recorded there as late as the end of the sixteenth century, but Gothic as a language is now extinct. It has had no influence on the development of our language, there being neither personal nor cultural contact between the peoples.

North Germanic is the language spoken by what are now the Scandinavian tribes in the north. They were originally a purely northern group, but probably moved into the area which is now Denmark after the central group had moved away. They occupied Iceland in the ninth century, and later settled in Greenland, the Orkneys, Faroes, and Shetlands, in Scotland, Ireland, and England, and even crossed to North America, as extant Norse records show. The earliest records are third-century inscriptions. During the Viking Age the language sub-divided into East and West Norse, the former including Old Swedish, Old Danish, and Old Gutnish, the latter Old Norse and Old Icelandic, and these eventually developed into the modern languages of the Scandinavian countries. Danish and Norwegian exerted considerable influence on English in the ninth and tenth centuries, and this influence will be the subject of a later chapter.

Finally we come to West Germanic, the immediate ancestor of our own language. It was the language spoken by the original Southern group, which later divided into a Low German and High German group, the former being established on the plains of northern Germany and the shores of the North Sea, the latter in the highlands of southern Germany. High German is distinguished from Low German chiefly by the effects of the Second Consonant Shift.

Of these West Germanic languages, Old English and Old Frisian are closely related, and will be considered together below. The other West Germanic languages have developed into the modern languages, Dutch having developed from the dialects of the western coastal area after independence from the German Empire had been secured, and German, or New High German, as it is sometimes called, developed from the languages of the eastern and central areas, and later spread considerably, eventually being divided into Low and High German, which are still differentiated today in pronunciation and partly also in vocabulary.

After the departure of the central group mentioned above, other tribes appear to have moved into Jutland from Schleswig-Holstein; these people appear later as Angles, living in Angeln. They had probably lived originally between the Elbe and the Oder, and had moved west-ward, either driving out or absorbing the original Celtic population. Alongside them were the Frisians and the Saxons. These three are often referred to as the Anglo-Frisian group, and the three languages, Old English, Old Frisian, and Old Saxon, shared in certain sound-changes peculiar to the group and possess sufficient common features for us to group them together in distinction to Old High German, though Old Saxon was later influenced by High German. Saxons and Frisians established settlements on the northern coast of France in the fifth century and from there, and probably also directly from their home-land, they settled in these islands also, while the Angles settled chiefly in the east midlands and north, perhaps somewhat later. According to Bede, the first settlements, in Kent, the Isle of Wight, and Hampshire, were effected by the Jutes. The Saxons eventually became the political leaders, largely as a result of the destruction of the earlier Anglian civilization by the attacks of the Vikings, and West Saxon, the language of King Alfred, became the official and standard language of Old English, though much of the earlier work had been written in Anglian and was later transcribed by West Saxons. West Saxon was the earliest non-Latin official language in Europe.

The four dialects of Old English, West Saxon, Kentish, Mercian, and Anglian, retained their differences into the Middle English period, but West Saxon was not to remain as the official language. Instead, the East Midland dialect, the descendant of Mercian, gradually developed into a new standard language, because of the growing importance of London, and also because it was the language of the area in which were established the two ancient universities. West Saxon itself developed into the modern dialects of the south and south-west, just as Anglian developed into the northern dialects and Lowland Scots, and the dialects of the west and north-west Midlands into the modern regional dialects of those areas.

At this point, having traced the development of our language from its earliest form, spoken somewhere in Central Europe or Asia, right up to the present time, we may conclude our short survey of the families of languages and the relationships established between members of these families. The scope of this book allows of only the bare details, for comparative linguistics is not our purpose here: accordingly, many details have been omitted, and arguments side-tracked. It is sufficient here to mention and in part classify the chief families of languages, so that when later an alien language is mentioned as having influenced English it may not be altogether unfamiliar.

We have already seen how it is possible, by means of comparative philology, to reconstruct at least some of the features of the parent Indo-Germanic language; let us now see how far it is possible, using the same methods, to arrive at some idea of what words these peoples used, and also, since these words will throw light on the objects and ideas familiar to those peoples, to see what kind of life they led, what stage of civilization they had reached.

Only comparatively recently, thanks to the discovery that Sanskrit was related to our European languages, and also, largely as a result of this, to the knowledge we have gained of the operation of certain phonological changes affecting the Indo-European family of languages, has it become possible to investigate comparative vocabulary scientifically. We know little of the Indo-European peoples before about 1000 B.C., nothing with historical certainty. Historical records, art, and literature throw some light on developments of the peoples and their language since that time, and archæology, ethnology, and folk-lore have contributed something to our knowledge of the earlier period, but in the present state of our knowledge linguistic material is by far our safest guide to the prehistoric period. The obvious method of study, as in the field of comparative grammar, is by taking points of similarity; it is reasonable to assume that if all, or a majority, of the languages in this family have, for a particular idea, a word which can be shown to have been developed from a common form, that common form is likely to have been in the parent language. Indeed, it is not necessary to insist on the presence of a word in the majority of the languages; if two widely-separated languages, such as a Germanic language and Sanskrit, have such forms, and it can be shown that the forms are indigenous, we may take it that they formed part of the stock of words of the parent language. Conversely, some scholars have extended their reconstruction of the period by making use of the argument that if a common word is not found for an object in the various languages, that object could not have been known to the parent-race. However, though we may rely on positive evidence, the value of the negative type is much more doubtful. There are many very common objects which must have been familiar to the Indo-European peoples, yet we have no common word for them; as an extreme example, it has been argued that, because we have no common word for *sea*, these peoples were not acquainted with the sea until they had split up, as a result of migration; this is commonly accepted, and is indeed quite feasible. But we also have no common word for *hand;* are we to argue similarly that these people did not develop hands until they had been separated into small groups? There is also no common word for *milk*, yet we know these people had flocks and herds.

With this reservation in mind, then, we may ask ourselves now, basing our investigation purely on linguistic grounds, who these people were, where they lived, and what type of life they led. Comparative philology tells us that they were the ancestors of the Hindus, the Persians, the Greeks, the Romans, the Armenians, the Slav peoples, the English, the Germans, the Scandinavians, the French, the Portuguese, the Spaniards, the Rumanians, and the Celtic peoples in Wales, Ireland, Scotland, and Brittany. Such a wide range of types at once suggests that we have here not a race, but a linguistic and cultural community made up of different races, and indeed the idea that the Indo-Europeans were a homogeneous race has been generally abandoned.

Early views on the original homeland of these peoples were based largely on the Scriptures, the view being that in the Garden of Eden, possibly somewhere in Eastern or Central Asia, perhaps in Mesopotamia, these people lived in idyllic pastoral conditions, in an earthly paradise. Much of this, too, has now been abandoned, and, as we have seen, modern scholars incline to believe that the Indo-European homeland was situated on the steppes of southern Russia and the forested plains of Central Europe. From here, as we have already seen, it seems probable that the Hindus and Persians emigrated south-east, the Greeks, Romans and Celts along the northern shores of the Mediterranean, and the Germans and Slavs west and north-west, through the forests of Germany.

Let us see now what we may learn of the common vocabulary. In such an investigation we must always bear in mind that we are dealing with a prehistoric period, with no written evidence, and if, in the following pages, an effort is made to divide the period into three, it must be understood that the evidence is not always clear for such a clean-cut differentiation, and there may be some overlapping. If words are to be considered as part of the common Indo-European stock we must expect to find them in both eastern and western branches, in Sanskrit or Persian, and in Greek, Latin, Celtic, Slavic, or Germanic. In this section no imposing lists of cognates will be provided, and, as the general reader will hardly be interested in the reconstructed forms of Indo-European, the forms given will be the Modern English develop-ments of the words. The first group of words to come to mind shows us at once that these people had already developed a strong family sense, for the common words of relationship *father*, *mother*, *son*, *daughter*, *brother*, *sister*, *widow* are found in most of the languages. We find later, in Germanic literature, that there seems to have been a particularly strong tie between a man and his sister's son, and the archaic *neve* – nephew (OE *nefa*, cognate with Latin *nepos*) is also common to several languages. There is also evidence of some substantial place of abode, perhaps only temporary, for the peoples were apparently nomadic in the earliest period. *Door* is a word common to several of the languages, and we also have *timber* (apparently from the stem which gave Latin *domus*) and *thatch*. There is, however, no common word for *window*. The word *wand* may perhaps throw light on the character of the build-ings, for, while it has the meaning of *thin stick* in English, it has the sense of *wall* in German. This may mean that the walls of Indo-European dwellings were of wattle. The word seems to be connected with OE *windan* – to wind, and Go *wandjan* – to turn round, and perhaps the basic sense is of 'something pliable', which would suit admirably the thin rods plaited to form a wattle wall. An established family life is also suggested by the names for domesticated animals, such as *goat*, *goose*, *hound*, *sow*, and OE *eoh* – horse (cognate with Latin *equus*), a word which has since died out in our language. A further group of animals throws even greater light on the type of life led by our ancestors, for

we find as common words *cow*, *ox*, *ewe*, *wether*, *steer*, and *herd*, all
suggesting a nomadic people, driving their flocks and herds before
them. The relationship between these flocks and herds and their conception of wealth is to be seen in the OE *feoh* – cattle, property (cognate
with Latin *pecu* – cattle). In King Alfred's translation of Orosius, in the
late tenth century, we are told something of conditions in Scandinavia
at the time in the interpolated passage which gives an account of
Ohthere's voyage: 'Ohthere was a very wealthy man in such possessions as make up their wealth, that is, in wild beasts. He still had six
hundred tame deer unsold when he came to see the king. . . . He was
among the first men in the land, although he had no more than twenty
horned cattle, twenty sheep, and twenty swine, and the little that he
ploughed he ploughed with horses'. The English word developed to
fee, and the relationship is still further brought out in the later loan-word,
from Latin, *pecuniary*. We have also some evidence of the way in which
they were able to move their property around in their wanderings in
the survival of common words for *axle*, *nave*, *wheel*, *yoke*, and a common
root giving *wain* or *wagon*. Apparently their wheels were solid, for
there seems to be no common word for such a thing as a spoke, but
it has already been pointed out that assumptions on such evidence are
unreliable. Some of the domestic arts were known to them, for there is
a common word *weave*, also for *wool*, showing a connection with the
flocks, and their knowledge of brewing fermented liquors is shown in
the wide currency of *mead*. As might be expected in a nomadic people,
they were little concerned with manufacture, and there seems to be
only one common word for a name of a metal, the word which has
given us *ore*, and which seems then to have had the sense of 'copper',
and perhaps later 'brass'. There are, in contrast with the clear evidence
for a nomadic life, few fully-authenticated words connected with agriculture, though the root which has given us *sow* and *seed* may belong to
this period. As we shall see later, agriculture seems to have developed
only when the European group emigrated westwards and the other
group to the south-east, for most words connected with agriculture are
not common to the two groups, but it is likely that, even in the earliest
days, there would be some elementary knowledge of crops and the
sowing of seed. Finally, to conclude our investigation of this earliest
period, we may ask if there is any evidence throwing light on the area
in which these people lived. There is a common word for *snow* –
though, strangely enough, it came to mean 'damp' in the languages of
the eastern group. From this it has been concluded that snow was
familiar to them in their original homeland, but that as the eastern
group moved south-east into warmer countries they passed through an

area of melting snows before reaching the hot plains; this is feasible if, as seems likely, they entered India from the north-west. There are also common words for the seasons *spring*, *summer*, and *winter*, suggesting an area in which the seasons were sharply differentiated, and the presence of both *snow* and *winter* suggests an area with cold weather at one period of the year; this would fit in admirably with the centre of a continent, but that does not help us in differentiating between Asia and Eastern Europe. The word *birch* is also common, but that tree is found very widely, and so is no help. There seems to be no common word for *sea*, nor for *fish*, suggesting that the original home was inland, and apparently well inland, away from navigable rivers leading to a sea, for the words *row* and *rudder* suggest a knowledge of primitive navigation. We get a little more evidence in words connected with flora and fauna; we have the common word for *tree*, and also, as noted above, for *birch*, and among names of animals we find *beaver*, *hare*, *mouse*, *otter*, and *wolf*. Perhaps we might conclude the study of this first period by quoting Bender: 'There are no anciently common Indo-European words for elephant, rhinoceros, camel, lion, tiger, monkey, crocodile, parrot, rice, banyan, bamboo, palm, but there are common words, more or less widely spread over Indo-European territory, for snow and freezing cold, for oak, beech, pine, birch, willow, bear, wolf, otter, beaver, polecat, marten, weasel, deer, rabbit, mouse, horse, ox, sheep, goat, pig, dog, eagle, hawk, owl, jay, wild goose, wild duck, partridge or pheasant, snake, tortoise, crab, ant, bee, etc'.[3]

In conclusion we may note that all the words which have survived from the earliest period are, as is to be expected, simple words, and names of concrete objects or words indicating the simple actions of everyday life.

We come now to the second period in this primitive age, and we shall now look for evidence in vocabulary for the great migrations which were eventually to produce two sharply-differentiated groups, the eastern, or satem, group, and the western, or centum, group.

As the different tribes, or races, moved away from each other in their migrations they were placed in a state of linguistic isolation, the conditions for the development of an individual speech. Although there may have been slight differences in the parent-speech, due perhaps to geographical distribution, there was probably something approaching a norm over the whole area. Any deviations from this norm which might develop among individual speakers or communities would be toned down or eradicated by intercourse with the others, but as soon as migration prevented this free intercourse, conditions would arise for the development of individual dialects. So deep and varied were the differences which arose that we learn that the Greeks had no idea of any relationship between their own language and that of their enemies, the Persians, nor did the Romans see any resemblances between their own Latin and the languages spoken by the Celts and Germans.

These migrations were almost certainly not highly-organized mass movements such as that which took the Israelites out of Egypt, but rather they were a succession of smaller movements, occasioned perhaps by some inquisitive spirit inherent in these peoples, perhaps by war among the tribal rulers, resulting in some being driven out, perhaps by compulsory emigration from unsatisfactory territories. Whatever the cause, it seems that the races who are the ancestors of the Persians and Hindus moved south-east, and the ancestors of the Greeks, Romans, Celts, Germans, and Slavs moved westwards, perhaps from the treeless steppes of what is now southern Russia to the pasturelands of the forested plains of Eastern and Central Europe. The words we shall now look for, as evidence of this movement, and possibly changed occupations resulting from new surroundings, are those which are common to the European group but which have no counterpart in the languages of the eastern group.

We shall find that quite a large proportion of the words peculiar to this European group relate to agriculture, suggesting that the new surroundings induced a change of occupation, and that the tending of flocks and herds, in nomadic communities, gave way to settled communities tilling the land in areas cleared from the forests. It may be that the forested plains of Europe did not provide sufficient pasture for their flocks and herds, and that these people were compelled to adopt an agricultural life, for the change from an easy nomadic life to the hard toil of agriculture is hardly one to be made by choice. Among the words illustrating this change of life we find *corn*, *grain*, *ear* (of corn), *furrow*, *bean*, *meal*, and the verbs *to mow* and *to ear* (OE *erian* – to plough), archaic now, but found in the Authorized Version of the Bible and in Shakespeare. *Acre* also seems now to have changed from its former meaning of 'enclosed land' to 'cultivated land', as in Latin *ager*.

There are also some words indicating a geographical change. As the European stream moved westward they passed through the area immediately to the north of the Mediterranean, and so apparently came into contact with the sea for the first time, and as a result they share a word *mere* (Latin *mare*) not found in the eastern group, and also *salt* and *fish* (Latin *piscis*). From *mere*, now generally used only in place-names and in poetry, has developed *mermaid*. Further evidence of this kind is again to be seen in names of flora and fauna. We find *beech*, *elm*, *hazel*, and *finch*, *starling*, *swallow*, *throstle*. The words *beech* and *bee* have been quoted by Professor Bender[4] as evidence for the area inhabited by these peoples. He points out that there is a common word for *honey* or the drink made from it, citing forms for the former from Latin, Celtic, and Germanic languages, but not from Aryan and Slavonic, and from Aryan, Slavonic, Greek and Germanic languages for the latter. He also notes that the bee is found everywhere in Europe, but in Asia is native only within a narrow band extending from Syria to Tibet, and most of the Asiatic areas formerly supported are outside that area. He shows that *beech* is found in several languages, and was almost certainly in the parent language, and that the beech is native to Central Europe and is not found north and east of a line from Danzig to the Caucasus. It should, however, be noted that the word is used in some languages for such trees as the oak, elm, and elder. Further evidence exists from the word for *silver birch*, and Bender finally favours Eastern Europe, Russia, Poland, and Lithuania, where conditions seem to favour alike the flora and fauna, the wide plains necessary for a nomadic people, and fertile valleys for the later agriculture.

Against this use of word material to establish the original homeland we should note that in some cases, as, apparently, in that of *beech*, there may be a change of the object and the name remain unchanged, that old names could be carried to new regions and then be afterwards adapted to similar objects, as has happened recently in America and Australia, and also that there may be widespread common words for objects not native to an area, as, for example, *tobacco* in European countries today.

After a lengthy period together – no one as yet knows how long – these European peoples again separated, the Greeks making their way south into the Grecian archipelago, and the other peoples moving west and north-west. Linguistic considerations suggest that the Italic and Celtic people remained together for some time, probably travelling west through the regions to the north of the Mediterranean, and that the Germans and Slavs moved north or north-west through the forested plains of Germany.

We are concerned now with Germanic – the development of the Italic and Celtic peoples will be considered below, when we examine the influence they exerted on the Germanic peoples – and there is again linguistic evidence for the breakaway of the Germanic peoples from the Greeks, Italic races, and Celts. The words providing this evidence will be those found in the Germanic languages, for which there is no counterpart in Greek, Latin, or Celtic, and, of course, in the eastern group, but we shall, from now on, concern ourselves less with establishing linguistic divisions than with building up the vocabulary common to the Germanic peoples, in order to accomplish our first purpose, of establishing the language brought here by the tribes about 450 A.D. First of all we may note a group connected with home life, among which we find *bowl, brew* (although we know this process must have been known to the Indo-Europeans, from the common word *mead*, further proof that the evidence of vocabulary is not always reliable), *broth, dough, home, house, knead, loaf*, and *quern*, for grinding the corn, is also common. Words also occur which show a more organized type of life, as *borough*, and *king* and *earl*. There is also evidence for the growth of trade in such words as *buy, cheap* (OE *cēapian*, from which we get such words as *Cheapside* and *Eastcheap, chapman*, originally the name for a trader, but now surviving only in the personal name), *ware*, and *worth*. Some scholars consider that *cheap* is a Latin loan-word; this is not unlikely, although cognates are found in all the Germanic languages, and the point will be touched upon when we come to consider Latin influence on the common Germanic language. Alongside developments in trade might come an increasing use of metals, further proof of an advanced state of civilization, and in comparison with the one word noted in the earliest period we now find *gold, silver, lead, tin, iron*, and *steel*, though *silver* and *iron* may possibly again be loan-words, the former from Salube – cf. the Germanic form of the word, **siluðr* – a town on the Black Sea which, according to a passage in the *Iliad*, was the original source of silver, and the latter from a Celtic source. The fashioning of precious metals is shown in a common word for a ring, cognate with OE *bēaʒ*, a form related to *būʒan* – to bend. There is also evidence of a geographical nature. As the Germans and Slavs moved north-west they would come in contact with the Baltic, and with the shores of the North Sea and the Atlantic. As a result of this the Germanic peoples developed an intense love for the sea, a characteristic of the people from early times, as we see from their literature, and one which has not weakened with the passage of time. It is not surprising, therefore, that we find quite a large group of words connected with the sea and sea-faring, such as *cliff, island, sea, sound, strand, whale, seal*, and *mew*, and *ship, steer*, and *sail*. There are also common Germanic words for *north, south, east* and *west*. We have also further information on the area in the form of names for new birds – the word *fowl* is common to Germanic – animals, and trees, and a further extension of the agricultural vocabulary, such as OE *bere* – barley, and *wheat*. We also find words connected with the arts, such as *book, learn* and *lore, write*, and the word *leech* in several forms, all connected with healing. Something of their religion is shown in common names for their gods, including *Tīw, Woden, Thōr* and *Frīʒ*, preserved still in *Tuesday* (OE *Tīwesdæʒ*), *Wednesday*

(OE *Wōdnesdæʒ*), *Thursday* (OE *þuresdæʒ*) and *Friday* (OE *Frīʒedæʒ*). OE *blōtan*, to sacrifice, has cognates in several Germanic languages, as also has OE *hearh* – a temple, and *bless* (OE *blētsian*) also throws light on early times, for though the word is found only in Old English it is related to *blood* (OE *blōd*), the original meaning being 'to sprinkle with blood', as a priest does at a sacrifice (c.f. *blōtan* above).

We see, however, that, although the Germanic peoples had certainly made progress since they left their Indo-European homeland, there is practically no evidence of their having acquired any culture. They were still living in rudely-fashioned houses, probably of wattle, practising primitive agriculture, and worshipping heathen gods. They were, as their more polished neighbours from the south called them, barbarians, and it required contact with Mediterranean civilization to draw them from this barbarism. We have, so far, examined the language as it had developed among the Germanic peoples, which seems to have been, at first, fairly pure, with few words adopted from non-Germanic languages. But it is probable that no language is absolutely pure; even among the very primitive tribes, speaking languages which can express their thoughts only in an elementary manner, we should probably find that they had borrowed the names of unfamiliar objects and ideas from neighbouring tribes. For several centuries before the Angles and Saxons came to this country the Germanic peoples had been in contact with other non-Germanic races, notably the Celts and the Romans, and some linguistic influence had naturally been exerted. Although the words we shall now study are loan-words, and therefore not purely native material, they had been incorporated in the Germanic language on the continent and were therefore part of the language brought here by the Angles and Saxons in the middle of the fifth century. In order to study these words it will be necessary to digress a little and consider what had happened to these non-Germanic tribes after they had separated from the Germans and Slavs and continued their way south and west, in order to see what progress they had made towards civilization, and the ways in which they were likely to influence the barbarian Germans.

There can be little doubt that the Greek and Italic peoples, by turning their steps towards the Mediterranean, made the happier choice, for by so doing they put themselves in contact with the earlier civilizations of Egypt and what we now call the Near and Middle East. Here they learnt how to build in stone, they became acquainted with the science of navigation, and with art, mathematics, and writing, all of which they were to develop still further, until the final result should be the great classical civilizations of Greece, and later Rome. From the great literature of Greece many words were later to find their way into English, such words as *epic*, *nectar*, *ambrosia*, but this is material for a ater chapter, when the influence of the Greek and Latin languages in the Renaissance period will be examined.

The Celts probably travelled for some considerable time in company with the Italic races who were eventually to found Rome, but later, when the Italic tribes turned south into the peninsula of Italy, they continued their way through the mainland of Europe. They were, therefore, the people in closest contact with the Germanic peoples, and as the latter moved further and further west towards the North Sea coast they drove the Celts before them. It is at least likely, therefore, that Celtic influence is first in point of time, though there is very little that can be fully authenticated. On the other hand, as the Celts and Germans were probably in close contact in Western Europe for some centuries, more words were perhaps borrowed than is now apparent. It is likely that some Celtic tribes may have been absorbed in the North-west European coastal area, from the Elbe to the mouth of the Rhine, settled later by the Saxons and Frisians, and if the women were kept as slaves, or mixed marriages took place, some linguistic contamination would be probable. It seems, however, that the superiority of the Celts lay in war, and organization and government, for authenticated loans are in those classes. OE *rīce* – power, powerful, and later formations from it, such as the verb *rīcsian*, is a fairly certain loan, from a Celtic stem *rīg-* connected with Latin *regere*. As it is to be found in all the Germanic languages, including Gothic, which was the first to break away from the parent Germanic, it must be very early. It survives as a suffix in such forms as *bishopric*, and as a part of such personal names as *Frederick* and *Roderick*. Another Celtic word was borrowed not only by the Germanic peoples but also by the Romans, but the meaning of the word makes it likely that the word itself might be adopted. OE *ambeht*-servant, may have been borrowed through Latin, though Gothic also has the word as *andbahts*, and Old High German has *ambaht*. Cæsar uses the word *ambactos* (*de Bell. Gall.* vi, 15), and Festus writes: '*Ambactus lingua Gallica servus appellatur*', leaving us in no doubt of the origin. Modern German keeps the word as *amt*, but the related words *embassy* and *ambassador* in Modern English are new borrowings from French. *Iron* has been proposed as a Celtic loan, but it seems at least possible that OE *īsern* (Go *eisarn*) is connected with the early root which gave us *ore*, and which appears in Gothic as *ais* – brass, money. OE also has the forms *īren* and *īsen*, the vowel of which appears to be in the same Ablaut series as the forms just mentioned. *Welsh* has also been suggested, as a loan from *Volcae*, the name of a particular Celtic tribe. The word may be common Germanic, as it appears also as ON *Valskr* and OHG *Walhisc*. It appears early in Old English; *walas* is used for the British in the A. S. Chronicle entry for 465 – '*Her Hengest and Æsc gefuhton wiþ Walas, neah Wippedesfleote and þær XII Wilisce ealdormenn of slogon.*' The noun perhaps had the general sense of 'foreigner', and it was used as a gloss for *barbarus*, just as it was used in the sense of 'Romanus' in Old High German. *Dūn* – hill, with cognates in several other Germanic languages, may be another example, but some scholars consider this doubtful. In any case, we see that authenticated examples of Celtic loan-words borrowed on the continent are few, and the proved influence is slight, whatever the actual influence may have been.[5]

The case is different when we come to Latin, and we need not look far for the reason, which is at the root of the whole psychology of borrowing. Foreign words are, as we have seen, adopted into a language in many different ways, and for many reasons, but the examination of the acceptance of loan-words into any language shows that in almost every case the language from which the words are borrowed is that of a people of superior culture and civilization; when a nation possesses objects, operations, and ideas of any kind which are superior to those of the other nation we find that usually not only the object or idea, but also the name, will be adopted. There are, of course, exceptions to this, for some peoples are more inclined to make use of the resources of their own language, rather than borrow foreign words. This paramount reason for borrowing will often help us to solve what may at first seem difficult problems; for example, we may wonder why the Germanic peoples apparently borrowed many more words from the Romans than they did from the Celts, with whom they were in much closer contact, and probably for a much longer period. The Celts may not have been very much superior, if at all, to the Germanic peoples, though their prolonged contact with the Romans and the possibility of closer contact with Mediterranean civilization would certainly have given them opportunity for advancement, but there was no doubt about the respective cultures when the Germans came into contact with the Romans, even if the latter were chiefly represented, as was probably the case, by merchants and soldiers.

Latin influence on the vocabulary of English up to the end of the Old English period may conveniently be divided into three periods; first there is the period of contact with the Romans themselves on the Continent, which was largely an influence exerted on the common Germanic language; then, much later, comes the period of indirect contact with Roman civilization through the Britons in the early years after the Anglo-Saxon conquest, and finally the period, extending from about 600 A.D. through some four and a half centuries, during which the conversion to Roman Christianity brought the English into close contact not only with religious ideas, but with many aspects of Roman culture and scholarship. It is with the first period that we are now concerned.

The influence of Latin on the Germanic vocabulary in the continental period was largely of a commercial nature, though some evidence is also to be seen of a rise in the standard of living conditions generally. This, according to the reasons for borrowing which we have just examined, suggests that these were the aspects of Roman life which most impressed the Germanic tribes, and we shall find that this was so. But first of all let us see how the presence of these Latin words in the common Germanic language can be substantiated, before discussing the words themselves. It is not sufficient to examine the Old English language alone, for that language is known to us only from a time when the English had been settled for a long period in a country which had been a province of the Roman Empire, and the presence of a Latin word in Old English, even in the earliest texts, is no proof that it was already in the language at the time of the Settlement. A word could, as we have seen, be borrowed in any one of three periods; the presence of a Latin loan-word in an early text does not help us much, for this merely shows that the word must have been adopted sufficiently early to pass into current use by the period of the text, but we do not know whether the word was borrowed direct from the Romans on the Continent, from the Britons in the years immediately after the Settlement, or later, as a result of the efforts of Roman missionaries and teachers. Again, the late appearance of a word is no proof of late adoption, for, apart from the fact that it could have been recorded in one of the many earlier MSS which have failed to survive, the word may not have been of a type which would occur frequently in literary records. But there are two tests which give reasonably accurate results – comparison with other early Germanic languages, and the evidence of phonological changes. If we find a word in use among several Germanic tribes, in Gothic, Old English, Old High German, Old Saxon, or other related languages, we may reasonably assume that it was in general circulation among the Germanic tribes on the continent, and was therefore brought over here by the Angles and Saxons, though we must not lose sight of the fact that in some exceptional cases such words may have been independently adopted at a later date if they reflect influences which might then have been operative over the whole area; such an influence would be, for example, the independent conversion of the tribes to Christianity, and the consequent introduction of Latin words in religious

works. Quite a number of words borrowed from Latin are to be found
in the various Germanic languages, and many of these must have been
borrowed at an early period. The second test is one of the sound of the
word. There are certain phonological developments in later Latin which
can be dated with reasonable accuracy; one of these is the change of
Classical Latin intervocalic *p* to *b*, and later to *ƀ*. OE *copor* (ON *kopar*,
OHG *kupfar*) must have been adopted before this change took place;
for the later development we may compare French *cuivre*, which shows
the development of the voiceless stop to the voiced spirant. We may
similarly compare OE *pipor* and French *poivre*. We may note, in passing,
that these words must be borrowed from Latin, or a non-Germanic
language, for had the word come into Germanic from Indo-European
the operation of Grimm's Law would have changed *p* to *f*. Similarly,
intervocalic *t* became *d*, and later *đ*, so that OE *strǣt* and *butere* must
have been borrowed before this change took place. But OE *cæfester*
(Latin *capistrum*), OE *cæfl* (Latin *capulus*), and OE *abbod* (Latin *abbatem*),
OE *eced* (Latin *acetum*) were borrowed when the changes had taken
place in the Romance language. Further phonological tests are possible
within the Old English period itself, for loan-words adopted early
enough would naturally undergo all the phonological changes operative on native sounds at the time. For example, Latin *a* passed unchanged
into Germanic, and then in Old English would undergo all the normal
changes, such as slight raising and rounding before a nasal, as *candel*,
condel; fronting to *æ*, as *tæfel;* retraction again to *a* in an open syllable
followed by a back vowel, as *draca;* breaking, under favourable conditions, as *earca;* and similarly diphthongization by initial front
consonant, as *ceaster;* and i-mutation, as *celc*. But words borrowed at a
later period retain *a*, or change *a* to *æ* if the borrowing took place after
the fronting to *æ* had ceased to operate but before i-mutation was completed. Similarly early loans retain *i*, as *biscop*, but later loans often show
e, as *seglian*, thus reflecting a late Latin change, (cf. French *évèque* as
against OE *biscop*). Similarly Latin *ā* appeared in Old English as *ǣ*, the
development of West Germanic *ā*, if borrowed early, as in *strǣt*, but
later loans retain *ā*, as *pāpa*. Other Old English tests of this kind may
also be applied, but sufficient has already been said to show the value
of the tests. There is a need, however, to be on guard against sound-
substitution and analogical levelling, but it will be seen that when a
word is ascribed to a particular period it is not a question of fortuitous
guesswork, but rather of demonstrable fact, though there may sometimes be difficulty in differentiating between loan-words of the Continental Period and those of the period in England before the conversion
to Christianity.

We may now examine some of the loan-words of the continental period in more detail, starting with commercial terms. All the words quoted have related forms in the other Germanic languages, thus suggesting borrowing during the period when the tribes enjoyed a common language and culture. Cognates will be given in one or two cases only, merely by way of illustration, but to give the available cognates for each word would swell the material unreasonably, and would be of little use to the general reader, while the philologist knows well where such material is available. Most examples, therefore, will give only the Modern English form and the Old English word. *Chest* (OE *ciest*) and *ark* (OE *earca*) are probably from this period, and would be originally the receptacles in which the traders carried their goods. For the trader himself we have -*monger* (OE *mangere* – merchant and *mangian* – to trade, OS *mangōn* – to trade, OHG *mangari* – trader), from Latin *mango*, a fraudulent trader. The word survives today in *fishmonger*, *ironmonger*, *fellmonger*, etc. Another word of similar meaning has already been mentioned as a possible loan-word, for OE *cēap*, goods, and *cēapian*, to buy, may be from Latin *caupo;* here we may compare German *kaufen*. This word was confined to wine-selling in Latin, but developed a more general sense in English. It survives, as we have already seen, in *Cheapside*, *Eastcheap*, the personal name *Chapman* – originally a huckster – and the adjective *cheap*. The dialect word *cheapen* is a perfect survival, for it means 'to bargain for, ask the price of', and not 'to make cheap'. The *wine* (OE *wīn*) sold by these traders was, as may be expected, another early borrowing, from Latin *vinum*. The trader's terms for his weights and measures and money also passed over; *pound* (OE *pund*, Go *pund*, OHG *pfunt*), the measure of weight, derives from Latin *pondo*, and *inch* (OE *ynce*) is also a loan-word, from Latin *uncia;* the money he used, Latin *moneta*, from the Latin goddess Moneta, in whose temple at Rome money was coined, appears in Old English as *mynet* (cf. Modern English *mint*, which kept the meaning 'money' until the sixteenth century), alongside *mynetere*, a coiner. We also find OS *muniteri* – coiner, and *munitōn* – to coin, and OHG *munizari* – coiner, *munizōn* – to coin. The road along which he travelled, Latin *strāta* – used also, of course, by the legions – yielded OE *strēt* (OS *strāta*, OHG *strāza*, O Fris. *strēte*), and the measure of distance *mīlle* (*passuum*), originally the 'thousand paces' of the legionary, gave OE *mīl*. Weekley notes an interesting word of this type: 'The word *dicker* will be unfamiliar to some of my readers. It means a bundle of ten skins. It is found, in some form or other, in practically all European languages, and it comes from Latin *decuria*, a set of ten. The *decuria* was the unit of barter or tribute wherever the Roman came in contact with the barbarian. In America it is still used of bargaining or haggling, originally in connection with the fur trade with the Indians, so that it has had a continuous history of nearly two thousand years'.[6] The names of many of the articles carried by the merchant were also borrowed, including domestic objects and strange products from the Mediterranean regions, such as *dish* (OE *disc*), *candle* (OE *candel*), *cheese* (OE *cīese*), *butter* (OE *butere*), the word *kitchen* itself (OE *cycene*), and *cook* (OE *cōc*), *vinegar* (OE *eced*, Go *akeit* – cf. the later loan-word *acetic*), *oil* (OE *ele*), *pepper* (OE *pipor*), *turnip* (last part in OE *nǣp*), *pea* (OE *pise*), *onion* (OE *ynne*), and fruits such as *pear* (OE *pirie*), *cherry* (OE *cires*) and *plum* or *prune* (OE *plūme* < Lat. *prunum*). The etymology of *apple* is doubtful, but it may be an early loan from Latin, one suggestion being that the word derives from Abella, a town in Campania famous for its apples. We also find such common words as *wall* (OE *weall*, OS *wall*), from Latin *vallum*, with a connection here perhaps with both domestic building and fortification, though the latter sense was perhaps the first with which the Germans were acquainted, and *port* (OE *port*, OS *porta*, OHG *phorta*) from Latin *portus*. Other building terms include *chalk*, used in the sense of *plaster* or *lime* (OE *cealc*), *tile* (OE *tiȝele*), and *pitch* (OE *pic*). A word which now survives only as a place-name element, OE *wīc* (Go *weihs*, OS *wīk*, OHG *wīch*), derives from Latin *vīcus*, a village. The influence on domestic life is to be seen in names of cooking and kitchen receptacles, such as *bin* (OE *binn*), *cup* (OE *cuppe*), *dish* (OE *disc*), *flask* (OE *flasce*), *kettle* (OE *cytel*), and in *table* (OE *tæfel* – a chessboard), *pillow* (OE *pyle*) and *carpet* or *curtain* (OE *teped* – Latin *tapetum*); numerous plants and fruits were also introduced, many of which undoubtedly raised the standard of living of the Germanic peoples. Names of animals and birds include *ass* (OE *assa*), *mule* (OE *mūl*), *peacock* (OE *pēa*, *pāwa*), and *turtle*(*dove*). We also find *fever* (OE *fefor*) from Latin *febris*.

All these words show the intercourse between Romans and Germanic peoples, which is proved not only by the testimony of the Roman historians, but also by the presence of nearly two hundred words in the Germanic language; Dr Serjeantson lists one hundred and seventy-two words in the continental period,[7] of which thirteen are 'military, legal, official', eight are 'trade, measure, etc.', four are 'coins', five are 'metals, etc.', twenty-three are 'dress, textiles, etc.', nine are 'household and other useful objects', seven 'food, drink, cooking', nineteen 'vessels, etc.', twenty-four 'towns, houses, building', thirty-seven 'plants and agriculture', twelve 'animals, birds, fish', three 'disease and medicine', and eight 'miscellaneous'; the borrowings in this period are thus summed up by her: 'In the earliest stratum there are moderately large

E

groups of military and official and general trade terms; a longer list for dress and textiles (twenty-three words), and equally long ones for vessels and receptacles, and for towns, houses, and building. But words for plants and agriculture form the largest group; many of the plant-names are ultimately of more remote origin than Latin (some are from Egyptian and Asiatic sources) and imply the gradual introduction into Western Europe of plants from the south and east. A number of the animal names, too, are non-European, and indicate the increasing acquaintance of Europe with the Eastern world'.[8]

As a result of this contact we find young Germans serving in the legions in different parts of the Empire; in addition, the constant flow of traders in both directions must have brought about the adoption of many Latin words into the Germanic language, and as the tribes later split up these words are found not only in the regions bordering the Empire, but even as far north as the Scandinavian countries, where Roman traders penetrated, and across the sea in this island. All of these words, no matter what their class, reflect the influence of the superior Roman civilization on the Germanic peoples, but one or two points still need to be stressed in connection with this influence.

In the first place, these words are invariably short and simple, of a type which would fit easily into the pattern of the Germanic language, which favoured this type of word. They are chiefly words of a concrete nature, being for the most part names of objects and simple actions, and are generally nouns, any verbs and adjectives being usually derivatives of nouns. The influence is exerted not so much through ideas as through things, and, numerous as are the words adopted which were names of objects, there is little evidence of any borrowing of the ideas which represented the superior mental characteristics of the Romans. The Germanic peoples were attracted by the practical and material things which their barbarian minds were able to appreciate. The long list of words covering household objects and food, cooking, and clothing shows how much must have been learnt in the domestic sphere, and how barbarous must have been the conditions under which the Germanic peoples lived, for there is no reason to suppose that they would have adopted Latin names for objects and operations already familiar to them. These were things which would make life more pleasant and more enjoyable from a material sense, but words indicative of an appreciation of the nobler ideals and concepts of life are almost entirely lacking. It may be argued that intercourse with soldiers and traders was not likely to lead to the introduction of philosophy and culture, but on the other hand we know that many of the Germanic peoples occupied relatively high posts in the Empire and they would naturally come into contact with the nobler aspects of Roman life and might be expected to bring back some traces of it to their own people. If it be argued that the number of such was relatively small, yet their influence would be great, as they would command a good deal of respect amongst their fellow-countrymen by reason of their success in the Empire.

There is, however, one aspect of life on a higher level represented. Although the Germanic peoples were heathens, there is evidence that they were familiar with one or two Christian words during this early period, as related forms appear in several of the languages. The word *church* (OE *cirice*), which derives originally from Greek, may have been adopted in the east, or perhaps as the result of pillaging raids on the Christian churches, which were obviously attractive targets by reason of their gold and silver vessels. It is worthy of notice, however, that it was the Greek word which was borrowed, and Latin *ecclesia* (Fr. *église*), which was later to give us *ecclesiastical*, was not borrowed until much later. *Angel* and *devil* were also probably borrowed in this early period; both were originally Greek words, but may have been adopted through Latin. *Bishop* (OE *biscop*), *monk* (OE *munuc*) and *minster* (OE *mynster*) also probably belong to this period.

In considering these words, it should be borne in mind that it is not always possible to distinguish between words borrowed in this earliest period and those borrowed in the second period, between the Settlement and the period of earliest recorded Old English, and it may be that a few words generally placed in the first period might equally well belong to the second; for example, some scholars consider that *ceaster* was adopted from the Romans on the Continent, while others think it was an indirect borrowing, through the Britons, in the second period, since there is little evidence for it in the continental Germanic languages.

One final point is to be noticed. These words were, of course, learnt by word of mouth, not through books, and will therefore in most cases reflect Vulgar Latin, not the classical language.

Such then was the language brought to this country by the Angles and Saxons in the middle of the fifth century, a language in the main pure, but already containing a few of the loan-words which were later to be so characteristic of English. This is our common language, consisting of homely, practical, down-to-earth words, words which provide us with a dim picture of our earliest ancestors as they moved with their flocks and herds over the plains of Europe and Asia, living in tents or primitive huts, transporting themselves and their few goods from one pasture to another in simple carts with solid wheels, splitting into smaller groups and migrating further and further afield as necessity or curiosity compelled them; words which go on to reflect the changed conditions of life of our less remote ancestors as they gradually forsook their nomadic pastoral life and began to till the soil, which reflect the new scenes, new objects, new ideas with which they came into contact, and which finally reflect the influence of a great civilization, so far as it was able to affect a still-barbarian people, on our Germanic ancestors living around the Baltic. These are words which have echoed down the corridors of time, the property of peoples who were to be the ancestors of the greatest and most powerful nations of the present day, and these words, handed down from father to son, from mother to daughter, through countless centuries, can now, thanks to the labours of philologists, be used to establish a bond of kinship between east and west, between the great nations of Europe and the New World on the one hand, and on the other the peoples of Russia, India, and Western Asia.

From this common language we pass now to the study of our own particular language, and a most important part of the fascinating story will be the discovery of how our language has stretched out to its sister languages of the great Indo-European family, to enrich itself still further with the treasures which were handed down to them but which it had perhaps itself lost in the earliest days, and also to share in the gains which they had made from contact with other peoples.

CHAPTER FOUR

★

THE ANGLO-SAXONS

We come now to the study of our English vocabulary as it has developed in these islands during the last fifteen hundred years, and our starting point is the language discussed in the last chapter, that brought to this country about 450 A.D. by the Angles and Saxons, and any other Germanic tribes who may have accompanied them. Bede mentions also the Jutes, and the evidence of language leads us to believe that Frisians, or at any rate Saxo-Frisians, also came here.

In this chapter we shall consider the development of the vocabulary between this Anglo-Saxon settlement and the Norman Conquest, except that the influence of Scandinavian will be reserved for a later chapter. The discussion will fall naturally under two heads, the native vocabulary and its normal development, and, secondly, the influence exerted from outside, either by the introduction of loan-words, or modification of the native language itself.

When we compare the huge bulk of our modern vocabulary, extending to at least half a million words, by far the larger part of them borrowed after the Anglo-Saxon period from Latin, Greek, French, and other languages, we may wonder how the Anglo-Saxons, with only about a twentieth of our word stock available to them, managed to express themselves adequately. If we think of the numerous Latin and French loan-words which we find almost essential for expressing our thoughts in everyday conversation we may think the Anglo-Saxon must have been severely handicapped. From what we have seen of the language he brought with him we know that he would be able to express himself tolerably well when it came to dealing with the practical things of everyday life, yet it seems he would find it difficult to make nice distinctions in meaning, to express complicated arguments, and to employ words with the exactitude and taste demanded in literary work. We might, for example, think that he would be in the position in which a first-class literary man would find himself today if he were to be confined to Basic English. This, however, is to see one side only of the picture. We may rule out of our consideration the very early period after the Settlement, for at that time the state of culture of the people was probably such that their language proved adequate for their needs. In a further examination it is perhaps necessary to distinguish between poetry and prose. As is the case with most peoples, poetry came before prose for the Anglo-Saxons; they brought with them from their continental homeland a lengthy and highly-developed tradition of poetry, but Anglo-Saxon prose does not begin much before the end of the ninth century. From the remains we have of Anglo-Saxon poetry, some of it apparently from a very early date originally, we can have little doubt that the *scop*, with his developed poetic diction, his kennings and extensive traditional poetic vocabulary, his command over compounding, and his stock of alliterative expressions, would find little difficulty in saying all he had to say on the traditional subjects, and later his vocabulary and technique was carried over successfully into religious poetry. The case was different with prose. There we see the writer obviously struggling with a strange and difficult medium. He had trouble not only with accidence and syntax, but also with meaning, and often he found it difficult to express himself with the words available to him. This, however, was but a temporary phase, for Old English was an extremely flexible language. New words could be formed by derivation and compounding – more than a hundred words are found formed by these two processes from OE *mōd* – and the meaning of existing words expanded or even changed. As a result, we find that by the end of the Old English period such masters of prose as Ælfric and Wulfstan have little difficulty in expressing themselves adequately in their homilies, and their prose is very different from that of the early *Anglo-Saxon Chronicle* and the Alfredian translations of only a century earlier. From what we can see of the development of Old English prose we may agree with Jespersen when he says: 'There can be no doubt that if the language had been left to itself, it would easily have remedied the defects that it certainly had, for its resources were abundantly sufficient to provide natural and expressive terms even for such a new world of concrete things and abstract ideas as Christianity meant to the Anglo-Saxons'.[1] He points out that a very similar language, Old Norse, was able to develop an admirable narrative prose style. Moreover, when Old English prose got away from translation and servile dependence on Latin we find passages which promise well for the future of English prose, passages such as the original interpolations in the Alfredian *Orosius* of the voyages of Ohthere and Wulfstan, some of the later homilies, and, much later, passages in the *Peterborough Chronicle*, for that work, although it was carried on until 1150, is Old English in language, style, and spirit.

In our examination of the vocabulary of Old English we have a much easier task than that which confronted us in our study of the Indo-European and Primitive Germanic periods. Admittedly we have no written records dating from the time of the Settlement, in the middle of the fifth century, but there are records from about the end of the seventh century, and from that time onwards, in spite of the loss of many manuscripts, for many have, of course, failed to survive from that early period for one reason or another, we have available an adequate, if not abundant, body of evidence for the language in use at that time. There is, however, one great deficiency in our knowledge of Old English which must always be borne in mind. Our extant MSS, with only one or two minor exceptions, are all purely literary works, and, moreover, since all copying of manuscripts was carried out in the scriptoria of monasteries, they are confined to the types which would be likely to appeal to monks, and be considered by them worthy of preservation. As a result, we have not at our disposal a great body of secular literature, and the loss of this – for there is some evidence of its existence – has inevitably meant the loss of part of the vocabulary. In addition, apart from one or two examples such as Ælfric's *Colloquy*, and the account of the voyages of Ohthere and Wulfstan in the Alfredian *Orosius*, which seem to reflect the questions and answers passing between the King and the seamen, perhaps recorded in note form at the time by clerks, and transcribed and expanded later, we have no evidence for colloquial Old English, the language in everyday use among the people.

With these reservations in mind we may now go on to examine the purely native aspect of the Old English vocabulary, which consists in large measure, as we are able to see by the presence of cognates in the other Germanic languages, of words inherited from the common Germanic stock. Many of these words, then, might have been included in the treatment of the native element in the previous chapter, and their mention now does not necessarily mean, therefore, that they are words peculiar to the Anglo-Saxons.

We may expect the everyday vocabulary of a people to reflect the life, tastes, and occupations of that people, and therefore, just as in the earlier period, the words we find in use among the people will throw light on their conditions of life. Although we have no written evidence for the very earliest period, and therefore find it difficult to distinguish between the periods when new words were coined and added to the language, we have knowledge on one particular point which does help in this respect. We know that for a considerable time before they settled in this country the Angles and Saxons were sea-pirates, just as were their neighbours, the Danes and Norwegians, who were later to attack them just as they themselves attacked the Britons. There is evidence for their raids on Britain in the mention of the appointment by the Romans of '*Comes Littoris Saxonici per Britannias*' – the Count of the Saxon Shore

– whose duty it was to protect the coast from Southampton to the Wash against the attacks of Saxon raiders. But once they had established themselves in the land which was henceforth to be known as Engla-land – the land of the Angles – these sea-raiders seem to have largely forsaken the sea and become farmers, or followed some other occupation on land. One definite piece of information in support of this shows how much they had lost their old skill in seamanship and fighting at sea; when Alfred set himself the task of building an English navy, in order to beat off the attacks of the Danes before they landed in his country, he not only had to seek the assistance of the Frisians – at that time noted as the best shipwrights in Europe – to plan and build his ships at first, but he also had to hire Frisians to sail the ships and teach the English how to handle them. It seems unlikely, then, that any large number of words connected with the sea would be coined once the Angles and Saxons were established here, and therefore any words denoting the sea, ships, or seamanship which we find recorded in Old English are likely to have been brought over to this country by the original settlers in the fifth century. It is to be noted, moreover, that most of the words connected with the sea are found in poetry; this is perhaps to be expected, for the bulk of the prose is but little concerned with affairs at sea, whereas the old epic poetry, which derives its heroes, locality, atmosphere, and spirit largely from the continent, naturally reflects accurately the emotions of the peoples, and, which follows naturally, their love for the sea. It will be of interest, therefore, to consider these words as reflecting the spirits and tastes of the original settlers, for, though some of these words have been lost, and our language is not now so rich in sea terms as Old English was, yet this love of the sea has never been lost by the English people. There is perhaps hardly an Old English poem which does not mention the sea in some way or another, and several are largely, if not entirely, connected with the sea. But the mere fact of the sea's having played so large a part in Old English poetry has probably had some influence on the extensive vocabulary used for reference to affairs at sea, for whereas a prose writer is often satisfied to repeat a basic word a poet who has to repeat an idea frequently is likely to try to express his thought in different words as far as possible. This may perhaps explain why there are more words connected with the sea in poetry than in prose, and Wyld, in his essay *Diction and Imagery in Anglo-Saxon Poetry*,[2] says of the subject of the sea and ships, 'A whole article might easily be devoted to the Anglo-Saxon poets' treatment of them'.

First let us look at the simple terms for the sea itself. There are a great number of these; indeed the modern reader may wonder why there are so many, but it must be remembered that we today find it difficult to put ourselves in the place of the Anglo-Saxon and not only be familiar with the objects he knew, but also understand the exact meaning of the words he used. Sweet has pointed out that a language always contains many terms for daily tasks and operations, things connected with everyday life, and objects and operations in which people are particularly interested. Jespersen also points out that primitive people have many highly-specialized terms, but lack general terms, as if they were unable to appreciate the common factor in the various members of the group, but also points out that, just as the different characteristics of the objects called for special names, so many words in Old English which seem to us perfect synonyms may not have been so, and that when the words were originally coined they probably did represent some difference of idea. Wyld has said: 'It is difficult for us today to reach back through the centuries and grasp the precise shade of meaning which each of these apparent synonyms once expressed, to recapture the mood or emotion which they called up, or to be fully alive to the grace and glamour with which, for our forefathers, this or that word may have lighted up a line'.[3] Words which seem synonymous to us may have had different meanings for the Anglo-Saxon, and we are, therefore, not able to be quite certain that he could not express subtle differences in his conception of the sea by a careful selection from among the words available to him. Indeed, the original meanings attached to some of these words suggests that, when used to denote the sea, they may have expressed different aspects. The simple words used to express the sea are as follows: *brim, dēop, eolet, fām, faroþ, flōd, flot, ford, garsecз, зelād, зeofon, hærn, heafu, holm, hrycз, laзu, mere, sǣ, strēam, sund, wadu, wæter, wǣз, ȳð* – twenty-four in all. Several aspects are at once apparent even in these simple words; for example, *strēam* suggests the current or tide of the sea, and *flōd*, meaning flood or tide, has possibly the same significance, *ford* and *зelād* suggest a passage over the sea, *dēop* the depth of the sea, *holm* and *hrycз* the rising of the waves, for *holm* seems to have meant something rising from the sea – it also means 'island' – and *hrycз* – back, ridge, also suggests the top of a wave, and the original meaning of *ȳð* is 'wave'. *Sund* suggests the power of the sea, for the original sense is one of swimming, and the poet was therefore perhaps thinking of the strength in the sea itself, or that needed to overcome the power of the sea. We still keep one of these words, *fām*, in poetic language, where *foam* may be used meaning 'sea'. Most of these words are found in at least one other Germanic dialect, suggesting that they were probably common Germanic.

But it is in compounds that we really see the force and power of the words used in poetry to denote the sea. The first type of compound is that which merely links two words which alone may signify the idea; although this should not lightly be considered needless compounding, with no extension of thought, for we cannot be sure, for example, that *sǣ*, *strēam*, and *sǣstrēam* were synonymous, it is a simple process, and may be dismissed briefly: the words which occur most frequently as second elements seem to be *strēam* and *flōd*, as in *mere-strēam*, *laȝustrēam*, *ēastrēam*, *wǣterflōd*, *brimflōd*, *mereflōd*, and many others, and we also find such compounds as *sǣ ȳð*, *wǣȝholm*, *ȳðmere* and *merefaroþ*. A second type of compound introduces a further idea, perhaps of some physical aspect of the sea, as, for example, its power, in *drencflōd* – the drowning flood, *wǣterþrȳðe* – the might of the sea, *holmprǣcu* – the violence of the sea, *ȳðewinn* – the struggle of water, or the fear it arouses, as in *wǣtereȝesa* – the horror of the sea; or it may be its breadth or depth, as in *merestrēama ȝemet* – the expanse of the sea, or *sǣgrund*, expressing its depth, or, even stronger, *garsecȝes ȝīn* – the ocean-abyss. Others suggest its movement, not always friendly, as in *flōdwylm* – the surging of the flood, *strēamfaru* – the moving (flowing) of the sea, *ȳðeblond* – the stirring, mingling of the sea, probably by violent storms. Other compounds reflect the main purpose of the sea to these people, as a highroad, and so we find a word denoting 'sea' compounded with one meaning 'path' or 'road', as *brimlād*, *flōdweȝ*, *merestrǣt*, and from there it is an easy step to looking upon the sea as the highway or domain of the creatures they encountered there, as *hronrād* – the whale's road, *swanrād*, *seȝlrād*, *hwǣlweȝ*, and others, and as the home of these creatures we find *hwǣles ēþel*, *mǣwes ēþel* – the mew's domain, *fisces ēþel*, and the common expression such as *ganotes bæþ*, *seolhbæþ* – the seal's bath, and *fiscesbæþ*, and even *bæþweȝ* – the bathway, perhaps a recollection of the results of storm and shipwreck. *Beowulf* alone has about twenty words for 'sea': other poems bring the number up to fifty or more concrete terms; in addition there are figurative expressions. If we were to take into account the lost literature of the Anglo-Saxons we should probably not be far out in estimating that they had available at least a hundred different terms, simple and compounded, and including figurative expressions, for sea, water, and related ideas.

As practical seamen these peoples were equally concerned with ships, and we find just as rich a vocabulary here also. Although there is a good deal of later Low German and Dutch influence in the part of our vocabulary relating to shipping, yet very many of the basic words were already in use in Old English, and indeed almost all the words in common use, as distinct from learned terms, are Germanic, for Low German and Dutch are also Germanic languages. Of the simple terms

used by sailors we find that *bāt* – boat, *helm* – helm, *mæst* – mast, *ār* –
oar, *rōðer* – rudder, *scip* – ship, and *seȝl* – sail are part of our Germanic
heritage, but this is really only a small part of the material used in Old
English. As we saw above when we examined words denoting 'sea',
many of these were part of the language of poetry, rather than of prose,
and once again we find in poetry many words for 'ship', generally with
some extension of meaning. Some simple terms occur in poetry, and
apparently not in our prose records, such as *fær* (connected with *faran* –
to go, and indicating the primary purpose of a boat) and similarly *lid*
(connected with *līþan* – to go), and also *naca*. *Flota* (lit. floater) is another
word for ship, emphasizing one particular aspect. Some words are
hardly poetic, as, for example, those referring to the material from
which the ship is made, as *brimwudu*, *sǣwudu*, *wǣgbord* (lit. wave-
board), and *wǣȝþel* (lit. wave-plank). Other words reflect a particular
purpose of the boat; these pirates must have spent long periods with a
boat as their headquarters – indeed we know that the Scandinavian
'sea-kings' almost lived upon the water – and so we often find a word
denoting 'boat' is compounded from words for 'sea', etc. and 'house',
as *mere-hūs*, *holm-ærn*, *ȳp-hof*. *Flota* is also frequently compounded, as
sǣflota, *wǣȝflota*, and the journeys undertaken by boat are reflected in
the use of *gangan* – to go, in compounds denoting 'ship', as *sǣgenga*
(lit. 'sea-goer'). An extension of this transfers the voyage on horseback
on land to a voyage on water by looking upon the ship as a horse, and
so we find *sǣhengest*, *sǣmearh*, and many other examples of *hengest* and
mearh compounded with a word denoting 'sea'. *Beowulf* has about a
dozen words for 'ship', and forty or more are found in other poems.

Next we may consider names for the seaman himself; naturally the
most frequent is our modern type, as in the word just quoted, where we
have a simple compounding of a word for 'sea' and a word for 'man',
as *sǣmann*, *brim-mann*. The idea of the sailor as a traveller by sea is also
frequent, as might be expected, and we find the same words being
compounded as were used for ship, for the two ideas are obviously
related; thus we have *sǣlida*, *ȳplida*, *brimliþend*, *merefara*.

Finally there is the actual voyage over the sea, and once again the
same two ideas are combined, as in *brimlād* (lit. sea-way), where *lād* is
connected with *līþan* – to go. The word *rād* – road, is also compounded,
as in *strēamrād;* one cannot be quite certain whether this is the same
image, of riding over the sea, which made a ship into a sea-horse, or
whether *rād* was merely conceived as a 'road, path', and therefore the
course of the ship, but the latter is certainly the case in *mere-strǣt* (lit.
sea-street), and perhaps in *flōdweȝ*, *holmweȝ* (lit. sea-way). The journey
itself is emphasised in *sǣsīþ* (lit. sea-journey).

The subject of sea and ships has been treated at some length – some may think at undue length – but the justification must be Wyld's remark quoted above and the fact that the sea did play such an important part in the lives of our ancestors, particularly before they settled here.

Another aspect of their life on the Continent, indeed what we may call one of the essential characteristics of the Germanic peoples, was their love of war, and supreme admiration for prowess in fighting and personal bravery. The heroic poems abound in instances of fearless fighting, and the heroes and incidents date back to continental times. It is not surprising, therefore, to find that the poet has at his disposal a large stock of words connected with fighting. The focal point of the fighting-machine was the lord, to whom every retainer owed the utmost loyalty, being expected not to leave the battle alive after his lord had been killed, and this conception of a militant lord, the defender of his people, comes out in the words used to denote prince or lord, such as *æscwiʒa* (spear-warrior), *beadorinc* (battle-warrior), *byrnwiʒa* (corselet-warrior), and *ēþelweard* (guardian of the native land). In return for this loyalty he was expected to be generous to his followers, as such words as *brytta* and *bēaʒʒyfa* (ring-giver) show. *Beowulf*, a poem concerned, like *The Faerie Queene*, in fashioning a good man, and therefore with great emphasis on the prince or leader, has nearly forty synonyms for this one idea. For 'battle' itself there are many words, of which the following occur most frequently: *beadu, ʒefeaht, guþ, heaðo, hild, ʒewinn, wiʒ;* it will be noticed that only one of these has survived, and even then 'fight' is used today in a much more limited sense than the French loan-word 'battle'. Many words are found for 'warrior', for his chief virtue, bravery in battle, and for his weapons. As we shall see later, many words concerned with warfare were later replaced by Norman words, after the Anglo-Saxon aristocracy had been wiped out. It would obviously require more space than we have available here to examine the whole vocabulary of warfare in Old English, but we may perhaps look at the words in one poem which, though late, does reflect remarkably the old spirit. In *The Battle of Maldon* we find the following: for 'battle', *beadu, beaduræs* (rush of battle), *ʒecamp, fǣhð(o), feld* (field of battle), *feohte, ʒefeoht, gārræs* (spear-rush), *guð, guðplega* (battle-play, fighting), *ʒetoht, wiʒ, wiʒpleʒa, ʒewinn;* for 'warrior' occur the following: *beorn, cempa, dreng, fyrdrinc, gārberend* (spear-bearer), *guðrinc, hæleð, hilderinc, hyse* (young warrior), *rinc, sǣrinc* (sea-warrior, viking), *scealc* (retainer, warrior), *secʒ* (retainer), *þeʒen* (retainer), *wiʒa, wīʒend,* and the metaphorical *wælwulf* (slaughterous wolf). For 'army' we find *folc, fyrd, æschere* (viking army), *here,* and such related words as *feða* (troop, force), *werod* (troop), *heorðwerod* (household troop), *heorðʒeneatas* (personal bodyguards), *hīredmen* (household retainers), and *prass* (proud array). Among names of weapons are included, for 'spear', *æsc, æscholt, daroð* (dart), *franca, ord* (lit. point), *sceaft* (shaft of spear), *spere, wælspere* (slaughter-spear); for 'sword' we have *bill, ecʒ* (lit. edge), *īren* (iron blade), and *mēce*, and the related *sceð* (sheath). For 'shield' are found *bord, lind, rand, scyld*. We also have *flān* (arrow, dart) and *boʒa* (bow). Related words include *byrne* (corselet), *hringlocan* (linked rings of corselet) and *hereʒeatu* (war gear). Knowledge of fighting tactics is gained from *bordweall* (shieldwall), *scyldburh* (shield wall) and *wīhaʒa* (battle-hedge, perhaps a row of spears). The ultimate result of the fighting is seen in *wæl* (slaughter) and *wælreste* (death in battle, rest among the slaughtered), the man who did the killing, *bana* (slayer), and a less fatal consequence in *wund* (wound) and *ʒysel* (hostage). We also have *frið* (peace) and *grið* (truce, peace), and *rēaf* (booty, plunder). The inclusion of verbs connected with shooting, striking, cutting, hewing, defending, attacking would add considerably to a list which is already surprisingly long when we remember the poem is of only three hundred and twenty-five lines. But again we may note how few of these words – not more than about ten of those actually quoted – survive in the modern language.

Several times reference has been made to poetic diction and a specialized vocabulary for the poet. There can be little doubt that Old English did have a particular poetic vocabulary, distinct from the language of prose. Reference to Old English dictionaries which mark words found only in poetry soon prove that this is so. It would be useless to attempt to list these words, so numerous are they, but it is clear that to a large extent the language of Old English poetry was traditional and archaic, and that, like so many poetic words today, it no longer represented either the language of formal prose or the colloquial speech of the people, but rather it reflected the life and thought of an earlier age on the Continent.

We may now turn to the life they led in England, a life not so full of fighting and plundering as the life on the Continent. This, unfortunately, will not be so well reflected in poetry, for the Old English poem, unlike some of the Old Norse poems, is largely of the heroic type, and concerns itself little with everyday life. In the prose we shall be more fortunate, and particularly in what we may call 'non-literary' prose, for the collections of words in glossaries, often arranged by class rather than alphabetically, preserve words which reveal many aspects of Anglo-Saxon life, and in Ælfric's *Colloquy* we have, in question and answer form, much material made easily available to us. This is really designed to teach Latin vocabulary, by question and answer between teacher and pupil on aspects of everyday life, and several occupations are dealt with specifically. Fortunately for us the Old English words have been added by way of interlinear gloss, and so we know the words in common use among the Angles and Saxons for these aspects of their life.

First we may take the occupations discussed, *yrþlincgas* – ploughmen (lit. earthlings), *scephyrdas* – shepherds, *oxenhyrdas* – oxherds, *huntan* – hunters, *fisceras* – fishermen, *fuʒeleras* – fowlers, *cypmenn* – merchants, *scewyrhtan* – shoemakers, *sealteras* – salters (men who salted meat), and *bæceras* – bakers. Of these only *shepherd* and *baker* survived, but *fisher* and *fowler* are in use still, even if archaic, and *chapman*, as we have seen, survives in the personal name, as does *salter*.

Then we learn of the work they do, OE *weorc*, with but little change. The ploughman takes his oxen (OE *oxon*) to the field (OE *felda*) and dare not stay at home (OE *ham*) even in the coldest of winters (OE *winter*), but has to yoke (OE *ʒeiukodan*) the oxen, adjust the plough-share (OE *sceare*) and the coulter (OE *cyltre*), and plough a full acre (OE *æcer*) every day (OE *dæʒ*). He is helped by a boy, who urges the oxen with his goad (OE *gadisen* – lit. goad-iron). He also has to fill the bin, or manger (OE *binnan*) with hay (OE *hiʒ*) and water (OE *wæterian*) the cattle. The shepherd drives (OE *drife*) his sheep (OE *sceap*) to the pastures, or leas, (OE *læse*), guards them with dogs, or hounds (OE *hundas*) against wolves (OE *wulfas*), milks them (OE *melke*), and from the milk makes cheese (OE *cyse*) and butter (OE *butere*). The hunter uses nets (OE *nettum*) to trap wild animals (OE *wildeor*), and captures harts (OE *hartas*), boars (OE *baras*), and hares (OE *haran*). The fisher-man goes out in his boat, or ship (OE *scyp*), and uses a hook (OE *ancʒil* – cf. angle and angling). Among other things he catches eels (OE *ælas*), lampreys (OE *lampredan*) and sprats (OE *sprote*). Although he prefers fishing in rivers to going out to sea, yet at sea he catches herrings (OE *hærincʒas*), oysters (OE *ostran*), crabs (OE *crabban*), mussels (OE *muslan*), cockles (OE *sæcoccas*) and lobsters (OE *lopystran*), but he has no desire to catch whales (OE *hwælas*). At sea he also catches the porpoise or dolphin (OE *mereswin* – lit. sea-pig, and 'sea-pig' is still used as a name for the porpoise). The bird-snarer catches fowls (OE *fuʒelas*), the word then having a wider sense than now, of birds in general (cf. German *Vogel*), taking them with nets, with lime (OE *lime*), decoying them by whistling (OE *hwistlunge*), or with hawks (OE *hafoce*), which he tames himself (OE *temian*), or traps (OE *treppan*). The merchant (OE *mancʒere* – cf. monger) brings from over the sea gold (OE *gold*) and gems (OE *ʒymmas*), wine (OE *win*), oil (OE *ele*), brass (OE *ær* – cf. ore) and tin (OE *tin*), and glass (OE *glæs*). The shoemaker has to buy hides (OE *hyda*) and skins (OE *fell* – cf. fellmonger), and works at them by his craft (OE *cræft*) or skill in trade, producing shoes (OE *sceos*) and garters or leggings (OE *leperhosa* – lit. leatherhose), and other leather goods. The smith talks of fashioning the fisherman's hook, the shoemaker's awl (OE *æl*), or the needle (OE *nædl*) of the tailor (OE *seamere* – lit. seamer), and we hear how the ploughman provides food (OE *hlaf* – lit. loaf) and drink (OE *drenc*). Later a pupil in the monastery school tells of his life, how he arose from his bed (OE *bedda*) when he heard the bell ring (OE *cnyll* – cf. *knell*), and after singing various offices with the brothers he ate (*æton*), drank (*druncon*), and slept (*slepon*). He tells us of his food, of meat (*flæscmettum* – lit. fleshmeat, just as today we speak of butchers' meat in distinction to poultry and fish), vegetables (OE *wyrta* – cf. wort as an element of plant-names), eggs (OE *æiȝra*), fish, cheese, butter, and beans (OE *beana*), and drinks ale (OE *ealu*) or water (OE *wæter*), but not often wine, because that is not a drink for a child (OE *cilda*).

Here we have evidence, in one short passage, of a rich store of words connected with everyday life; this, of course, by no means exhausts the vocabulary of this text, for words have been chosen for their interest, as revealing common things of life, and only when the word has come down to us with little change. An examination of some of the vocabularies and glossaries, such as, for example, that of Ælfric, soon shows how rich a vocabulary Old English had in practical terms in common use, but to attempt anything like a representative selection of native words in regular use in Old English would involve us in long lists taking up far more space than is possible in a work such as this. We may, however, note just a few more, before going on to deal with foreign influences, for this will be our last opportunity to deal at length with the native element in its original state, unaffected by outside influences. As most of the words which follow have come down from OE with but little change, only the modern form is given. Most of the parts of the body had names in Old English which we still use today, as *body* itself, *hand*, *foot*, *arm*, *eye*, *ear*, *head*, *chin*, *heart*, *bone*. Among words connected with natural features we find *land*, *mead*, *meadow*, *field*, *ford*, *earth*, *wood*, *hedge*, *hill*. Words connected with the home and domestic affairs include *house*, *home*, *bower*, *yard*, *stool*, *door*, *floor*. *Sun* and *moon* are also found, and *day*, *month*, *year*. Among abstract nouns we find *strength*, *depth*, *love*, *care*, and many others. The names of many trees are almost unchanged, as *beech*, *birch*, *oak*, *ash*, *elm*, and so are the names of many domestic or wild creatures, as *horse*, *mare*, *cow*, *sheep*, *lamb*, *goat*, *deer*, *swine*, *goose*, *hen* (feminine form of *hana* – cock, connected with Latin *canere* – to sing), *mouse*, *dog*, *fish*, *seal*, and *bear*. Many of our common adjectives had recognizable forms in Old English, as *black*, *white, high, deep, wide, broad, narrow, long, small* (though in Old and Middle English it had the meaning of 'slender', as has its German cognate today), *fresh, sound, swift, good, wise, merry, greedy, busy, dark, light, glad, sorry, many, few, little, much, old, young, new, bitter, sweet.* There are so many Anglo-Saxon verbs preserved almost unchanged in our language today that a representative list is impossible, but we may note a few common ones, taking them in the order of their OE classifi- cation, strong verbs first: *drive, abide, bite, ride, rise, shine; choose, bow, brew, float, fly, lie* (tell an untruth), *shoot, shove; bind, climb, drink, find, sink, sing, spring, swim, win, help, melt, swell, milk, yield, fight, carve, starve, burst; bear, steal, tear, shear, come; see, lie, break, speak, tread, weave, eat, sit; fare, shake, heave, bake, wake, waken, wade, wash, shape, step, stand, swear; let, dread, sleep, hold, beat, blow, know, mow, grow, crow, weep, fold, fall, wield, hew, leap; set, answer, knit, lay, lead, greet, deal, deem, feed, hear, heal, leave, rear, fill, send, spend, meet, kiss; dwell* (with later change of meaning), *sell, stretch, buy, bring, think, seek; love, earn, ebb, end, follow, gather, learn, look, sail, wound; have, live, say; shall, may; will, do, go* and the forms of the verb *to be.*

Again we have limited the list to words which have come through without change, apart from the usual phonological developments through the centuries. Many other common words existed which have been omitted from the lists because they have been replaced by other forms, as, for example, OE *wlite* – countenance, was replaced by the French loan-word *face*. The loss has been particularly great in words connected with abstract and reflective thought, and learning generally, and this is perhaps because those who had encouraged learning and culture among the Anglo-Saxons were replaced by a new ruling-class, both lay and clerical, speaking another language, after the Norman Conquest.

Two further points may be made about the Old English vocabulary, both of which have been touched upon already, and which will be raised again later in the chapter. The first is the capacity for forming compounds, one of the simplest and easiest methods of filling out a vocabulary, though sometimes the results may be clumsy, as they are so often in modern German. Compounds, by introducing a double image for a single idea, may even be objectionable, in that they con- fuse the issue. Some Old English compounds are as simple and clear as our modern types; *meoduheall, framweorc, ʒymmwyrhta* are as clear as *railway, steamship, drawing-room,* and many others we use today, but a word such as *mere-hengest*, poetic as it is, does provide a double image. Some of the compounds are extremely lively, as *wælwulfas* – slaughterous wolves, for the invading Scandinavians. Compounding has always been a favourite device of English poets, but nowhere is it used so freely as in Old English poetry. It may be, indeed, that this also was a part of the poetic tradition, a craft brought over from the continent, for it is certainly not so prevalent in prose. One poem, *The Wanderer*, contains more than fifty compounds in just over a hundred lines.

The other point to be noticed is the Old English capacity for derivation, the addition of affixes to existing words to extend the meaning or vary the function. When we come to study the influence of Christianity on the Old English vocabulary we shall see that it was exerted to a great extent by such modification of existing native material, suggesting that the process was already well established in the pre-Christian era, and indeed we find in the common Germanic material a plentiful supply of prefixes and suffixes used to modify existing words. Native prefixes in use in Old English are almost too numerous to mention – Wright lists thirty-one for nouns alone in his *Old English Grammar*. There are about a dozen different verbs formed from *settan* by adding different prefixes, or, to look at the process from the opposite point of view, more than fifty OE verbs are compounded with *wiþ-* and about a hundred and twenty with *ofer-* in Sweet's *Students' Dictionary of Anglo-Saxon*. We find a similar state of affairs with suffixes; Wright lists twenty-two for nouns, seventeen for adjectives.

A striking instance of the way in which a word could be modified by these two processes is supplied by *mōd*, which, by the addition of prefixes and suffixes, or by compounding, appears as an element of more than a hundred words.

Vocabulary was also extended by forming derivative verbs from nouns, adjectives, or other verbs; for example, *talu* – tale, *tellan* – to tell (of numbers or stories); *salu* – sale, *sellan* – to sell; *tūn* – enclosure, *tȳnan* – to enclose; *blōd* – blood, *blēdan* – to bleed; *fōd* – food, *fēdan* – to feed; *blāc* – white, pale, *blǣcan* – to bleach; there is also the causative type, such as *fiellan* – to fell, from *feallan* – to fall, *rǣran* – to raise, from the preterite of *rīsan*, to rise, *cēlan* – to cool, from the adjective *cōl* – cool, or the preterite of *calan* – to cool. Many of these are at least as early as the common Germanic period, as other languages show similar formations.

Other ways, which there is time only to mention, and which really need little illustration, include deliberate change of function, as when an adjective is used absolutely, to replace a noun, or a noun used in such a way in a compound that it seems to be almost adjectival in function, and also the method, found already in the parent language, of forming new words by mere change of the stem-vowel within a regular Ablaut series.

All these show how flexible was the native Germanic stock of Old English, and how much more resourceful it was in adapting native material than is our modern language, which depends so much on borrowing.

We now leave the native vocabulary and go on to examine outside influences on the language, but here again we shall be in part concerned with the native element, for in the Old English period the influence from other languages was exerted not so much through actual loan-words as through the stimulus given to the native language to express new ideas by using its own resources.

The first foreign influence on the Germanic language after it had been brought to this country would be exerted by the Britons, in the period immediately after the Settlement. The influence could be that of either Latin or Celtic, and in order to decide this we must know what language the Britons spoke. It was, as we know, the custom of the Romans to introduce their civilization, language, and way of life into the countries they conquered, but the extent to which they were able to do this would naturally depend upon the completeness of the conquest, the character of the conquered people, and the duration of the occupation. There is much more evidence for the imposing of the Latin language and way of life upon the people of Gaul than there is for its imposing upon the people of Britain, though we have, of course, plenty of evidence of Roman civilization in this country. We may still see traces of their great roads; the sites of their cities and towns have been excavated, and the remains of villas, theatres, temples, and baths have been uncovered; pottery, glassware, and ornaments from the Roman period may be seen in our museums. The Britons had been, at any rate in part, converted to Christianity, and there is a record of the attendance of more than three hundred bishops from Britain at a council held in Gaul in the fourth century. Inscriptions in Latin have been found, and the contents of these show that Latin was apparently the official language. We hear of Britons who proved apt scholars and showed great interest in Latin literature and culture generally. But there is no proof that this holds good for the Britons in general, and indeed it is more than likely that such people were isolated exceptions. When the Settlement was effected the Romans had been gone for forty years or more, and, though we have little direct evidence of the language spoken when the Angles and Saxons came, it seems probable that Latin had not survived, at any rate among the majority of the people, and that the Angles and Saxons found a people speaking Celtic. For some time scholars thought that some form of Latin – we might call it a Brito-Roman dialect, a sort of Vulgar Latin as spoken in Britain – was spoken by the Britons at the time of the Conquest. This was the opinion at first of Pogatscher,[4] who inclined to the view that, if there had been no Anglo-Saxon Settlement, some form of Romance language would now be spoken in England. Later, however, Loth[5] suggested that Latin became extinct in Britain after the withdrawal of the Roman garrisons, and that all borrowings in Old English which show Romance sound-changes were taken over from the Continent at a later period. Pogatscher later admitted the force of Loth's arguments, but still clung to the theory that Latin may have survived to some extent among the inhabitants of the larger towns, and we must remember that the Romans established over a hundred cities and towns in Britain. It is reasonably probable that the inhabitants of these towns, and perhaps the upper classes living in the country, in contact with Romans of their own class, spoke Latin, and retained it for some time after the Romans left, and from inscriptions in debased Latin scratched on tiles and pottery it seems that some work-men also understood something of Latin, as, for example, stonemasons, who may have spoken some regional form of Latin picked up from their masters. At the end of last century Freeman wrote: 'I think that most likely things were then much the same in all Britain as they are in Wales now. In Wales, English is the language of the towns, and in the large towns most people cannot speak Welsh at all. And a Welsh gentleman can very seldom speak Welsh, unless he has learned it as he may have learned French or German. But the country people commonly speak Welsh, and some of them cannot speak any English. So I fancy that in these times men spoke Latin in the towns, and also those whom we may call the gentry spoke Latin, but that the country people still spoke Welsh'. These wealthier townsmen, and the country gentry who spoke Latin, would be the very people able, through their wealth and position, to escape westwards before the advance of the English. The poorer people and servants would probably have to remain behind for lack of money and means of escape, and they would be the people who became the slaves of the English. Apart from the fact that they had little, if any, Latin, they would also have no influence upon their English masters, so that, when the Angles and Saxons settled here, they probably found the people with whom they came into real contact using Celtic, with some words adopted from the Latin. It has been estimated that several hundred Latin words were adopted into the Celtic languages, but the number available to the English was not great, and probably not more than a hundred Latin words were adopted by the English from the Britons.

It is not easy to differentiate between Latin words adopted on the Continent and those adopted after the Settlement but before the

conversion of the English to Christianity. Both will show the effect of
the primitive Old English sound-changes. The words were, of course,
adopted by word of mouth, from the colloquial Latin in the mouths of
the ordinary people, and they are generally similar in type to those
borrowed on the Continent, being chiefly nouns, names of domestic
articles, plants, words connected with agriculture, and a few with
learning and religion. They are usually referred to as Latin of the First
Period, and the influence of this period on our language is slighter than
the influence exerted by Latin at any other time. A classified list of just
over a hundred words borrowed from Latin in this early period in
England, between 400 A.D. and 650 A.D., is given by Dr Serjeantson.[6]
She describes them as 'Words probably borrowed in Britain, 450–650.
These are still loans from the spoken language'. The various classifica-
tions usually contain only a few items, but there are nine words under
'Dress, Textiles, etc.', twelve under 'Vessels', seven under 'Towns,
Houses, Building', thirty-three words connected with 'Plants and
Agriculture', eight names of 'Animals, Birds, and Fishes', and fifteen
connected with 'Medicine' and 'Religion and Learning'. OE *ceaster*,
Latin *castra*, was perhaps borrowed at this time, and possibly *-coln*, Latin
colonia (e.g. Lincoln), though the latter has been doubted. One of the
principal reasons for the establishment of a town or city by the Romans
was the siting of a garrison for defensive purposes, and just as Catterick
is today often called Catterick Camp, so these Roman towns had
-castra attached to them, the word often being added to Celtic elements,
as *Dorchester*, *Gloucester*, *Winchester*. *Chester* was particularly renowned as the headquarters of the Twentieth Legion, and its name
derived from *Legionis castra*, OE *Legaceaster* (A. S. Chron. 894). The
Latin form has provided two forms in the modern language; in the
south the initial consonant was fronted, and then later diphthongized
the vowel to give *ceaster*, and this developed to *-chester*, as in *Gloucester*,
Winchester, *Cirencester*, *Towcester*, *Leicester*. In the northern dialects,
by either Anglian or Scandinavian influence, the initial consonant was
preserved as a velar stop, and there was no diphthongization, so that we
find in the northern area such forms as *Doncaster*, *Lancaster*, *Tadcaster*.
Such forms as *port* (Latin *portus*) and *wīc* (Latin *vīcus*) may belong here,
or to the continental period, but if they had been borrowed earlier their
use, along with that of other words which would be heard frequently,
such as *strǣt*, *weall*, and *wīn*, would be strengthened by their use among
the Britons. Among words which probably belong to this period, and
are still in use today, we find master (OE *mæʒester*, Lat. *magister*),
provost (OE *profost*), cowl (OE *cuʒle*), strap, strop (OE *stropp*), anchor
(OE *ancor*), oil (OE *ele*), chest (OE *ciest*), cup (OE *cuppe*), pail (OE

pæʒel), pot (OE *pott*), fork (OE *forca*), mattock (OE *mattuc*), cock (OE *cocc*), though this, and O Fr. *coc* and Lat. *coccus* may all be independent imitative formations, trout (OE *truht*), Latin (OE *læden*), monk (OE *munuc*), minster (OE *mynster*), mount (OE *munt*), and Saturday (OE *Sætern-dæʒ*), this being the only day of the week whose name is not of Germanic origin. Some of these words may perhaps have been brought over from the Continent; several have already been mentioned as possible loans in the earlier period, and OE *pott* is paralleled by Du *pot* and ON *potr*.

The other linguistic influence which may be ascribed to the Britons in this period was that of their own language. To understand the effect of this influence we need to know two things, the relations between the English and the Britons, and the state of culture of the two races. A close examination of these two points will make quite clear why the English not only adopted so few Latin words from the Britons, but also borrowed surprisingly few Celtic names. First let us examine the way of life, the culture, the civilization of the two races, for words are borrowed only when a nation has something new and superior to offer, something which will compel the attention and respect of the other nation, so that borrowing takes place when the culture of the foreign nation is superior to that of the nation which borrows. To examine the problem from another angle, it is a question of the ability of the Britons to force their language on their conquerors because of the inherent superiority of either themselves or their language. The Britons had probably absorbed something of Roman civilization as a result of four hundred years of Roman occupation, and some of the words quoted above, and particularly the words listed by Dr Serjeantson under dress, textiles, houses and building, vessels, and, to a lesser extent, religion and learning, suggest that the Britons had something to offer to the English, but on the other hand the Britons would hardly be considered by the Angles and Saxons as worthy of respect or admiration, as they had twice been a conquered nation. As Jespersen has said: 'There was nothing to induce the ruling classes to learn the language of the inferior natives; it could never be fashionable for them to show an acquaintance with that despised tongue by using now and then a Celtic word. On the other hand the Celt would have to learn the language of his masters, and learn it well; he could not think of addressing his superiors in his own unintelligible gibberish, and if the first generation did not learn good English, the second or third would, while the influence they themselves exercised on English would be infinitesimal'.[7] This is borne out by two other factors, the relative numbers of the two races, and the relations between them. At first sight it may seem that the Britons would greatly exceed the English in numbers, but in the case of linguistic influence it is really a question of numbers in actual contact. Lindelöf suggested that the English killed off all the Britons who did not seek refuge in the barren mountainous areas in the west, and indeed we read in the A. S. Chronicle that after one particularly bitter struggle, at Andredescester – perhaps Pevensey – not a single Briton survived (Her Ælle and Cissa ymb sæton Andredescester and ofslogon alle þa þe þær inne eardedon, ne wearþ þær forþon an Bret to lafe – Ann. 491). But, although there may have been few survivals in the east and south-east, where the conquest was first completed, and where place-name evidence suggests the absence of British villages, yet it is likely that quite a large proportion of the Britons managed to escape to the west. The existence of place-names such as Walton – the Welsh village – does not suggest that such communities were numerous, otherwise they would not have been so named, for 'the village of the Welsh' as a place-name seems very significant, yet it does indicate separate communities, and not existence entirely as slaves in English households. While there were kingdoms of Britons in Cornwall, Wales, and Cumberland, it is likely that these were the more fortunate ones, and that the others were either killed or became the slaves or subjects of the English. We know that some of the Britons, both male and female, were made slaves, for the Anglo-Saxon name for the Britons, *wealh*, or *wēalas* in the plural, is also used to translate *servus* and *mancipium*, and the feminine form *wīelen* corresponds to *ancilla*. But, though this does not suggest that the two nations lived amicably or on equal terms, yet there is also evidence that the English married British women – physical characteristics of the population in some parts of the country today suggest mixed blood – so that, at any rate in the later stages, the two races lived in close contact in some areas, and even on friendly terms. We know from the A. S. Chronicle that the English and Britons fought together against the Danes (e.g. Ann. 894). The reason, then, for the paucity of Celtic loan-words in this period may probably be put down to two causes, the lack of any cultural superiority on the part of the Britons, and the physical and material superiority of the English, who came in large numbers, wave after wave, in such numbers that the Britons were, except in their kingdoms in the west, an insignificant minority, and probably more or less a slave class, and under such conditions the language of the conquering invader will survive, although words will be adopted which denote new phenomena, including not only new natural objects, but also native products and customs, and, perhaps most of all, place-names. Celtic loan-words are of this type. Later we shall see, in the case of the Normans, how a conquest in which the invaders were numerically inferior had an entirely different effect linguistically. But Celtic influence is not important, and one of the least effective of outside influences on English.

Therefore, although more Celtic words may have been used by the Angles and Saxons than can now be authenticated, very few Celtic words – probably not more than a dozen, apart from place-names and place-name elements – were adopted in this period and found a permanent place in the language. The tendency in the past has been to overestimate the number of Celtic words in the language, and as a result the efforts of philologists have in recent times been directed towards a strict scrutiny of the proposed loans, and many have, as a result, been rejected. Gardiner relied upon four words in particular, *gown*, *curd*, *cart*, *pony*, to show that Celtic influence was exercised through females and agricultural labourers, but Jespersen[8] has since pointed out that *gown* came in from French in the fourteenth century, and *curd* is also a late borrowing, of about the same period, while *cart* is an Old Norse word, found admittedly in Celtic but there 'palpably a foreign word' (NED), and *pony* is Lowland Scots, from an Old French form. The words which were adopted were all popular words, names of natural objects, animals, and articles in everyday use, and were, of course, adopted by word of mouth; what may be called 'learned' words, adopted from books, are almost entirely lacking in the early period. Celtic loan-words adopted before the end of the Old English period were introduced in three different periods; the first of these, on the continent, has already been discussed, and the other two periods were, first, in the years immediately after the Settlement, and, at a later time, through Irish missionaries. The words of the second period were popular words, adopted through intimate contact with the Britons; those of the third period, from the seventh century, were of a religious nature, adopted as a result of the activities of the missionaries sent out from Iona by St Columba.

A list of Celtic loans appears in Serjeantson,[9] where three words are accepted in the continental period, seven in the second period, apart from place-name elements, four of which occur also as common nouns, and seven also in the third period, though some of these are of Latin origin ultimately, and it is not quite certain that they came in through a Celtic language. Of the words which are still in use today we find OE *bratt*-cloak (still used meaning 'pinafore' or 'overall' in Northern dialects), *bin* (OE *binn*), perhaps borrowed earlier from Latin, but the word is ultimately Celtic, *bannock* (OE *bannoc*, once only, as a gloss), and *dun* (OE *dunn* – grey, dark-coloured) in the first group, and also *brock*, still a common name for a badger (OE *brocc*), and perhaps *ass* (OE *assa*).

The four place-name elements found as common nouns are OE *carr* – rock, OE *luh* – lake, OE *torr* – rock, peak, and OE *cumb* – combe, valley. In addition, crock (OE *crocca*) may be a Celtic loan, though similar forms are found in Old High German and Old Norse. Skeat suggested *clout* (OE *clūt*) and *cradle* (OE *cradol*), but these are doubtful, especially the latter, and also cart (OE *cræt*), which has already been discussed. In the second group few have survived, for, as we have seen already, much of the vernacular religious vocabulary has been lost. OE *drȳ* – 'magician', survives, but only in a particular sense, in the Celtic plural, *druid;* the other commonly accepted loans, OE *clucȝe* – bell, OE *ancor* – anchorite, OE *stǣr* – story, OE *æstel* – bookmark, and OE *cīne* – a fourfold sheet of parchment, have not survived. *Curse* (OE *cursian*) may belong here, but is not certain, and *cross* (OE *cros*) may be either Celtic or from Old Norse, but, as the latter were heathens when they came to England, a Celtic source is at least possible. Two other words have been suggested on phonological grounds; Kluge considered that the form of OE *ælmesse* – alms, could perhaps better be related to O Ir. *almsan* than to Latin *eleemosyne*, and the long vowel in OE *Crīst* – Christ, seems to show more affinity with Celtic, which had the long vowel, than with Latin, which had a short vowel.

Other Celtic loan-words in the modern language are later, none before the end of the Middle English period, and so do not really call for consideration in this chapter on the Anglo-Saxon period, yet they are so few, and so scattered chronologically, that it will be more convenient to deal with them at this point, and so conclude our examination of Celtic influence.

Of Celtic loan-words after the Anglo-Saxon period Skeat[10] lists the following from Irish: '*bard, bog, brogue, dirk(?), fun, gallowglass, galore, glib, s., kern, lough, orrery, pillion(?), rapparee, shillelagh, skain (skene, skein), shamrock, spalpeen, tanist, Tory, usquebaugh*'. Many of these words have been used only in specifically Irish contexts, and several are today considered to be rather Irish words used in English than part of our vocabulary. In addition to these, certain diminutives, such as *colleen, mavourneen,* and perhaps *spalpeen* and *shebeen,* are used fairly commonly in English today. Of the last word, Skeat considers it to be 'merely a diminutive of *seapa,* a shop, which can hardly be other than the English word *shop* transplanted into Irish'. Yet *shebeen,* as we have it, and so far as we use it, is manifestly a borrowing from Irish, no matter what the origin of the word may have been. *Blarney* is perhaps sufficiently common today to deserve mention.

Skeat also lists Celtic words adopted from Scotch Gaelic. He separates them into earlier loans, not, of course, before 1066, and loans found only in modern writers. In the first class he includes *bog, crag, glen, loch, clan, inch, strath,* and *galloway* ('ambling horse'), also *spate, creel,* and *slogan,* and for all of these he quotes examples before the end of the sixteenth century. As loans of the later period he quotes, '*banshee, cairn, cateran, claymore, collie (colly), cosy, gillie, gowan, macintosh* (from a personal name), *philibeg (fillibeg), ptarmigan(?), reel* (a dance), *spleuchan, sporran, whiskey.* Moreover, we have *ingle, kail,* and *plaid,* three words which are not original Celtic, but adopted from Latin'. *Cairngorm* and *Glengarry,* both from place-names, are now fairly common. *Brose* he considers to be merely a re-borrowing, the Celtic word being from English *broth,* and *pibroch* merely a form of English *pipe,* borrowed in the sixteenth century.

Again, leaving aside the question of place-name elements, apart from *spate, slogan, collie, cosy, macintosh,* and *whiskey,* and perhaps *creel* and *crag,* the words listed by Skeat are found only in contexts relating to Scotland, and several, such as *cateran, philibeg,* and *spleuchan,* can hardly claim a place in the vocabulary of English.

Skeat adds: 'We may also draw two conclusions; that the English has borrowed more freely from Gaelic than from Irish, and that the borrowing began at an earlier time. This is the natural consequence of the respective geographical positions and political relations of Scotland and Ireland to England'. Yet there could have been but little direct contact with the Gaelic-speaking Highlands in the earlier period.

Among words borrowed from Welsh after the end of the Anglo-Saxon period Skeat includes *coble, clutter, flannel,* and such specifically Celtic words as *coracle, cromlech,* and *metheglin,* hardly ever heard outside Celtic contacts. *Penguin* may be a Welsh form, from *pen* – head, and *gwyn* – white, but its etymology is doubtful. *Eisteddfod* has become more frequent, but is, of course, also reserved for Welsh contexts. Skeat continues: 'Amongst the words which perhaps have the most claim to be considered as Celtic, or founded upon Celtic, are some of which the origin is very obscure. It may suffice to mention here the words *bald, bat* (thick stick), *boggle, bots, brag, bran, brat, brill, brisk, bug, bump, cabin, char* (fish), *chert, clock* (originally a bell), *cob, cobble, cock* (small boat), *coot, cub, Culdee, curd, cut, dad, dandruff, darn, drudge, dudgeon* (ill humour), *fun, gag(?), gown, gyves, jag, knag, lad, lag, lass(?), loop, lubber, mug, noggin, nook, pilchard(?), pony, puck, pug, rub, shog, skip, taper, whin.* As to some of these there does not seem to be much known. I wish to say distinctly that I feel I am here treading on dangerous and uncertain ground, and that I particularly wish to avoid expressing myself with any *certainty* as to most of these words'.

Mention should perhaps also be made of Cornish, which has died out within recent times. Cornish has had little influence on the vocabulary of the standard language; *gull* may be a loan from Cornish, and also *dolmen*. Some Celtic words remain in the modern dialect of Cornwall, and there is, of course, plenty of place-name material in the county. From Breton, carried to the continent from Cornwall at the time of the Anglo-Saxon invasion, only one word, *menhir*, has been borrowed, and that is not a word in common use.

Skeat concludes: 'The net result is, that the Old Celtic element in English is very small, and further research tends rather to diminish than increase it. The greater part of the Celtic words in English consists of comparatively late borrowings; and the whole sum of them is by no means large. A wild comparison of English words with modern Celtic forms, such as is so commonly seen in many dictionaries, savours more of ignorance than of prudence'.

Many of the words are, indeed, comparatively late. Spenser uses some Irish words in his *View of the Present State of Ireland*, but thinks it necessary to explain them, as do also Johnson and Boswell in the eighteenth century, in their accounts of their Scottish travels. The great bulk of the words are later, and it is to Scott, in his romantic novels and poems dealing with Scotland, that we owe many of the most picturesque.

We find a different state of affairs when we come to consider place-names,[11] for by far the greatest evidence for Celtic in our English words is to be found here. This is, of course, to be expected, as place-names and names of natural features are usually adopted freely by invaders. Names containing Celtic elements are to be found in all parts of England – Kent and Sussex, for example, where the Anglo-Saxon conquest was earliest and most thorough, have *Fordcombe* and *Balcombe* – but they are more frequent in the west and north-west, and, of course, in Cornwall, Wales, Scotland, and Ireland. Some of them seem to have been borrowed at an early period, as might be expected, for they show the effect of some of the Old English sound changes, though comparatively few have been found in very early sources.

Perhaps the first Celtic place-name element to be considered should be the name of the people themselves, OE *wēalas* and *Brettas*. It has already been pointed out, as evidence for the survival of Britons among the English, that towns and villages with these elements are found, suggesting British communities. Care is needed with the first-named element, which is generally reduced to *Wal-*, as it could also have developed from OE *weald* or OE *weall*, but forms such as *Walcot* and *Walton* may indicate British communities, and *Wallasey*, in Cheshire, was apparently the 'island of the Wealas'. Forms such as *Bretton*, *Bretby*, and *Birkby* (DB *Bretebi*) are apparently derived from the other name, Brettas.

The old kingdom of *Kent* derives its name from a Celtic word *Canti*, and the two old northern kingdoms, *Deira* and *Bernicia*, whose names no longer survive, also had Celtic names. The first element of *Devonshire* is the name of a Celtic tribe, the *Dumnonii*, and *Cumberland* is obviously the 'land of the Cymry'. Two survivals far to the east are to be noted. *Lindsay*, in Lincolnshire, is almost certainly Celtic, from the old name for Lincoln, and *Kesteven*, also in Lincolnshire, may also have a Celtic element.

Many of our rivers have preserved their original Celtic names, such as *Aire, Avon, Calder, Cam, Dee, Derwent, Don, Esk, Ouse, Severn, Tees, Thames, Trent, Wye*. Many of these preserve a Celtic word for water, such as *Avon, Esk, Usk, Ouse, Stour*, and *Wye*, and the use of such a word in Celtic describing a stream to the Angles and Saxons may be the source of the use of such a general single term. The Celtic word for 'hill' is also found as an element of place-names as *Great Barr* (*bar* – summit), *Breedon-on-the-hill*, and *Bredon* (*bre* – hill); *torr*- rock, peak, is found in *Torr, Torrcross, Loughtor*. Space forbids the inclusion of fully-illustrative material, but among Celtic elements commonly found in place-names are the following: *cumb*, a valley on a hillside, found in such names as *Ilfracombe, Babbacombe, Winchcombe;* this element is rare outside the south-west. The Celtic *brocc* – badger, is found in *Brockholes, Brockhall*, but some names with this element may go back to OE *brōc* – brook. The element *funta* – spring, well, is found in such names as *Havant, Bedfont. Aber* – mouth, is found in *Aberdeen, Lochaber; caer* – castle, in *Caerleon, Caernarvon; dun* – a fortified place, in *Dunbar, Dundee, Dunfermline; inch* – island, in *Inchcape; inver* – river-mouth, in *Inverary; kill* – church, in *Killarney, Kilkenny; llan* – holy, in *Llandaff*.

Some of our ancient cities and towns also have Celtic names, as *London*, the etymology of which is not quite certain, though it probably goes back to Celtic, *Canterbury, Leeds, York, Dover, Carlisle, Crewe*, and the Latin element has also been added to Celtic elements, as *Gloucester, Leicester, Winchester*, and *Lincoln*, and *Salisbury* and *Lichfield* have Celtic elements to which has been added an Old English element, *-bury* and *-field*.

These Celtic place-names and personal-names may sometimes be misleading; an example is *Churchill*, which usually has no connection with a church, but derives from Celtic *cruc* – a hill, so that what we really have here is a synonymous pair, one word Celtic, the other English, compounded.

Finally we come to the influence exercised on the Old English vocabulary by the conversion of the Angles and Saxons to Christianity, an influence which was operative for nearly five hundred years. With the departure of the Roman occupying forces direct contact with Roman civilization had been broken, and in the following hundred years things must have gone back, with the land a wide battleground, and finally in the power of ruthless heathen invaders. But within a century and a half of the first settlement the Romans were back, on a different footing, and the two Indo-European streams which had diverged in Central or Southern Europe several centuries before, and had since made only sporadic contact, were once more brought together, this time on a peaceful footing, and the impetuous heathen Germanic people came into friendly contact with the great classical civilization of the Mediterranean, Roman culture based on an earlier Greek founda-tion, and the whole strengthened by a powerful new influence for good – Christianity.

The conversion of the Angles and Saxons to Christianity did not officially begin until 597 A.D., when Augustine and his fellows, after a year's delay in Gaul, landed in Kent, but this was not the first time they had encountered Christianity. There is, as we have seen, proof in the common Germanic vocabulary, in such words as *church*, *angel*, and *devil*, that they were at any rate familiar with some of the more obvious features of Christianity. The use of a word such as *church* does not necessarily mean that the Germanic peoples were Christian; it has, indeed, cognates in most of the Germanic languages, and has been strong enough to resist the encroachment of Latin *eglesia*, so widely adopted elsewhere, but churches were probably more familiar to the Germanic tribes as opportunities for looting, enriched as they were with gold, silver and precious stones, than as places for worship, though Trèves, in the centuries immediately before the Settlement a prosperous Roman city, with Christian churches, must also have been known to the Germanic peoples, for it lay only just beyond their borders. Some scholars think that these early words may have been borrowed by the Goths direct from Greek in the second, third and fourth centuries of the Christian era; they are all ultimately from ecclesiastical Greek. But in some cases the phonological development is not clear, and Gothic has no word recorded cognate with the Germanic forms for 'church'. Moreover, two other points need to be considered; first, it is by no means clear how much intercourse there was in the early stages between the Goths in the south-east and the Germanic tribes in the north-west, and these loan-words are all early—though some can be postulated later from the presence in the west of the Visigoth Empire, and the Aryan church, to which the Goths belonged. But there was also the possibility of another contact with Christianity before Pope Gregory sent his missionaries over at the end of the sixth century. The Romans had in part at least established Christianity in Britain, and from there it passed over to Ireland, where the church continued to flourish after it had been destroyed in Britain by the Angles and Saxons. Missionaries from Ireland came over after the invaders were firmly established and were probably at work in the north before Augustine landed in Kent, and we have already seen that some words passed into the vocabulary of Old English as a result of this Celtic conversion.

The Latin conversion was completed within about a hundred years; entries from the Anglo-Saxon Chronicle tell the bare facts of the work carried out by the missionaries. The annal for 596 records: 'This year Pope Gregory sent Augustine to Britain with many monks, to preach the word of God to the English people', and in 597: 'This year Augustine and his companions came to England'. In 601: 'This year Pope Gregory sent the pall to Archbishop Augustine in Britain, with very many learned doctors to assist him; and Bishop Paulinus converted Edwin, King of the Northumbrians, to baptism'. In 604: 'This year Augustine consecrated two bishops, Mellitus and Justus. He sent Mellitus to preach baptism to the East Saxons', and in another MS the annal for the same year reads: 'In this year the East Saxons received the faith and baptism'. In 626: 'This year Eanfleda, King Edwin's daughter, was baptized on the holy eve of Pentecost. And within twelve months the king, with all his people, was baptized at Easter', and in 627: 'This year King Edwin was baptized at Easter, with all his people, by Paulinus'. Edwin was king of Northumbria. In 632 the king of the East Angles followed his example: 'In this year Eorþwald was baptized'. In 634: 'This year Bishop Birinus preached baptism to the West Saxons, under their king Cynegils', and in 635: 'This year King Cynegils was baptized by Bishop Birinus at Dorchester; and Oswald, King of the Northumbrians, was his sponsor', and in the following year, 636: 'This year King Cwichelm was baptized at Dorchester, and died the same year. Bishop Felix also preached to the East Angles the belief of Christ', and in 639: 'This year Birinus baptized King Cuthred at Dorchester'. In 646: 'This year King Kenwal was baptized'. In 653: 'This year the Middle-Angles under Aldorman Peada received the true belief'. In 655, after the death of Penda, 'the Mercians became Christians'. In 661: 'Eoppa, a mass-priest, by the command of Wilfrid and King Wulfere, was the first man to bring baptism to the people of the Isle of Wight'. And finally, as Bede tells us, Wilfrid preached the gospel to the South Saxons. This rather rapid conversion suggests that there must have been some earlier knowledge of Christianity amongst the Angles and Saxons.

As we learn from the Chronicle, and from Bede, the establishment of churches and monasteries soon followed, and, as a natural result, Latin was once more spoken in England, this time as the official language of the church. Schools were also set up in the monasteries, some of which were later to become famous all over Western Europe; Theodore of Tarsus and Hadrian established a school at Canterbury, Aldhelm taught at Malmesbury, and Benedict Biscop founded two famous schools at Wearmouth and Jarrow. Bede was a pupil at Jarrow. Bede's most famous pupil was Alcuin, who eventually took charge of the school at Charlemagne's court. These men were not content with religion only, and contact with religious communities on the continent meant contact also with the whole body of secular learning accumulated there. Benedict Biscop visited the continent several times, and Wilfrid lived for a time in Gaul and Rome. England held the intellectual leadership in Western Europe in the eighth century, and, as Alfred said later, in the Preface to the *Cura Pastoralis*, 'foreigners came to this land in search of wisdom and instruction'. We see, then, how the conversion of the English to Christianity introduced Roman scholarship and civilization. The boundaries of learning were considerably extended as a result of the conversion, and this could not but affect the English language, for all this time Latin words were continually in the mouths of the monks, who were the people able to influence the development of language. While we cannot say with certainty what the language would have been like had there been no conversion, for we have no literary remains of the pre-Christian period with which to compare the later works, yet it is reasonable to assume that language benefited as much as did learning, that not only ecclesiastical terms were introduced in the early period but also many words unconnected with religious matters, and indeed the influence of the conversion is to be traced eventually in many aspects of life.

But this influence of the Roman church and Roman civilization on our language cannot be estimated merely by counting the Latin words borrowed in this period. It is, indeed, better to consider the influence we are now to examine as that of an event rather than of another language, for the influence is to be measured rather by the effect it had, in the widest sense of the word, on the English language than by the number of loan-words introduced. Indeed, if we compare the religious vocabulary of Old English with that of our own times we shall be struck most of all by the absence in Old English of the Latin forms of what seem to us basic words, words without which we should find it impossible to express thoughts on religious subjects; we shall be struck by what was apparently not borrowed, rather than by what was.

There would naturally be many new objects and ideas introduced by the missionaries, and quite a number of Latin words were adopted along with the idea they expressed. There would also be great zeal and impetuosity among the new converts, a desire to make rapid progress in understanding to the full the new beliefs, and it is likely that, at any rate in the earliest period, the native language would be quite incapable of coping with the new ideas and objects demanding expression, and, self-reliant as the English proved themselves to be in matters of language, it would be absolutely necessary to adopt many foreign expressions. Again, it is probable that the new converts would feel great respect for the already-accepted terms of their new religion, would like to use the words used by their teachers, and their fellow-Christians abroad, and many words connected with the authority and organization of the church would therefore be borrowed. *Biscop* (*bishop*) had probably been borrowed earlier, and now we find most of the names of the officials of the church borrowed from Latin, as *pāpa* – *pope*, *prīor* – *prior*, *provost*, *abbod* – *abbott*, *abbudesse* – *abbess*, *prēost* – *priest*, *decan* – *dean*, *diacon* – *deacon*, *acolitus* – *acolyte*, *clēric* – *clerk*, words connected with organization, as *capitol* – *chapter*, *reogol* – *rule*, words connected with the church, vestments, and church fabric generally, as *scrīn* – *shrine*, *alter* – *altar*, *earc* – *ark*, *candel* – *candle*, *cælic* – *chalice*, *organ* – *organ*, *cuȝle* – *cowl*, *pæll* – *pall*, *stōl* – *stole*, *tunece* – *tunic*, and words connected with services, such as *antefn* – *anthem*, *ymen* – *hymn*, (*e*)*pistol* – *epistle*, *letanīa* – *litany*, *mæsse* – *mass*, *salm* – *psalm*, *psalter*, *crēda* – *creed*. Two points are to be noted in connection with this list; first, the Old English forms show how little many of the words have changed throughout the centuries, and, secondly, it is remarkable how so many of these words have held their place in the later language, when so many other Old English religious terms were replaced, but the answer is perhaps to be found in the fact that these words are really part of the technical vocabulary of Christianity, and, as such, likely to be preserved.

It is also to be noted that these are chiefly short words, similar to the Germanic words, and capable of bearing Germanic inflexions; they are also chiefly nouns, though adjectives and verbs (both generally derivatives of nouns), also occur. There was also another important difference; previously words had been borrowed from the spoken language, but now they are adopted equally from the written language, as the knowledge of Latin writings and scholarship extended. But it was the works of the early fathers rather than those of the great classical writers which were the sources. The reasons for study at this time were purely religious, and some secular works were even proscribed by those in authority.

Simple words such as have been quoted above do not, of course, represent the full total of direct Latin influence, for, once the words had become established in English their use was extended by derivation and functional change. Probably this came at a later stage, after the first spate of direct borrowing, for it is only when a word has been thoroughly accepted into the language that derivatives are formed; and indeed it is only when a word has been so thoroughly assimilated that its use is no longer confined to its original meaning, but prefixes and suffixes may be added to extend that meaning, that it may be said really to have become part of the language. As an example of derivation we may note the root of Latin *dictare*, which appears in Old English as *dihtan*, and also *diht* – order, *dihtend* – director, *dihtere* – expositor, *dihtnere* – steward, *dihtnian* – to dispose, *dihtung*, *dihtnung* – disposition. New verbs were formed from nouns, as *crīstnian* and *biscopian* – to confirm (lit. to bishop). The latter had its related noun *biscopung* – confirmation, lit. 'bishoping', with which we may compare a term still in use today, the 'churching of women'. The boundary between derivation and compounding is very indistinct in some cases, when we can not be sure if the element added is dependent or independent, but there can be no doubt that the process of derivation was further extended by the addition of what were in Old English independent elements. This resulted in the formation of such hybrids as *priesthood* (OE *prēosthād*), *biscop* was compounded to yield *biscophād* and *biscopscir* (now replaced by the later loan *diocese*), and another Old English element added to a Latin loan yielded Christendom (OE *Crīstendōm*).

Dr Serjeantson[12] has listed some two hundred and fifty words, religious and secular, borrowed between 650 A.D. and the end of the Old English period, though some of these, such as the names for the whole scale of clerical offices, are what we may call technical vocabulary, and others do not occur frequently, yet this by no means represents the influence of the conversion upon the Old English language. The number of loan-words is no guide whatsoever, for of the most obvious effect of outside influence, the direct adoption of foreign words, Old English is remarkably free. Rather we shall need to discover how far English itself, as a medium of expression, was affected by these outside influences, how far the new ideas stimulated English to independent creative effort, to make use of its own resources. We shall find that Old English, as revealed in the literature which has come down to us, was affected, but not in the obvious way, by the influx of a large number of foreign loan-words. A comparison of the religious vocabulary of Old English with that in use a few centuries later shows how slight was the direct borrowing, how few Latin words, comparatively, Old English adopted and made a real part of the language, and this fact needs to be emphasized continually in any study of the vocabulary of Old English, for the presence of between four and five hundred recorded Latin loans in Old English, out of a vocabulary of between twenty and thirty thousand words, suggests a much greater proportion of Latin loans in common use than was actually the case.

Indeed, there was a tendency for some of the words adopted early to begin to pass out of the language before the end of the Old English period, and it is not easy to see why a word, once adopted, should be later rejected. We have seen the reason for the large influx of loans in the earliest stages of the conversion; in the first outburst of religious zeal many new ideas would demand expression, the resources of the native language would be for the time inadequate, and so foreign words would be adopted in fairly large numbers. Possibly some of these proved indigestible, and had to be replaced by native forms, particularly as the knowledge of Latin decreased as a result of the Scandinavian invasions. It is certain that learning declined, and the swing-over to the native stock becomes apparent by the time of Alfred and the Vespasian Psalter and Hymns. Alfred often translates terms, which suggests that they were not understood by the ordinary people and the lower orders of clergy, for whom he wrote.

But what strikes us most is the fact that so many apparently basic words were never adopted in the first place, and that the English should have made as much use of the resources of their own language as they did. Not only did they extend the scope of what foreign words were actually borrowed, by the use of native affixes, but they also modified the meaning of Old English words already in existence, and also coined new words from native stems. The example which springs first to mind is *God*, originally a neuter noun, and used to designate the heathen gods, as the use of the cognate word in the plural in Gothic clearly shows. *Metod* was formed from the root of the verb *metan* – to mete, measure, and referred to the heathen Fates; it is used regularly in Old English in the sense of 'God the Creator'. *Easter* takes us back to the old pagan spring festival, and an old heathen goddess of spring, the root of whose name, *Austro* (cf. Latin *Aurora*), yielded Old English *Eastru, Eastron*. *Tēoða* was originally an ordinal, meaning 'tenth', and later developed the sense of *tithe*. *Hūsl*, the Old English word for the Sacrament, still surviving in the archaic and dialectal *housel*, was originally a pagan sacrifice, *scrīn* was originally merely a box or chest, and then developed to the religious sense of a box or chest to house relics, and *scrift*, from a root which gave Latin *scribere* – to write, was merely 'a writing', later a written form of penance. Perhaps the most striking, from the point of view of meaning, is the Old English use of *weofod* to mean 'altar', for

F

it has developed from *wiȝ-beod* – idol-table. Perhaps it was used because phonological development had obscured the original connection with *wiȝ* – idol. *Blētsian* meant originally 'to sprinkle with blood', the verb being a derivative of the noun *blōd* – blood; just as the old heathen priest sprinkled blood from the sacrifice over the worshippers to give them some magical power or virtue, so the benediction of the Christian priest gave Christian virtue, and so we find that, instead of adopting a form of Latin *benedicere*, the English used *blētsian* – to bless, with a change of meaning. Perhaps the reason for some of these changes in meaning is to be explained by the difficulty the early missionaries would encounter in explaining the facts of Christianity. Latin would, of course, be useless, as most of the people would not understand it, and so perhaps the missionaries fell back on the native idiom, and sought in familiar things and old heathen beliefs resemblances of what they were trying to teach, as, for example, the great Christian festival of Easter and the old pagan spring festival, or the heathen sprinkling of the sacrificial blood and the Christian blessing. The missionaries were there to give a message to the people, and therefore used the Old English word *bodian* – to give a message, rather than Latin *prædicare* – to preach; they wished to teach that baptism made a man completely holy, and therefore used the English term *ful-wihan* – to make fully holy, which became *fulwian*, and then developed the noun *fulluht*, which later developed such compounds as *fulluht-bæþ* – font, *fulluht-stōw* – baptistry, *fulluht-nama* – Christian name, and others.

Some of these, such as *tēoða*, *bodian*, and *fulwian*, are really translation words, the Latin term being replaced by its English equivalent, and much use was made of this in forming the new Christian vocabulary of Old English. Sometimes it is not easy to see how much has been added to the meaning of a word, or whether we have a word with extended meaning or a mere translation; for example, *scaru*, from the verb *scieran* – to cut, apparently was extended by adding a religious significance when it was used for 'tonsure', yet it is really no more than a translation, the Latin being from a form of *tondere* – to clip, shear. OE *gōd-spell* is a literal translation of Greek *euaggelion* – the good news: with later shortening before the consonant group it became *godspell*, and afterwards the loss of the medial consonant, giving *gospel*, obscured the connexion with *gōd*. An interesting development is to be seen here; Old English had a derivative noun, *godspellere*, but this, like so many other Old English religious terms, was later replaced by a foreign loan-word, so that we now have *evangelist* instead. But in recent years the wheel has come full circle, and by a new process of derivation the Americans have their *hot gospellers!* OE *þrynnes* – trinity, is an obvious translation, and *heathen* (OE *hǣþen*) is said to be derived from *heath* (OE *hǣþ*) by the same reasoning as had given Latin *paganus* (NE *pagan*) from *pagus* – a country district. A centurion is, quite literally, *hundred-man*, and the approach to Jewish ceremonial is equally realistic in *ymb-snide* – circumcision (*snide* – a cut, incision, *snīþan* – to cut). The Hebrew *synagogue* is literally translated, as *ȝesamnung* – a gathering together, and the Tabernacle is simply *ȝeteld* – tent. Prayer is *ȝebed* – lit. asking, and the verb is *biddan*, originally 'to ask'. *Fulwian* – to baptize, has already been noted, but alongside this is found a translation word, *dyppan* – lit. to dip. Although these translation-words are not very numerous, and are indeed the exception rather than the rule, they were very useful. Neither the abstract ideas of Christianity, foreign in every way to the temperament of the Germanic peoples, nor the Latin names for them, would be easily acquired by the English, but this method accomplished two things; first, it explained the word by reference to known things, for *þrynnes* – the quality of being three, was easily understood, and it also avoided the use of foreign technical terms. We can be quite sure that the conceptions underlying the Passion, or martyrdom, were better understood when the OE *þrowung* – suffering, was used than if the Latin word had been adopted, that *þrowere* – a sufferer, gave a clear picture of a martyr, and that OE *dǣd-bōt*, a recompense for a deed, had a livelier meaning for the English, familiar as they were with *wergild* and compensation for crimes, than the Latin loan *penance* would have had. As we shall see later, in studying the secular vocabulary, this process proved extremely useful later in providing words which would express clearly and simply the ideas of the new learning, and such words were used by later scholars, such as Ælfric, to express the ideas of philosophy, grammar, and science.

The boundary between this class of pure translation-words, in which the foreign word is merely replaced by its literal native counterpart, and another process, by which the foreign idea, rather than its mere name, is expressed by a native term, is indistinct, and some of the later examples in the last paragraph belong rather to the last-named process. Here it is almost as if the idea behind the word had been conveyed, without the use of the actual word, and then a native word had been coined to express the idea. For example, Latin *scribere* provided the later loan *Scripture*, but Old English preferred *ȝewritu* – a writing, from which we have *Holy Writ*. Old English might have used some form from Latin *scribere* for *scribe* – the root had been used in *shrive* and *shrift* – but instead a new word was coined, *bōceras* – lit. bookers, or bookmen, and *wrītere* – writer, was also used. *Pharisee* was expressed by *sundor-halga* – the holy man who kept himself apart; a simpler term

was used for 'pharisee' in the northern dialects, where they were called
ǣ-larwas – teachers of the divine law. Prophet was expressed by witeʒa
– lit. the knowing one, the wise man, and by extension the idea of the
Magi in the Christmas story was conveyed by tungol-witeʒan – men
learned in the stars. The chaplain, or family priest, had his duties clearly
shown in hīredpreost – lit. 'family priest', and the duties of the acolyte
were as clearly portrayed in the words used as alternatives to the Latin
loan-word acolitus, already noticed; we find huslþegn – servant of the
Sacrament, taporberend – taper-bearer, and wæxberend – wax-bearer. The
primary idea of God as the Creator is expressed by Scieppend, a verbal
noun from scieppan – to fashion, create. The ideal Germanic leader was
expected to care for and protect his people, and we get a mingling of
Christian and Germanic traditions when God, as the protector of His
people, is identified with the Germanic prince in such words as dryhten
– prince, wealdend – ruler, þēoden – prince, weard – guardian. These words
were also applied to Christ, who sacrificed himself for His people as
Beowulf, the ideal prince, sacrificed himself for his tribe, and we also
find Neriend – the Preserver, and Hǣlend – lit. the Healer, Saviour. With
the later Latin loan-word Testament, from testāri – to bear witness, testify,
may be compared sēo ealde ʒecȳpnes and sēo niwe ʒecȳpnes (ʒecȳpnes –
witness, testimony). Genesis appears as cnēores-bōc – lit. the generation-
book, and Exodus is ūt-færeld – lit. the out-journey. Religion is ǣ-fæstnes
– lit. firmness in religious law, consecration is halgung – a hallowing,
making holy (< hāliʒ – holy), and salvation is hǣlu – a wholeness, an
abstract noun formed from hāl – whole. The two words for hermit
show that two different aspects had been seized upon, ansetla emphasizing his solitude (ān – alone, solitary), and wēstensetla his retirement to a
desert or waste place (wēsten – a waste place).

Examples in this last class are all, in a sense, translation-words, but
whereas in the earliest examples we have respect and reverence for the
authority of the original, an exact imitation, the later examples show
more freedom of treatment. Many of these words must have been
extremely forceful at the time, and it is to be regretted that so few of
them have survived.

This preference for a native word instead of the Latin word ready to
hand cannot be put down to ignorance of Latin, at any rate among
the higher ranks of the clergy, for we have evidence from Bede of the
learning of men such as Tobias, bishop of Rochester, Albinus, abbot of
Canterbury, and Aldhelm, abbot of Malmesbury and later bishop of
Sherborne, and others, such as Theodore of Tarsus, Hadrian, Benedict
Biscop, his pupil, Bede, and Bede's pupil, Alcuin, have already been
mentioned. Yet the ordinary people were ignorant of Latin, and if the

learned Latin words had been introduced they would not have been understood. But, although there were probably excellent Latin scholars in England at all times from the end of the sixth century to the Norman Conquest, learning sank to a low level in the ninth century, for the culture and civilization of the northern kingdoms was destroyed by the attacks of the Danes, and Alfred[13] himself tells us that matters were no better in the south, for of learning in England he writes: 'so general was its decay that there were very few on this side of the Humber who could understand their rituals in English, or translate a letter from Latin into English; and I believe that there were not many beyond the Humber. There were so few of them that I cannot call to mind a single one south of the Thames when I came to the throne'. And later in the same passage: 'I remembered also that I saw, before it had been all ravaged and burned, how the churches throughout all England stood filled with treasures and books; and there was also a great multitude of servants of God, but they had very little knowledge of the books, for they could not under-stand anything of them, because they were not written in their own language'. It seems then, that during the ninth and early tenth centuries the ordinary people did not understand Latin, and the lower orders of the clergy also knew little or nothing of that language. In the preface to his Grammar Ælfric says: 'Until Dunstan and Æþelwold revived learning in the monastic life no English priest could either write a letter in Latin, or understand one'. We can, then, understand a state of affairs such as is found in Old English, where nearly all the terms in common use are native, and therefore easily understood, as against a later period when the language relies almost entirely on loan-words to express the same ideas. It seems not unlikely, then, that it was in this middle period, between the beginning of the Scandinavian raids and the time when the effects of the Benedictine revival began to be felt, that the native religious terms were coined, but there is no direct evidence for this. If this decay in learning had not taken place, if the clergy had continued to be zealous Latin scholars throughout the whole Old English period, perhaps more Latin words would have been adopted, and older ones retained, and fewer English words coined or adapted, but even then we must take into account the ignorance of the laity.

It was not until Alfred had achieved peace, and tried to remedy the ignorance of his people, an effort which was supported, so far as the religious orders were concerned, by the tenth century Benedictine revival under Dunstan and Æþelwold, that learning revived and Latin was again studied. It is this later period, especially after the Benedictine revival, which gives us the large influx of learned Latin words in Old English, for Latin influence was almost completely dependent on

church influence, and not until the religious orders had been reorganized could Latin learning again flourish. The regular study and
translation of Latin, and the familiarity of the best English prose-writers
with Latin could not but result in an influx of foreign words to express
new ideas where English proved inadequate or unsuitable for learned
purposes.

These new words were often not of a popular nature, but expressed
ideas rather of a scientific and learned nature. They also occur far less
frequently than the popular words, and some are found once or twice
only. It is probable that a large proportion of the later loan-words
occurred only in writing, and were never really living words, part of
the spoken language. Some of them, indeed, may be said not to have
penetrated into the language at all, for they even retained their foreign
inflexions. In particular, many of the words found in glosses are little
more than Anglicized forms of foreign words. The words are found in
scientific manuals such as that of Byrhtferth, or in the collections of
charms and herbal recipes, and in the collections of homilies and works
on religion and philosophy written by men such as Ælfric and Wulfstan.
Many technical terms in scientific subjects came into English at this
time, many names of trees and plants, but we shall find that, numerous
as they are, they have added but little to our English vocabulary, for
very few survived, and of the large body of loans of which the examples
listed below are merely a selection only a handful can now be found in
our language.

The secular knowledge which flowed into England as a result of the
conversion was by no means limited to Latin in the narrow sense of the
word. It was, indeed, Latin civilization which was introduced, but this
Latin civilization had imbibed knowledge and culture from Greece, and
from civilizations of Asia and Asia Minor, of Egypt, and other civilizations of the remote past. All these were to contribute in some measure
to the learning which now came to England. Eastern words were
absorbed through Latin, and in this early period we have names of
fruits and spices such as *orange*, *ginger*, *hyssop* (*ȳsope*), *myrrh* and *cassia*,
trees such as *palm* (*pælm*, *palm*[a]) and *cedar* (*cēder*), glimpses of the
wonders and marvels of the East in *lion* (*lēo*) and *camel* (*camel*[l]), and
the romantic names, *India* and *Saracen*, both recorded in the Old
English period. The word *silk* probably travelled from China across the
caravan routes of Asia before reaching the Mediterranean, and passing
thence to our own language. Greek civilization is represented by *school*
(scōl) and *scholar*, *verse*, and *philosopher* (philosoph).

From Latin itself we have OE *cubit* and *talent* (OE *tālente*); among
metals and precious stones we find OE *amber*, *aðamans* – diamond (cf.

the later loan *adamant*), *cristalla* – *crystal;* in music and poetry we find *cimbal(a)* – *cymbal, fiðele* – *fiddle, fers* – *verse;* OE *scutel* – *dish* (NE *scuttle*) was borrowed in this period. We have also *clauster* – *cloister, tempel* – *temple,* and *ðēater* – *theatre.* Among plants we find *alewe* – *aloe, balsam* – *balsam, balm, bēte* – *beet*(root), *cāul* – *cole, cucumer* – *cucumber, fēferfūge* – *feverfew, lilie* – *lily, rōse* – *rose;* included among animals and birds are *fenix* – *phoenix, tīger* – *tiger, pard* – *leopard, pellican* – *pelican,* and among scientific words, and words connected with learning generally, are *comēta* – *comet, circul* – *circle, grammatic* (*cræft*) *grammar, paper* – *paper, plaster* – *plaster.* Not all these were originally Latin, but all came into Old English through Latin, some having travelled far before then. OE *panther* – *panther,* came originally from Sanskrit, as did also *pipor* – *pepper.* Old Persian was the source of *pard* – *leopard,* and *tīger* – *tiger.* OE *camel(l)* – *camel, balsam* – *balsam,* and *ʒeaspis* – *jasper,* all derive ultimately from Hebrew.

In the third period Dr Serjeantson lists ten military, legal, and official terms, nine names of metals and precious stones, eleven connected with clothing and eleven with domestic affairs, forty-eight names of plants, etc., seventeen of animals and birds, ten medical terms, forty-five words connected with religion, thirty-two connected with books and learning, and eighteen with music and poetry.[14] Here are literary and learned words, not those of everyday life, and the lists are very different from those of the first two periods. They were not really part of the vocabulary of Old English, but many of them were reintroduced later, and so are part of our vocabulary today. Some of these words may have been adopted earlier, but it is difficult to be sure of the exact date of adoption, and unless a word of this type occurs so frequently in the other Germanic languages as to make it probable that it was adopted on the Continent, or occurs in pre-Alfredian literature, it is better to consider it as one of the learned loan-words of the tenth or eleventh centuries.

But, just as was the case with religious words, there is another side to the picture; once again native words are used for these new ideas and objects. The seven liberal arts of the old trivium and quadrivium have native names; *stæf-cræft* – grammar (cf. OE *stæf* – letter, *cræft* – art), *þylcræft* – rhetoric (cf. OE *þyle* – orator), *flit-cræft* – logic (cf. OE *flit* – dispute), and *tungol-ʒescead* – astrology (OE *tungol* – star, *ʒescēad* – reason), *eorþ-gemet* – geometry (OE *ʒemet* – measure), *rīm-cræft* – arithmetic (OE *rīm* – number), and *sōncræft* (the first element a Latin loan) or *swinsung-cræft* – music. Astronomy was *tungol-æ* (lit. *star-law*), equinox was *efen-niht,* solstice was *sunn-stede,* both translation words, and medicine was *lǣce-cræft* (cf. NE *horse-leech*). Ælfric made use of native terms to describe grammatical features, as *nama* – noun, *word* – verb, *fore-setnes* – preposition. Even such an abstract idea as 'fertility' was rendered by the native word – *wæstmberendnes* – 'fruit-bearingness'. The meanings of all these terms are clear today to an ordinary reader with but little knowledge of Old English, and must originally have been much clearer to the English than the learned loan-word would have been.

We have seen two effects of contact with Latin civilization, the direct adoption of the Latin word, and the stimulation of Old English to provide a translation-word or coin a new word to express the idea of the Latin original; there was also an intermediate stage, partaking of the nature of both the others, for we find recorded pairs of words, one foreign, one native, for the same idea. For example, we have seen how Ælfric used native grammatical terms, yet he also used derivatives of the classical *gramma*. The Latin *ærce-* is found alongside the native *hēah* – high, in *ærcebiscop* and *hēahbiscop*. We find *predician*, from the Latin, once, alongside the regular native *bodian*. There is a learned loan (e)*pistol*, but we also have *ǣrend-ʒewrit* – lit. errand-writing. The Latin verb *saltare* – to leap, dance, appears as *saltian*, and there is a related noun *sealticʒe*, but *saltavit* is also translated by the native *tumbude* (cf. *tumbler* – dancer, acrobat). Alongside *alter* we find *weofod*, alongside *offrung* – a hybrid – was used the native *lāc*. As an extreme example, Old English adopts *discipul*, but also uses no fewer than ten native synonyms – *cniht, folʒere, ʒingra, hīeremon, lǣringmon, leornere, leorningcniht, leorningman, under-þēodda,* and *þeʒn*. In all these cases we see that, to say the least, Old English would have proved sufficient without the Latin.

The number of loan-words may seem considerable[15] – some four hundred or so basic forms – but even if we take into account all the derivatives from these loan-words, yet the number really forms but a small part of the total Old English vocabulary. And it is not merely a question of the actual number of loans, for we have already seen that some were technical words and others occurred infrequently, both of these types being therefore hardly part of the living vocabulary, so that the foreign material in general use was inconsiderable compared with the full range of the Old English vocabulary.

One other point remains to be discussed in connexion with the native terms illustrated above. It will be noticed that very few indeed of these have survived, and that we now use the foreign loan-word. For example, *halʒa* (cf. *hālig* – holy) was used for a holy man, but this was later replaced by *saint;* Latin *sanct* is found also, but rarely. The Old English form remains in *All Hallows,* and, as a verb, in *hallowed,* in the *Lord's Prayer. Tonsure* has now replaced OE *scaru,* and *ʒesomnung* has given way to *congregation*. Sometimes the replacement has not been for good; OE *prowung* and *prowere*, later replaced by *martyrdom* and *martyr*, seem to hold more meaning, more of the spirit of English, than do the rather colourless loan-words, and the American *gospeller* certainly suggests a livelier and more vital personality than does *evangelist*. No real purpose would be served by listing the secular words which have failed to survive, for the examples given are sufficient; in each case the Old English form is unfamiliar, and the translation given is the word in common use today. It is not easy to see why native words, once used, should be replaced by foreign loans. It may have been some form of intellectual snobbery, as the priesthood once more became educated, or the lower orders of clergy, and some of the laity, felt superior if they could use Latin. It may have been the authority of the established church, and the desire for more uniformity. Many words must have been introduced as a result of the Benedictine Revival, but no certainty is possible unless we know just when the replacement took place. Undoubtedly some of the replacements are later, and the result of displacement from positions of authority in religion and learning of the English by Normans or Frenchmen after the Norman Conquest.

Our study of this aspect of Old English vocabulary may perhaps be concluded with a short examination of a particular text. Bede's account of the manner in which Cædmon received, by divine means, the ability to compose religious verse was originally written in Latin, but was later translated into Old English either by Alfred himself or by some scribe commissioned by him. This translation was made at the end of the ninth century, some three hundred years after the beginning of the Conversion, and since it is fairly general in scope it may be taken as being representative of the religious prose of the period.

In about a hundred and forty lines (in Sweet's *Anglo-Saxon Reader*) we find six undisputed Latin loan-words, all technical terms connected with the ranks of the Church, or its organization; they are *mynster*, *munuchād*, *abbudisse*, *apostol*, *reʒollecum*, and *canōn* (in *canōnes bēc* – the canonical books). We also have *Crīst*, an essential word which could hardly be replaced, from either Latin or Celtic, and a Celtic loan-word, *stǣr* – story, not specifically religious, but used here in a religious sense.

It may be that if the passage had been more concerned with the ranks of the priesthood, with doctrine, discipline and regulation, and general organization we may have had more loans. The presence of the first five above suggest this, but to go further is mere hypothesis.

We find also native and heathen words adapted to a Christian purpose. *God* is used, as may be expected, and, as usual, is found in the masculine singular, as against the use in the neuter plural for the old heathen gods.

Heofen and *hell* are also old heathen concepts common to Christian doctrine. The basic meaning of the latter word is 'hole', perhaps 'secret hole', and in the case of the former we may note how this word has retained only a religious or poetic significance, having now been replaced as a general term by *sky*, an Old Norse loan-word. *Metod*, applied to the heathen idea of fate, and connected with the verb *metan* –to mete out, measure, is also applied to the Christian God, and the basic word *Gāst* – spirit, to the Holy Ghost, as in modern English. *Hūsl*, originally a pagan sacrifice, is used for the Christian sacrament, suggesting that it was the idea of sacrifice rather than a memorial which was uppermost in the minds of the Anglo-Saxons.

We note also two derivatives, *godcund* (lit. godlike) – divine, and *halwende*, the basic idea of the stem *hāl* being 'whole, safe, sound'.

Also to be noted are general native words used with special force, as *Drihten* and *Frēa* (both lit. lord), *Weard* (lit. protector, guardian) for God, *brōþor* and *leorneras* (lit. learners – novices) for the monks, and *ʒesomnung* (lit. a gathering) for the Christian congregation, some of these being purely translation words, as are also *Scyppend* (derived from *scieppan* – to fashion, create), used for God, and, related to this same verb, *frumsceaft* – Creation. The native term *lār* is used for the teachings or doctrines of the apostles, and for the writing of hymns we have *scopʒereorde* – the language of the scop (the Germanic court poet). Other words which are pure translation forms are *menniscnes* – Incarnation, *þrowung* – Passion, *up-āstiʒnes* – Ascension, *ut-gong* (lit. outgoing) – Exodus, *ʒehātland* – promised land, *uht-sang* (lit. dawn song) – matins, and the abstract terms *æfestnesse* (lit. firmness in the law) – piety, and *ārfestnesse* (lit. firmness in honour) – virtue. *Weʒneste* (lit. food for the journey) is also a straightforward translation of the Latin *viaticum*.

Among compounded forms are *heofenrīces* – heavenly kingdom, *Wuldorfæder* – the Father of Glory, *munuchād*, already mentioned, and a hybrid, and a pure native compound in *weoroldhād* (lit. world-order) – secular or lay order.

Finally we may note a pair of native synonyms, *synn* and *māndǣda*.

It will be seen that the proportion of loanwords is small in this passage, and that much use has been made of the native material. It may perhaps be argued that Alfred's purpose was to teach people who were unfamiliar with learned words, but we also find that passages from the works of Ælfric or Wulfstan show a similar preference for the native words, particularly when the works are original, and not translations.

In conclusion, it would seem, then, that if English writers could handle, in their own language, religious and scientific subjects, in which

Latin influence might be expected to be paramount, they must have been satisfied with the capacity of their language to meet all normal needs. We may compare this attitude with that of the Greeks, who so developed their language that it proved capable of dealing with the most difficult abstract and technical subjects without recourse to outside help. Moreover, this reliance on native material shows a greater understanding and grasp of the new ideas than might be shown by indiscriminate borrowing of foreign words. The man who coined *sundor-halʒan* for 'Pharisees', holy men who kept themselves apart, or *ʒesamnung* for 'synagogue', certainly understood to the full the real meaning expressed by the foreign word. The contrast with modern English is very striking, and the number of native words once capable of expressing abstract conceptions, and later replaced by foreign loan-words, is very great indeed. From the way in which our modern language has borrowed so freely it would seem that the old word-forming capacity has been lost, and that the conservatism which has objected so strenuously to borrowing at different periods in our history has now been broken down; indeed, it would seem, from the difficulty experienced last century in reintroducing *handbook*,[16] a word used already in Old English, that the objection in our own time is to the very reliance on native material which was so strong a feature of Old English.

CHAPTER FIVE

*

THE SCANDINAVIANS

The Anglo-Saxons came here, as we have seen, about the middle of the fifth century, and for some four hundred years they were left in peace by the outside world, to establish their new kingdom and create for themselves a new way of life. At the end of that period their language was still in the main Germanic, and, so far as vocabulary is concerned, perhaps but little changed from the language they had brought over from the continent, for, although it had been subject to the influences of two foreign languages, Celtic and Latin, these had made surprisingly little difference to the ordinary speech of the people.

But about the middle of the ninth century they were themselves subject to the same kind of attacks, first plundering raids, and later attacks with the object of establishing settlement, as they had earlier inflicted on the Britons. As a result of this they suffered grievously at the hands of the Scandinavians, chiefly Danes and Norwegians, for nearly two hundred years, and eventually the Saxon ruling dynasty was replaced by a Scandinavian line. The Scandinavians had been near neighbours of the Angles and Saxons on the continent, and had sprung from the same parent Germanic stock. They were perhaps rivals, but yet of the same kindred, and even after the Angles and Saxons had established themselves in this land relations between them and the Scandinavian races were probably peaceful, and it is not unlikely that there was literary contact between the two peoples. King Alfred, as we know, was visited by two Scandinavian seamen, Ohthere and Wulfstan, who told him of their voyages to the White Sea and in the Baltic, and these stories Alfred included in the account of European geography in his translation of *Orosius*.

The story of the contact between the English and the Danes and Norwegians in the ninth, tenth, and eleventh centuries is a remarkable one. Sometimes, not infrequently, an unknown nation comes out from its obscurity, takes its place with the great ones for a time, and then just as suddenly, retires into its former obscurity. An obvious example is the Gothic nation, a minor Germanic tribe who moved from the Baltic to the Black Sea, and afterwards sacked Rome and ruled Italy, and established empires in France and Spain, only to disappear later, leaving hardly a trace of their former greatness. The history of the Scandinavians

168

in the Viking Age is a similar story. For centuries they had lived in their northern home, but conditions changed suddenly in the eighth century, and from these northern lands there came a steady stream of fierce fighting men who left hardly any part of Europe, from Iceland to Constantinople, untouched. The Swedes established a kingdom in Russia, Norwegians settled in Ireland, England, Scotland, the Faroes, and Iceland, and went thence to Greenland and Labrador. The Danes settled on the northern coast of France, where their leader, the Duke of Normandy, became more powerful than the King of France himself, and from there came to England. In the eleventh century Cnut conquered England, and from his new capital, London, governed England, Norway, and his native Denmark.

These changes may have been the result of economic or political conditions, or merely the natural outcome of the character of these Scandinavian people. Their lands were by no means extensive, and were far from fertile. In Alfred's account we read: 'Ohthere said the land of the Northmen (Norwegians) was very long and very narrow. All of it that can be either grazed or ploughed lies alongside the sea, and that is very rocky in some places; and wild moors lie to the east, running alongside and overlooking the cultivated land'. Norway was perhaps less fortunate in this respect than Denmark, where the land was more fertile, but southern Norway, southern Sweden, and Denmark were also subject to inundation, and we read of Goths and Burgundians driven from their island homes in that area by floods centuries before the Viking Age. Political conditions were no happier. There were a number of petty kings, each ruling his own tribe, and war between them was ceaseless. The heroic poems which have come down to us tell of struggles in these lands before the English left the continent, and they continued in the Scandinavian lands until Harold the Fairhaired brought all Norway under his control. Many minor chiefs must have been overcome and driven from their kingdoms, and for them the future offered few problems, for they were all seamen by nature, and so took to the sea when driven from their kingdoms. Ohthere and Wulfstan, we know, were both experienced seamen and navigators, as much at home on the sea as on land, and we have no reason to believe that they differed from their fellow-Scandinavians. In the *Ynglinga Saga* we are told of sea-kings who were served by many men, and yet they had no lands, and indeed were entitled to be called sea-kings only if they never slept under sooty beam, never drank at chimney corner. We can easily imagine, then, a fight between two petty rulers, and the loser, driven from his kingdom, seeking his fortune by plundering at sea. We know from their literature of their love for the sea, a love amounting in some cases almost to rejection of life on land, and piracy was no crime in their eyes. Indeed, we read in one saga of a young man who was reproved by his father for not following the example of his ancestors and acquiring by plundering raids honour for himself and treasure which should not be inherited by his sons, but buried with him when he died. Most of the raids of the earlier Viking Age, which lasted from around 750 A.D. for about three centuries, were carried out by the younger landless sons, and landless princes, but later the purpose of the raids changed, and plunder gave way to conquest and settlement.

The Scandinavian attacks on these islands may be divided into three phases. From 787 to about 850 there was a series of plundering raids, carried out probably by small isolated bands, such as that we read of in the A. S. Chronicle, in the annal for 787: 'In Beorhtric's time there came first three ships, and the reeve rode up to them, and intended to bring them to the king's town, because he knew not who they were, and he was slain. These were the first ships of the Danes that visited the land of the English'. The annal for 793 tells of the plundering of the monastery at Lindisfarne, and of Jarrow in the following year. The main objects of attack were the rich religious foundations, and the towns which had grown up around them; the sacred vessels and the shrines, resplendent with gold, silver, and precious stones, provided rich loot, as did also the costly and magnificent ecclesiastical robes, and slaves were also carried off. The first attack was chiefly in the north, and after this first series of raids there was a break of nearly forty years, until, in 832, as the Chronicle tells us, 'the heathen men plundered Sheppey'; in the following year thirty-five ships appeared off the coast of Wessex and ravaged that kingdom, defeating the English under Egbert at Charmouth, and again in 840 a similar number appeared and the English were defeated again at Charmouth, this time under Ethelwulf. The raids increased in number and strength, and the Vikings gradually spread over the whole of England, though these raids were, in the main, carried out by comparatively small bands.

The second stage began about 850, with the arrival of a huge Danish fleet. In 851 they stayed throughout the winter, for the first time, in the Isle of Thanet, the A. S. Chronicle recording: 'Heathen men for the first time remained through the winter'. Before this they had carried out extended raids, but always returned to their ships on the approach of winter, and left for home, but this second stage is the work of larger armies, marching through the whole country on plundering raids, and establishing large settlements, with well-organized winter quarters, though no actual settlements seem to have been made before 865, when a large army landed in Thanet, and in the following year the Vikings wintered in East Anglia and then struck north, seized York in 867, and captured Northumbria. Various accounts mention large fleets, one of seven hundred ships, one of three hundred and fifty in the Thames, recorded in the annal for 851, and twelve thousand men are reported to have been killed in one battle. There were two lines of attack, the Danes from the east, driving into Yorkshire and the East Midlands, and the Norwegians, who sailed round Scotland, settled in Ireland, and then drove into north-west England and even round along the Channel coast. The midland kingdom of Mercia was next to fall, and soon Wessex itself was threatened.

The annals of the A. S. Chronicle make dismal reading in this period: in 870 'King Eadmund fought against the Danes, and they gained the victory, slew the king, and over-ran all the country', in 874 'the host went from Lindsay to Repton, and established winter-quarters there, and drove the king, Buhred, over the sea, when he had reigned twenty-two years, and over-ran the land', in 875 'Healfdene advanced with some of the army against the Northumbrians, and established winter-quarters on the Tyne, and the host over-ran that country', in the following year 'Healfdene divided the land of the Northumbrians, so that they became their harrowers and ploughmen', in 877 'at harvest time the host marched into Mercia, and divided up some of it, and gave some to Ceolwulf', and in 878 'about mid-winter, after twelfth-night, the host stole to Chippenham, and rode through the land of the West Saxons, and settled there, and drove many of the people over the sea, and brought them to their will, except King Alfred, and he, with a small force, with difficulty made for the woods and the security of the moor'. But Alfred finally gained a great victory at Ethandun, and this stage came to an end in 878, with the Treaty of Wedmore, when Alfred and Guthrum divided the land between them, and the Danelaw, roughly north and east of a line from London to Chester, along Watling Street, was established. Guthrum and his followers accepted Christianity, and this perhaps helped to improve relations between the two races. The truce was, however, naturally uneasy, and sporadic fighting continued, and by the middle of the tenth century a great part of eastern and central England had been reconquered by Alfred's son, Eadward, assisted by his sister Æþelfleda, the 'Lady of the Mercians', and later by Alfred's grandson, Æþelston, and the Scandinavians, it is to be noted, were neither exterminated nor driven out, but quietly absorbed into the English nation. Relations between the English and the Scandinavians who had settled in England improved, and the latter were converted to Christianity. They became landowners, and so were likely to suffer as much as the native English if raids were resumed, and later, when

new bands of Vikings appeared, they did actually fight for the English
kings.

The third stage began in the last decade of the tenth century, when
another great fleet, under Olaf Tryggvason, appeared, and now the
invasion took on a more national aspect, and mere local settlement was
replaced by an attempt at political conquest, the campaigns being conducted by two great kings, Olaf of Norway and Svein of Denmark.
The third stage really began when, in 994, after a few sporadic raids,
during one of which there occurred the Battle of Maldon, celebrated
in a fine Old English heroic poem, these two kings sailed up the Thames
with ninety-four ships and besieged London. They failed to take the
city, but terrible ravaging raids continued for five or six years. The
treacherous massacre of St Brice's Day, 1002, when Svein's sister,
Gunhild, was among the victims, really brought matters to a head, and
Svein once more attacked England. The struggle continued, and several
times the English bought off the Viking attacks. In 1013 Svein himself
reappeared, quickly conquered Northumbria and the Danelaw, and
marched south, ravaging the whole country in English hands. In the
same year he was acknowledged king of the whole country, Eþelred
having fled in the ships of his Scandinavian bodyguard, Purcytel and
his followers, who had joined the English in 1012. Svein died the
following year, and Eþelred was again proclaimed king by the English
witan, and Svein's son, Cnut, was driven from the country. He soon
returned, and by the following year the whole country was in his
hands. After the death of Eþelred there was bitter fighting between his
son Eadmund and Cnut, and finally the kingdom was divided between
them, but Eadmund died in 1016 and in the following year Cnut was
acknowledged king. Thus the Scandinavian raids came to an end, and
Cnut, who valued England more than his native country, and became
more of an English than a Danish king, made London the capital of his
empire of England, Denmark, and Norway, and appointed Englishmen
to important positions. For the remainder of his reign England was
untroubled by foreign invaders. Probably further Scandinavian settlements were effected, but now by peaceful means, and although fighting
broke out again after his death it was then a question of civil war, and
not fighting between English and Danes, and in the last twenty-five
years or so before the Norman Conquest the fusion of the two races
living alongside each other in England proceeded rapidly.

This long period of struggle had, however, not been one of continuous fighting. Even in the earliest days some of the invaders may
have tried to establish themselves in England, instead of returning home
with plunder, and many of the places in England, chiefly in the Danelaw,

in the north and east, and also in the north-west, in Lancashire, West-morland and Cumberland, whose names suggest that they were once Scandinavian settlements, must have been established soon after the Treaty of Wedmore, if not earlier. It is, therefore, not only a question of invading bands ravaging the countryside, but also of some of the invaders settling peacefully, setting themselves up as farmers, and marrying English women.

So long as the contact between the peoples was confined to plunder-ing raids, or to bitter fighting within the country, there would be little effect on language, but once the Scandinavians began to settle, and comparatively peaceful conditions prevailed, as in the Danelaw after 878, and throughout the country after Cnut had been accepted as king, then the influence of Scandinavian on the English language would be felt. The bare facts of history prove that the influence must have been exerted before the Norman Conquest, for after 1066 Scandinavian influence, except in the north, was replaced by French influence. It may be noted in passing that Northern dialects preserve many Scandinavian words not found in the dialects of the south, so obviously Scandinavian influence was deeper, and lasted longer, in these northern areas. The influx of Scandinavian words before the Conquest must have been considerable, though the words which actually appear in Old English works are extremely few. In Sweet's *Students' Dictionary of Anglo-Saxon* only about fifty words are marked as Scandinavian, and Kluge, who covers the early transition period also, up to 1150, lists only about a hundred and fifty, some of which are doubtful.

The periods of influence may be divided as follows: (*a*) 787–850, a period of plundering raids, with little appreciable influence on the language; (*b*) 860–990, the period of early settlements, and some fusion after the Danelaw had been established, when the two languages would be spoken side by side throughout most of northern and eastern England; (*c*) 990–1016, with renewed waves of Scandinavians, and consequent strengthening of linguistic influence by mere weight of numbers, in spite of the fact that the state of war would militate against the influence, as it did in the first period; (*d*) 1016–1050, the period of Danish rule and the beginnings of real fusion, with English the official court language, and Scandinavian beginning to give way, though leaving its marks on the language; (*e*) the post-Conquest period, with the English and Scandinavians united in opposition to the Normans, with the two races fused completely, the two languages finally merged, and Scandinavian no longer spoken, except perhaps in isolated communities. Or we may look at the question in another way; there is little trace of loan-words before the ninth century, then we have a period covering the tenth and eleventh centuries, when many new words were introduced, as a result of the peaceful fusion of the two peoples, although they do not appear in literature. This is perhaps a simpler division than the more detailed one already proposed, for it resolves itself into two periods, one of warfare and hostility, with no loan-words worth mentioning, the other of peaceful fusion, when the foreign influence is great.

Dr Serjeantson[1] has analysed the introduction of these loan-words chronologically. In the first period, which she takes as up to 1016, very few words were introduced; about fifty of these survived into Middle English, and about twenty-five are in use today. They are largely of a technical type, concerned chiefly with legal procedure and the sea. In the second period, which she puts at 1016–1150, thirty-three words are listed, with about twenty only surviving into Middle English, and about a dozen still in use. In the Middle English period itself, particularly in the thirteenth century, hundreds of words appear for the first time, though almost certainly adopted earlier. It is not easy to deal with the Middle English loans chronologically, and a regional survey is easier, and probably more fruitful.

Although the Scandinavian words are slow to appear in literature, for reasons to be discussed later, and represent an inconsiderable part of the recorded vocabulary up to the end of the twelfth century, yet the influence of Scandinavian on Old English colloquial speech was almost certainly greater than that of Latin, for so many of the Latin words adopted in the Old English period, particularly in the later Old English period, were 'book' words, learned or technical words, and unlikely to be in frequent use in the spoken language.

The Scandinavian loan-words found recorded in the early period fall into two classes, words connected with warfare, and especially warfare at sea, with the names of ships used, and sea-terms generally, and words connected with law and government. In the first group we find such words as *barda* – beaked ship, *cnearr* – warship, *floege* – little ship, *liþ* – fleet, *scegð* – light ship, *hæfen* – haven, *sweʒen* – in *bātsweʒn*, boatswain; *dreng* – warrior, *targe* – small shield, *orrest* – battle, *fylcian* – to marshal, *griþ* – truce, peace. In the second group are *hūsting* – assembly, *wapentake* – administrative district, *laʒu* – law, *ūtlaʒa* – outlaw, *hold* – freeholder, *līesing* – a freedman, *crafian* – to demand at law, *māl* – legal action, *þryðing* – Riding (one of the three divisions of Yorkshire). There are also some general words, such as *cnīf* – knife, *feolaʒa* – fellow, *hūsbonda* – householder, *niðing* – villain, *ðīr* – maidservant, *þræl* – slave, *dieʒen* – to die, *eggian* – to egg on, *scinn* – skin, *rōt* – root, *tacan* – to take, *marc* and *ōran*, both coins, and a few others, including perhaps *ceallian* – to call, though this has recently been doubted. Both the warfare terms and the legal terms later disappeared, when the Normans conquered the country and took control of those two spheres of life.

The real worth of the loan-words of the early period is not very great, for some occur only infrequently, and many, especially legal terms, were hardly part of everyday speech. Moreover, as Dr Serjeantson pointed out, less than forty have survived to our own time.

But, as we have seen, the bulk of these Scandinavian words were slow to appear in the literary language, there being comparatively few before 1200. The main reason for this is to be found in the sphere of influence. The areas most affected by Scandinavian influence in the Old English period, in the early Middle English period, and, so far as dialects are concerned, in the modern period, were the northern, north-eastern, east-midland and eastern counties as far south as East Anglia, and the north-western counties. Scandinavian influence is least in the southern, western, and south-western counties. To illustrate this point by reference to Middle English, there are few Scandinavian words in the *Brut* (c. 1205), probably less than forty, but the east-midland *Ormulum* (c. 1200) has quite a large number, about a hundred and twenty which are certainly Scandinavian, and others which may be. As a result of the Scandinavian invasions, learning decayed in the north, which had previously been in the forefront in European learning, and because of this decay there seem to have been practically no important works written – or at any rate they have not survived – in the areas where Scandinavian influence was strong from the beginning of the invasion until the thirteenth century. Accordingly, it is not possible for us to be sure what Scandinavian words were in use in those areas at that time. Most of the literature which has survived was written in the West Saxon area, where the Scandinavian influence was least likely to be strong, since King Alfred was able to encourage his people to resist the Danes: moreover, by Alfred's efforts West Saxon became the official language of England and the most important literary dialect. Again, it may be that many of these Scandinavian words were not the type to appear in literary works, though we should expect most of the legal terms in common use to appear in records. But there must have been many more in the spoken language, for words which appear first in the Middle English period have evidently been borrowed early enough to fall in with native words and undergo the same vowel and consonant development; for example, spirants in Scandinavian loan-words fall in with a preceding vowel to form diphthongs, just as they do in native words, and vowels in Scandinavian words undergo lengthening before consonant-groups under the same conditions as do vowels of native words.

Any deep and abiding linguistic influence will ultimately depend, as we have already seen, upon racial fusion, the relations between the two peoples, and their respective cultures and civilizations. As we have already noted, relations became much less hostile in the early eleventh century, and most of the Scandinavians became Christian. Any question of difference of nationality almost certainly disappeared in the common struggle against the Normans. It seems likely, too, that although there were exceptions, the invaders did not bring their own womenfolk, and the settlers therefore married English women. We need to remember here that, in spite of the hostility occasioned by the invasion, we have now to deal with two nations which were closely akin, which had a good deal in common, and this would certainly facilitate the eventual fusion of the races. Moreover, the Scandinavians, in their contacts with peoples of all types and nationalities, from Iceland and Russia in the north to Italy and Turkey in the south, had proved themselves a very adaptable people, and this adaptability would obviously be more marked in contact with people of another Germanic tribe. It may be noted here, as an example of this adaptability, that the Scandinavians seem to have made no effort to impose their language on the English, but on the contrary, as happened on the continent in Northern France, they eventually gave up their own language. We might have expected the opposite in England in the first half of the eleventh century, when they had close contact with their native country, and were constantly reinforced from there, conditions favouring the establishment of the conquerors' language, but Cnut's known fondness for England and the English, and his use of English as his official language, were apparently sufficient to ensure the final supremacy of English over Scandinavian.

As we are considering the relations between the two peoples purely from the point of view of the effect on language, we may perhaps leave out of consideration the period of hostility before the Treaty of Wedmore in 878. Articles in this treaty give us an idea of what the relations between the two peoples would be likely to be after the treaty became effective. The equality of English and Scandinavians in the eyes of the law is clearly shown: 'If a man be slain, we all estimate equally dear English and Danish'. Intercourse between the two peoples was apparently already common, for an article setting forth the conditions under which such intercourse would be permitted was also drawn up: 'We all agreed that neither bondservant nor freeman should go over to the Danish people without leave, no more than any of them to us. But if it happen that, from necessity, one of them wishes to have dealings with us, or we with them, it is to be carried out in this way; hostages are to be given as a pledge of peace, and to show that a man has a clean back' (i.e. is acting above board). It seems, therefore, that by the end of the ninth century large numbers of Scandinavians were settled in the northern and eastern parts of England on an equal footing with the English, and when the English kings began to reconquer the Danelaw – or when the Danes in this area submitted to English rule, for it may have been arranged peacefully – they accepted this mixture of population and attempted to devise regulations for the mingling of the two races to continue on peaceful lines. That the Scandinavians were co-operative is seen from an entry in the Chronicle (annal 924) referring to Alfred's son, Edward: 'and then was he chosen father and lord by the King of the Scots, with all his people, and by Regnald, and the son of Eadulf, and all that dwell in Northumbria, both English and Danish, both Northmen and others'. But we also see from the last two phrases that the Scandinavians were still considered alien, of another race. Further evidence for the acceptance of Scandinavians, and Scandinavian customs, on at least an equal footing, is provided in the annal for 959, where we are told that the Northumbrian king was blamed because he loved foreign tastes too much and allowed heathen customs to be too quickly and firmly established in the country, and enticed vicious foreigners to come to the land, and a letter surviving from the Old English period censures the English for adopting Danish customs and Danish dress and forsaking English ways.[2] Many of the Scandinavians also became Christian, as is shown by the frequent appearance of Scandinavian names in lists of monks and abbots, and among those making bequests to the Church, and this would help to improve relations between the two peoples. It seems, therefore, that in England, as elsewhere, the Scandinavians quickly adapted themselves to a new way of life, and, as Green puts it, 'when the wild burst of the storm was over, land, people, government reappeared unchanged. England still remained England: the conquerors sank quietly into the mass of those around them; and Woden yielded without a struggle to Christ. . . . The life of these northern folk was in the main the life of the earlier Englishmen. Their customs, their religion, their social order were the same; they were in fact kinsmen bringing back to an England that had forgotten its origins the barbaric England of its pirate forefathers. Nowhere over Europe was the fight so fierce, because nowhere else were the combatants men of one blood and one speech. But just for this reason the fusion of the northmen with their foes was nowhere so peaceful and so complete'.[3]

And so, after the early years of warfare, we have to do with a peaceful settlement by the Scandinavians, inter-marriage between the two races, and the gradual adoption of the English way of life. Such a fusion is to be seen, of course, in other spheres than that of language; we may

trace it in manorial organization, in legal procedure, in local government, but with these we are not concerned here. Not only do we find
the two peoples living side by side, but with marriages taking place
between the two races – John of Wallingford tells how the Danes
attracted the English women because they combed their hair and
washed weekly, and evidence for the marriages themselves is provided
by the number of Scandinavian personal names in early charters, wills,
and other documents – bilingualism would be greatly increased, at first
between the parents, and even more so among the children. Even with
the two languages existing quite distinctly side by side, as they would so
long as the Danes were considered as foreigners by the English, we
should find a Dane occasionally using an English word, an Englishman
using Danish words, and later, when the two races came to have a
working knowledge of each other's language, the Dane would need
Danish words to help out his English, and Danish words would, in
many cases, come to be used alongside or instead of English words. It
would be during this period that fresh loan-words would be introduced
in considerable numbers, so that, when Danish finally ceased to be
spoken here, it would at any rate leave traces of its existence in an
English rich in Scandinavian words. Conditions would probably be
much the same then as are found today in areas, such as in the United
States, where large-scale immigration has taken place; in isolated groups
the Danes would probably soon adopt English, but where large communities were established Danish would remain for some time the
usual language. Probably bilingualism lasted in some areas until the
twelfth century, and in some parts of Scotland a type of Norse was
spoken as late as the seventeenth century.[4]
     The fusion of the races would be greatly assisted by the similarity
between the two languages, particularly in the north, where the Scandinavian influence was strongest, for Anglian resembled the Scandinavian
languages in some points where West Saxon, the official language established by King Alfred, showed divergence. We know from Ohthere's
account of his voyage that the Angles had originally lived in lands
adjacent to the Scandinavian areas. There were differences in grammar,
and differences in some sound developments, but there was a good deal
of the common Germanic vocabulary in both languages, and in many
cases corresponding words in the two languages were almost identical
– we can think of many examples among words in frequent use, such
as *folk, man, wife, father, mother, brother, sister, ground, land, town, tree,
house, room, life, sorrow, summer, winter, full, wise, better, best, mine, thine,
will, can, come, bring, hear, meet, see, set, sit, stand, think, over, under,* and
many others – so that the speakers would easily understand one another,

more easily perhaps than a Yorkshire farmer and a Somerset farmer would today, and words introduced from one language into the other would have little of the appearance or sound of foreign words. The similarity is not so obvious today, after the two languages have developed in isolation for a thousand years, and, moreover, been subject to very different influences, English having been influenced by Romance languages, particularly French, and Danish by Low German, yet even now there are many similarities, though not so many as there were in the Viking Age. In some cases in which the word is recorded for the first time in Middle English we cannot be sure whether its origin is English or Scandinavian, and we should be uncertain whether many words now in common use are English or Scandinavian in origin if we had no records from the Old English period. Contemporary evidence exists for the similarity of the spoken language; in *Gunnlaugssaga Ormstungu* we are told that in the time of William the Conqueror the same language was spoken in England as in Norway and Denmark, but this was not quite true, as is proved by the story told of the Marshal of Norway after the Battle of Stamford Bridge, when a Yorkshire carter from whom he tried to obtain a coat as disguise recognized him as a Scandinavian by his speech. Yet the two could at least understand each other, and there is no doubt that the languages were in many respects very similar. There is an inscription in the church at Aldboro' (Yorks.) which shows how the two languages could easily be used side by side. It reads, '*Ulf hēt ārǣran cyrice for hānum ond Gunware sāule*', and the intrusion of the Scandinavian pronoun *hānum* in a sentence otherwise English, and the un-Anglicized form of the Scandinavian name in an English community, shows how little distinction was made between the two languages. But there were, as we shall see later in the more detailed examination which follows, forms where, although there was an obvious similarity, there were also recognizable differences in vowels or consonants, and in these cases modification took place in both directions, sometimes a Scandinavian vowel or consonant being used for the Old English equivalent, and sometimes the reverse, as when Middle English has *swein*, with OE *swān* influenced by ON *sveinn*, or *shift*, with ON *skipta* influenced by the sound of the Old English initial consonant combination, or ON *bruðlaup* partly modified to *brydlop*. NE *get* may be directly from ON *geta*, as Old English uses the cognate verb only in compounded forms, and in any case OE *ʒietan* would have yielded *yet*, not *get*. But it is not impossible that an Anglian dialect may have had the word in its simple form, and with a velar stop in the initial position. Similarly, OE *ʒiefan* would have yielded *yive*, so here we may have modification by ON *gefa*. However, as will be noted in the mention of dialectal variants below, the evidence for the pronunciation of these consonants in Old English and the Scandinavian languages is not clear.

One point, however, does need to be kept in mind in discussing borrowing from these Scandinavian languages. The written records of these languages are all considerably later than the period during which they influenced the English language, and developments must have taken place in the intervening two or three hundred years, so that, strictly speaking, we ought to use the Primitive Scandinavian forms when considering the influence, especially if phonological questions are likely to arise. Another point also arises: the A. S. Chronicle speaks almost invariably of Danes, but it is known that Norwegians were also concerned in the raids, and settled in different areas from those occupied by the Danes. In the later period the languages of the two races diverged, Danish belonging to the East Scandinavian group and Norwegian to the West Scandinavian group, but it is by no means certain that there was a great deal of difference in the two dialects in the early Viking period. Much work has been done on the problem of linguistic differences as revealed in the loan-words adopted and there is no general agreement, though most do agree that some words were Danish, some Norwegian. It is very difficult to be certain in many cases, though there are one or two phonological differences which help, but their consideration lies beyond the scope of this present work.

When two similar languages are spoken side by side in a country minor modifications, to remove what are considered to be unimportant differences, are more likely to be made than if the languages were very different. We have already seen that in some cases where there were slight differences in vowel or consonant development from the parent language, modifications were made. This was one way of dealing with variant forms, but in some cases the variants were not modified, and a new common form created, and as a result we have pairs of words, sometimes with a divergence of meaning, in the modern period. Among the double forms which once existed, and are still used in Standard English, are the following, the native form being placed first in each case: *whole, hale; no, nay; shirt, skirt; from, fro; -less, loose*. An interesting set of three related forms has arisen through the introduction of a Scandinavian variant. OE *rīsan* gave NE *rise;* from the preterite of this verb a new weak causative verb had been formed, which gave OE *rǣran*, NE *rear*. Then the ON *reisa*, cognate with OE *rīsan*, was adopted, to give NE *raise*. Other examples, where both have not survived into the modern period, include *eʒe, aʒe; dǣlan, deila; ǣʒ, egg; ǣ, laʒu; trēowe, trigg*. The natural result of the existence of such pairs would be a struggle between the native and foreign forms, and not often did the two manage to survive side by side.

For example, in the case of *eʒe* and *aʒe*, both forms are found in Orm (c. 1200), but within about a century the Scandinavian word is appearing more and more frequently, and finally the English form disappears. The same thing happened in the case of *ǣʒ* and *egg*, and the struggle going on between such pairs, and the consequent conflict in the minds of the people, is well shown by the story told by Caxton:

'. . . And certaynly it was wreton in suche wyse that it was more lyke to dutche than englysshe I coude not reduce ne brynge it to be vnderstonden / And certaynly our langage now vsed varyeth ferre from that. whiche was vsed and spoken whan I was borne / For we englysshe men / ben borne vnder the domynacyon of the mone. whiche is neuer stedfaste / but euer wauerynge / wexynge one season / and waneth & dyscreaseth another season / And that comyn englysshe that is spoken in one shyre varyeth from a nother. In so moche that in my dayes happened that certayn marchauntes were in a shippe in tamyse for to haue sayled ouer the see into ʒelande / and for lacke of wynde thei taryed atte forlond. and wente to lande for to refreshe them And one of theym named sheffelde a mercer cam in to an hows and axed for mete. and specyally he axyd after eggys And the good wyf answerde, that she coude speke no frenshe. And the merchaunt was angry. for he also coulde speke no frenshe. but wold haue hadde egges / and she vnderstode hym not / And thenne at laste a nother sayd that he wolde haue eyren / then the good wyf sayd that she vnderstod hym wel / Loo what sholde a man in thyse dayes now wryte. egges or eyren / certaynly it is harde to playse euery man / by cause of dyuersite & chaunge of langage.'[5]

In some cases the native word has proved victorious so far as the standard language is concerned, but the Scandinavian word has been preserved in regional dialects, as in *trigg*, against Standard English *true*, *loup*, *laup* against *leap*, *nowt* against *neat* (animal – cf. *neat's foot oil*), and *garth* against *yard*. Pairs with a velar stop alternating with an alveolar fricative are often quoted, as *kirk*, *church; kist*, *chest; kirn*, *churn; brig*, *bridge;* and *rig* (back), *ridge;* but it is by no means certain that this is Scandinavian influence, for we have no certain information on the pronunciation of the consonant in the Scandinavian languages, and it may be that Anglian retained the stop pronunciation in these cases.

The usual result, however, was for one or other of the forms to be ousted completely, and it is interesting to note that in the majority of cases the native form has survived. Thus, to take just a few examples of such pairs, we use *goat*, not *gayt*, *gray*, not *gra*, *leap*, not *loup*, *yarn*, not *garn, bench,* not *benk,* and *worse,* not *werre;* but we also use *window* (ON *vindauga*), not *eyethril* (OE *ēaȝþyrel,* lit. eye-hole), *egg,* not *ey, weak* (ON *veikr*), not *woak* (OE *wāc*), and *sister* (ON *systir*) not *swester* (OE *swooster*), *wrong* (ON *wrangr*), not *unright* (OE *unriht*), *birth,* not *birde* (OE *ȝebyrd*), *swain,* not *swone* (OE *swān*), *boon* (ON *bōn*), not *been* (OE *bēn*), *loan* (ON *lān*), not *lean* (OE *lǣn*), though the last-named is not quite certain, as there was also a rare OE *lān,* but Scandinavian influence is not unlikely. Sometimes two words, very different in form but identical in meaning, clashed in this way, and usually one of them disappeared; for example OE *niman* – to take, was replaced by ON *taka;* OE *weorþan,* to throw, gave way to ON *kasta,* only for the latter to be at least partly superseded by another native verb, to throw (OE *þrāwan*). Old English had two words for *cut, snīþan* and *ceorfan;* the latter remains, in a special sense, as 'carve', but the general sense is now expressed by *cut,* which appears first in Middle English and, from its form, may be developed from a lost Scandinavian form. Similarly, Old English had several words to express *anger,* including *torn, grama,* and *ierre,* but all gave way to our modern word, from ON *angr.* A form of OE *wolcen* survives in the archaic *welkin,* but the common word, *sky,* is from ON *skȳ* (cognate with OE *scēo* – cloud); we may note here how the native word *heofen* came to have a religious significance, and a limited use in poetry, and the Scandinavian loan-word was used as the general term. *Rind,* from the OE *rīnd,* is now less general in meaning than *bark,* and where we should now say *feather* (OE *feþer*) for both *wing* and *feather,* the admission of ON *vengja* has allowed us to differentiate.

In a few cases Old English and Scandinavian had words identical in form, or developed from the same Germanic root, but different in meaning. OE *drēam* had the sense of 'joy', and our modern meaning of *dream* is developed from that of ON *draumr.* OE *brēad* meant 'a crumb, fragment'; the Scandinavian word had the sense of NE *bread,* and the meaning of the latter may have been influenced by the Scandinavian meaning. OE *blōma* meant 'a mass of molten metal', and NE *bloom* is still in use with that sense in the metallurgical trade, but the word corresponding to the sense of NE *bloom* (flower) in Old English was *blōstma* (NE *blossom*). The sense of the modern word has been influenced by ON *blōmi.* In Old English *holm,* as we have seen already, was used with the meaning of sea, perhaps with the sense of the rising of the waves, and Scandinavian has influenced the modern meaning of 'island'.

There is an interesting example of modification of both sound and meaning. OE *ȝiefu* – gift, would have yielded NE *yive.* OE *gift* – the price paid for a wife (and plural – marriage) would have developed to *yift.* NE *gift* owes its meaning, and perhaps the initial consonant as a velar stop, to Scandinavian *gipt*. OE *dwellan*, *dwelian* – to lead astray, was apparently influenced in meaning by ON *dvelja* – to dwell, tarry, abide, and so our modern word apparently owes its meaning to Scandinavian influence.

Occasionally the Scandinavian languages had a word which was either unrecorded in Old English, or had been lost. Old English had *dēaþ* – death, *dēad* – dead, and *dīedan* (< *dauþjan*) – to put to death, but apparently had no intransitive verb 'to die' from this stem, having to rely on two unrelated words, *steorfan* and *sweltan*, the first of which has survived with a modified meaning, and the second has been lost. ON *deyja* – to die was nearer to the first group in Old English, and so was accepted, to give NE *die*. Similarly Old English had *sittan* – to sit, *sēt* – ambush, *setl* (NE *settle* – a seat), and *ʒeset* – seat, but NE *seat* shows at any rate in its meaning the influence of ON *sǣti* – seat, and may indeed be a Scandinavian loan-word.

One important effect of the existence of variant forms side by side has been the possibility of making finer distinctions in meaning; for example, the adoption of ON *skinn* has enabled us to differentiate between *skin* and *hide*, and we have already seen the distinction made between *rise*, *raise*, and *rear*. Another example has not survived to our own times, but the adoption of ON *lagu* allowed that word to be used for secular *law*, while the native word, OE *ǣ(w)*, was reserved for divine and ecclesiastical law, and for a few special uses.

Another influence of Scandinavian may be seen in the way in which native words which were becoming obsolete have been strengthened. The NED says *dale* 'appears to have been reinforced from Norse, for it is in the North that the word is a living geographical name', and the northern survival of *bairn* is also probably due to Scandinavian influence.

With such a similarity between the language as we have just seen in common forms with practically no difference, and variant forms with but little difference, it is obviously very difficult to assess the influence of one language on the other, for examples such as we have seen above, of modification in sound or sense, are not numerous, and it is not always easy to be sure of the origin of a word recorded in Scandinavian but not in Old English, and occurring in our language for the first time in Middle English. We need to be very careful before accepting a word as a loan from Scandinavian. The tendency might be to ascribe every Germanic word found in Middle English, but not recorded in Old English, to Scandinavian influence, but this is far from being true. Hundreds of words appear in our literature for the first time in Middle English, but very many of these, whether native or Scandinavian, must have been in common use for centuries before. The fact that a word has not been recorded in Old English is no proof that it did not exist, for much of Old English literature has been lost, many words would not appear in literature, and colloquial language is rarely identical with the literary language. Therefore, unless the form of a word, or its meaning, suggests a Scandinavian origin, we should be very careful not to accept it too easily as a Scandinavian loan-word. We must also remember that the northern dialects, in the early mediaeval period, were in many respects very like Scandinavian, and words may therefore be ascribed to Scandinavian influence which really owe their form to these northern dialects, but were not actually recorded there. On the other hand, the colloquial language, so little represented in literature, would be most influenced by Scandinavian, and it is almost certain that most of the words which appear for the first time in literary works in Middle English and may be ascribed to Scandinavian sources were first borrowed in the Old English period. We have very little material from the east midlands or the north for the tenth, eleventh, and twelfth centuries, and in any case many of the words borrowed were not the kind to find their way into literature, so it is likely that the language actually in use contained far more Scandinavian words than may be inferred from a study of the literary remains. We may compare here the modern dialects of those areas, which still retain in regular use many words of Scandi-navian origin not found in the standard language. Although, therefore, we should not accept words as Scandinavian too easily, yet when a word which is recorded for the first time in Middle English is not found in Old English, but has a satisfactory Scandinavian cognate, and occurs in Middle English in an area where Scandinavian influence is known to have been strong, there is at least a strong probability that it may be a loan. Only the careful application of certain phonological tests can confirm the probability.

We come now to an examination of the cultures of the two peoples, in order to see whether or not we have, as in the case of the Romans and the Celts, a dominant and a submerged race, one people much more advanced than the other from a cultural point of view, with ideas worthy of respect and adoption. We shall see that the Scandinavian peoples were not able to make any marked contribution to English culture, and this is really what we should expect. We may take it for granted that at about the middle of the fifth century the Angles and Saxons on the continent had been at very much the same stage of culture and civilization as the Danes and Norwegians, perhaps a little more advanced, for the Scandinavian peoples, living further north, were more remote from the influence of Roman civilization. We have no reason to suppose that the Scandinavians were brought into contact with any new civilizing experience between the fifth and the ninth centuries, whereas the English had been in direct contact with Roman civilization, first through the Britons, and later through the introduction of Christianity. We may, therefore, be fairly certain that the culture and civilization of the invaders was very similar to that of the English, as they had sprung recently from a common stock, that it was not at any rate superior to that of the English, and that it was probably somewhat inferior. There were, however, certain aspects in which they surpassed the English; they were, by reason of the fact that they had not become either a peaceful or an agricultural people, as had the English after the Settlement, superior in the arts of war and shipbuilding, as we have seen from the fact that words connected with these spheres of life were borrowed in the early period, and from remains which have been discovered it has been claimed that they were also more advanced in certain types of handicraft. To the culture and learning absorbed by the English as a result of their conversion to Christianity and later contact with Roman civilization and scholarship the Scandinavians had no pretensions. We may expect, therefore, that apart from the early loans, already noticed, connected with warfare and the sea, we shall find no large groups of words connected with particular aspects of life and knowledge, as we did in the case of Latin influence, because there were no broad, general aspects of culture which the English could adopt from the Scandinavians. There was, however, one aspect of Scandinavian character which had an effect, powerful at the time, if not permanent, on the English language; we see many examples in their literature of the fondness of these Scandinavian people for litigation and for legal procedure generally, and there are quite a number of words connected with law and administration which are probably borrowed from Scandinavian. These have been examined by Steenstrup, and he has been able to show, from the evidence of vocabulary, by the number of new legal terms, probably of Scandinavian origin, which appear at this time, that the Scandinavians modified the legal system, and also the system of local government, of the English, so that, as Jespersen says, basing his remarks on a summary of the results of Steenstrup's investigations, 'The Scandinavian settlers reorganized the administration of the realm and based it on a uniform and equable division of the country; taxes were imposed and collected after the Scandinavian pattern; instead of the lenient criminal law of former times, a virile and powerful law was introduced which was better capable of intimidating fierce and violent natures. More stress was laid on personal honour, as when a sharp line was drawn between stealthy or clandestine crimes and open crimes attributable to obstinacy or vindictiveness. Commerce, too, was regulated so as to secure trade'.[6] We see from this how the investigation of vocabulary may throw light on social history. These legal terms, and the periods in which they were borrowed, have already been discussed. It is interesting to note that, if there had been no Norman Conquest to wipe out Scandinavian influence, our legal vocabulary would probably have consisted largely of Scandinavian words, and not French words, as it does today.

Apart, then, from these three classes of loan-words, those connected with warfare, the sea, and law and administration, most of the loans are words used in everyday life by peoples of the same cultural standard, there being no groups at all pointing to cultural superiority on the part of the Scandinavians. There is little, too, in the character of the words adopted to suggest that the Scandinavians were of a higher social standard than the English with whom they mixed, the words being homely terms for the objects and actions of everyday life, and so very different from the words introduced later by an aristocratic Norman ruling-class. They are, too, typically Germanic words, being short, often monosyllabic, and therefore agreeing well with the character of the vocabulary into which they were introduced. As Jespersen has said, 'Scandinavian words will crop up together with the Anglo-Saxon ones in any conversation on the thousand nothings of daily life or on the five or six things of paramount importance to high and low alike. An Englishman cannot *thrive* or be *ill* or *die* without Scandinavian words; they are to the language what *bread* and *eggs* are to the daily fare'.[7]

We may now consider some of these loans, remembering what has been said about the difficulty of being certain of Scandinavian origin. The lists which follow are merely representative, and do not pretend at inclusion of even all the words about which there is no reasonable doubt, for there are perhaps at least a thousand of these. As the Scandinavian influence is reflected chiefly in the common affairs of life, we may perhaps begin with nouns, the words which express everyday objects and ideas; among these we find, using now the modern form rather than the Old or Middle English form in which it is first recorded, *anger, awe, band, bank, billow, birth, bloom, bole* (tree), *boon, brink, bull, calf* (of leg), *crook, down* (feathers), *dregs, egg, fellow, gate* (*gait*), *girth, hank, haven, husband, husting, keel, kid, knife, law, leg, ling, link, loan, loft, mire, outlaw, race, root, scab, scale, scrap, seat, sister, skill, skin, skirt, skull, sky, slaughter, stack, steak, swain, tarn, window, wing.* The adjectives are equally diverse in character, and include *awkward, flat, happy, ill, loose, low, meek, muggy, odd, rotten, rugged, same, scant, seemly, tight, ugly, weak, wrong.* The list of verbs is a very long one, covering all the common actions of everyday life; included among them we find *bask, batten, call, cast, cow, crave, die, droop, drown, egg* (on), *gape, gasp, get, give, glitter, guess, hit, kindle, lift, lug, raise, ransack, rive, scare, scowl, scrape, scream, scrub, skulk, thrive, thrust, want*. We should expect words of this kind to be borrowed, particularly nouns and verbs, for these are words which pass easily from one language to another, but in addition to these we also find pronouns, adverbs, and even prepositions passing from Scandinavian into English. Old English was poor in pronouns, and this poverty often caused ambiguity, and when OE *hē* – he, *hēo* – she, and Anglian *hēo* (WS *hīe, hȳ*) – they, weakened to the same form in Middle English matters became worse. Scandinavian, however, had *h*-forms in the singular and *þ*-forms in the plural. It is not surprising, then, to find that eventually the native forms were confined to the singular, and, instead of the development of OE *hie, hiera, him*, we have *they, their, them*, from the Scandinavian forms, adopted for the plural. These plural forms first became established in the northern dialects; for example, the northern 'Pricke of Conscience' has *þai, þair, þam*, while the Kentish 'Aȝenbite of Inwyt', of approximately the same date, uses *hi, here/hare, ham*. The conjunction *though* is from Scandinavian, for OE *þēah* could not have developed to our modern form. *Aloft* and *athwart* are adverbs adopted from Scandinavian. The use of *at* with the infinitive, surviving still in *ado*, and of *till*, which does occur in Old English, in *Cædmon's Hymn*, but is rare until the Middle English period, is also probably due to Scandinavian influence. *Both* is probably to be explained as the result of Scandinavian influence, as is also *same*, for Old English used *self* or *ilca*, though *swa sāme* – similarly, is found, and *same* as an adjective is recorded first with its present meaning in the *Ormulum*, which contains many Scandinavian words. Of such words Jespersen says: 'It is precisely the most indispensable elements of the language that have undergone the strongest Scandinavian influence, and this is raised into certainty when we discover that a certain number of those grammatical words, the small coin of language, which Chinese grammarians term "empty words", and which are nowhere else transferred from one language to another, have been taken over from Danish into English'.[8] In this Jespersen sees not a failure of one test for borrowing, cultural superiority, but a more intimate fusion of two closely-related peoples.

As the two languages were very similar in structure, few changes were needed when words were taken over into English. At the time the words were being adopted analogical influence was powerful in Old English, and much levelling was taking place, particularly in the nouns, which were tending to simplify the inflexions. Some Scandinavian nouns had -*r* as the inflexion of the nominative singular, and this was dropped, on the analogy of the OE masculine a-stem nouns, but there is otherwise little to note about the forms of Scandinavian nouns and adjectives as they were adopted in Old English. Most of the Scandinavian verbs passed into the weak conjugation in Old English – ON *taka* is a notable exception – just as the French verbs were to do later. Scandinavian, alone among the Germanic languages, had a passive conjugation formed by the addition to the verb of the pronoun *sik* as a suffix, and English has retained a few of these, such as *bask* and *busk*, though the passive sense was lost.

The main differences between English and Scandinavian were the inflexional endings of nouns, adjectives, and verbs, for in many cases, allowing for one or two differences in phonological development between the languages, the stem-forms were identical, or nearly so. It is not surprising, therefore, to find that it was these inflexions which were first discarded, as a troublesome barrier between the two races, and in the northern and midland areas, where Scandinavian influence was strongest, the weakening of inflexions, which is generally regarded as a characteristic of Middle English, was well established before the end of the Old English period, and that part of the country carried out these developments as much as two hundred years earlier than the more conservative south and west, where Scandinavian influences were hardly felt. In the northern dialects the earlier forms of the definite article, which had varied for gender, number, and case, had been simplified to a common form *the* by the middle of the eleventh century. This did not take place in midland dialects until a century later, and not until about the end of the thirteenth century in the south. It is not unreasonable, therefore, to connect this weakening of inflexions with the existence of a bilingual population in the areas most affected by Scandinavian influence, with the Danes satisfied merely to make themselves understood, and not concerned with all the finer points of inflexion so long as what they had to say could be grasped by the English, and with the English later adopting some of these simplified forms.

What has just been noted in connexion with inflexion holds good generally, for in the Middle English period we have evidence that the dialects of the north, north-west, and the north-east midlands show many effects of Scandinavian influence, in vocabulary, phonology, accidence, and syntax, but the southern and south-western districts are hardly affected, and London, which was outside the sphere of sustained Scandinavian influence, would therefore not be much affected. This explains why our standard language, developed in the fifteenth century from the dialect of the London area, shows much less of the effect of Scandinavian influence than do the regional dialects of the areas in

which the Scandinavians settled. Although we are concerned here only
with the vocabulary of the standard language it would be misleading to
ignore the extent of the Scandinavian influence in regional dialects.
There are many examples of Scandinavian words in the ballads, and for
the northern dialects material was collected by Wall in his paper *A contribution towards the study of the Scandinavian Element in the English
Dialects* (Anglia xx). To anyone familiar with northern, north-western,
north-midland and east-midland dialects Scandinavian influence will
be very obvious. Wright, in editing the *English Dialect Dictionary*,
pointed out that there are thousands of words of Scandinavian origin
in use in the dialects of the north and east, including over eleven hundred
words beginning with *sc-* or *sk-* not common to the dialects and the
standard language, and, if the survey of regional dialects now proposed
is eventually carried out, no doubt the number of authenticated Scandinavian words will be very great indeed. Among words relating to the
simple things of everyday life we find, taking a representative sample
only, such forms as *addle* – to earn, *arr* – a scar (cf. *pock-arred* – pock-
marked), *claggy* – heavy with clay, *dag* (a variant of *dew*) – to drizzle,
flit – to move (especially to move house), *gain* – short, direct, *gar* – to
make, *glegg* – clear-sighted, *haver* – oat (cf. *havercake*), *hoast* – cough
(and *hoarse*), *keek* – to peep, *ket* – carrion, *lake* – to play, *lathe* – barn,
mug(gy) – of hot, damp weather, *neave* – fist, *red up* – to tidy, *sile* – to
strain, *spink* – chaffinch, *stor(e)* – great, *tang* – sting, *trigg* – true, and
war – worse (cf. ME *werre*, in Chaucer). Many of these dialect words
have been used by writers to achieve local colour, or an archaic effect,
and so we find a few have moved across from the dialects to the standard
language; *batten, beck, billow, doze, gill* (or *ghyll*) and *nag* were probably
regional dialect words originally, and in this way passed over to the
standard language.

So far as the actual number of words borrowed is concerned, Skeat's
Etymological Dictionary lists about five hundred, but there are in the
standard language nearly a thousand words denoting objects, actions,
and ideas connected with everyday life about whose origin there is not
much doubt, and there are probably as many more where a Scandinavian
origin is at least possible. This is far from a true picture of the real
influence exerted, for there were a great number of words in common
use in Middle English, and therefore presumably in Old English, which
have failed to survive. But of those words which have survived Professor
Wrenn has rightly said: 'Looking at all the foregoing Norse words and
comparing those of Latin origin, one is struck, for the most part, with
the completeness with which they have become one with the language
and the way they have exactly the same kind of feeling and connotation

G

as words of purely Anglo-Saxon origin. Indeed these Norse loans do not really lessen the "homogeneousness" of the language; it is Latin, and to a less extent French, of the greater sources of linguistic borrowing, that do this for us'.[9]

More than once mention has been made of the difficulties encountered in differentiation between native and Scandinavian words. Bjorkmann, who has confined himself almost entirely to the phonological side of the question of Scandinavian loan-words in ME, maintains that no tests are more reliable than phonetic tests. He says: 'Although the vocabularies of the two languages were to a very great extent identical, there must of course have been a considerable number of words peculiar originally to one or the other of the languages in question, but subsequently adopted by one language from the other. But we shall never be able to make out wholly in what points the vocabulary of one language differed from that of the other, and consequently the results drawn from presumed differences of vocabulary must be regarded as very uncertain'.[10] The phonological tests are beyond the scope of this work, for they are not easy for the layman to apply.

Finally, we may perhaps note how Jespersen has summed up the difficulties of the problem: 'As for the language, it should be borne in mind that the tongue spoken by the Danes was so nearly akin with the native dialects that the two peoples could understand one another without much difficulty. But it was just such circumstances which made it natural that many *nuances* of grammar should be sacrificed, the intelligibility of either tongue coming to depend on its mere vocabulary. It is in harmony with this view that the wearing away and levelling of grammatical forms in the regions in which the Danes chiefly settled was a couple of centuries in advance of the same process in the more southern parts of the country. A fully satisfactory solution of the question of the mutual relations of North English and Scandinavian at that time must be regarded as hopeless on account of the small number, and generally inadequate character, of linguistic records; and, unless some fresh sources become accessible to us, we shall probably never learn clearly and unequivocally which points of correspondence in the two languages are attributable to primitive affinities, which others to loans from one language to the other, or, finally, how much may be due to independent parallel development in two areas which offered such striking analogies in so many essential particulars. But, as I hold, any linguistic change should primarily be explained on the basis of the language itself, while analogies from other languages may serve as illustrations and help to show what in the development of a language is due to psychological causes of a universal character, and what is, on the other hand, to be considered the effect of the idiosyncrasies of the particular idiom'.[11]

We turn now to a less general part of vocabulary, names of people and places. Scandinavian personal-names, or names containing a Scandinavian element, are found in the mediæval records, in late Old English and Middle English wills, charters and other documents of areas in which Scandinavian settlements were made. Bjorkmann has collected about two hundred, and does not claim that the list is complete.[12] Names surviving in the modern period with the suffix -son, such as Atkinson, Gibson, Jackson, Johnson, Robinson, Robson, Stevenson, Thompson, Watson, Wilkinson, Wilson, and others, all still very common in the northern counties, show, especially where a northern source can be verified, a Scandinavian formation, of which the English equivalent is the type with -ing, as, for example, Browning, Fielding, and, with transference to place-names, Reading, Worthing, and Birmingham.

The question of Scandinavian influence on the language through the adoption of Scandinavian names for natural local phenomena and their inclusion in place-names is far too big a subject to be treated adequately here, where reasons of space make it possible to mention only the essential features, and those who are interested are referred, for greater detail, to the article by Professor Ekwall in the introductory volume of the publications of the English Place-Name Society, and to the individual volumes dealing with the counties in which Scandinavian settlements were made. It has been estimated that well over a thousand places in England have Scandinavian names, and when the English Place-Name Society completes its survey that number will almost certainly have been substantially increased. Most of these names are to be found in the area formerly known as the Danelaw, as might be expected, and while they occur most frequently in Yorkshire and Lincolnshire they are also to be found plentifully scattered in Cumberland, Westmorland, Lancashire, and East Anglia, particularly in Norfolk. They may be divided roughly into two groups, those with elements indicating a Scandinavian settlement, and those containing an element which is a Scandinavian name for some natural feature, such as mountain, stream, or valley. First we may take the suffix -by, indicating a town or settlement (O Dan. by, ON bær, býr) such as Derby, Grimsby, Rugby, Selby, Whitby, and what we may call the perfect example, from our point of view, Normanby – the town of the Northmen; this may mean Northmen generally, or perhaps Norwegians, and as there are seven places so named in the eastern half of England, where settlements were essentially Danish, they may indicate Norwegian settlements in Danish territory. The West Riding of Yorkshire has many Norwegian elements,

probably because the Norwegians made their way east through the passes
of the Pennines, and *Denby Dale* and *Denaby* may perhaps indicate
Danish settlements in Norwegian country. There are about six hundred
places so far identified with this suffix. This element is also seen in the
code of laws drawn up for the regulation of life in these settlements, the
by-laws, or town-laws, a term now used in all administrative districts.
Next we may take *-thorp*, such as *Alverthorpe, Bishopsthorpe, Gawthorpe,
Ravensthorpe, Scunthorpe*, of which more than three hundred examples
have been identified. There was a similar native word, OE *þorp* –
village, and some forms in *-thorpe* may be English, but such forms are
more frequent in the Danelaw than elsewhere, and there Scandinavian
influence may be inferred. In the second group we find that almost as
numerous are place-names containing *-thwaite* (from ON *þveit* – clearing, meadow), such as *Bassenthwaite, Slaithwaite*. About a hundred
places have been identified containing the element *-toft* (ON *topt* –
homestead, piece of land), as *Altofts, Lowestoft*. Other Scandinavian
elements in common use include *beck* (ON *bekkr*), as in *Birkbeck, Trout-
beck, carr* (ON *kiarr*) – wet ground, as in *Batley Carr, force* (ON *fors*), as
in *High Force*, gill (or *ghyll*) (ON *geil* – ravine), as *Scalegill, Hugill*, *rigg*,
as in *Askrigg, Lambrigg*, scale (ON *skali*), as in *Scholes, Seascale*, scarth
(ON *skarð* – cleft, mountain pass), as in *Scarcroft, Scarcliff*, garth (ON
garðr), as in *Applegarth*, and among other elements found in place-names
Professor Ekwall also quotes *booth* (ON *bóþ*), as *Boothham, Boothroyd,
lathe* (ON *hlaða*), as *Lathes, Lathom*, denoting a building of some sort,
eng (*ing*) – a meadow, *fell* – mountain, hill, *breck* (ON *brekka*) – slope,
hill, as *Larbrick, Haverbrack, wath* – ford, and many others. ON *austr* –
east, is found occasionally, as in *Austwick*, but has usually been replaced
by 'east', even when the Scandinavian form was recorded in mediaeval
times. ON *karl* – freeman, is found in names such as *Carlton*, frequent
all over Scandinavian England, ON *kaupa*, in the sense of 'purchased
land' (cf. OE *cēapian*) as distinct from inherited land, in forms such as
Coupland, Copeland, ON *melr* – sandbank, sandhill, as in *Meols* and
Ingoldmells, ON *mýrr* – mire, as in *Mirfield* and *Myerscough*, and ON
saurr – mud, dirt, as in *Sowerby*.

It must be once more emphasized that in this account of place-names
there has been no more than a skimming of the surface: the justification
for this is twofold, first, in that these words are hardly part of our general
vocabulary, and secondly that, as has already been mentioned, a full
treatment is quite beyond the scope of the present work, and plentiful
material is easily available.

There remain now only the words borrowed after the end of the
Middle English period. These are not numerous, and Skeat lists only

about fifty, from all sources, both direct and indirect borrowing, and about half of these he considers to have been adopted through French.[13] Since the end of the Middle Ages contact between this country and the Scandinavian countries has not been either strong or continuous, and this accounts for our having borrowed so few words in the later period. Among these later loans we may note *batten*, *cosy*, *doze*, *eider*, *fiord*, *gauntlet* (only in the expression 'to run the gauntlet'), *geyser*, *keg*, *mælstrom*, *oaf*, *rug*, *saga*, *scrub*, *silt*, *ski*, *skit*, *skittle*, *slag*, *snag*, *troll*, and *tungsten* (lit. heavy stone). We may note also the late introduction of Norse words in special contexts, as in poetry, and works of a romantic or antiquarian nature, particularly in the nineteenth century; among such words are *norn*, *rune*, *saga*, *Valhalla*, and *Valkyrie*, rarely found outside Scandinavian contexts.

This concludes our study of the influence of Scandinavian on our language, an influence which, whether we confine ourselves to its effect on the standard language, or extend our field to cover dialects also, is perhaps the most interesting of all the foreign influences, revealing as it does the intimate fusion of two closely-related peoples and languages. It is also one of the most important, perhaps the most important, on the colloquial language, for, though Latin loan-words outnumber borrowings from Scandinavian, many of them are learned, or 'book' words, and many of the French loan-words, to be considered in detail in the next chapter, are not so much part of our everyday language as are the Scandinavian words.

CHAPTER SIX

*

THE NORMANS

The title of this chapter has been chosen deliberately, and for three reasons; in the first place it was Norman-French or Anglo-Norman which influenced English in the first period after the Conquest; secondly, although there was admittedly some influence of Central French later in the Middle English period, this influence could not have been exerted but for the conquest of England by the Normans. Finally, it seems the best way of distinguishing between the influence of French in the Middle English period and that exerted continuously since 1500, by reason of French literature and culture and the close physical relationship of the two countries.

It is impossible to understand the effect of the influence of French in the Middle English period without knowing the historical and social conditions operative at the time, the relations between conquerors and conquered, the language used by the two races, their respective standards of culture. Moreover, as we have seen, the question of dominant and submerged races, of superior and inferior cultures, is an important factor in the way one language may influence another, and so this factor must of necessity be considered in this particular case, where the effect is so obvious.

In spite of Latin, Celtic, and Scandinavian influence, the general character and vocabulary of Old English in the middle of the eleventh century was essentially what it had been five centuries before, but in 1066 came the Norman Conquest, an event which had more influence on the English language than any other from outside, important though the later influences of the Renaissance and the development of trade and the expansion of the Empire were to be.

Some French words – but very few – had been introduced into Old English before the Conquest, particularly in the time of Edward the Confessor, and probably more were in use than have been recorded, but we may perhaps date the beginning of the real influence of French from the time of the Conquest.

The Norman Conquest brought England into close contact with France at a time when France was about to enter on one of her most creative and glorious periods. Many of the Normans who settled in England were themselves men of great intellectual capacity, energetic,

purposeful, and wise administrators, and therefore capable of introducing into this country the best of French culture in its many and varied
aspects. We shall, therefore, expect to find French culture exercising a
profound influence on many aspects of English life.

There is an important difference between the influence now to be
examined and the earlier foreign influences. The native language was
not completely driven out, leaving little impression on the language of
the conquerors, as had happened when the Angles and Saxons conquered the Britons, nor modified by a related language, as in the case of
the Scandinavian invasion, but instead a second language was established
in the country, in use side by side with the native language. The comparison may be carried further; Scandinavian first came into, and
influenced chiefly, the north and north-east, whereas French was most
influential in the south and south-east, a fact which became of increasing
importance as a standard English language gradually developed in the
fifteenth and sixteenth centuries. Scandinavian modified the existing
language through related words and constructions, but French
introduced entirely new words. Scandinavian made its way into the
everyday speech of the people, whereas, although many French words
eventually became part of our everyday speech, and can hardly be
recognized today as foreign loan-words, the French element was in
the main composed of words reflecting a high state of culture, and
influenced at first chiefly the language of the upper classes. Or we may
look at the question from another angle: English had held its ground
easily against the competition of the native Celtic of the subject race;
it had had little competition from Latin, as a spoken language; it had
been but little affected by the closely-related Scandinavian, the language
of a conquering people, probably because the conquest did not last long
and was closely followed by another conquest, and also because the
peoples and languages were closely related. But now we find English
facing the competition of an entirely different language, and that the
language of a conquering people who were able to maintain their
position as distinctly foreign rulers for a comparatively long period.

The Norman Conquest was a thorough subjugation of the whole
country, carried out by a people of superior culture, who were in deed
as well as in name the rulers of the country, imposing their own ideas
of government and law, and keeping to themselves all the important
positions in Church and State. Moreover, they made little effort to
acquire the language of the country they had conquered, but merely
continued to use their own language for all purposes, private and official,
and expected the English with whom they had dealings to learn to use
it. Finally, they kept up a close contact with their old home, and brought

over large reinforcements from time to time, which tended to strengthen
the position of their own language. We may, then, expect that the
effect will be different from that of earlier influences.

One recent writer on the history of the English language has described
this effect as 'shattering'. In more sober language we may say that
English, which before the Conquest had been the official language of
the country, used by all classes of people, and in which an important
literature had been written, became merely the language of a subject
lower class. In addition, the knowledge of French gave access to a rich
literature. For nearly three centuries much of the literature written in
England was written in French, translated from French, or strongly
influenced by French models, and so it is not strange that the literary
language was enriched by many French words, and these gradually
made their way into familiar speech, so that today a large part of our
vocabulary consists of words introduced from French in the four
centuries following the Conquest. The influence which French exerted
on our language is seen in all aspects of life, social, political, and religious,
and hardly any walk of life was unaffected by it. Had the Conquest not
taken place it may be that English would have developed along entirely
different lines, keeping in the main its Germanic characteristics, particularly as regards vocabulary, much as the German and Scandinavian
languages, particularly Icelandic, have done, and therefore lacking the
tremendous number of Romance words which are now an accepted
part of our language. All this is, of course, a question of hypothesis, for
it is impossible to say what would have been the relationships between
this country and France if there had been no Norman Conquest, but
one thing we can be sure about, as things have actually turned out, and
that is the effect of the Conquest on the development of our vocabulary,
which underwent a complete change of character, and, indeed, on the
language in general, for French influence is to be seen also in grammar
and syntax, though that lies outside the scope of this present work.

Let us, as we have done in the case of the earlier influences, attempt
to see just what this influence was, how it was exerted, the characteristics
of the people introducing the influence, and their relationship with the
English, so that we may form some idea of the conditions under which
the English language was spoken and developed during the four
hundred years following the Conquest. We shall see that this period
can be conveniently divided into two, separated about 1204, when
Normandy was lost, French being predominant in the first period, and
English gradually regaining its old position in the second period. The
history of modern standard English really begins in the early part of the
fifteenth century, just after the English language had been restored to

its rightful place as the official and literary language of the country. Our task will be, however, much easier than when we examined the earlier Celtic, Latin, and Scandinavian influence. In the earlier periods historical documents and chronicles are scarce, and the evidence for the influence of Celtic, Latin and Scandinavian on our language has to be sought for in the actual texts. But after the Conquest documents are more plentiful, there are numerous records, some long, some mere scraps, of the Normans and their doings in this country, and we shall find that the evidence for the influence of Norman and Central French on the language in the Middle English period can be pieced together not only from the appearance of French words in literary texts but also from historical records which give us a reasonably adequate picture of the relations between the English and French languages in the centuries following the Conquest. We shall also find that, as usual, the history of the language cannot be separated from the national history.

The Normans themselves were, to a great extent, of the same general race as the English, or we may perhaps say of the English and Scandinavians, for many Danes and Norwegians had been absorbed into the English population in the two or three centuries immediately preceding the Conquest. The Normans were originally Germanic people – Northmen – who had settled on the northern shores of France, in the area still known as Normandy, in the ninth and tenth centuries, and had established a kingdom there at the same time as the Vikings were attacking England, so that by the early part of the tenth century their leader, Rollo, was acknowledged by the French king Charles the Simple as Duke of Normandy by the terms of the Treaty of St Clair-sur-Epte, and very soon the dukedom came to be even more powerful than the dominion of the King of France. We see, therefore, that in the early stages at least French words were introduced into English by men of the same race as those who were responsible for the Scandinavian influence examined in the last chapter.

Just as had happened in England, the Northmen who settled in France proved to be exceedingly adaptable, and they soon absorbed the best elements of French culture. In the process their way of life was almost transformed, for they acquired a new religion, new ideas on law and the organization of society, and generally acquired a knowledge of Latin civilization which had been denied them in their northern homes. Ideas were adopted from French military tactics, and these new ideas, joined with the traditional fearlessness, bravery, and physical skill in combat of the Germanic peoples, made them the most efficient soldiers of their day. They also adopted ideas of French law, combining them with their own already highly-developed legal system. They were converted to Christianity, and left behind proof of their new piety and devotion in the great cathedrals and churches they built. The Scandinavian language came into conflict with French here just as it came into conflict with English during the Viking invasions, and the result was the same, for they allowed their own language to give way to the language of the people they had conquered, and by the time of the Norman Conquest they had given up the Germanic language of their northern ancestors, and spoke a Romance language. Their civilization at that time was essentially French in character, their speech was French, and it was indeed as Frenchmen that they were regarded by the English, and by their fellow-countrymen who had settled in England.

There had been contact between England and France before the Norman Conquest. There was already contact in religious matters and trade in the tenth century. In 1002 Ethelred had married Emma, daughter of the Duke of Normandy, and when England was overrun by the Danes and Norwegians he sought refuge there. Their son, Edward the Confessor, was educated in France, and when he became King of England in 1042 he brought over many of his French friends, giving them the chief positions in both Church and State. Most of these were eventually turned out, but the French language spoken by Edward and his favourites must have affected in some ways the English spoken in the court. Admittedly the Norman Conquest took place very soon after his death, yet there had been a beginning of French influence before William landed, a fact not generally recognized. The words recorded are, however, so few that it is hardly necessary to separate them from the main body of French influence, and it was, therefore, not considered necessary to include them in the discussion of the language of the Old English period. *Castel* was introduced, distinguishing the nobler dwellings of the Normans on the continent from the *burȝ* of the English noble, and *tūr* – *tower*, apparently a loan through French and not direct from Latin, is recorded in the tenth century. *Market* occurs in a charter dated before the Conquest. *Capun* – capon, and *bacun* – bacon, foreshadow the host of words connected with French cooking which were to appear later, and *prūd* – proud, is also recorded before the Conquest, perhaps reflecting the haughtiness of the Norman. *Serfisc* – service, is found in the Chronicle, Annal 1070, and the early date, only four years after the Conquest, and before its effect could be expected in language, suggests that the word had been adopted in Old English before the Conquest.

It is probable that Edward had promised the throne of England to his cousin, William of Normandy, and the latter seems undoubtedly to have expected it, but the English had other ideas, and elected as their king, Harold, son of the great Earl Godwin of Wessex. Harold had evidently been considered a danger by William, for he had forced Harold to swear not to oppose him, but when Harold was elected king by the English witan he did not consider himself bound by an oath exacted under duress. William was compelled, therefore, to fight for his claim, and he gathered around him an army of men ambitious for gain. He made his position secure in France, obtained the blessing of the Pope on his enterprise, and landed in England in 1066. Harold was defeated at Hastings and William was later accepted as King, though there was hard fighting in several parts of the country before he finally established his authority over the whole country. This fighting, and the ruthlessness employed to subdue the rebellious English, had an important effect on the later history of the country. Not only was a foreign king accepted, but practically the whole of the English nobility was wiped out, so that the English ruling classes, and all that they stood for, were completely replaced by a foreign autocracy. Roger of Wendover says in his chronicle that hardly a single English noble remained alive: in 1072 only one of the twelve Earls of England was an Englishman. In the same way the other important power in the country fell into the hands of foreigners, for all the important offices in the Church were gradually filled by Normans as vacancies arose. Only two of the original Anglo-Saxon bishops, both resident in the West Country, outlived William. In 1075 the majority of the abbots signing the decrees of the Council of London were English, but by 1087 only three of the twenty-one were English. It is probable, too, that there was a corresponding influx of the lower orders, though written records, concerned only with the great, naturally provide less evidence for this. There must have been a large number of artisans, tradesmen, and workpeople who came over after Norman rule had been established, and no doubt many of the mercenaries who had come over to fight for William remained in England. The Normans would almost certainly use the English for the more menial tasks, and although the names of various trades and occupations, of which those showing most contact with the master or mistress seem to be French, may not be an accurate guide, since the Normans may have used their own terms for trades concerning them intimately, even if the workpeople were English, yet it is likely that the fastidious Normans would bring over their own workpeople to fashion clothes, furniture, and other personal things where a particular style would be demanded. Moreover, records show that some Norman tradesmen and merchants preferred London to their own country because trading conditions were better. Estimates vary as to the number of English killed or driven into exile, and the number of

Normans who settled in England – York Powell suggested twenty thousand for the latter figure – but whatever the number may have been, as the Normans eventually seized all the chief positions in Church and State their influence must have been out of all proportion to their number.

But from a linguistic point of view we are concerned chiefly with the ruling classes. No doubt some words would be picked up by the English lower classes from the Norman servants and tradesmen, but probably not more than they would acquire from their Norman masters. We have little evidence in favour of French being spoken by the English lower classes for some time after the Conquest, yet they would undoubtedly pick up some words quite early, and this may explain why some of the common French words became really well-established in English at an early date. As may be expected, the Norman rulers continued to use their own language after they were established in England, although they apparently made no conscious effort to impose that language on the English. Most of them would, of course, know no English when they came over – English was not yet sufficiently important to be widely known on the Continent – and, although they would no doubt pick up English words in their dealings with their English servants, they made no effort to adopt the language of their new country, as they had done in France. Robert of Gloucester tells us that they could speak nothing but French when they came over, that they continued to speak French, and taught their children to do so. It is not until towards the end of the thirteenth century that we find the foreign ruling-class using English to any extent. This was in direct contrast to their behaviour in France, but the reason for this difference is easily explained. French was at this time the most important of the European vernacular languages, rivalling even Latin in importance, particularly as the medium for composition of works intended for the entertainment of the chivalrous society of the time, so that there was every reason why the Normans should retain this language rather than adopt a culturally-inferior language. It is once again a question of superior culture; the Normans adopted French because it was in many respects superior to the Scandinavian they abandoned; had English been superior to French at this time we may be sure they would have adopted English in turn and abandoned French, but this was not the case, and French remained the language of the ruling-classes in England for something like two hundred years. Some of the French words they used would affect the English closely and we find that some of these words, indicative of a real ruling-class, a veritable dictatorship, were soon adopted into English. The Englishman who continued to hunt in his native woods soon found that his Norman master had preserved the game in the forest, and if he continued to hunt he would soon learn of *prisun* – recorded before the death of the Conqueror. The Normans were absolute masters, and the English had soon to learn words expressing the power and authority and the pleasure of their new masters.

Another important factor in the retention of French by the ruling-classes was the close connexion maintained with the Continent. We have seen already that one of the factors tending to maintain the language of a conquering nation in the conquered territory is contact with the homeland and constant reinforcement from there, and this took place to a marked degree in the years immediately following the Conquest. We may be certain that if this close contact and constant intercourse with the French had not taken place the linguistic influence of Norman and Central French would have been much less, as we see from the development once the link was broken. Most of the nobles had estates in both England and Normandy, and spent considerable periods abroad. In addition, as we have seen, there was a continual stream of William's former friends and followers once his authority was established. Moreover, this state of affairs continued for some long time, and indeed both factors became increasingly effective in the hundred and fifty years following the Conquest. During this time, apart from a brief period immediately following the death of William, the King of England was also Duke of Normandy, and, because of this maintained contact with France, and political marriages resulting from it, the territories in France of the King of England were considerably extended, so that by the time of Henry II we find that he is ruling more of France than the King of France himself. It was natural for the Kings of England to maintain close contact with their territories abroad, and records show that until about 1200 most of the English kings spent as much time in France as in England. Only one king – Henry I, who married Matilda, daughter of Malcolm, King of Scotland, and a direct descendant of Ethelred – married a wife from these islands before the middle of the fifteenth century. The same state of affairs is to be seen in the case of the nobles; practically all had estates in France demanding their attention, many chose their wives from among Frenchwomen, and, apart from this, we should expect to find them in France when the king himself was there, so that all the ruling-classes maintained close contact with their original home until the beginning of the thirteenth century. We can understand, then, that among them at any rate, purely as a matter of necessity, the French language was likely to maintain its predominant position. A similar close contact between religious leaders, and in affairs of trade, would further strengthen the position of the French language.

But, although it has been said that William and his successors attempted to replace English by French, there is no real evidence that they tried to impose their own language on the English. A fourteenth-century writer does tell us that William's aim was to destroy the English tongue, yet Orderic Vitalis also tells us that William actually tried to learn English in his later years. It seems likely that he would be able to understand the English language, even if he did not use it, and his reputation suggests that he was far too wise and statesmanlike to attempt to force upon the English something which would be distasteful to them and no advantage to himself. It is also likely that, once established as King of England, he would stress the English side of his possessions in order to offset his subordinate position, as Duke of Normandy, to the King of France. It is possible that William's youngest son, Henry I, was taught English as a child. The two languages must have been, from the earliest stages, what we may call class dialects, French being the language of the upper classes and English the language of the lower classes, because in the first place French had been the language of the ruling race, and even when distinctions of race eventually disappeared distinctions of class remained, and French was still the language of the upper classes, and a mark of distinction between them and the lower classes. Moreover, although the Normans were at first stern rulers, there was soon peaceful co-operation, intermarriage, and the beginning of the fusion of the two races. Probably the later kings understood English, if they did not speak it, and Giraldus Cambrensis tells us that this was true of Henry II at any rate. But, although this state of affairs continued up to about 1200, it is rather a question of indifference to a language which was of little practical use to them, on account of their preoccupation with continental affairs and the lack of any necessity to use it when in England, than of actual hostility to the language of a conquered people. English was just not necessary to them, so they made little effort to learn it, but they also apparently made no effort to discourage its use.

During the same period the predominance of French as the language of the court and of the upper classes generally was further sustained by the royal patronage of literature. Much literature written in French was produced in England from the early part of the twelfth century. Men of letters found encouragement at court in this period, particularly from the ladies of the court, among whom Adela, the Conqueror's daughter, both the wives of Henry I, Matilda and Adelaide, and Eleanor of Aquitaine, wife of Henry II, were noteworthy in this respect. An extensive Anglo-Norman literature developed on English soil, and among the works produced were Philip de Thaun's *Bestiaire*, written for Adelaide, Gaimar's *Estorie des Bretons*, and *Estorie des Engleis*, for a lady of the court, Wace's *Brut*, written for Eleanor, and the later *Roman de Rou*, in which the deeds of the Norman Dukes were treated in the same way as those of the British kings in the earlier work. There was a constant stream of poetry, history and romance, and also religious works, during the twelfth century, all written in French, a strong indication of the position occupied by the French language in the circles for whom these works were written.

But very soon, as a result of the fusion of the two races, and also as a result of happenings on the Continent, a difference arose in the relationship between English and French. At first, as we have seen, the two languages corresponded to class dialects, but after a time, when the bitterness of conquest had passed and the new order of things was accepted as a fact, the fusion of the two races proceeded rapidly, and we find that linguistic conditions were so changed that, irrespective of nationality, English became the language of people in this country, and French the language of those who had decided to make their home in France. The fusion of the two races began, no doubt, with inter-marriage, perhaps first among the lower classes, but probably many a Norman lord increased his wealth or made his position more secure, his claim to his lands better established, by marrying an English woman, wealthy in her own right, or the daughter of some wealthy lord, and Matthew Paris records that these mixed marriages were encouraged by the Conqueror. Evidence of quite another kind is to be found early, when William II was helped by English soldiers when his brother Robert of Normandy tried to seize the throne. The marriage of Henry I to Matilda must also have helped towards this fusion of the races, and his strict rule, by which Normans and English were treated equally at law, would tend in the same direction, and Walter Map tells us that Henry 'both by making marriages, and by all other means in his power, united the two peoples in firm concord'. The Normans began to feel that England, not Normandy, was their real home, and the fusion, once begun, gained ground so rapidly that towards the end of the reign of Henry II we read in the *Dialogus de Scaccario*: 'Now that the English and Normans have been dwelling together, marrying and giving in marriage, the two nations have become so mixed that it is scarcely possible today, speaking of free men, to tell who is English, who of Norman race'. Indeed, the distinction by then was no longer one of race, but of domicile, English being used for those living in England, Norman for those living in Normandy. The fusion was completed in

the following century, after the loss of Normandy and a resurgence of
national spirit, fostered by a feeling of hatred towards France, and the
union of the two peoples meant the beginning of the decay of French as
the language of the upper classes in this country, and the re-establishment
of English as the accepted standard language.

It is possible, by piecing together scraps of scattered information
available in contemporary records, to form some idea of what languages
were spoken in England during this first period, when French was
predominant among the upper classes, in the hundred and fifty years
preceding the loss of Normandy in 1204. Although we shall confine
ourselves chiefly to English and French, and to the spoken language, so
far as we have evidence for this, it should be remembered that for about
three centuries after the Conquest the written records are tri-lingual, in
English, French, and Latin, the latter the universal language of mediaeval
scholarship and culture. We are told casually from time to time of some
noble who could or could not speak English or French. Robert of
Gloucester sets out the conditions at the outset very clearly: 'Thus
England came into Normandy's hand, and the Normans at that time
could speak only their own language, and spoke French as they did at
home, and taught their children also, so that people in this country of
noble rank who come of their blood keep to the language they had
from them'. Books also, when we know the class of people for whom
they were written, as we do, for example, in the case of the *Ancren
Riwle*, give us information about the use of the two languages in
various social classes, and writers often tell us in a preface why they have
chosen one language rather than the other. We have also records of
evidence given in courts of law in English or French, and some information is also available from the language of town and guild records. In
the early stages, at any rate, all the evidence confirms the existence of
the two languages as class dialects; Robert of Gloucester, continuing
the passage quoted above, adds: 'But the lower classes hold fast to
English and their own language'. The position of French as a class
dialect is emphasized by the sentence which links these two passages:
'For unless a man knows French, he is considered of little account'.
These records not only show us that the Normans continued to use
their own language, while English was spoken by most of the native
population, but they also show when, and to what extent, the upper
classes learnt English and the lower classes French, so that we can
obtain some idea, even if very imperfect, of the fusion of languages
accompanying the fusion of the two races.

When French ceased to be regarded as a foreign language, the speech
of the conqueror, and became instead a class dialect, the speech of the

upper classes, we may be sure that the remnant of the English upper classes would soon acquire it; indeed, Higden tells us so in his Polychronicon: 'and oplondysch men wol lykne hamsylf to gentil men, and fondeþ wiþ gret bysynes for to speke Freynsch, for to be more ytold of' – an attitude not unknown today. And perhaps, though certainly not consciously or deliberately, they would find it necessary to use English words and so introduce these words among the Normans in their circle. The latter would be almost certain to pick up English words and phrases in their dealings with their English servants, and there is evidence that the Norman ruling class soon acquired some knowledge of English. Freeman says: 'There is distinct evidence that in the days of Henry II, men of high rank and Norman birth could freely speak, or understand English, though of course this does not exclude their speaking French also'. The fact that some of William's writs in English were addressed to Normans carries little weight, as very few men apart from clerics could have read them, no matter what language they were written in. A much weightier example is found in William of Canterbury's story of a warning uttered by Helewisia de Morville to her husband, a man of Norman descent. Her warning was in English – 'Huge de Morevile, ware, ware, ware, Lithulf heth his swerd adrage'. If this story is true, and the warning was spoken as recorded, two interesting facts are to be noted, namely the woman's use of English at a time of great emotional stress, and the fact that her husband obviously understood English. Geraldus Cambrensis tells a story which shows that Henry II could understand English, when addressed in that language by a Welsh countryman, even if he did not habitually speak it, and the fact is confirmed by Walter Map's statement that Henry was acquainted with all the languages spoken from the Bay of Biscay to the Jordan, though he used only Latin and French. The original language of the *Ancren Riwle*, written for three women of aristocratic family, was almost certainly English, although copies have survived in English, French, and Latin. The *Peterborough Chronicle* was continued in English until 1154, which proves the use of English in some monastic establishments. Orderic Vitalis, son of a Norman father and an English mother, was sent to Normandy to be educated, and there, he says, 'like Joseph in Egypt I heard a language which I did not know'. There is also evidence that some Norman bishops were able to use English in addition to Latin and French. Jocelyn of Brakelond tells us that Abbot Samson spoke French and Latin, but also 'was wont to preach to the people in English, but in the dialect of Norfolk, where he was born and bred'. Bishop Foliot, a Norman who supported Becket against Henry, also knew English, according to Walter Map. However, we hear of bishops who were censured because they knew no English, and in the thirteenth century the Archbishop of York refused to give benefices to some priests because they could not preach in English. Roger of Hoveden tells that William Longchamp, Chancellor of England, fleeing to France disguised as a woman, carrying a roll of cloth as if for sale, was unable to reply in English to a woman who wished to buy. But one wonders if his silence may not have been due to a lack of confidence in his ability to disguise his voice. The point to be noticed, however, is that most of the men thus spoken of as unable to speak English were men of foreign blood, and from the fact that the chronicler thought it worth while to note that they had no knowledge of English one may assume that a knowledge of English was fairly general among their fellows. It seems likely, then, that by the end of the twelfth century many of the upper-class Normans had acquired some knowledge of English, and that it was even expected among educated men.

But, just as the upper classes were beginning to adopt English, so there is evidence that a knowledge of French was not confined to the ruling classes, and in the thirteenth century we find authors stating that French was then understood by 'la laie gent' – the unlearned people – though evidence to the contrary is found in the *Romance of Richard the Lion-hearted*, where we are told that scarcely one out of a hundred unlearned men can understand French, and we have already noted the statement of Robert of Gloucester that the lower ranks kept to their native tongue. English knights seem often to have made an effort to acquire French, and we read of one who employed a Norman to teach his son French. It seems, indeed, that by the end of the twelfth century a knowledge of French was expected of a knight, for of four supposed knights concerned in a dispute between the Abbot of Crowland and the Prior of Spalding we are told that one did not even know how to speak French. The higher servants on Norman estates, those in constant contact with their Norman masters, would also need to know French. Men of the merchant class and the prominent townsmen, particularly in the larger towns and cities, probably had some knowledge of French, and we read of accounts being kept in French as well as the customary Latin. It is probable, however, that the great mass of the people knew no French, and Abbot Samson seems even to have considered such a knowledge undesirable, for he gave his manor of Thorp to 'a certain Englishman, a man adscript to the soil, in whose fidelity he had the fullest confidence, because he was a good farmer and because he knew no French'.

We see, therefore, by the end of the twelfth century, at least the beginnings of bilingualism among the upper classes, and some evidence of it lower down. We have also noted already that once the conquering race begins to be bilingual their own language is likely to give way, and we may therefore expect that to happen in England. That is, indeed, what actually took place, and the decay of French as the predominant language of the ruling classes in England was hastened by another factor which would tend in the same direction, the breaking of the close contact with France and the stopping of reinforcements from that country, a factor which began to develop in the early thirteenth century.

If contact with France had been maintained, and if the constant flow of Frenchmen to this country had not been checked, it may be that French might have remained the language of the upper classes and the official language of the country, at least until the rise of the middle class in the sixteenth century. But shortly after the end of the twelfth century conditions changed; Normandy and a considerable part of the possessions in France were lost, and although French was for some time, and for a variety of reasons, cultivated among the upper classes, it had ceased to be a necessity to them. Once the language had become thus an artificial adornment rather than a necessity it was more likely to give way before the native language, especially when conditions developed later in this country which strengthened the position of English.

In 1204 John lost his territories in Normandy, as a result of his marrying Anne of Angoulême when she was already betrothed to Hugh of Lusignan. John refused to appear as a vassal before his liege-lord, the King of France, to answer for his attack on the Lusignans, whom he had attacked first, in anticipation of their attacking him, and Philip declared John's possessions in France forfeit. In a very short time he had conquered Normandy, and so a contact was broken which had lasted for a hundred and fifty years. But there were still the extensive territories in the south of France, and many English nobles had large estates in France. This question of divided allegiance of English and French nobles who had estates in both countries and so owed loyalty to both kings came to a head when Philip overran Normandy and then confiscated the estates in France of several great nobles living normally in England, and supporting John. This was only a forcible expression of a process which had gone on since the early days of the Conquest; William himself had been the first so to divide estates in the two countries by leaving Normandy to his eldest son and England to his second son, and this example had been followed from time to time, thus establishing one branch of a family in France and one in England. But this action by Philip, and a similar action by John in retaliation, hastened the process and compelled nobles with estates in both countries to choose one or the other as their native land. The divisions continued throughout the first half of the thirteenth century, one example being that of Simon de Montfort, who writes: 'My brother Amaury released to me our brother's whole inheritance in England, provided that I could secure it; in return I released to him what I had in France'. The question of double allegiance was finally resolved in 1244, as Matthew Paris tells, when the French king Louis IX, saying that no noble could be loyal to two kings, commanded that those who still had lands in both countries should decide the matter for themselves, and relinquish their possessions in one land or the other. In retaliation, Henry III ignored any question of free choice, and confiscated the possessions in England of all Frenchmen and Normans. From this time forward English nobles were essentially English, they no longer had any need of French, and soon the distinction between those who spoke English and those who spoke French was no longer a matter of social class but of domicile.

As a result of this severance of possessions, and, which followed naturally, of interests, king and nobles were compelled to look upon England as their primary concern, and so we see national spirit and pride in England once more coming to the front. But another factor has to be taken into account, and although this factor was not allowed to operate for long it was very powerful while it lasted; yet in the end it also served to kindle the national spirit, for it aroused a violent antipathy to foreigners who came over to England and enriched themselves at the expense of the native English. When John married Anne of Angoulême he began to introduce into England a number of Poitevins, among whom was Peter des Roches, who eventually became the most powerful man in the land. English were dismissed from all high offices, as Roger of Wendover records, and replaced by foreigners, and Henry III recruited a large number of foreign mercenaries, soldiers and landless knights, and 'wherever the king went he was surrounded by crowds of these foreigners; and nothing was done in England except what the bishop of Winchester and his host of foreigners determined on'. Although a revolt against this state of affairs, organized by a number of bishops and backed by a threat of excommunication against the king, compelled Henry to dismiss Peter des Roches and the other foreigners, they were soon back in power again. Another influx occurred when Henry married Eleanor of Provence in 1236, and Matthew Paris tells of the horde of foreigners who obtained lands and money in England. After John's death his widow had married Hugh de Lusignan, the man to whom she had been first betrothed, and Henry showered wealth upon his half-brothers by this marriage, giving them rich positions and arranging rich marriages for them and their followers, so that the whole land was full of foreigners, battening on the revenue of Church and State.

The effect of all this was to foster a stronger spirit of nationalism, a feeling of antipathy towards the foreigners, and several attempts were made to get rid of them. We have already seen how the bishops compelled Henry to dismiss his favourite, and Bishop Grosseteste attacked the foreigners who were robbing the Church of her revenues. He claimed that the wealth obtained by these men from the Church greatly exceeded the king's own income. This antipathy towards the foreigners united all classes of the native English, and resulted eventually, towards the end of the thirteenth century, in their final dismissal. Not until the reign of Edward I do we find England once more governed by Englishmen, and this king's summons to Parliament in 1295, expressing this antipathy towards foreigners, is particularly interesting to us in our study of the linguistic conditions at the time, for in it he claims of the King of France that, '[he] planned, if his ability should correspond with his detestable purpose, which God forbid, to wipe out the English tongue wholly from the earth'.

Although these new arrivals from France might at first have tended to preserve the use of French among the upper classes, the ultimate result was to set a wide gulf between English and French. One of the common charges against the newcomers was that they knew no English, and so perhaps the ability to speak English became the sign of the patriotic Englishman. This hostility towards French is expressed as early as the middle of the thirteenth century, by William of Westminster, who writes that the common people considered anyone unable to speak the English language a vile and contemptible person. The eventual result was that where French survived among the upper classes in the latter part of the thirteenth century it was as a cultivated tongue, much as it is today. This was, of course, helped by the prestige of French literature and French civilization, at that time the most cultured in Europe, and the reputation enjoyed by the University of Paris, at that time unchallenged in Europe. France took the lead in the Crusades and in the movements for monastic reform, the university in Paris was the centre of mediaeval theology and philosophy, and the 'three matters' of mediaeval romance, the stories of the Trojan War, of Charlemagne, and of Arthur of Britain, originated in France. The French language was cultivated in many European courts, and celebrated European writers were proud to use French for their masterpieces; Marco Polo, a Venetian who travelled in China and met Khubla Khan, wrote an account of his travels in French. This 'fashionable' aspect of French language and literature was a strong reason for the retention of French by the upper classes in England, but it was retained more and more as an artificial, cultivated language, and English made steady progress, so that soon after the middle of the century, after the question of divided allegiance had been finally settled, most of the upper classes were beginning to adopt English, and there is evidence that by the end of the thirteenth century their children spoke English as their mother-tongue and were taught French as a foreign language by manuals provided with English glosses, as, for example, that of Walter of Bibbesworth, probably written about 1285, and others which followed, some of which paid particular attention to pronunciation, another sign that the language was not in common use.

It is in the hundred and fifty years from 1250 to 1400 that we find the greatest influx of French words, and one of the reasons for this is obvious; as the upper classes began to use English they would often need to help out with French words in expressing themselves, and some of these frequently-used words came to be adopted into English. Moreover, we have only the words found in writings; if we had a record also of the words used in everyday speech the total might be still larger. But there is a difference between the adoption of words in the early period and again in the later period. In the early period English borrowed from necessity, for the servants were compelled to adopt the terms used by their masters, and the borrowing is a sign of physical inferiority, the helplessness of a conquered people. The later borrowings are fashionable, and a tribute to the intellectual and cultural superiority of the French; they are borrowings by choice, not from necessity. As most of the early borrowings are from Norman French and the later borrowings from Central French it is not difficult to separate them and see the difference in type. We have direct evidence for these fashionable borrowings, for John of Salisbury says that in the twelfth century it was the fashion to interlard one's speech with French words. This may account for the adoption of many words which do not fit easily into the classes of loans to be discussed later.

Direct references to the use of English by particular persons, although they are to be found, are not so frequent in this later period, perhaps because it had by now become the general thing to use English. Yet this change did not take place all at once, nor was it completed within a short period. We have noted already that as late as the end of the thirteenth century Robert of Gloucester was able to write that a man was held of little account if he did not understand French, though, of course, it may be that he used English generally but a knowledge of French was expected of him. At the close of the century French was still being used in schools, in the law-courts, in parliament, and often in books intended solely for the upper classes, another sign that, although they had begun to use English in everyday speech, they continued to cultivate French in the written form, and another reason for the recorded appearance of still more French words at this time.

Yet there can be no doubt that by the beginning of the fourteenth century French was beginning to lose its hold, and we may even note attempts to bolster it up artificially, such as the regulations in monasteries and university colleges banning the use of English in favour of Latin and French, and Froissart tells of a decree in Parliament in 1332 requiring 'lords, barons, knights, and worthy men of great towns' to have their children instructed in French; even though the purpose of the decree was to ensure that they should be 'better equipped for their wars', yet it does show clearly that it was becoming more and more necessary to teach French as a foreign language, and that English was once more established as the mother-tongue.

Mention has already been made of the support given to the retention of French by the prestige of French literature and culture, but there was one important factor which militated against this. Even at the time of the Conquest there had been a difference between Norman French and the French of Paris. Indeed, at the time of the Conquest there was no recognized French language as we know it today, but merely a number of dialects, all descended from the colloquial Latin used in Gaul, and differentiated by the fact of their having developed in conditions of partial isolation. It was eventually Central French which became established as the classical French, largely because of the political supremacy of Paris, just as the political and cultural supremacy of Athens had made its Attic dialect classical Greek. But the language introduced into England as a direct result of the Conquest was Norman, and this, already differentiated from Central French, became still more different as it developed in isolation in England. But this 'barbarous' and dialectal Anglo-Norman was later modified by the influence of Central French, introduced in the twelfth century into court and fashionable circles with the accession of the Angevin dynasty. This language, in its turn, came to be looked upon as provincial, as we may gather from references, usually apologetic, to this 'false French of England', and so people who wished to retain French for cultural reasons might hesitate to use a language which could bring forth a scornful smile from a cultured Frenchman, and children were sent abroad then, as they are today, to correct their accents. We may perhaps use again the year 1204 as a division, for it is roughly true to say that influence up to the twelfth century is largely Norman, and Central French after that time.

But there were other factors besides the loss of French possessions and this shame in using a provincial dialect which helped in the decline of French and the re-establishment of English: most of them developed within the country, and were not due to outside influence. The nationalist feeling which had shown itself in the outburst against foreign favourites in the reign of Henry III was still further strengthened in the fourteenth century by the Hundred Years' War. During all this time French was the language of the enemy country, and this no doubt furthered the cause of the English language. Another factor was the decline in relative importance of the upper-classes, who had been instrumental in retaining French. The condition of the peasant-class had been gradually improving during the thirteenth century, and the Black Death increased the importance of this class by reducing the number of labourers and thereby increasing the value of the services of those left. Although the proportion of deaths was probably greater among them than among the upper classes, yet the loss among the ruling and educated classes was perhaps as high as forty per cent, and this must have affected the use of French. In addition, the merchant and craftsman class was becoming increasingly important in the towns, and these soon became established as a rich and powerful class ranking between the nobility and the peasants. Such an increase in the importance of the peasants and this new middle-class would undoubtedly lead to an increase in the importance of the language they spoke.

We have already seen that by the end of the thirteenth century English was understood by most people, and in the fourteenth century it became generally adopted as the language of the country in the widest sense of the word. English begins to be used almost universally in literature, and there are many instances recorded from 1300 onwards of writers giving their reasons for using English rather than French, which had previously been the fashionable language for polite literature. Several times we are told that works are written in English because, whereas only men who have been at Court, or clerics, understand French and Latin, all men in the country understand English, and in the opening lines of *Arthour and Merlin*, written early in the fourteenth century, the author adds that he has seen many nobles who could not speak French. Edward I could apparently use English with ease, and Froissart records that Edward III understood it and used it, and it was in his reign, in 1362, that history was made by the opening of parliament in English, and in the same year it was decreed that pleading in Court should be conducted in English. There is evidence for the use of English by high officials in the reigns of Henry IV and Henry V; the former made his claim for the Crown in English, which is expressly stated in records to be his mother-tongue, and it is likely that he used no other. He was the first English king since the Conquest whose mother-tongue was English. Ambassadors acting for Henry V so far distrusted their French that they refused to negotiate in that language. But this takes us into the fifteenth century, when English was fully established. Yet, although polite literature was written in English for the upper classes, it is likely that they were bilingual throughout the whole of the fourteenth century, or at least understood French if they did not speak it. Edward III apparently made his remark about allowing the Black Prince to 'win his spurs' at Crécy in French, and his even more famous remark when the Countess of Salisbury lost her garter was certainly in French. Richard II certainly used English to address the crowd after the death of Wat Tyler; he commissioned Gower to write his *Confessio Amantis* in English, yet he possessed romances probably written in French. Robert Brunne suggests that educated men understood French, and these educated men would include lawyers and clergy; there is plenty of evidence for the use of French in monasteries, but perhaps the position was that the higher ranks of the clergy understood French while the poor parish-priests knew only English and Latin, for in *Piers Plowman* we read that not above one in a hundred could understand a letter unless it was in Latin or English. Perhaps French was dying out even among the higher clerics, for we have already seen that it had to be forcibly kept in use in monasteries and colleges. French was also used for the records of town councils and guilds, but it is very much to be doubted if the members of these assemblies habitually spoke anything but English, and outside the larger towns we may be sure that few of the middle class and peasants could understand French, and fewer still used it.

The fourteenth century provides us with one long continuous record of the gradual re-establishment of English in all walks of life. Although French was still the language of parliament, English began to get a foothold there; the claim of Edward III to the throne of France was explained to the assembled parliament in English in 1337, to make sure that it was understood by all, and we have already seen that parliament was opened in English in 1362; this is a curious contrast to his use of French just mentioned, and shows how prevalent bilingualism was. There is a petition in English to parliament from the Mercers of London dated 1386. At the very end of the century the whole of the proceedings concerning the deposition of Richard and the accession of Henry IV were in either English or English and Latin, and French was not used at all. By the time of Henry VI petitions and bills are frequently in English, and after the middle of the fifteenth century only in the case of statutes did French hold its place alongside English. English began to be used in

matters concerning local government also, and also for the business of
guilds, as might be expected from the increased importance of the
merchants and craftsmen. In 1388, when parliament asked for information about the guilds, the majority of the returns were in Latin, but of
those not in Latin there were more in English than in French.

As early as the thirteenth century French had superseded English as
the second language, alongside Latin, in the law courts, and once
established it held its place firmly for at least a century, but with the
general spread of English throughout the country in the fourteenth
century the native language began to get a foothold there also. In 1356
the mayor and aldermen of London decided that proceedings in their
sheriffs' court should be in English, and, as we have seen, parliament in
1362, by the Statute of Pleading, decreed that lawsuits should be
conducted in English, because French was 'much unknown in the said
realm' and people could neither understand the laws nor follow what
judges and advocates were saying in court. Although this decree was
not obeyed completely at once, yet the fact that English had been
declared the language of the law shows that it had once more become
the acknowledged official language of the country, although French
continued to be used for the general proceedings of parliament until
1483, when regulations were introduced whereby statutes were for the
first time to be drawn up in English, and for legal documents, and the
mongrel French, often called 'Law French', was not finally abolished
until 1731.

As in the law courts, French had early become the language in
general use in schools. Higden, in his *Polychronicon*, written in the early
fourteenth century, tells how children did all their lessons in French,
and that the children of the upper classes were taught French from the
cradle. But when Trevisa made his translation of the book some sixty
years later he added a note that, thanks to the efforts of two school-
masters, Cornwall and Pencrich, things had changed a good deal, that
French was no longer the language of instruction, that English children
did their lessons in English, and that children of the upper classes were
not so commonly taught French. By the end of the century English was
the language regularly used in schools.

We see, then, that by the end of the fourteenth century English had
regained its position as the national speech, and was understood by all,
and that French, which had survived only as an artificial, cultivated
language, bolstered up only by fashion and class-snobbery, had been
unable to hold its ground against the newly-aroused national spirit, and
was not understood by all the upper classes even, and that those who did
understand it were bilingual. Usk, in his *Testament of Love* (c. 1385),

puts well what seems to have been the general opinion of his time: 'Let then clerkys endyten in Latin, for they have the propertee of science, and the knowinge in that facultee: and let Frenchmen in their Frenche also endyten their queynt terms, for it is kyndely to their mouthes: and let us shewe our fantasyes in suche wordes as we lerneden of our dames tonge'. During the course of the fifteenth century, English became still more important, and the decline of French continued. The upper classes not only ceased to speak French; some of them even ceased to understand it clearly. There is an interesting example (quoted in OHEL II, p. 177) of the difficulty encountered in the early transition stages by people used to French in expressing themselves in English in a letter, partly in English, partly in French, written probably in the early part of the reign of Richard II by Rose Mountefort. The Earl of March wrote to the king in English in 1400, excusing his use of that language by saying that he understood it better than Latin or French, and about the same time the Dean of Windsor, writing to the king, changes from French to English in the middle of a sentence as his feelings get the better of his ability to express them in French. This type of writing, partly English, partly French, with the two languages used naturally together without any self-consciousness, is frequent between 1375 and 1425, but rare at other times. It may reflect two things: bilingualism, when the two languages are used easily together, or, when English is used to help out the French, the use of French, in deference to fashion, by people who did not understand it well enough to use it well. We have already seen how two of the king's ambassadors refused to negotiate in French, pleading their ignorance of that language, and by the middle of the century parliament needed a 'Secretary in the French Language'. The general position at the end of the century is concisely expressed by Caxton, who says 'the mooste quantyte of the people vnderstonde not latyn ne frensshe here in this noble royame of englond'.

But French was still cultivated during the fourteenth century, as it has been almost continuously ever since, as a language of fashion and culture, and as a necessity for those having dealings in France, either for business or pleasure. Books began to appear written expressly for those who wished to learn French for utilitarian purposes, and Caxton published his *Dialogues in French and English* chiefly for merchants who wished to trade with France.

Once English had again been acknowledged as the common spoken language, it was only a matter of time before it was used regularly in writing also, both official and private. Apart from its use in purely literary works, which will be examined in more detail below, it appears in the fifteenth century in many other types of prose writings. The

records of towns and guilds are generally in English after the middle of
the fifteenth century because, as we are told, townsmen and members
of the guilds can write and read English, but not Latin and French.
English also began to get a hold in the proceedings of parliament, and
shortly before the end of the fifteenth century the process was completed,
when the statutes themselves no longer appear in French. Although a
few letters in English date from the end of the fourteenth century, it is
only in the fifteenth century that the practice becomes common, and
letters ranging from those of the king and his ministers down to those
of simple merchants and their womenfolk are found. This is the age of
the Pastons, the Celys, and the Stonors. After a break of nearly four
centuries, wills begin to appear again in English; the earliest in the
London Court of Probate is from the year 1387; such minor prose
records as treatises on fishing or hawking, medical and herbal recipes,
calendar notes, and so on also appear now in English, written by people
with no pretensions to Latin or French scholarship. The end of the first
quarter of the fifteenth century has been suggested as the period when
English began to be generally used again for writing.

Thus we see the long struggle between English and French resolved
finally in favour of English. The story of the struggle has been illustrated
so far from the facts of history and from contemporary records, but,
as may be expected, the language used for the literary works of the
Middle English period also provides valuable evidence, and serves to
confirm the main features of the development traced above, though the
comparatively small amount of literature preserved from the hundred
and fifty years following the Conquest makes it difficult for us to know
just how soon French influence began to make itself felt in English.
Although there have been periods of decadence in English literature,
there is no period, from the time English records appear, in the Old
English period, right up to the present day, from which we have no
record at all of writings in English. From the end of the great period of
Old English prose until well into the twelfth century, a span of nearly a
hundred and fifty years, records are sparse, but after that they present
a continuous picture of the language as it has developed over nearly
seven centuries. But it is not until the fifteenth century that a standard
language develops, and so our study of the vocabulary of Middle
English is further complicated by the fact that every author used his
own dialect, Northern, Midland, or Southern, with the many sub-
variants of these. Although the influence of the Normans was not
strong enough to accomplish the subjection of the language, as they
had conquered the people, so that English continued to be written
throughout the whole period, yet, so long as French continued to be

the language of the ruling classes so long would they demand works in French. At first they made use of French literature, until works could be written for them in England, and we have already noticed this French literature written on English soil. Therefore, any poet seeking court patronage at that time had to write in French, and most of the works which appear in English before about 1250 are not of a courtly type, but consist chiefly of religious works, such as the *Ancren Riwle* and *Ormulum*, lives of saints, paraphrases, historical records, and so on, the bulk of which were intended for the instruction of the lower classes, as we read in the preface to *Handlyng Synne* (c. 1303): 'For lewde men y vndyrtoke On englyssh tunge to make þys boke', and in *Cursor Mundi* (c. 1320) where the author says: 'To lewid and Englis men I spel / þat understandis quat I can tell'. There are two notable exceptions, Layamon's *Brut* (c. 1205) and the debate poem of *The Owl and the Nightingale* (c. 1195), but, in general, works for a courtly audience were not written in English in this period, and the type of work which has survived from the period up to about 1250 confirms that French was the language of the court, English of the middle and peasant classes. After 1250 the spread of English among the upper classes is reflected in literature, and types of literature for the courtly class, previously written in French, such as, for example, the romance, now begin to appear in English. Alongside the earlier religious works we begin to find a body of secular writing. By the time we come to the middle of the fourteenth century the swingover is complete, and we have a body of literature written in English between 1350 and 1400 which is the high-water mark of mediaeval English literature, with such writers as Chaucer and Langland, who, surprisingly enough, used more French words than most other writers of the time, Wyclif, and the writer of *Sir Gawayne and the Grene Knight*, and the tradition was carried on in the fifteenth century, though perhaps sometimes on a lower plane, by Lydgate, Hoccleve, Skelton, Malory, and Caxton, all writing in English for English people.

Yet the influx of French words was not halted. These works in English contain many French words. In the thirteenth and fourteenth centuries writers could assume that their audience would be familiar with French, and even in English works they felt free to introduce French words as and when they pleased, particularly to meet the demands of rhyme and metre and to comply with the rules of alliterative verse. A large number of new words from another language, varying little if at all in meaning, would provide a wealth of synonyms or near-synonyms which would be extremely useful to the poet, not only for the three reasons already mentioned, but also to enable him to vary his vocabulary. On the other hand it is likely that many French words so used would have been

replaced by English words under normal conditions. Yet these words
were introduced also into prose works; for example, the *Peterborough
Chronicle*, continued in English until the middle of the twelfth century,
and essentially English in its vocabulary, yet contains a number of
French words, including *acorden*, *bataille*, *cancelere* (chancellor), *carited*
(charity), *castell*, *cuntisse*, *curt* (court), *duc*, *emperice* (empress), *iustise*,
miracle, *pais* (peace), *processiun*, *rent*, *tresor*, *tur* (tower), and others.

Although we find these words in the middle of the twelfth century in
East Anglia, yet the number of French words in the *Ormulum* (c. 1200)
is negligible; Dr Serjeantson quotes eleven French words used by Orm,
including *prophet*, *castle*, *rich*, *charity*, and *bulten* (to boult, sift flour), and
Kluge found about twenty French words in over twenty thousand lines.
On the other hand, Layamon's *Brut*, of about the same date, contains
more French words; Skeat found one hundred and fifty words in
fifty-six thousand lines, and in the A-text eighty-seven words have been
identified in just over thirty thousand lines; the second version, some
fifty years later than the first, contains more French words, and some
English words in the first text are replaced by French words in the
second. Among the French words in the *Brut* we find *admiral*, *barun*,
conseil (council), *contre*, *crūn*, *folie*, *grace*, *gyle* (guile), *image*, *lettre*, *mon-
taine*, *nonnerie*, *paie*, *rout* (assembly), *scarn* (scorn), *seruise*, *soffri* (suffer),
and *weorre* (war). In the *Ancren Riwle*, written in the twelfth century,
though the extant MSS are considerably later, the number of French
words is much larger, and Jespersen mentions the use of about five
hundred French words in two hundred pages. In this text we note a
practice found commonly in didactic texts in the Middle English period,
a tendency to use the French word and its English equivalent side by
side, so that the work might be more easily understood. As the versions
which have come down to us are later than the original, they may
contain French words substituted for English forms in the original
text, but even then the proportion is high. The number of abstract
terms is large, as may be expected in a work of this kind. Among the
French words in this work we find *abit* (dress), *autorite*, *auenture*, *broche*,
burgeis (burgess), *chastete*, *cite* (city), *dette*, *deuocion*, *eresi* (heresy), *gelus*
(jealous), *jugement*, *jurneie*, *kunscence* (conscience), *nurice* (nurse), *pacience*,
reisun, *trecherie*, *turnement*, *wardein* (guardian), and many others, far too
numerous to mention. There is a great difference between the early and
the later works, such as those of Chaucer and Langland, in which the
French words are almost too numerous to count, whereas the *Cursor
Mundi* (c. 1300), a Northern work, contains only about five per cent of
French words, though the area from which it came may partly account
for the low proportion. The number of French words in the romance

of *Havelok the Dane* shows that there was strong French influence in the north-east midlands in the fourteenth century.

Many estimates have been made of the number or proportion of French words used by well-known writers, but in studying these it should be borne in mind that even in the same author the vocabulary will vary with the type of work, and Chaucer, for example, varies between ten per cent and fifteen per cent in different works. Chaucer was much influenced in his writing by foreign models, and it has been estimated that, of the eight thousand or so words used in his work, about half are from Romance sources. Dr Serjeantson has estimated that Chaucer and Langland use about ten per cent of French words. In the first eighteen lines of the *Prologue* there are eighteen French words, *Aprille, March, perced, reyne, licour* (liquor), *vertu, engendred, flour* (flower), *inspired, tendre, cours, melodye, nature, corages, pilgrimages, palmers, straunge, specially, martir*. Noting that Chaucer varies in his different works, Dr Serjeantson has analysed passages from four different types of writing, the *Nun's Priest's Tale*, *Boece*, *Balade to Rosemounde*, and *Troilus and Criseyde*, and finds 13.5 per cent, 12.3 per cent, 15.6 per cent and 11.6 per cent respectively, an average of 13.2 per cent, which she considers rather high for a general average.[1]

Apart from original works in English, many French works were translated by English writers, and this contributed to the great increase in the number of French words recorded for the first time between 1250 and 1400. Lydgate translated *The Fall of Princes* and the *Troy Book* from French texts in the first half of the fifteenth century, and later in the century Caxton, Malory, Rivers, and others also translated from the French, and Caxton, as he tells us in his introduction to the *Eneydos*, was blamed by some people 'sayeng yt in my translacyons I had ouer curyous termes which coude not be vnderstande of comyn peple'.

The general rate of introduction of French words into literary English also provides an interesting parallel to the evidence just examined of the use in individual works as a confirmation of the picture already presented in this chapter of the use of the two languages. There are very few before 1100, and probably not more than five hundred before 1250; the total is doubled in the next fifty years, and Skeat found about three thousand four hundred words in some thirty-one works written before 1400. The influx was greatest between 1250 and 1400, with the highest rate of borrowing in the last half of the fourteenth century. Jespersen compiled a table based on a thousand words in the first half of the alphabet,[2] and a similar list, based on the whole alphabet, was compiled by Baugh;[3] these lists confirm in their detail the general picture, and Baugh summarizes: 'For a hundred years after the Conquest there is no increase in the number of French words being adopted. In the last half of the twelfth century the number increases slightly and in the period from 1200 to 1250 somewhat more rapidly. But it does not become really great until after 1250. Then the full tide sets in, rising to a climax at the end of the fourteenth century. By 1400 the movement has spent its force. A sharp drop in the fifteenth century has been followed by a gradual tapering off ever since'.

Such a lengthy struggle between the two languages, with French remaining the regular speech of the dominant class for nearly two hundred years, with most of the literature during the same period written in French, followed by a period nearly as long when most of the ruling class were bilingual, and the important business of the country was still transacted in French, cannot but have had a great influence on the vocabulary of English, and we come now to examine in some detail the particular aspects of expression which were most affected. Once more, as in the case of Latin, we shall be able to see to some extent what aspects of Norman and French civilization and culture appealed to the English, or at any rate in what aspects the conquerors were most influential, for often we shall see that it is not so much the question of the introduction of new ideas as the replacement of an English word by a French word expressing the same idea. But we shall also find, as was the case with Scandinavian influence, many everyday words taken over, again replacing English words previously in common use, and sometimes we shall perhaps be surprised to discover that words in common use today were actually borrowed from French during this period, and have managed to become so thoroughly absorbed into the language that we no longer think of them as loan-words.

Before we go on to consider the loan-words in groups, classified according to the ideas they express, it may be interesting to consider the general implication of such a large adoption of French loan-words into English. The first point to be emphasized – and this has already been touched upon – is that here we are not dealing with completely new ideas introduced from a different type of civilization and culture, but rather the imposing by a dominant race of their own terms for ideas which were already familiar to the subject race. Such a state of affairs obviously means that there will arise pairs of words, the native and the foreign term, for the same idea, and a struggle for survival between the two, so that one of the words was eventually lost from the language, or else survived only with some differentiation of meaning.

Let us first take examples of native words replaced by French words; it is possible to compile a very long list, so here we must confine ourselves to a few, merely by way of illustration. As we have seen, the

Anglo-Saxon dynasty was replaced, and although *king* has been retained, many words intimately connected with royalty were replaced
by a French word; for example, *cynelic* was replaced by *royal*, *cynestōl*
by *throne*, *cynehelm* by *crown*. The Anglo-Saxon *witenaʒemot* – meeting
of wise men, was replaced by *parliament*. *Dēma* was replaced by *judge*,
firen by *crime*, *rihtǣw* by *justice*, *sacu* by (law) *suit*, and *scyldiʒ* by *guilty*.
Among religious words we find *dǣdbōt* replaced by *penance*, *lof* by
praise, *mildheortnes* by *mercy*. OE *lēod* was replaced by *people*. *Friþ* has
given way to *peace*, *wiʒ* to *war*, *siʒe* to *victory*, *fierd* to *army*, *cempa*
to *soldier*, and *onwald* to *power*. *Æþeling*, *frēa*, and *dryhten* gave
way to *prince* or *noble*, *wuldor* and *wuldiʒ* yielded to *glory* and *glorious*,
wlite and *wlitiʒ* were replaced by *beauty* and *beautiful*. Much of the
loss of Old English vocabulary can be accounted for by the influx
of French words for the same or a similar idea in the Middle English
period.

Sometimes both the words have survived side by side, but in that
case there has usually been some differentiation of meaning. The second
element of *witenaʒemot* still survives in the local *Moot Hall*, though only
rarely now are the local council meetings held in it, and the *moots* of
the law schools, at which cases are argued; we still speak of a *moot point*,
one sufficiently important or involved to be debated at a moot, and we
have a verb *to moot* (OE *mōtian*) – to raise a point, all connected
semantically. Although *dēma* has given way to *judge* we still use the
verb *deem*, in the Isle of Man they still have the *deemster*, and the judgement may still be referred to as *doom*, which is the development of OE
dōm, the unmutated form related to *dēma* – judge, and *dēman* – to judge.
Cynelic has given way to *royal*, but alongside that word we have its
native counterpart, *kingly*, although the two words are far from being
synonymous. There are many examples of these pairs of words, one a
native word, the other a Romance loan, originally of either identical
or similar meaning, with some distinction made today, such as *begin*
and *commence*, *child* and *infant*, *depth* and *profundity*, *freedom* and *liberty*,
happiness and *felicity*, *help* and *aid*, *hide* and *conceal*, *holy* and *saint(ly)*,
love and *charity*, *meal* and *repast*, *wedding* and *marriage*, *wish* and *desire*,
and there is the list, familiar to all, of *ox* and *beef*, *sheep* and *mutton*, *swine*
and *pork*, *calf* and *veal*, *deer* and *venison*, *pig* and *bacon*. The list could be
extended so as to cover Latin or later French loans also, such as *friendly*
and *amicable*, *hearty* and *cordial*, *house* and *mansion*, *lonely* and *solitary*, and
in both cases we should find that the native word has a more emotional
sense, is homely and unassuming, whereas the loan-word is colder,
aloof, more dignified, more formal. Sometimes, though very rarely,
the native word may have the higher tone, as in *deed* and *act* or *action*.

H

An obvious example to illustrate this point is the native *stink* and *stench* alongside *perfume* and *scent*.

There are examples of pairs surviving with practically no difference in meaning, as in *bloom* and *flower*, *fight* and *battle*, *folk* and *people*, *kingdom* and *realm*, *shire* and *county*, *thief* and *robber*, *weapons* and *arms*, though here again the sensitive ear may detect the difference mentioned in the previous passage.

Sometimes the word may have disappeared from the standard language and yet have survived in regional dialect. OE *ēam* was replaced by *uncle*, yet *eme* still survives in Scots dialect; *flītan* disappeared from the standard language, but some dialects retain *flite* – to struggle, contend, especially with words.

This large-scale adoption had two other effects on our vocabulary. We saw that in the Old English period many ideas new to the English were expressed by a native form derived from a combination of native material, such as *bōcere*, *dǣdbōt*, *sundor-halʒa*, *prowung*, and many others. Another characteristic of Old English had been its ability to form many derivatives from a single root, thus extending the vocabulary at will by forming noun, verb, adjective or adverb, once the basic root was available. The adoption of these numerous French words in the Middle English period marks the beginning of the decline of these two native characteristics. In spite of the wholesale change in the character of the vocabulary, this change in the nature of the language is perhaps the greatest effect of French, and later Latin, influence. We have an entirely new approach to language, which is now expanded chiefly by borrowing, not creating.

Finally, before illustrating the loan-words in classes, we may perhaps once again stress the chronological aspect, taking the first half of the thirteenth century, when the break with France was effected, as the dividing-mark. Before that, as we have seen, the loans are likely to be from Anglo-Norman, whereas later loans will show the influence of Central French. In the first period most of the loans are words which might have been picked up by servants from their masters, and words of a religious nature. The words adopted in the second period are the type which would have been in common use among the French-speaking upper classes in the early period and which were introduced into English in the speech of these people when they began to use English, either to supply deficiencies in the newly-acquired English vocabulary, or else merely by habit, because the words were so familiar and so much in everyday use. To put this in another way, the loans of the first period are such as might be adopted by English people from contact with people speaking French, those of the second period such as

terms denoting rank and position are French. Instead of words such as
æpeling and *dryhten*, and the many synonymous words used in Old
English for petty kings and princes, we have the French terms, such as
baron, count and *countess, duke* and *duchess, esquire, marquis* and *marchioness,
noble, page, peer, prince* and *princess, squire,* and *viscount.* We note that
earl (OE *eorl*) has remained, though his *lady* now has the French title,
countess, and that the native terms *lord* and *lady* also survive as designations of rank; OE *cniht* survives in form, but with change of meaning,
perhaps because the longer French form, *chevalier,* was more remote
from the genius of the English language. Some of the words specifically
connected with such an organization of society, such as *chivalry,
courtesy, courtly,* and *honour,* may also be noted here. Finally, again
closely connected with such a society, are the terms used in heraldry,
most of which are from French, though the present-day meanings often
bear little resemblance to the earlier meanings. Dr Serjeantson has
written: 'Many heraldic terms are now unfamiliar to most people,
though some are fairly widely current, e.g. azure, quatrefoil, cinquefoil,
chevron; others are used commonly in non-heraldic senses, e.g. bend,
chief, displayed, label, lozenge, proper; some are fairly easy to guess,
e.g. rampant, roundel, argent, sable; but many people would find it
impossible to say what was meant by mullet, saltire, caltrap, garb, fess,
mascle, flaunch, maunch, gules, passant, guardant, formée, pattée, paly,
semé, ragulée, gemel, gorged, segreant, engrailed'.[4]

We saw, in examining Scandinavian influence, that the Danes and
Norwegians had brought over here a highly-developed legal system,
and quite a number of Scandinavian words relating to the law had been
adopted in the Old English period. This Scandinavian legal system,
carried into Northern France at the same time as it was being introduced
into England, had been further improved by the incorporation of
details of the French system which had appealed to the Normans. This
Norman-French legal system was in turn introduced into England, and
imposed upon the English. Of all aspects of government introduced by
the Normans the legal system was the most prolonged, and although
English was established by decree in 1362 as the official language of the
law courts, yet 'Law French' continued in use for several centuries
longer, and was not finally abolished until 1731. We may therefore
expect French, so long the official language of the law, to have had
strong influence on our legal vocabulary, and in Pollock and Maitland
– *History of English Law* (I, pp. 80–1) we find: 'It would be hardly too
much to say that at the present day almost all our words that have a
definite legal import are in a certain sense French words. . . . In the
province of justice and police with its fines, its gaols and its prisons, its

constables, its arrests, we must, now that outlawry is a thing of the past, go as far as the gallows if we would find an English institution'.[5] And our French-named institution, *parliament*, recently considered doing away with even that survivor.

As an extreme illustration of the way in which French words replaced native words already in use to express ideas with which the English were acquainted, we may note that even the most fundamental concepts of the law are involved; OE ʒerihte is replaced by *justice* or *equity* – though *right* has survived, and, in a more limited sense, *righteousness* – dōm by *judgment*, firen, undǣd and mandǣd by *crime;* though synn and ʒylt have survived, yet the former has almost ceased to be a legal term, and its use is now almost entirely confined to religious contexts. *Thief, theft,* and *steal* have all survived; perhaps they were too well-known to be replaced, though one would think this argument would apply to many words which have been replaced. *Law,* from ON laʒu, which replaced the native ǣw, has itself survived, but the related adjective, *legal,* is a foreign loan. So numerous are words of French origin among our legal terms that it is possible to give only a representative selection; among names of crimes we find *adultery, arson, assault, battery, burglary, felony, fraud, larceny, libel, perjury, slander,* and *trespass;* very few English terms remain, of which *murder* and *theft* are most noteworthy. The names of people connected with the *court* – itself a French word, as are also *assize* and *sessions* – are usually French, as *advocate, attorney, bailiff, coroner, defendant, judge, jury, plaintiff.* Among the various processes of court we find *bail, bill, decree, evidence, fine, forfeit, gaol,* and its variant *jail, inquest, petition, plea, prison, proof, punishment, ransom, sentence, suit, summons, verdict.* Actions involving succession or possession of property introduced *assets, chattels, dower, entail, estate, executor, heir, heritage, lease, legacy, patrimony, property, tenure.* Verbs were adopted to deal with actions taking place at law, such as *accuse, acquit, arraign, arrest, banish, blame, condemn, convict, embezzle, indict, pardon, plead, pledge, seize, sue, warrant.* There are also adjectives such as *culpable, innocent, just.*

All the words quoted above have a distinct legal flavour, yet are in common use, and many have been carried over out of the court into ordinary life. Very many more examples might be quoted, from among French loan-words, of legal words which have remained the particular property of lawyers, and are hardly ever used by the layman, such as *amerce, eyre, implead, mainour, jeofail, seisin.*

There are also interesting pairs of words, sometimes almost synonymous to the layman, one native, the other a loan, which have survived, such as *theft* and *larceny, steal* and *rob.* The last-named example is an interesting form; it is really a Germanic word, and cognates are found

in several Germanic languages. The native word *rēafian*, with OE medial *f* for Germanic *b* (cf. OHG *roubon*, Dutch *rōven*), has been replaced by a Romance borrowing of a Germanic cognate.

We also find numerous legal terms in which the adjective follows its noun, which, by their word-order, show evidence of French influence; examples include *attorney general*, *court martial*, *fee simple*, *heir male*, *letters patent*, *malice prepense* (alongside *malice aforethought*, with the second element English), *proof positive*, and many others.

In some cases the French form has remained unchanged, or almost unchanged, in legal forms, as in *lèse majesté*, *malfeasance*, *tort*, and *puisne*, with an Anglicized pronunciation.

Oyez, used by the crier, is an interesting form; it is the imperative of the A Fr. verb *oyer* – to hear. We may be sure that many who use it, and most who hear it, know little or nothing of its source, or real meaning.

The Normans, as we have seen, soon obtained for themselves most of the chief positions in the Church. After settling in Northern France they had been converted to Christianity, and the race as a whole developed a strong feeling for religion, one aspect of which is to be seen in the noble churches they built in France and in this country. In fact, we might say with truth that one of the chief evidences for Norman influence in ecclesiastical matters is their contribution to church architecture; but we are concerned with linguistic influence. In addition to the fact that Normans occupied the chief offices, and took their language with them, there were many monastic establishments peopled entirely by Normans, where French would be the language in normal use, and records show that, when it seemed likely that English would displace French as the speech of the upper classes, rules were made in some of these religious houses insisting on French as the second language alongside Latin. We may, therefore, expect to find evidence of French influence in the religious vocabulary. This leads us to an interesting point; we saw in the OE period that quite a number of ecclesiastical terms were adopted from Latin, and many of the words denoting the orders and organization of the Church remain after the Conquest. But the French words which were introduced, many of which replaced the native words, were themselves developed from Latin. Thus we see that the words which had been coined in the OE period, as translation words from the Latin, or which had been adapted in meaning to express new ideas, and which during the OE period had been able to hold their own against the Latin invaders, now have to give way before this new wave of Latin in its Norman-French form. These new French loan-words cover almost every aspect of religious life, including the ranks of

the clerical orders – *cardinal, chaplain, clergy, dean, evangelist, friar, palmer, pardoner, parson, vicar* – words connected with monastic life – *abbey, chapter, chantry, convent, hermitage, priory* – with the services of the church, vestments used in these services, etc. – *altar, baptism, chancel, chant, confess, crozier, homily, lectern, mitre, orison, praise, preach, psalter, sermon, service, surplice* – words denoting the abstract ideas expressed by Christianity, many of which had earlier been expressed by native words – *absolution, communion, conversion, creator, miracle, paradise, pardon, passion, penance, penitence, religion, sacrifice, salvation, sanctuary, saviour, trinity* – and words expressing abstract ideas, both moral and religious – *charity, chastity, conscience, devotion, duty, faith, grace, mercy, patience, peace, piety, pity, purity, vice, virtue*, and many others, including such varied terms difficult to classify as *angel, feast, prophet, relic, saint*, and *virgin*. A chronological examination of these loans shows that the earlier adoptions are largely connected with formal Christianity and the organization of the Church, while the later loans perhaps reflect the influence of the preaching friars in that they represent the more personal aspect of religion, that which would concern the villagers and humble townsfolk to whom these friars devoted themselves.

As absolute rulers of the country the Normans were of course concerned with the means for its defence: to their natural warlike qualities they had added the best of French military ideas, and they were undoubtedly one of the most efficient races in Europe from a military point of view. When we bear in mind that they kept in their own hands all the positions of authority in matters connected with war, it is not surprising that this aspect of our vocabulary also shows strong evidence of French influence. Possibly, too, the fact that much of our fighting at that time was done in France may have had some effect. Again we shall find few new ideas are introduced; rather is it that common ideas, previously expressed in English, are now expressed by the Normans in their own language, and the English words are displaced. Such basic words as *war* itself, and *peace, army*, which replaced OE *fierd, here*, and other synonyms, *enemy, battle* – though *foe* and *fight* survived to a limited extent – *soldier, armour, arms* – though again *weapon* has also survived – are all French, as are also *defence, garrison, lieutenant, sergeant, siege*, and many others, including individual weapons and items of gear such as *buckler, dart, hauberk, lance*, and *mail*, though here again such common English words as *shield, spear*, and *sword* have withstood the French. It may be that it was because the English were themselves a warlike race, and had a very rich vocabulary of war terms, that so many of the native words have remained; it is also true, to a great extent, that the French words are concerned with rank and position, though two

obvious examples in this group, *captain* and *colonel*, were not borrowed until later, and with tactics in general, the abstract affairs which would affect the leaders rather than the rank and file, such as *advance*, *attack*, *besiege*, *conquer*, *defend*, *forage*, *pursue*, *retreat*, *surrender*, and *vanquish*, whereas native words connected with the more practical aspects of fighting – such as *fight*, *helmet*, *shield*, *spear*, *sword* – words which would be used by the soldiers – have managed to survive. Some of the native words which are now obsolete did manage to survive for quite a long time; for example, *fird* and *here* are found as late as the fifteenth century.

Next we may consider the organization of society, in particular of the upper classes, including the ideas introduced by the feudal system, by which that society was regulated. We have already seen that, although *king* and *queen* have survived, most of our words denoting rank and nobility are of French origin. More abstract conceptions connected with the organization of society, such as *feudalism*, *chivalry*, and 'feminism', the latter due to the influence of the literature of the courts of love, all reveal evidence of their French origin in the terms employed. Words such as *allegiance*, *fief*, *homage*, *vassal*, and most of the terms employed to express the many and varied social distinctions of the time can be traced back to the organization of society under the feudal system. The influence of chivalry in the society of the time is to be seen in the words used to express the qualities of the 'preux chevalier', later our 'gentleman': *bounty*, *courage*, *honour*, *loyalty*, *mercy*, *pity*, and *valour* are all introduced from French, as is, of course, the word *chivalry* itself. Moreover, our word *manners*, the characteristic of the true gentleman, is French, as are also most of the words expressing the social graces, such as *agreeable*, *amiable*, *courteous*, *debonair*, *gracious*, *pleasant*.

Society at a more intimate level, that of the family, also shows the effect of French influence: the native forms *father*, *mother*, *brother*, *sister* were all strong enough to resist the invader, but *aunt*, *uncle*, *nephew*, *niece*, and *cousin* soon replaced their native counterparts, perhaps because the connexion was more remote. *Grandsire* and *grandam* were formations which originated in England, and were never used in France; such formations are chiefly of interest because of the hybrids *grandfather* and *grandmother*, and, later, in the sixteenth century, *grand-daughter* and *grandson*, which were probably modelled on them. *Sire* and *dame*, originally titles of respect, also developed in England the meanings of 'father' and 'mother', but later suffered a rather remarkable decline from their original position of eminence, for, in the forms *sire* and *dam*, they are now used in ordinary speech only with reference to animals.

We come now to the second stratum, the less obviously dominant aspects of the ruling class. We may, perhaps, begin with literature, for the influence of France in the world of literature between the eleventh century and the fifteenth century was very great indeed. This influence was felt throughout the whole of Europe, and not only were French models copied and French works translated into the vernacular tongues of most European countries, but some of the greatest writers in European centres of culture wrote works in French, as we have already seen. We may, therefore, expect to find evidence of French influence in terms connected with the technique of literature. The new words introduced into our vocabulary are not, however, so numerous as might be expected, for Old English had a sufficiency of terms, both native and Latin, and these seem largely to have been carried over for use with the new type of poetry, the 'courtois' lyric poetry, the poetry of love and feminism, and the romance, which developed in France in the twelfth century, displacing the older heroic poetry and the *chansons de geste*, and gradually spreading from France throughout all Europe. The French verse technique, rhyming and syllabic, largely replaced the Old English alliterative measure, and so it is not surprising to find two basic terms, *rhyme* and *refrain*, taken over, the former at first in its French form *rime*, and changing later to its present form through the influence of the Latin word. *Poem* is also a French loan-word. New types of poem, such as the *ballad*, *carol*, and *lay*, were introduced, and their French names adopted with them, while the word *romance* is also obviously a French word, as its very meaning originally suggested.

Next we may consider the arts, taking that word in its widest sense, and architecture. The Anglo-Saxons had been able to resist the influx of Latin words connected with the mediaeval arts, learning, and education, native words being either coined or adapted to meet the needs as they arose, but now we find many words borrowed. The Normans are justly renowned as great builders; we have evidence of their influence in this field in many of our cathedrals and great buildings. It is, therefore, not surprising that many of our architectural terms have been borrowed from French. So numerous are these loan-words that it is beyond the scope of this work to attempt even a representative sample, but among them we may note *aisle*, *belfry*, *buttress*, *cathedral*, *chapel*, *choir*, *cloister*, *pew*, *reredos*, *transept*, *vault*. The religious flavour is very strong, as we may expect, but we also find terms connected with military works, such as *castle*, *dungeon*, *fortress*, *moat*, *portcullis*, *rampart*, *tower*, *turret*, and such general architectural terms as *arch*, *balcony*, *bay*, *ceiling*, *cellar*, *chamber*, *chimney*, *column*, *garret*, *latch*, *lattice*, *lintel*, *manor*, *mansion*, *palace*, *pavement*, *pillar*, *porch*. Many of the names of workers, tools, and processes in architecture are also derived from French, as *carpenter*, *joiner*, *mason*, *painter*, *plasterer*, *chisel*, *trowel*, *cement*, and *mortar*.

In art French influence was extensive, for the French and Italians have been our chief teachers, and French loan-words are numerous. Among them we may note three basic terms, *art*, *painting* and *sculpture*, and also *colour*, *design*, *figure*, *image*, and *ornament*.

Many of our musical terms are borrowed from Italian, but French loans are also numerous, and included among them are to be found *chant*, *chord*, *concord*, *discord*, *descant*, *harmony*, *melody*, *music*, *sound*, *tone*, and its variant, *tune*.

As we may expect, since all education was in the hands of the Church in those days, many mediaeval words connected with education are derived directly from Latin, but, although it is not always possible to be sure whether the source is Latin or French, it seems likely that such words as *college*, *degree*, *gender*, *grammar*, *lesson*, *noun*, *study*, and *university* are derived from French, though, of course, the ultimate source was Latin. It is, however, worthy of note that the two basic terms, *reading* and *writing*, have retained their English forms, but *spell* may possibly be a French loan-word, though a native source is more likely, and the names of two basic materials, *ink* and *paper*, are also of French origin. The influence of French on the vocabulary of mediaeval learning will be considered later in this chapter, but it may be mentioned here in passing.

French influence was apparently as paramount in the world of fashion then as it is now, and the fact that the upper classes were extremely interested in dress is obvious from illustrations of the fashions of the time. We may expect, therefore, to find French loan-words here too, and again we find that many of the basic words, such as *apparel*, *attire*, *costume*, *dress*, and *fashion* have been borrowed from French, as have also the names of many *garments* – itself a French word – such as *cape*, *cloak*, *coat*, *gown*, *habit*, *robe*, and what we should now call trimmings, or accessories, such as *buckle*, *button*, *collar*, *embroidery*, *lace*, *tassel;* the names of the more luxurious materials, such as *satin*, *taffeta*, and the names of many furs used in trimming garments, such as *sable* and *ermine*, are also derived from French.

Closely connected with dress are jewellery and costly articles of personal adornment, the particular concern of a wealthy ruling class, and here again many of the words used have been borrowed from French, such as *brooch* and *jewel*, and the names of many precious stones, though derived originally from many languages, have come to us through French: among these we may note *amethyst*, *diamond*, *emerald*, *garnet*, *pearl*, *ruby*, and *turquoise*.

We have already noticed French influence in the names of workers, tools, and processes in architecture and, extending our view of this class of word, we find that a great number of trade terms are derived from French, particularly the names of those trades with whose workers the ruling classes would have close and direct contact. Thus *baker*, *builder*, *fisherman*, *miller*, *saddler*, *shepherd*, *skinner*, *smith*, *wainwright* – now found only as a personal name – *weaver* and *wheelwright* kept their English forms, but *barber*, *butcher*, *chandler*, *cutler*, *draper*, *grocer*, *haberdasher*, *hosier*, *mercer*, *painter*, *spicer*, and *tailor* are all French, as are also *bargain*, *customer*, *profession*, *merchandise*, *merchant*, *money*, *price*, *purchase*, *value*, and although *shoemaker* appears to be an exception there is also the now obsolete term *cordwainer*, used now only as the title of one of the Companies of the City of London. We may note that, while the cloth is actually being made, we have the English term, *weaver*, but when the finished cloth is brought into the presence of the Normans it is the *tailor* who handles it. We may, however, wonder why *purchase* was introduced, when *buy*, the native term, was shorter and more convenient. When we remember the number of artisans introduced into the country after the Conquest, and bear in mind also that the capacity for organization already noted in the ruling classes might be expected to be paralleled by keen business ability in the lower orders, we can understand why so many of our trade terms are of French origin, and also why it is that it is perhaps the more homely, less skilled, and less remunerative trades which have retained their English names, though *founder*, *fuller*, *miner*, and *tanner* are derived from French, while those giving most scope for profit attracted the Norman artisan, who used for them his own word. It is worthy of interest too that the *merchant* seems to occupy a higher rank than his counterpart, the *dealer*, the name of whose occupation is native. The trade that *catered* – also a French word – for travellers also has French terms, as *hostelry*, *tavern*, and *vintner*, but *inn* is a native word. In view of this possible division of labour we shall expect French influence on our agricultural vocabulary to be slight, for it is likely that the Normans would leave the arduous task of cultivating the land to the subject race. Yet we do find words connected with life on the land, some of them, such as *peasant*, *serf*, and *villein* concerned with the organization of rural society, a few words connected with agricultural operations, such as *graft*, a few materials used in the more laborious manual tasks, such as *marl* and *manure*, the words *grain* and *fruit*, expressing in general terms the products of agriculture, and a few flower-names, such as *flower* itself, *dandelion*, *pansy*, and some others.

Now we may pass to the large group of words connected with household affairs, food, and cooking. Most people are familiar with the remark made first by John Wallis in 1653 in his *Grammatica Linguae*

Anglicanae, known better probably from its repetition by Scott in *Ivanhoe*, that so long as the domestic animals remained in the stall, fold or sty they retained their English names, *boar, calf, cow, deer, ox, sheep, swine*, because apparently they were then the concern of the English servants, but immediately they came into the kitchen, as food for the upper classes, they became *brawn, veal, beef, venison, mutton, pork* or *bacon*. It may be that French cooking was even then superior, and that the Normans preferred their own countrymen as cooks, and that this is the reason for so many of the names of utensils and operations in the kitchen being derived from French. The word *kitchen* itself survived, rather astonishingly perhaps, but cooking operations such as *boil, fry, grill, mince, pickle, roast, souse, stew* and *toast* are all denoted by words of French origin, as are also many of the results of the cooking, such as *jelly, pastry, pasty, sauce, sausage, soup*, and many of the ingredients, such as *cream, spice, sugar, vinegar*, the names of many herbs, such as *cinnamon, clove, mustard, nutmeg, parsley, sage*, and many of what we may term the luxury articles of food, such as *oyster, partridge, pheasant, salmon, sole*, and *sturgeon, almonds, cherries, dates, figs, grapes, lemons, oranges* and *peaches*, and even some of what we may now call everyday foods, as *endive, flour, gruel, lettuce, mushroom, onion, salad, treacle*. *Breakfast* retained its English name, but *dinner* and *supper* are both French, and while we still have the homely *meal, banquet, feast*, and *repast*, which suggest a different level of society, all came to us through French. On the other hand, it can hardly be assumed that all these foods and processes of cooking them were introduced by the Normans. In some cases we know that foods which now have a French name were known to the English before the Conquest, and, although some new and better methods of cooking were probably introduced, we may be sure that the English housewife in the tenth century was familiar with boiling, roasting, and many other ways of cooking, and that, even if the names of most of our spices, condiments and seasonings are derived from French, the English people ate their food neither raw nor unseasoned. As has been emphasized already, we do find a tremendous number of new words introduced in the four centuries following the Conquest, but we can be sure that in many cases the idea conveyed by the new word was already known to the English, that there would be, therefore, a word to express the idea, and that what we have to deal with so often here is the replacement of a native word by a French word with approximately the same meaning.

In the same way many words connected with the household, and with what may perhaps be called improvements in social life and creature comforts, such as *furniture* itself, *blanket, carpet, chair, chimney*, *counterpane, curtain, cushion, couch, lamp, lantern, quilt, table,* and *tapestry* were introduced, but most of these things must have been known to the Anglo-Saxons: we do know, from linguistic evidence, that they were familiar with *washing,* and we need not suppose, because the word *towel* is a French loan, that they ran around in the open until they were dry. We may perhaps care to see a social distinction in that *chair* is a French loan-word, whereas *stool* is a native word.

Again, *juggler, melody, minstrel, music, revelry* are all French words, but we know of the Anglo-Saxon 'joy in hall', the singing of the scop, the feasting, and the merrymaking generally. If we have to agree that so many of the words which signify a capacity to appreciate and enjoy the pleasures of life are French, such as, in addition to those already quoted, *comfort, dance, ease, joy, leisure, pleasure,* and *sport,* and most words connected with *sports* – itself a French word – and gaming, including most of the terms used in riding and the *chase* – though *hunt* was never displaced – such as *covert, falcon, kennel, leash, park, quarry, scent, track, warren, cards, dice, chess, joust* and *tournament,* it is not so much a question of the Anglo-Saxon nobility lacking all these things which make life pleasant as the fact that most of the upper classes were killed in the years following the Conquest, and replaced by a new ruling aristocracy, with a great zest for these things, and speaking not English, but French. We need always to be very careful in distinguishing between the introduction of words and the introduction of ideas.

As may be expected, French influence has not been great in seafaring terms, for the Anglo-Saxons had a vocabulary exceedingly rich in such terms, which had later been strengthened by borrowings from Scandinavian, and, moreover, by the time they conquered the English in the eleventh century the Normans had largely ceased to be a seafaring nation.

Another outstanding exception to French influence may also be noted. Apart from *face,* which was perhaps adopted because it was shorter and more convenient than the native words *onlete, onsene,* and *wlite,* the native names for the parts of the body have all survived. A related term, *voice,* has however, replaced OE *stefn.*

Naturally, not all words can be easily divided into groups according to meaning, as has been done with the examples so far quoted, and there are very many French words in our language which are of a general nature, and would not therefore fall into the main groups already discussed. But they are, in many cases, part and parcel of our everyday speech, and should therefore not be neglected in a discussion of the French influence on our vocabulary. It is obviously impossible to list even a representative selection of these, but some are so common as to demand mention, including, among nouns, *action, adventure, age, air, business, calendar, cause, chain, chance, choice, city, coast, country, cry, custom, damage, error, escape, fame, fault, folly, force, grain, grief, hour, labour, language, manner, marriage, matter, metal, noise, number, order, pair, part, people, person, piece, point, powder, rage, reason, river, season, sign, sound, success, use, waste.* Among verbs we find *advise, aim, allow, a ly, arrange, arrive, carry, change, count, cover, declare, defeat, defy, desire, destroy, endure, enjoy, enter, grant, join, move, obey, pass, pay, please, praise, prove, pursue, receive, refuse, rejoice, reign, reply, save, serve, spoil, suffer, suppose, turn, wait.* There are also many adjectives, including *able, active, amiable, brief, calm, certain, chief, clear, close, common, cruel, dangerous, double, false, feeble, fierce, final, firm, frank, gentle, honest, large, mean, natural, nice, original, perfect, plain, poor, probable, pure, real, safe, second, secret, simple, single, strange, sudden, sure, tender,* and *usual.* All these words were firmly established before the end of the Middle English period. Only words in common use today and not related to the groups already discussed have been included, and the list could easily have been increased tenfold without introducing unfamiliar words.

We may perhaps conclude this examination of classes of loan-words by reference to their occurrence in literary texts. It would be an impossible task within the limits of this book to investigate the various works surviving from the ME period, or even to take a representative selection, from different areas and of different periods, so numerous would the examples of French loans be. But it is perhaps possible to choose a fairly short text which contains material on most aspects of life. The *Prologue* to Chaucer's *Canterbury Tales* is often described as a picture of English life at that time, and although Chaucer was limited in his choice by setting his scene on a pilgrimage, thus losing the very extremes of society, we do get a fairly complete cross-section of the English people of Chaucer's time. If, therefore, we examine the *Prologue* for French loan-words, in their classes, it will give us some idea of the penetration of French words into English by the end of the fourteenth century, for Chaucer wrote at a time when borrowing from French was at its height, and, being a court poet, wrote for an audience representative of the superior culture to whom such work would appeal, and who could be expected to understand the French loan-words employed. It is to be noted that Chaucer rarely thinks it necessary to explain these terms, there being only a handful of French loan-words specifically explained by a native synonym, so we may take it that Chaucer's language was not unlike that of the Court.

The *Prologue* contains only eight hundred and fifty-eight lines, and so is a comparatively short work, yet it contains nearly five hundred words derived from French. The words to be quoted now will, unlike those already mentioned, be given in their ME form, since they are quoted from a specific text.

A large proportion of the French terms found in the *Prologue* are religious terms, or terms connected with morality and teaching, both of which were the particular concern of the mediaeval church. *Monk* and *nonne* survive from the OE period, as does also *preest*, but among the clerical ranks we find *chapeleine, clerke, curat, ecclesiaste, frere, licenciat, limitour, palmer, pardoner, persoun* (parson), *prelaat, prioresse, somnour*. Among the administrative divisions we find *diocyse* and *parisshe*, also *celle* and *cloistre*, the latter two being used also in the physical sense; *chapel* and *chaunterie* belong also to the last-named group, the latter denoting also the singing of masses. Many words are found connected with Christian faith, dogma, and traditions, and the regulation of the services; among them we may note *absolutioun, anoynt, assoillyng*, alongside the native word *y-shryve, confessioun, dyvyne services, feith, grace, lessoun, offertorie, pardoun, penaunce, pilgrims, pilgrimages, preyeres, preche, relikes, repentaunt, reule, service, text, vigilyes*. Among abstract conceptions we find *religioun* itself, and *charitee, conscience, ensample, pees, reverence*, and *solas*, and among adjectives denoting qualities of the nature just discussed are to be found *charitable, devout, honeste, pitous, solempne*, and *vertuous*. Among other abstractions, not specifically religious, are *adversitee, disdeyn, flaterye, maistrie*, and *resoun*.

Next we may consider the social divisions of the people at that time, such divisions being immediately brought to mind by *condicioun* (rank), *degree, estaat*, and *ordre*, which separate the whole *nation*, from king to *poraille* (poor people). The native word *king* is retained, as are *lord* and *lady, alderman, knight, reve*, and *yeman* (yeoman), but alongside them we find *bachiler, burgeys, governour, marshal, squyer, vavassour*, the *baillif*, the *frankeleyn*, and the *maunciple*, the terms of address, *sire* and *madame*, and the larger division of *nacioun*. At the other end of the scale we find *servaunts*.

Closely connected with this latter group are the terms denoting the social graces of the time, the qualities of the *preux chevalier:* among these we find *corage, chivalrie, curteisie, grace, honour, port* (carriage, bearing, behaviour), *renoun, vertu*, and *amyable, benygne, deyntee, digne, diligent, discreet, estaatlich* (stately, dignified), *fetys, gentil, pacient, parfit, plesaunt*, and also, indicative of a quality to be avoided by the *veray parfit gentil knyghte, vileynye* and *rudeliche*.

Here we may note also words connected with the leisure times of the ruling classes, their sports and pastimes. Chaucer uses *daliaunce, daunce, disport, cours*, and *venerye* (hunting) – though *hunters* occurs. Musical terms abound, as *burdoun, entuned, melodye, rote*, (probably a kind of fiddle), *sautrye, soun, tromp*, alongside native *fithele, baggepipe*, and *harping*, and we also note *purtreye* and *endite*, and *chere, delyt, felicitee*, and *jolitee*. Among words connected with entertainment we note *hoost*, *hostelrye* and *tavernes*, and *goliardeys* (buffoon).

Chaucer's pilgrims are drawn from a very wide circle: the higher classes in the social scale are represented by the Knyght and his son, the Squier, and they are accompanied by a servant, the Yeman. The Church is represented by the Prioresse, the Nonne, the Monk, the Frere, the Persoun, the Somnour, and the Pardoner. These two groups have already been mentioned. Amongst tradesmen, manual workers, and the ranks of society below the Knyght we find the Marchant, the Shipman, the Haberdassher, the Carpenter, the Webbe (weaver), the Dyere, the Tapycer (upholsterer), the Millere, the Cook, and the Plowman, and the Frankeleyne, the Reve, and the Maunciple. Amongst the professional classes are the Clerk, the Sergeant of the Lawe, and the Doctor of Phisik. The Wif of Bathe, in more senses than one, is in a class by herself! With so many varied occupations, it is not unlikely that we shall find many words connected with trade and the professions, although some are in the more distinctly laborious occupations into which, as we have already noticed, the Normans probably did not enter, and which therefore show little evidence of French influence.

So numerous are the words connected with commerce that one may be excused for thinking that nearly all trade must have passed into the hands of the Normans. *Marchant* itself is a French loan-word, and *haberdassher* may be derived from French, as are also *carpenter* and *tapycer*. Among related words we find *achat* (buying), *achatour, arrerage* (arrears), *auditour, bargaynes, chevisaunce* (dealing for profit), *cost, countour* (accountant), *dette, dispence* (expenditure, expense), *eschaunge, gover-naunce* (handling of affairs), *mercenerie, moneye, pay, profit, purchace, purchasour, rente* (revenue, income) and *taille* (account, cf. NE *tally*). But we also note such basic native words as *bye* (buy) and *chapman*, and also *rekenynge*. The terms *lyueree* and *fraternitee* (guild) are also used here in a commercial sense. Continuing our study of occupations we note that there is little French influence in the agricultural vocabulary, Chaucer using native terms such as *flok, folde, herde, shepherde, sheep*, and also little influence in words connected with the sea and shipping, where we find the native terms *shipman*, and *havenes, herberwe, stremes*, and *tydes*. We do, however, find *dayerie, forster* (forester), *gerner* and *pultrye* in the first class, and in the second class we have a hybrid, *lodemenage*, and perhaps *barge*, from Italy through French.

Medical terms are also numerous, including such basic words as *doctour, phisik, apotecarie, pacient, surgerye, maladye* (illness generally), and *pestilence* and *sawceflem*, two particular diseases, and *cordial, drogges,* such as *boras, ceruce, litarge,* and *oille, lectuaries, oynement, remedyes* (alongside *boote*), and reminders of the old system of medicine in *colerik, complexioun, humour, sangwyn,* and *superfluitee* (of a particular humour), and *astronomy* (to us, astrology), the (astrological) *houres,* and *practisour.*

There are also many legal words, although the native *lawe,* borrowed from Scandinavian, survived; in fact we may almost say that everything except the actual name was borrowed. We may note here *assyse, caas, catel* (property), *composicioun* (agreement), *conseil* (agreement), *covenaunt, decree, fee, justyce, juge, jugement, mariage* (in its legal sense), *sessiouns, statut, termes,* and *verdit.*

The profession of the soldier is suggested by the Knyght and his son, the Squier; military words occur frequently, such as *werre* itself, and *pees, armee, bataille, champioun, chivachie, chivalrye, listes, sege, viage* (armed expedition), and among names of articles of equipment and related words we find *bokeler, bracer, gypon, habergeon, targe,* and the comprehensive *harneised;* but we also find such basic native words as *fight, foe,* and *arwe* (arrow), *bowe, sheef* (of arrows), *spere, swerd,* and *takel,* confirming the distinction made earlier in this chapter, though *daggere* seems to have replaced the Anglo-Saxon *seax* for fighting at close quarters.

Chaucer describes the appearance of his pilgrims in some detail, so that there is no lack of words denoting articles of dress and ornament, and, as may be expected, the bulk of these are words of French origin. We have the general term *array;* alongside the native terms *girdel, hat,* and *sho* (shoe), we find *medlee cote* and *mottelee, baudrik, belt, botes* (boots), *broche, coral, coverchiefs, gipser* (pouch), *gowne, hosen, laas, mantel, pouches, robes, sleves, tabard, veyl,* also *pers* (stuff, material), *sendal* (silk), *taffata,* and *grys* (gray fur), and *embrouded* (covered with embroidery).

There remains only one large specialized group, of words connected with domestic life, food, and cooking. For the less delicate and refined kinds of food we find the native word, as in *breed* (bread), *chiknes, fish, flesh, garleek, lekes, marybones* (marrow bones), and *milk,* but alongside these are *breem, luce* (pike), and *oistre, partrich, wastel* (best bread), *blankmanger, deyntees, galingale, poudre marchant, mortreux, licour, oynons, pye, sauce poynant, soper, spice,* and *vitaille,* and *table dormant,* expressing the rich man's hospitality, against native *bord.* Alongside native *bake, carve, sethe* we find *boille, broille, frye, rooste.*

To extend this list to include all French words in the *Prologue* would be to lengthen it unduly, but enough examples have been quoted, in these classified groups, to show how thoroughly French had permeated the language, and it is not claimed that all the relevant words have here been quoted. Moreover, it will be noted that most of these words are in common use today.

A final point may be made about these French loans. The early loans have been, in the main, completely absorbed into our language, and many of the examples quoted in this chapter would not easily be recognized as loan-words. Naturally, some technical words, especially legal terms, which were hardly part of everyday speech when they were adopted, have still remained the particular property of the specialist, and some loans are still felt to be un-English, even though, like *naïve* and *bizarre*, they may be in fairly common use.

One other point arises which, though mainly of a phonological nature, is yet concerned with vocabulary. Although the Normans brought French to this country, it was not, of course, French as we know it today. Indeed, just as there was no standard language in England in the eleventh century, but a number of regional dialects, so also there was no standard French language, but a number of dialects, all descended from the colloquial Latin spoken earlier in France, and all in one way or another different. The dialect brought to England by the Normans was one of these dialects of French. Later in the period, as we have seen, we have the influence of Central French on our language, and, as these two dialects differed in several important points, we get pairs of doublets, the early loan-word showing the Norman-French form and the later loan-word the Central-French form. Later again we may even have triple forms arising, for sometimes the Latin word which had been the source of the Norman-French and Central-French forms was itself borrowed directly from Latin, and this Latin form naturally did not show the phonological decay to be seen in the French words. Let us start by examining words in the first two groups: Norman-French had [k] in some words where Central-French had *ch* (although *ch* had also developed in some parts of Normandy, so that early *ch*-forms may perhaps be Norman); as examples we may note *catel* (NE *cattle*) alongside *chatel* (NE *chattels*), both from Latin *capitale*, *cacchen* (NE *catch*) alongside *chacen* (NE *chase*), from Latin *captiare*, *cariteth* alongside *charitee*, *kenel* (NE *kennel*) alongside *chanel* (NE *channel*). Norman-French also had *ch* where Central-French had *s*, as in *launch* alongside *lance*. We find *w* in Norman-French words and *g*, *gu* in Central-French words, as in *wage / gage*, *ward / guard*, *warden / guardian*, *warrant(y) / guarantee*, and perhaps *wile / guile*; the forms with the stop consonant are found chiefly in and after the fourteenth century. Norman-French had *g* in words where Central-French had *j*, which leads us to an interesting pair, for whereas we spell *gaol* with the Norman-French

form we pronounce it with the Central-French form, and later a new
form, *jail*, influenced by the pronunciation, arose. Here we may compare the Norman-French form, surviving in *gammon*, with Fr. *jambon*.
Finally, although the point concerns us only in part here, we may note
that the pronunciation of French has changed since these early loans
were adopted, so that variations of pronunciation may arise according
to the date when the loan-word was adopted. An early loan from a
French word having *ch* shows an affricate [tʃ] in English, as in *chandler*,
charge, *chief*, but the later loan will show the later French pronunciation
[ʃ], as in *chandelier*, *champagne*, *chef*. Similarly, we find [dʒ] in the
earlier loans, as in *age*, but the modern French pronunciation [ʒ] in
later loans, as *camouflage*, *garage*.

Among doublets showing a second borrowing direct from Latin in
the later period, alongside forms borrowed earlier from French, we may
note, with the French forms in each case placed first, *balm / balsam*,
benison / benediction, *blame / blaspheme*, *chance / cadence*, *count / compute*,
danger, *dungeon / dominion*, *diamond / adamant*, *dainty / dignity*, *fancy /
phantasy*, *palsy / paralysis*, *sure / secure*, and, with a complete divergence
of sense, *reason / ration*.

We have already seen above an example of a Germanic form adopted
from French in the word *rob*. Another example reveals an interesting
pair; *choose* is developed regularly from OE *cēosan*, but its related noun
choice is derived from O Fr. *chois* (Fr. *choix*), developed from the verb
choisir, which is itself from OHG *kiosan*, cognate with OE *cēosan*.

In conclusion, we see, from the lists of words examined above, how
widespread was the influence of French in replacing native words, and
that the words introduced were at first of the type likely to be used by a
dominant upper class, but that gradually the influence spread to the
speech of the lower classes, and finally that, unlike the influence of Latin,
we have to deal here not with the adoption of new words to express
new objects and ideas, but that very often the object or idea was already
known to the English, so that the influence consists in the replacement
of an English word already in use by a new French word.

In this chapter our study of French influence has been confined to the
Middle English period, but, once begun, the borrowing of French
words never really ceased, and we shall see later that very many French
words have been adopted into the English language in the five centuries
since 1450.

CHAPTER SEVEN

★

THE RENAISSANCE AND THE
LANGUAGE OF LEARNING

After the period of Norman-French influence there is no period in the history of our language in which the influence of any one language may be said to be predominant. From the fifteenth century onwards English has been enriched almost continuously, and words have been borrowed from very many languages. It will, therefore, perhaps be best now to discontinue the method so far followed, of isolating particular influences, and instead to examine the development of vocabulary according to the particular field in which such development has taken place, and we shall begin with what we may call the language of learning. It is no part of the purpose of this book to discuss scientific vocabulary as such, (the subject of a separate volume in *The Language Library*), but the general reader will be surprised to discover how many words which were first introduced as particular terms in natural science, theology, philosophy, and other specialized branches of learning have found their way into the everyday speech of the average educated man.

In order to study the fashioning of the language of learning in English we shall need to go back a little further than the usually accepted starting-point, the Renaissance, for quite a number of words had made their way from the East into English before the end of the Middle English period. But as we move forward from the fifteenth century we shall be conscious of a change in the development of English, though one which concerns us but partly, since our study here is confined to vocabulary. In spite of the extension of vocabulary through borrowing from Latin, Scandinavian, and French during the thousand years from the Anglo-Saxon settlement to the end of the Middle English period, the outstanding feature of the development of the English language during that period had been the loss of inflexions and a consequent extension of the use of prepositional phrases, the change from an inflected to an analytic language. After the end of the Middle English period there are but few changes of importance in the grammatical structure of the language, but the development of vocabulary, particularly in the sixteenth and seventeenth centuries, and later again in the nineteenth century, is of greater importance. Yet we should not lay too much emphasis on this later development of vocabulary, for, though many of the words which have entered our language since 1500 are familiar to most speakers of English, it is nevertheless true to say that the great majority of the words in everyday use were firmly established in the language before that date, as we have already seen in the preceding chapters.

We now move clearly from the mediaeval period into the modern period, for it is with the end of the fifteenth century that mediaevalism draws to a close, and the world enters on a new phase. The discovery of the route to the east round the Cape of Good Hope was to the advantage of the Western European countries, and did much to lessen the commercial superiority of the Mediterranean peoples. With increased knowledge of navigation seamen became more venturesome, and the boundaries of the known world extended rapidly, particularly westwards. After the capture of Constantinople by the Turks the scholars who had worked there fled to the west, finding refuge in the courts of the Italian princes, and the learning which they brought with them soon extended throughout all Europe, the chief result being the study of the great classical literatures. Naturally, all this influenced language, and in two ways particularly may the effect on vocabulary be traced. In the first place ancient things, previously lost, were rediscovered with the introduction into western Europe of the learning hitherto hoarded in Constantinople, and the exploration of the seamen brought to Europeans objects and ideas hitherto unknown, and both these increases of knowledge demanded some increase in vocabulary if they were to be expressed in words. Another factor is also to be noted: just at the time when the boundaries of knowledge were being widely extended, and language developed to cope with the need to express the new ideas introduced, there was invented a means of spreading this knowledge more quickly and more widely than had ever been known before, and, moreover, of making such records more permanent. One may safely say that the results of the adventurous voyages of the people of these times, both physically into uncharted seas and unexplored continents, and mentally into the treasure-houses of Greek and Roman literature, would not have been so great nor so permanent had there been no invention of printing. Works which before had been laboriously, and often inaccurately, copied by hand could now be reproduced accurately in great numbers, and, as a result, books, which had before been the luxury of the wealthy classes, now became available to all who had the ability to read them, and the number of such readers was a good deal larger than most people imagine. There can be little doubt that, as these books became more easily available, there would arise conditions favourable to the spread of ideas and the consequent stimulation of the language to express these ideas. It will be our purpose in the next two chapters to examine the effects of this in two particular fields, the world of learning, and the aspect of language influenced by exploration and trade.

Before going on to examine the influence of the Renaissance on English vocabulary, we may take note of two earlier influences which call for attention. As we have just seen, the Renaissance made available to Western Europe the learning of scholars driven from Constantinople by the Turks, but ideas of various kinds had penetrated from the east before then, and indeed the influence to be examined now might have been studied in the last chapter, for the bulk of the words were being introduced, through French, during the period of Norman-French influence investigated in that chapter. Some of these eastern words appeared very early, and *ginger* and *galingale* – the latter used by Chaucer in the Prologue, as we saw in the last chapter – had actually been recorded before the end of the Old English period. Other words, such as *pard* (leopard), *tigris* (tiger) and *paradis*, had also made their way into our language before the end of the Old English period, and during the Middle English period many more words were introduced through French, which may be further traced back into Latin and Greek, and, in many cases, ultimately to the varied dialects of the Eastern Mediterranean countries. As Pearsall Smith has said, 'they represent, indeed, the wrecks and fragments of Greek learning which had been absorbed into Roman civilization, and which, after the destruction of the classical world, were handed on through the Dark Ages from compilation to compilation, growing dimmer and more obscure, more overlaid with errors and fantastic notions, in this process of stale reproduction'.[1] A formidable list of such words could be compiled, but we shall confine ourselves here to the commoner words, and those which have survived in our modern language. Three such common words are *cotton, orange*, and *sugar*, all perhaps brought into Western Europe as a result of the Crusades, as were also probably *assassin* – originally the 'hashish-eaters' sent out to murder the Christian leaders – *caravan, lute, mattress, miscreant*, which is merely 'an unbeliever', a term applied by the French to their Mohammedan enemies, and the obvious *Bedouin*. *Saffron* is an early loan, recorded from the twelfth century, *admiral, almanac, alkali, amber, camphor*, and *syrup* had all made their way into English from the East, through French, by the end of the fourteenth century, and in the following century appear such words as *antimony, caraway, lemon*, and *mosque*. In addition to the leopard and tiger, already noted in the Old English period, we find *elephant* (OE *elpend*), *hippopotamus, ostrich, panther*, and *rhinoceros* all recorded in English by the end of the fourteenth century, along with such fabulous creatures as the *basilisk*, mentioned already in Old English, *chimera, griffin, salamander*, and the *unicorn*, or *monoceros*.

The marvellous qualities attached to the last-named group of fabulous beasts had their parallel in the powers ascribed to some of the precious stones introduced from the east in the mediaeval period; among them we find *amethyst*, whose possessor was immune from drunkenness, the *beryl*, the *coral*, proof against enchantments, the *diamond*, the touchstone for poisons of all kinds, the *emerald*, the *pearl*, and the *sapphire*, all recorded in English by the end of the fourteenth century, and introduced, through French, from many tongues, *coral, emerald*, and *sapphire* being from Semitic languages, and *diamond* from Greek; *pearl*, whose etymology is uncertain beyond mediaeval Latin, appears in OE as *meregrota*, the source of NE *Margaret*, and a Sanskrit word which reached us through Greek and Latin.

Words connected with medical science also appeared early, though they are, of course, the vocabulary of the alchemist rather than of the doctor in our sense of the word. Among these we note *alchemy* itself, *alembic, alkali*, and *tartar*, all recorded before the end of the fourteenth century, and derived through French from Arabic. The Arabs were also skilled in the lore of the heavens, and as mediaeval medicine was closely concerned with astrology it is not surprising to find words of this class also introduced early, such as *almanac, azimuth*, and *zenith*.[2]

Other terms of learning, introduced from Latin, but almost certainly in most cases through French, are the names of the trivium and quadrivium, the seven liberal sciences of the mediaeval schools, for which, as we have seen, Old English had coined native terms, but which soon appear in their more familiar forms, *Grammar* (cf. OE *grammatic cræft*), *Logic, Rhetoric, Arithmetic, Geometry, Music*, and *Astronomy*, probably derived through the Latin which was then the universal language of instruction in schools, and other Old English native terms were replaced by later borrowings.

Latin words were also borrowed direct during the Middle English period. The early loans were technical terms, generally of a religious nature, and some of them, such as *benedicite, gloria*, and *requiem*, can hardly be said to be anglicized, though such ME loans as *collect, diocese, mediator, psalm* are in fairly general use. Latin terms were also introduced into the legal vocabulary during this period, some of which, such as *arbitrator, client, conviction, custody, equivalent, extravagant, implement, legal, legitimate*, and *pauper*, have survived to be used in a wider sense. There are also medical terms, such as *diaphragm, dislocate, ligament, recipe*, words connected with several particular spheres of learning, such as *allegory*, *comet*, *dissolve*, *equator*, *essence*, *library* and *scribe*, and many general terms difficult to classify, such as *admit*, *adoption*, *collision*, *combine*, *commit*, *compact*, *conclude*, *conductor*, *confide*, *depression*, *discuss*, *exclude*, *expedition*, *imaginary*, *immortal*, *index*, *inferior*, *interest*, *interrupt*, *moderate*, *necessary*, *picture*, *polite*, *reject*, *solitary*, *submit*, *subordinate*, *temperate*, and *tolerance*.

Among early Greek words, introduced usually through French or Latin, we find *theology* and *philosophy* in the fourteenth century, *comedy* and *tragedy* are both in Chaucer, *astronomy* and *astrology* had both been used earlier, and *microcosm* is recorded in the twelfth century.

All these words appear before the end of the Middle English period, and it is not unlikely that they were introduced through translations. Trevisa uses a great number of new Latin forms in his translations, and Wyclif and his followers, according to Dellit,[3] introduced more than a thousand hitherto unrecorded Latin forms. To take only a single verse from Wyclif, if we compare his version of St Matthew iii, 7, we find that he has replaced OE *sundorhalgena* by *Pharisees*, OE *rihtwisendra* by *Saducese*, OE *fulluhte* by *bapteme*, and OE *kin* by *generaciouns*. This single verse shows the extent to which he replaced native words by the learned words of the Vulgate. In spite of the difficulty of distinguishing between Latin and French loans in this period it is fairly certain that most of the technical words such as those quoted above were adopted directly from Latin, and there are in addition a large number of doubtful words.

One of the reasons which make it difficult for us to be sure whether a word was taken over directly from Latin, or through French from Latin, is the fact that at this time French was also borrowing a large number of Latin words of these kinds, and with identity of subject it follows that often the same word is found adopted in both languages. When a certain amount of decay is noticeable in a French word the source of the borrowing may be obvious; for example, *fact* is clearly adopted direct from Latin, and not through the French form, *fait*, which does actually occur as a loan-word in ME, with a rather different sense, as *feat*. In such cases the Latin form is usually longer, as in *blaspheme*, as against the decayed French loan-word *blame*. Again, English has often constructed a verbal infinitive from the Latin past participle stem, and if French adopted a type from the present stem the source would again be obvious; for example *confiscate* is from the past participle stem, and not from the French *confisquier*, from the present stem. The French form was actually borrowed, and occurs in Caxton as *confisk*, but failed to survive. Similarly, *instruct* must be direct from Latin, and not through French *instruire*. Yet there are many forms adopted in this period which

might have been borrowed from either language, since the English
form would be the same from either source, and numerous examples
occur of abstract nouns in -*ity* which might equally well be developed
from Latin stems with -*itat*- or French forms with its development, -*ité*,
or of adjectives in -*able* from Latin -*bilis* or French -*able*. The difficulty
arises chiefly in the case of technical words, likely to have been adopted
fairly late in both languages, for when the French word is a normal
survival of earlier spoken mediaeval Latin the form will usually be so
far from the classical Latin form that no confusion is possible, as in
blaspheme and *blame*, quoted above, or NE *sever*, from French *sévrer*,
as against *separate*, which not only cannot develop from French *séparer*,
since it is a past participle type in English and a present stem type in
French, but also does not show the change of *p* to *v* in mediaeval Latin.
Or we may note *surety*, found from the fourteenth century, which is
obviously French, against *security*, the borrowing either direct from
Latin or from the French *securité*. There is a further test for these doubtful
words which may not be so scientific, yet works in most cases. We
may say, speaking generally, that if a doubtful word is recorded for the
first time after the end of the fifteenth century, and has not an unmistakably French form, it is more likely to have been adopted directly
from Latin than through French, for after that time it was to Latin
rather than to French that scholars went for their learned terms.

   Another and different set of Latin loan-words, also recorded earlier
than the Renaissance, is the use of what are generally called 'aureate
terms',[4] a style to be found in some of Chaucer's successors, becoming
noticeable in Lydgate's writings, and gradually developing during the
following century. This was pure affectation, and the 'halff chongyd
Latyne' forms never became a part of our real English vocabulary, and
so need not be discussed at further length here, or illustrated, since our
concern is not with such 'precious' words.

   We pass now to the Renaissance, and its effect on English vocabulary.
The interest in classical learning which had been aroused in Western
Mediterranean countries by the appearance of fugitive scholars from
Constantinople after 1453 began to show itself in England early in the
sixteenth century. Wolsey encouraged the teaching of Latin and Greek
at Oxford, and Erasmus taught Greek at Cambridge. At first conservative opinion was against Greek studies, largely because the reformers of
the faith went back to the study of the New Testament in Greek, and at
Cambridge the Greek Testament of Erasmus was banned, but conditions
later were not so difficult.

   As a result of the Renaissance, two problems became of paramount
importance so far as our language was concerned, one being merely an

old problem intensified, the second an entirely new one, arising out of a new set of circumstances. The first was the position of English itself relative to the universal language of European scholarship – Latin. We have seen how English had to some extent resisted Latin influence in the OE period, but later there was a further challenge, more difficult to resist, and one which faced not only English, but all the other vernacular languages of Europe. For most of us today Latin is a dry, dead language, something of academic interest only, and it is hard for us to realise that in the sixteenth century in England it was a vital, living language, used in the services of the Church, the accepted universal language of philosophy, theology, and science, and even the language on which most emphasis was placed in grammar-schools, for the teaching of English then occupied a very subordinate position, and we often hear of men who are able scholars in Latin, but write English less well. More wrote his *Utopia* in Latin in 1516, and it was more than thirty years before it was translated into English. Calvin wrote in Latin. Both Montaigne in France and Bacon in England distrusted their native languages, and felt that only Latin would be permanent. It will also perhaps be remembered that Milton occupied the post of Latin Secretary to the Council of State from 1649 to 1660. Moreover, it was felt that the classical languages represented linguistic perfection, compared with which the vernacular languages were rough, immature, unpolished, and incapable of being used so exactly as the classical tongues. This comparison was always in the mind of the mediaeval scholar, and when he thought about the improvement of his own language it was only with a view to bringing it up to the standard of the classical languages. Although, then, English had finally withstood the challenge of French and had re-established itself as the popular national language, it was not the accepted vehicle for learned writing even in this country, and, to name but two of our great scholars of the time, More and Bacon both wrote in Latin. The rediscovery of the great literary records of the classical world could not but strengthen the position Latin had always held as the language of mediaeval scholarship, but even in the fifteenth century there had been champions of the vernacular languages in Europe, particularly Alberti in Italy and later du Bellay in France, in the sixteenth century, and in England we find Mulcaster, Ascham, Elyot, Wilson, and Puttenham all defending the use of English for learned purposes. The attitude is perhaps best summed up by Mulcaster: 'I do not think that anie language, be it whatsoever, is better able to utter all arguments, either with more pith, or greater planesse, than our English tung is. . . .' One notable result of this was to make the treasures of the Renaissance available to all, Latin or Greek scholars or

not, for in the spate of Tudor translations the works of most of the
great classical writers appeared in an English form, particularly those of
the historians and poets and dramatists. Although it is likely that the
primary purpose of most of these translations was to meet a popular
demand, that there was another side to the question is proved by Elyot,
who declared in the introduction to his translation of the *Doctrinal of
Princes* that he had translated it from the Greek 'to the intent onely that
I wolde assaie, if our English tongue mought receive the quicke and
proper sentences pronounced by the greekes'. And by the end of the
century the battle was so far won that Pettie was able to declare, coun-
tering the charge that English was 'barren', 'barbarous', and 'unworthy
to be accounted of', 'I durst my selfe undertake . . . to wryte in it as
copiouslye for varietie, as compendiously for brevitie, as choycely for
woordes, as pithily for sentences, as plesauntly for figures, and every
way as eloquently, as any writer should do in any vulgar tongue whatsoever', and Sidney maintains 'for the uttering sweetly and properly
the conceit of the minde, which is the end of speech, that hath it
equally with any tongue in the world'.

The second point concerns us more closely in our study of vocabulary; it is the question of how English would be able to adapt itself to
the expression of the new ideas which came in with the Renaissance,
ideas of arts and science known to the ancient world, and long forgotten,
the information and inspiration enshrined in classical literature, and the
wisdom of the old philosophers. In addition to this we have new ideas
arising as a result of the Reformation, new ideas in astronomy, as the
Copernican theory replaced the Ptolemaic, and the new ideas introduced
as a result of exploration. Once before, as we have seen, the learning of
the Mediterranean world had penetrated northwards to our islands,
and the Anglo-Saxons had been able to make use of the resources of
their own language to express most of the new ideas, but we find a
very different picture in the sixteenth century. As a result of French
influence English had lost much of the power which it had possessed
earlier to form compounds, to refashion its own material, and now we
find that nearly all the words needed to express the new ideas are
borrowed from Latin. This is a habit which has never left us, and, as
Jespersen has pointed out, when 'the ideas derived from classical authors
were no longer sufficient for the civilized world. . . . New ideas and
new habits of life developed and demanded linguistic expression, and
now the curious thing happened that classical studies had so leavened
the minds of the educated classes that even when they passed the bounds
of the ancient world they drew upon the Latin and Greek vocabulary
in preference to their own native stock of words'.[5] We shall have

abundant illustration of this later in the chapter when we come to examine scientific and technical language.

English, then, proved inadequate to deal with the huge influx of new ideas, and many foreign words were introduced. The need would be particularly apparent in the translations, already mentioned, and in many cases the writers, unable now to call upon the linguistic powers which had served the Anglo-Saxons so well, felt that they had no alter-native but to borrow the words of their originals for which English seemed to offer no adequate parallel, and indeed this point is specifically made by the translator, when he has occasion to defend himself for having borrowed too frequently. The words were often deliberately introduced with the idea of enriching the English language, and making it comparable with the classical languages; this was one of the purposes of Elyot, as he says: 'I intended to augment our Englyshe tongue, wherby men shulde as well expresse more abundantly the thynge that they conceyved in theyr hartis'. The method of introduction has been summed up as follows: 'free use was made of classical diction in the attempt to obtain increased power of literary expression. The beginning of this influence is seen in the translations, where numerous words of the originals were, perforce, retained; then, again, in the fashion of introducing classical quotations into works of various kinds'.[6]

Most of the new words were borrowed from Latin, but many also came from Greek, and the other European languages were also called upon to enrich our vocabulary at this time. The extent of borrowing from Latin is clearly shown in an examination of vocabulary made by Greenough and Kittredge; they have investigated all the Latin loan-words, adopted in all periods, and they conclude: 'we have counted the words beginning with A in *Harper's Latin Dictionary* (Andrews-Freund, revised by Lewis), excluding proper names, doublets, parts of verbs, and adverbs in -*e* and -*ter*. Of the three thousand words there catalogued, one hundred and fifty-four (or about one in twenty) have been adopted bodily into our language in some Latin form, and a little over five hundred have some English representative taken, or supposed to be taken, through the French. Thus we have in the English vocabulary about one in four or five of all the words found in the Latin Lexicon under A. There is no reason to suppose that this proportion would not hold good approximately for the whole alphabet. . . . Roughly speak-ing, then, we are safe in asserting that our language has appropriated a full quarter of the Latin vocabulary, besides what it has gained by transferring Latin meanings to native words'.[7] And, so far as our study of the sixteenth-century borrowing is concerned, we must remember that in that period far more words were borrowed than were destined to remain in the language, so that we can understand why Sir Thomas Browne commented that if the practice continued of writing so elegantly 'we shall, within a few years, be fain to learn Latin to understand English'.

The borrowing of these Latin words, where they really supplied a need, could only be for the ultimate good of our language, but we have already noticed licence in borrowing, in the 'aureate' language of the preceding century, and again we find some writers, deficient in critical powers, who are guilty of excess of borrowing in this period, and the practice of such writers led to the first conscious and deliberate effort to control the vocabulary of English, for there arose a group of writers who protested strongly against what they called 'inkhorn terms', language which used words favoured only by pedants, and never spoken or written by the ordinary man. Wilson, in his *Art of Rhetorique*, attacks those who 'affect straunge ynke-horne termes', and 'seeke so far for outlandish English that they forget altogether their mothers language'. Yet, in their zeal for purity, these defenders of our native language attacked many words which we now use every day.

The objection to the new words was based chiefly on two grounds, strangeness and obscurity. Elyot, defending his borrowings, talks of people who 'doo shewe them selfes offended (as they say) with my strange termes', but there can be little doubt that these 'strange termes' would cause a good deal of difficulty to the unlearned, as we shall see later when some of the more remarkable examples are mentioned, and they did indeed call forth our first real English dictionaries, the collections of 'hard words' explained for the benefit of those who found them difficult. The objection on the score of obscurity is well put by Ascham when he says: 'Many English writers . . . usinge straunge wordes as Latin, French and Italian, do make all thinges darke and harde', and Puttenham refers to 'many straunge termes of other languages . . . and many darke wordes'. Wilson comments: 'I know them that thinke *Rhetorique* to stande wholie upon darke wordes, and hee that can catche an ynke horne terme by the taile, him they coumpt to be a fine Englisheman, and a good Rhetorician'.

Others, however, took up the struggle as a matter of principle, and this attitude is perhaps best put by Cheke: 'I am of this opinion that our own tung shold be written cleane and pure, unmixt and unmangeled with borowing of other tunges, wherein if we take not heed by tijm, ever borrowing and never payeing, she shall be fain to keep her house as bankrupt'. Yet he does partly qualify this by adding later: 'and if she want at ani tijm (as being unperfight she must) yet let her borow with such bashfulnes, that it mai apeer, that if either the mould of our own tung could serve us to fascion a woord of our own, or if the old denisoned wordes could content and ease this neede, we wold not boldly venture of unknowen wordes'.

But this question of the admission of Latin and Greek words into English is often referred to as the 'inkhorn *controversy*', and the argument was by no means one-sided. There was no lack of writers prepared to defend their use of Latin words, and they pointed out that this was nothing new, for earlier languages had increased their stock of words in the same way. Mulcaster pointed out that strange terms become familiar by use, and Elyot rebutted the charge of obscurity, so far as his own writings were concerned, by declaring that all the new words he used were clearly explained 'by one mene or other to a diligent reder that no sentence is therby made darke'. Pettie defended the practice in general terms when he said: 'And though for my part I use those woords as little as any, yet I know no reason why I should not use them, and I finde it a fault in my selfe that I do not use them: for it is in deed the ready way to inrich our tongue, and make it copious, and it is the way which all tongues have taken to inrich them selves'. Almost at the end of the seventeenth century Dryden still feels the need to defend borrowing: 'I trade both with the living and the dead, for the enrichment of our native tongue. We have enough in England to supply our necessity, but if we will have things of magnificence and splendour, we must get them by commerce'.

The eventual result of the controversy was the adoption of a 'middle-road' policy. It was clear that English could not really do without some of these words, as even the purists had to admit, and soon objection was not to the loan-words as such but to excessive use of them. But the struggle had its value, as has been pointed out by Atkins: 'The conservatism of the purists proved a useful drag upon the energies of the reformers; it tended to preserve from obsolescence the native element in the language, and was a wholesome reminder of the necessity for moving slowly in a period of rapid change and hot enthusiasm. The efforts of the innovators, on the other hand, made great things possible. The language under their treatment became more supple, more ornate and more responsive to new ideas and emotions; but this was only after a certain amount of licence had been frowned out of existence'.[8]

Having discussed briefly this struggle between those who wished to enlarge our vocabulary by borrowing freely whenever the need arose and those determined to resist such a practice, we may now examine the effect of all this on our vocabulary. That the purists had right on their side is seen in the large number of words introduced which have

THE WORDS WE USE

failed to find a permanent place in the language. The usual reason for the rejection of a word which has actually been introduced into the language is that it does not meet a real need, and we can see clearly in some of the examples quoted below that this is so. Our examination of such forms will not be extended unduly, for we are concerned with the words we use, or which have been commonly used, and these can hardly be said ever to have formed part of the real living language. Perhaps we cannot do better than begin with a letter quoted at the time in order to pour scorn on the practice. Wilson, who was the author, and who claims that similar letters have been written, 'and praised above the Moone', calls it 'a letter devised by a Lincolnshire man, for a voyde benefice, to a gentleman that then waited upon the Lorde Chauncellour, for the time being'. He writes: 'Pondering, expending, and reuoluting with my selfe, your ingent affabilitie, and ingenious capacity for mundaine affaires: I cannot but celebrate, and extol your magnifical dexteritie above all other. For how could you have adepted such illustrate prerogative, and dominicall superioritie, if the fecunditie of your ingenie had not been so fertile and wonderfull pregnant. Now therefore being accersited to such splendente renoume, and dignitie splendidious: I doubt not but you will adiuuate such poore adnichilate orphanes, as whilome ware condisciples with you, and of antique familiaritie in Lincolnshire. Among whom I being a Scholasticall panion, obtestate your sublimitie, to extoll mine infirmitie. There is a Sacerdotall dignitie in my natiue Countrey contiguate to me, where I now contemplate: which your worshipfull benignitie could sone impetrate for mee, if it would like you to extend your sedules, and collaude me in them to the right honourable lord Chaunceller, or rather Archgrammacian of Englande. You know my literature, you knowe the pastorall promotion, I obtestate your clemencie, to inuigilate thus much for me, according to my confidence, and as you knowe my condigne merites for such a compendious living. But now I relinquish to fatigate your intelligence, with any more friuolous verbositie, and therfore he that rules the climates, be euermore your beautreur, your fortresse, and your bulwarke. *Amen.*

Dated at my Dome, or rather Mansion place in Lincolneshire, the penulte of the moneth sextile. *Anno Millimo, quillimo, trillimo.*

Per me Johannes Octo.

Among other words used in the sixteenth and seventeenth centuries which have failed to survive in common speech are *acroame, allectyve, anacephalize, annect, armipotent, attemptate, charientism, commorse, deruncinate, deturpated, discruciating, eximious, fatuate, furibund, illecebrous, immorigerous, inquisiturient, lapidifical, lubrical, magnificate, matutine, oblatrant, obstupefact, polypragmon, prorumped, suppeditate, temulent, turgidous,* and *vadimonial.* Doubtless many good words have been lost, and much time could profitably be spent on an examination of loan-words or coinages of this period which for one reason or another have been replaced by another word, or failed to hold their place against an existing word, but lost words of this type are not our concern, and we pass on to the words adopted in this period which, in spite of the fact that new words at that time tended to be learned and technical, have become part of our everyday speech.

Although the words introduced were of the learned type, it would be wrong to assume that they were all pedantic, and countless words which seem indispensable to us today were adopted in the sixteenth and early seventeenth centuries, and they now seem so obviously right and necessary that it is not easy for us to picture their ever having been threatened with rejection. On examining the list which follows, we can have little doubt that our language would have been considerably poorer if the extreme purists had had their way. No distinction is made here between Latin and Greek loans, for most of our Greek loans have come in through either Latin or French, though, of course, some have been introduced direct, and also no account is taken here of changes in meaning since the time of adoption, it being considered sufficient for our purposes to record the use in that period of a word which subsequently became a part of our regular vocabulary. So numerous are the words from which choice might be made that it is possible to give only a small selection, but this has been made as representative as possible, and has been limited to words in common use today. Classification according to meaning is hardly possible in such a list, and so division will be made into nouns, verbs, and adjectives. Among nouns we find *abdomen, anachronism, allurement, allusion, alphabet, antipathy, appendix, area, arena, apparatus, atmosphere, autograph, catastrophe, chemist, circus, crisis, critic, cynic, decorum, delirium, denunciation, dexterity, disaster, emphasis, energy, enthusiasm, equilibrium, excursion, exit, function, genius, idea, idiom, impetus, impression, irony, machine, method, omen, patriot, premium, scene, scheme, skeleton, squalor, system, terminus, theory, thermometer,* and *vacuum.* Verbs include *adapt, benefit, consolidate, emancipate, eradicate, erupt, excavate, exert, exist, extinguish, meditate,* and *penetrate.* To be found among adjectives introduced at this time are *abject, agile, appropriate, audacious, compatible, conspicuous, enormous, expensive, external, extravagant, habitual, insane, jocular, malignant, metrical, numerous, pathetic, pernicious, precise* and *scientific.*

Once established, this practice of borrowing learned words from

I

Latin and Greek, or coining words from elements in those languages, thus forming words unknown in the classical age, has never ceased. Much additional material will be noted when we study the development of scientific language, but we may note here, although it does not strictly belong in this chapter, some later loans from the classical languages. Again we shall avoid unusual words. Among words first recorded in the seventeenth century, additional to early seventeenth-century words already mentioned, we find *appreciation, approximate, crater, criterion, dispel, elastic, fluctuation, forceps, hallucination, hesitate, heterodox, longevity, loquacity, momentum, museum, orchestra, pallor, pendulum, precarious, query, scintillate, series, siphon, specimen, spectrum, stamen, stimulus, tonic, torpid, ultimate,* and *valediction.* In the eighteenth century are *bonus, camera, deficit, extra, inertia, maximum, nucleus, propaganda, prospectus.*

We may now turn from Latin and Greek to what was then called 'oversea language'. Experiments were made with various words from Romance languages, and although, again, many of these were later rejected, a great number did survive to enrich our vocabulary. One difference to be noted from the words discussed above is that these Romance borrowings are less abstract, pedantic, scholarly, that they denote objects rather than ideas, and are of the kind which might find their way into speech as well as writing. Again, as in the case of Latin and Greek, many of these words came into our language as the result of translation, for many works in French, Italian, and Spanish were translated into English during the fifteenth and sixteenth centuries: Ascham, in *The Scholemaster*, mentions books 'of late translated out of Italian into English and sold in every shop in London'. Other languages, too, had provided material, and by the seventeenth century English had borrowed words from more than fifty languages, so that extreme purists no doubt felt that they had right on their side when they protested against the importation of 'oversea language' into English. Wilson says: 'Some far journayed gentlemen at their retourne home, like as thei loue to goe in forraine apparell, so thei will pouder their talke with ouersea langage. . . . He that cometh lately out of Fraunce, will talke Frenche Englishe and never blush at the matter. Another choppes in with English Italianated, and applieth the Italian phrase to our Englishe speakyng'.

Words which were introduced as the result of exploration and trade will be considered in a later chapter, and so are excluded from the lists which follow.

Of French words borrowed at this time we may note *alloy, battery, comrade, detail, entrance, essay, flank, genteel, minion, moustache, pioneer, serviette, ticket, trophy*, and *vogue*. There are also many specialized naval and military terms, which do not concern us here.

Some Spanish words had appeared in English before the sixteenth century, having usually reached us through French, but borrowing takes place freely from the middle of the sixteenth century, though the number of words borrowed was never very large, and indeed is inconsiderable if words connected with the sea, exploration, and commerce are excluded. *Cork* and *cordwain* date from the Middle English period, and of general terms borrowed during the sixteenth and seventeenth centuries we may note *apricot, bravado, brocade, cask, cavalier, dispatch, embargo, escapade, guitar*, and *tornado*. The main bulk of the borrowings from Spanish and Portuguese will be found in the chapter on exploration and trade.

Although many of the words introduced into English in this age of experiment in language were soon discarded, it is probable that more than five thousand words first used at this time have remained permanently in the language. The words were, as we have seen in the examples quoted, largely of a learned nature, and some have remained so, but a great number soon passed out of the hands of the specialists and became current in ordinary, everyday language, as we may see by referring to almost any Elizabethan play, and many are in common use now in the everyday spoken language.

We pass finally in this chapter to a rather specialized type of vocabulary, that of science and technology. In some ways this is outside everyday vocabulary, and therefore outside the scope of this present work, yet many words used originally purely in a scientific sense have tended to become part of our general vocabulary, and so call for mention here. It is, however, not proposed to deal with the subject exhaustively here, but merely to outline the development of scientific vocabulary, to ask ourselves why such a vocabulary was originally necessary, how the words were formed, from what sources, and how much of it has remained the particular province of the scientist. But before doing this we perhaps ought to find out just what this scientific language is, and we cannot do better than start with a sample. Dr Victor Grove, in *The Language Bar*, quotes an extreme example, requoted by Savory:[9] 'Begoniaceae, by their anthero-connectival fabric, indicate a close relationship with anonaceo-hydrocharideo-nymphaeoid forms, an affinity confirmed by the serpentarioid flexuoso-nodulous stem, the liriodendroid stipules, and cissoid and victorioid foliage of a certain Begonia, and if considered hypogynous, would, in their triquetrous capsule, alate seed, apetalism, and tufted stamination, represent the floral fabric of Nepenthes, itself of aristolochioid affinity, while, by its pitchered leaves, directly belonging to Sarracenias and Dionaceas'. Or we may note an example, not quite so fearsome, quoted by Weekley: 'A gulf divides the exaltations of the mystics from the tachypraxia of the microsplanchnic hyperthyroidics or the ideo-affective dissociations of the schizothymes'. From this we pass with relief to Whewell's definition: 'When our knowledge becomes perfectly exact and intellectual, we require a language which shall also be exact and intellectual; we shall exclude alike vagueness and fancy, imperfection and superfluity; in which each term shall convey a meaning steadily fixed and vigorously limited. Such is the language of science'. An obvious comment has been made on the value of such a utilitarian language: 'Efficiency and lucidity are two great virtues in writing, but they are far from being the only virtues'. The scientist's answer to this is, of course, a defence of his purpose. He does not seek to arouse emotions, to present beauty, but only to make himself understood, leaving as little margin for error as possible, and if he achieves this he is content to leave the 'purple patches' to literary men.

Before discussing the development of science since the Middle Ages, the new substances, processes, and ideas discovered, and the rise of a language to express these ideas, we may perhaps ask why the scientist should demand his own vocabulary, and, moreover, why he should insist on using words or elements from foreign languages instead of the native material ready to his hand. Semantics is not an easy subject for the layman, but one aspect of it can be understood by most people – the gradual extension of meaning which develops as a word becomes more widely used. We have many words whose meaning is clearly circumscribed, words which refer to a definite object or idea, but this is not true of the bulk of our everyday vocabulary. The meaning of a word is often vague and indeterminate, and even where the basic sense is clear the boundaries are vague and fluid, and each speaker is inclined to fix his own boundaries. We may represent this definition of meaning by a series of concentric circles, the innermost enclosing the basic idea, and the outer circles becoming more and more unstable as they expand, needing more and more help from context if the meaning is to be grasped. This diffusion of meaning is largely due to association of ideas, the extent to which various speakers are familiar with an object, what it means to them, and the precise way in which they limit the definition. Words, then, may be inadequate as tools for exact and logical communication. St Augustine says neatly what so many of us have often felt when asked to describe an object or idea unfamiliar to the hearer: 'What is time? If no one asks me, I know: if I am asked and attempt to explain, I do not know'. But this power of exact and logical communication is the first requirement of the scientist. His one demand is for mono-significance, for terms that have a precise meaning and one meaning only, and which enable him to express his ideas with no possibility of ambiguity or confusion. He must know exactly what his word means, and he must be able to rely absolutely on his hearer's attaching to a particular word exactly the meaning which he attaches to it. Our ordinary vocabulary, with its vague boundaries to the sense of common words, is obviously, therefore, of no use when scientific precision is required, and so we must admit the claim of the scientist for a specialized vocabulary.

But, we may ask, why should he make things more difficult by using words and elements with which we are unfamiliar? To answer this question we must go back to the time when this particular vocabulary was first being fashioned, and the reason we shall find there is still being emphasized by present-day scientists, and, indeed, inventors of universal languages, for scientific language, to be most efficient, must be universally intelligible. In the sixteenth century, and indeed for some time after, scientific and philosophical works were written in Latin: Bacon wrote in Latin in the sixteenth century, Harvey's *De motu cordis et sanguinis* appeared in 1628, and Newton's *Philosophiae Naturalis Principia Mathematica* in 1687. We may, then, expect that when scientists felt the need for new words they would look for them in a language with which scientists in all countries were familiar. In the seventeenth century the newly-formed Royal Society attempted to encourage the use of English, and printed contributions in both English and Latin, but their efforts met with no success so far as the use of native words as scientific terms was concerned, and even today, when few scientists are trained in the classical languages, they persist in coining their new words from elements in languages with which they are largely unfamiliar, their knowledge of them being usually limited to the meanings of the particular elements they use. This is one reason; another is that Greek – and many of our scientific words are taken from Greek, either direct or through Latin – was the language of the people who had led the world in art, science, and philosophy. Moreover, the Greek language, as it had been developed by such clear thinkers, is eminently suitable for the formation of compounds with a precise meaning. But we have already seen that Old English had well-developed powers in this direction, too, and modern German still uses the process of compounding native words to form scientific terms. Apart from the fact that by the sixteenth century English had largely lost the habit of compounding and derivation, there are other reasons, well put by Bradley: 'it is often a positive disadvantage that a scientific word should suggest too obtrusively its etymological meaning. A term which is taken from a foreign language, or formed out of foreign elements, can be rigidly confined to the meaning expressed in its definition; a term of native formation cannot be so easily divested of misleading popular associations. If, for example, the English founders of the science of geology had chosen to call it "earth-lore", everyone would have felt that the word ought to have a far wider meaning than that which was assigned to it. The Greek compound, which etymologically means just the same thing, has been without difficulty restricted to one only of the many possible applications of its literal sense. Sometimes also a scientific term embodies in its etymology a notion which the progress of discovery shows to have been erroneous or imperfect: thus the name *oxygen*, formed by the French chemists from Greek elements, literally implies that the element so called is the distinctive constituent of acids. If our chemists, instead of adopting the word as it stands, had framed a native compound of corresponding meaning (as the Germans have done in their *Sauerstoff*), the retention of the name would have had the inconvenient result of suggesting to beginners in chemistry an erroneous notion. As it is, we can continue to speak of "oxygen" without thinking of its etymology, while if we do happen to know the literal sense we may learn from it an interesting fact in the history of science'.[10]

Another point which is often made today in support of our present scientific vocabulary is that the meaning of the Latin and Greek is so well known throughout the world that words compounded of such elements are readily understood by scientists the world over. There might be more truth in this if scientists were classical scholars – which, indeed, they are not, or they would never have coined some of their terms – yet it is probably true to say that the majority do understand the meanings of most of the elements in common use, even if they have no working knowledge of Latin or Greek, and this is really all they need. It is certainly easier for scientists of all nations to learn the meanings of elements in two fixed languages than to learn the corresponding elements in all the contemporary vernaculars. To this extent scientific vocabulary may be considered international, or supranational.

But, as Jespersen has pointed out, all this really applies only to words which are the particular property of the scientist. When scientific words filter into everyday speech the case is different; Jespersen comments: 'If the thing to be named is one of everyday importance, national convenience should certainly be considered before international ease; therefore *to wire* and *a wire* are preferable to *telegraph* and *telegram*. Scientific nomenclature is to a great extent universal, and there is no reason why each nation should have its own name for *foraminifera* or *monocotyledons*. But so much of science is now becoming more and more the property of everybody and influences daily life so deeply that the endeavour should rather be to have popular than learned names for whatever in science is not intended exclusively for the specialist'.[11]

These scientific words are almost invariably long words, and this means that the language of science must clash with precepts suggested at one time or another by different writers on English and English style – that Anglo-Saxon should be preferred to foreign words, and the short word preferred to the long. This last piece of advice is useless to the scientist, who just has not sufficient short native words available for all the ideas he wishes to express, and, which seems something of a paradox, the long foreign compounds are most serviceable to the scientist just because they are extremely unfamiliar to the ordinary man. Because they are strange they are kept apart from ordinary vocabulary, and therefore do not undergo the phonological and semantic changes suffered by many words in common use.

This mention of the way in which scientific words are kept apart from ordinary vocabulary leads us to consider the nature of such words. In the first place it will surely be agreed that most scientific words are extremely ugly, both in appearance and sound. No scientist would reject a newly-coined word on account of its ugliness, as a sensitive literary man undoubtedly would. The scientist does not concern himself with the beauty of a word, but merely with its efficiency. If a word expresses clearly the idea the scientist has in mind that is all he demands of it. This power of easy definition leads us to another characteristic: almost all scientific words are easily translatable, are, indeed, self-explanatory. Admittedly, the student of science needs to know the meaning of a few basic elements, but once they have been mastered there is little difficulty in discovering the meaning of a compounded scientific word, no matter how long it may be, for these basic elements, especially the prefixes, are used over and over again in all kinds of words. To take an easy example, even the layman could quote *telephone*, *telegram*, *telegraph*, *telescope*, and *television*, but he might be surprised to know that the NED lists nearly sixty words with that prefix, and Savory[12] points out that the same dictionary lists twelve words beginning with *phono-*, thirty-five with *pyro-*, forty-four with *thermo-*, and fifty-four with *photo-*. If we were to consider instead the use of suffixes, it would be something of a task to list all the words ending in *-itis!*

The next characteristic is inflexibility of meaning. One of the fascinating aspects of language-study is the way in which words change their meaning during the course of years. This is not true of scientific words, and such words coined in the fifteenth and sixteenth centuries are as limited in sense now as they were then; indeed, they would cease to be of value as scientific words if they had in any way extended or varied their original sense, for in that case they would not perform their primary function of clearly and unmistakably defining a particular set of conditions. But this constancy is to be expected, for change in meaning is dependent upon association, upon the picture aroused in the mind of the hearer by a particular word. Such changes take place usually in what we may call the penumbra, the outer, less clearly-defined circles, but the scientist, by his very training, has his mind concentrated on the basic idea in the innermost circle, and changes are extremely unlikely there.

Only when scientific words pass into everyday language do they undergo this semantic change and even then only for the layman, and not for the scientist. Savory[13] has pointed out two interesting examples of this kind. *Peroxide* was originally purely a scientific word, with no emotive content, but because of the power of hydrogen peroxide to bleach hair, and the opinion once held of women who used it for that purpose, it now has a derogatory sense when used as an adjective in such an expression as 'peroxide blonde'. Similarly, he points out that, to the layman, *atomic* suggests 'menace, terror, and undreamed-of destruction', because of the effects of the explosion of the bomb at Hiroshima. Yet to the scientist, at any rate while in his laboratory, there has been no such extension of the meanings of these two words.

The constancy to be noted in scientific vocabulary may be illustrated by reference to languages which have diverged within the last few centuries. An Englishman and an American, writing on a scientific subject at the end of the seventeenth century, would use a common vocabulary, and there would not be a great deal of difference in the language of an Englishman and an American writing novels, biography, or essays at that time. If we now move to the present day we find our English and American scientists still using a common vocabulary, but the language of the literary men has changed considerably. If we were to consider speech instead of serious literary work the difference would be still greater.

There are three main types of scientific word. The first is a word taken from the scientist's native vocabulary, and used with a particular force. This means that a particular word will have one meaning for the ordinary man and another for the scientist – a confusing state of affairs. Savory[14] has discussed several words, including *life*, *time*, *current*, *resistance*, *fruit*, *berry*, *force*, *weight*, and *work*, all of which have different meanings for the layman and the scientist, but the clearest example is perhaps the word *salt*, a word which means the same thing the world over to everybody except the scientist, who would insist on calling our 'salt' *sodium chloride*, and instead use our word for a chemical compound in which one element of an acid, hydrogen, has been replaced in whole or in part by another element – a metal. Here, then, is one danger, that of confusion, if ordinary words are pressed into the service of science, and this possibility of confusion justifies the scientist in his preference for unfamiliar terms.

The second type is also a borrowed word, but this time from another language, usually either Latin or Greek, and, since the language from which the word is adopted is not so familiar as the vernacular, the danger of confusion is less. This class of words differs from the third class, to be discussed below, in that a word which already exists is borrowed, that is, a word already found in another language is adopted without any change of either form or meaning. This is, of course, a method which would be widely adopted in the early period, when scientists were familiar with the classical languages, and had the whole classical vocabulary at their disposal. Among common words adopted without change we may note *axis*, *bacillus*, *fulcrum*, *pollen*, *saliva* and *species*.

Later, as the words whose meanings most closely coincided with scientific ideas were gradually adopted, the material from which the scientist could make his choice was reduced, and so he was compelled to make his own words, by taking formative elements from the classical languages and compounding them to produce forms which were unknown to Greece and Rome – the third type. In this coining the scientist is fortunate, for he has few restrictions to worry him. He need not worry about the emotive power of a word – indeed, he will avoid this; he will not concern himself with beauty of sound or form; he will certainly not be dismayed if he is accused by the classical scholar of coining words unknown to the ancients, or of coining hybrids. He will probably reply that the ancients would very likely have coined his word if they had been confronted with the need to express the same idea, and, as for hybrids, he is not concerned with purity of language or philological principles, but merely with the power of his word to express his meaning clearly and accurately: his concern is with intelligibility, not beauty.

We may now proceed to examine the growth of this highly-specialized vocabulary, and we must begin in a period before science as we understand it was known, the age of mediaeval alchemy. We may go right back to the Old English period, with *aspide*, *circul*, *grammatic*, and *lenticul*. There is, as we have already seen, a long list of names of plants and animals, usually derived from Latin, and some others such as *fefor* – fever, *mamme* – breast, *plaster*, *scrōfel* – scrofula, *ūf* – uvula, *comēta* – comet, and *termen* – fixed date. These, however, are of merely academic interest, and from them we may turn to the Middle English period. In the fourteenth century we find Arabic words making their way into the language, for science, and especially astronomy and mathematics, had been developed among the Moors. We find *alchemy*, *alembic*, *alkali*, *tartar*, *elixir*, and terms of astronomy such as *zenith*, *azimuth*, *almanac*, and *cipher*.

Scientific words from Latin or Greek are also found in Middle English, particularly in astronomy, alchemy, and the related science, medicine, and we also have names of plants, animals, and minerals. We find, for example, choosing only common words, *diaphragm*, *digit*, *fomentation*, *ligament*, *recipe*, and *saliva*, *dial*, *eccentric*, *equator*, *equinoctial*, and *ether*, and *mercury*, and *calcine*, *distillation*, and *essence*.

There is one fourteenth-century work which presents itself as an obvious choice in a search for early scientific words, Chaucer's *Treatise on the Astrolabe*, written for 'Lyte Lowys my sone', and based chiefly on the work of an Arabian astronomer, Messahala, who lived in the eighth century. It would be tedious to quote all the scientific words in this work, but some of those in common use today may perhaps be noted, taking them in the order of their appearance in the work: *sciences*, *nombres*, *proporciouns*, *tretys*, *orizante* (horizon), *latitude*, *regioun*, *astrologiens*, *fraccions*, *longitudes*, *declinacions*, *meridian*, *kalenders*, *celestiall*, *almenak*, *zodiak*, *planete*, *ecliptik*, *statutes*, *doctours*, *equaciouns;* all these are to be found in the Introduction. Continuing a little further, we note *clymates*, *orientale*, *occidentale*, *firmament*, *degre*, *minutes*, *houre*, *Aries*, *Taurus*, *Gemini*, *Cancer*, *Leo*, *Virgo*, *Libra*, *Scorpio*, *Sagittarius*, *Capricornus*, *Aquarius*, *Pisces*, *divisiouns*, *cercle*, the names of all the months in succession, *reule*, *mediacioun*, *Pool Artik*, *consentrike*, *equinoxiall*, *secundes*, *solsticium*, *tropik*, *equator*, *cenyth* (zenith), *azimutz*, *mesure*, *eclipse*, *compas*, *influence*, *operaciouns;* these words occur in the short first part, describing the Astrolabe itself. The introduction and first part take up about a quarter of the whole work, and although there will of necessity be much repetition in the later part, we may gain from this partial analysis some idea of the vocabulary then available to the scientist in one field only. It is not suggested that Chaucer was the first to use these words – in some cases he was, in many more not – but they are quoted merely as examples of what may be found in one work. In the *Canon's Yeoman's Tale*, one of Chaucer's *Canterbury Tales*, we find much of the current vocabulary of alchemy, but to quote from this also would unduly increase the examples of scientific vocabulary in the fourteenth century, and the reader is referred to the *Tale* itself.

Some words were added in the fifteenth and sixteenth centuries, but not a great number, probably because most scientific works were written in Latin. Among them we may note, from Arabic, and first recorded in the sixteenth century, *algebra, alcohol,* and a number of names of plants and animals, and from Latin and Greek, up to and including the sixteenth century, *integer, pollen, fungus, area, peninsula, abdomen, centre, magnet, rheumatic, surgeon, artery, meteor, vacuum, species, terminus, radius, delirium, virus, chemist, cylinder, prism, skeleton, theory,* and, again, names of plants and animals. We find also in the sixteenth century many words connected with anatomy, and quite a number of names of diseases, as *catarrh, epilepsy, mumps,* and *scurvy.*

The advance of science in the seventeenth century was very rapid, and we have such famous scientists as Boyle, Newton, and Harvey. Latin was still being used for important works – as we have already noted, Newton and Harvey wrote in Latin – but English was also now being used, and science was also spreading, being now no longer the particular province of the specialist, and this meant a large influx of scientific words into English. A considerable number of scientific words still in common use date from the seventeenth century; *zero* appears, from Arabic, and also a few names of plants and animals, but the bulk of the words are now from Latin and Greek; among them we may note *equilibrium, specimen, apparatus, formula, impetus, focus, data, complex, vortex, pendulum, fulcrum, calculus, lens, momentum, acoustic, clinic, coma, tonic,* and *electric.* By the end of the seventeenth century most of the bones and organs of the human body had received the technical names by which they are now known, and the advance in medical knowledge is revealed by the recording for the first time of names of diseases such as *goitre, pneumonia,* and *rabies.*

It is noteworthy that progress was more rapid in some sciences than in others. Advances in the study of the human body and its weaknesses, in anatomy and medicine, and increased knowledge in natural history, in botany, and biology are revealed by additions to vocabulary, but chemistry was only slowly freeing itself from the limitations imposed by mediaeval alchemy, and physics was as yet largely undeveloped, so that new words connected with these two fields of study are less numerous.

The classification of natural phenomena, begun in the seventeenth century, was further developed in the eighteenth. The human body had been so thoroughly investigated that little scope remained there, but many animals and plants were examined, compared, and classified, and we find many zoological and botanical terms added to the vocabulary, but most of these are too technical to merit quotation here. New discoveries in chemistry brought about many changes, and the large number of words connected with that branch of science which are recorded first in the eighteenth century testifies to the advances made.

The influence of science on vocabulary in the nineteenth century is well illustrated by a statement by A. J. Lawrence, quoted by Savory:[15] 'From the end of the eighteenth century the trickle of new scientific words became a steady stream, and by the end of the nineteenth it had swelled to a flood'. Almost all the words adopted after 1800 are composed of Latin and Greek elements, usually newly-coined, for most of the available words in those two languages had already been taken over, and the use of native words almost ceases, in spite of the efforts of purists such as Morris and Barnes. Some of the suggestions of the latter for replacing these learned loans by native compounds are extremely interesting to the philologist, as a revival of an old practice, but they had no chance of acceptance by the scientist, who was concerned only with expediency and intelligibility, and had no feelings for tradition in language.

It is no part of the purpose of this chapter to quote a long list of scientific words which appear for the first time in the nineteenth century and the first half of the twentieth. Such a list, if compiled – and this would not be difficult, for our great dictionaries are crowded with such words – would perhaps be of interest to the scientist, provided great attention were paid to chronology, for it would tell in terms of linguistics the story of the extraordinary development which has taken place in almost all branches of science in the last hundred and fifty years, but such a list would be of little interest to the ordinary reader. There is another reason against the inclusion of such a list here: these are words used particularly by the scientist, and our concern is with the words *we* use. Savory quotes a dozen such words, selected, as he says, almost at random: '*adiabatic, allotropy, catadromous, coleorhiza, conidium, isomerism, lodicule, micron, neurilemma, phyloclade, pygidium,* and *typhlosole*'. He notes that these 'are all used commonly enough in the different sciences to which they belong, but which have no place outside the language of the laboratory. Their existence, and that of scores of others like them, is but evidence of the increasing degree of specialization which was, and is, the characteristic of the developing language of science. It would be intolerable to read a very long list of words like these, and quite purposeless'.[16] And with that we may leave the highly-specialized vocabulary of science.[17]

CHAPTER EIGHT

*

EXPLORATION, COLONIZATION
AND TRADE

In this chapter we shall take the above words in their widest sense, so that, for example, we shall feel justified in treating contact with foreign countries for any purpose, even belligerent, under the first two headings, and under the last we shall include the effects of any exchange of commodities or processes. As a result of this we are able to make a start earlier than might be expected, in that period when religious zeal for the liberation of the Holy Land brought many Englishmen in contact for the first time with the wonders and strangeness of the eastern world.

Not a few words have entered our language as a direct result of the Crusades. Before these religious expeditions carried men from all Western Europe to the Holy Land, contact with eastern countries had for long been indirect, through the rich merchandise, jewels, costly materials, spices, and rich dyes, rather than with the peoples themselves, but the gulf was once more bridged when the liberating hosts made their way eastwards. It will not always be easy to be certain how much of the influence to be examined is due to the Crusades themselves and how much to the thriving trade of the Mediterranean, so, as this chapter includes both exploration and trade, we may perhaps take as one group all the words from the east which came into our language in the very early period, apart from the scientific words, which have already been discussed in the last chapter, and avoiding as far as possible common words mentioned in the early part of the last chapter.

One of the earliest commercial loans is *mancus*, the name of a gold coin; this Arabic loan is recorded in the Old English period, as is also another Arabic loan, *ealfara* – a pack animal, but as neither of these words has survived into the modern period they need not concern us further here. *Assassin* and *miscreant*, both definitely arising from the Crusades, have already been mentioned. In the Middle English period we have *saffron*, *cubeb* (a berry used for flavouring), *camphor*, *cotton*, *amber*, *syrup*, *lemon*, *antimony*, and *tare*, all Arabic words originally, though usually not coming direct from Arabic into English. *Damask*, from Damascus, is an obvious example. Direct contact between England and North Africa and the Near East increased in the sixteenth century, but we may leave that to a later part of this chapter.

From Persian in the early period we have a few commercial terms, including *scarlet*, originally a fine rich cloth, usually red in colour, hence the change in meaning later, *taffeta*, *borax*, *arsenic*, *musk*, all recorded before the end of the fourteenth century.

The only Turkish word recorded before 1400 appears to be *khan*, used in Mandeville's *Travels*, and, although this word has been used frequently in English, it has been only in works with a definite Eastern setting, and it has never really become a living English word.

Of commercial terms borrowed from the Semitic languages before the end of the Middle English period we may note *hemp*, *endive*, and *cinnamon*.

Extending our study still further east, we find a few words from China recorded early, including *silk*, and before the end of the sixteenth century more words appear, chiefly in translations, of which we may note *litchi*, a special kind of plum, and *chaa*, probably the Portuguese form of the Chinese word, but perhaps more familiar as a soldiers' slang term made popular through service in India.

We pass now to the sixteenth century, when the influences of exploration and trade on our language become more noticeable: from that period we have an unbroken succession of loan-words, in most cases the native names for objects, customs, and ideas with which our people, merchants, travellers, adventurers, and pirates, first came into contact in their adventurous journeys over the whole world, and as a result the vocabulary of modern English contains words borrowed not only from all the civilized nations of Europe, but also from countless peoples from Africa, America, Asia, and Australia. The remainder of this chapter might easily develop into a brief history of the development of the British Empire, illustrated purely from linguistic evidence, and this is, indeed, what it really is; historical details cannot be entirely excluded, but they will be reduced to a minimum, and the emphasis directed to the linguistic aspect. In the sixteenth century the age-old struggle for sovereignty over France was given up, and Englishmen turned to the sea, to foreign trade, a change which was to result in the establishment of the Empire. The international relations between the British and other nations may be illustrated in all periods from the sixteenth century onwards; in that century we have Spanish words adopted, reflecting the fierce struggles between England and Spain for the possession of the New World, and from contact with that same area Portuguese words were also adopted. Words from Mexico, Peru, and Brazil show relations with the Western World, and later we also find words adopted from the Amerindian languages. The sovereignty over India is reflected in the many words borrowed from Indian languages, and words have also been adopted from East Indian and Pacific languages. The aboriginal languages of Australia have also swelled our vocabulary, as have also both native African words and Boer words from our contact with South Africa. We have noted that words from far-off lands, particularly the East, had earlier made their way into our language, but these had all been acquired at second hand, usually through French. From the middle of the sixteenth century Englishmen were urged to go abroad and see things for themselves, and as a result the later loans are usually adopted direct from the native languages.

This adoption of native names for new objects, products, and ideas is not characteristic of English; the objects have made their way into most countries, and in the majority of cases the native word has been adopted with the object or idea. As Jespersen has said: 'There is, of course, nothing peculiarly English in the adoption of such words as *maccaroni* and *lava* from Italian, *steppe* and *verst* from Russian, *caravan* and *dervish* from Persian, *hussar* and *shako* from Hungarian, *bey* and *caftan* from Turkish, *harem* and *mufti* from Arabic, *bamboo* and *orang-outang* from Malay, *taboo* from Polynesian, *chocolate* and *tomato* from Mexican, *moccasin*, *tomahawk*, and *totem* from other American languages. As a matter of fact, all these words now belong to the whole of the civilized world; like such classical or pseudo-classical words as *nationality*, *telegram* and *civilization* they bear witness to the sameness of modern culture everywhere; the same products and to a great extent the same ideas are now known all over the globe and many of them have in many languages identical names'.[1] But it is, perhaps, a characteristic of English that native words have in many cases been adopted unchanged, contrary to the practice of some other nations.

We may now pass to a consideration of some of the sources of the type of loan-word to be discussed in this chapter, arising from contacts made either through exploration of foreign lands or seas, or through trade. Chronological order will be followed only in part, as it seems better in this chapter to trace the influence of a particular nation unbroken, from its earliest appearance to the present day, rather than to attempt to deal with all influences century by century. The historical picture is perhaps better preserved by the latter method, keeping all sources of influences in the exact order of their appearance, but the first method gives a clearer picture of international relationships.

Among the earliest influences to be noted are those of Dutch and Low German,[2] and these two may be taken together, as they are in some ways complementary. Three languages are concerned in this influence from the Low Countries – Flemish, Dutch, and Low German – and because these languages were so similar in earlier times it is often difficult for us to decide exactly the origin of a particular word. There is a further difficulty here too, especially for words recorded early, for these three languages are closely related to English, and would therefore share originally a common vocabulary. Some of these words which may possibly be Low German could be native words not recorded earlier. This is the same difficulty as we noted in connection with early Scandinavian loan-words. Contact between England and the Low Countries has been close for nearly a thousand years, not only in ordinary mercantile relationships – there is some evidence that a league of German merchants was established in London in the tenth century – but also through settlement of refugees in this country, through a common interest in the sea – Alfred employed seamen and shipbuilders from Friesland – and business conducted on the sea, and, we must not forget, national hatred and rivalry, and bitter conflict, especially the naval conflict of the seventeenth century. In Chaucer's time, as we know from his writings, there was a flourishing trade in wool carried on between this country, then a producer of the raw article, and the Low Countries, already renowned for their skilful weavers. Later, because of religious oppression, and direct encouragement from merchants here, many of these weavers were tempted to set up their looms in this country; there was some feeling against this, and many settlers from the Low Countries, chiefly the wealthy woollen merchants, were killed in the Peasants' Revolt. The merchants of the Hanseatic cities also carried on business with this country, chiefly with east-coast ports such as Harwich, London, and Boston, and much of the carrying trade was in the hands of the seamen of these countries. It is, therefore, not surprising to find Flemish, Dutch, and Low German words being introduced into this country; the influence is particularly noticeable from the Middle English period until the eighteenth century, though one rather surprising fact is to be noted, that the establishment here of the House of Orange did not result in any great influx of Dutch loan-words: this may be due to the relative positions of the English and Dutch civilizations and cultures. Not many words have been introduced in more recent times, though some Dutch words came to us indirectly in the nineteenth century from the Boers of South Africa.

The words, as we shall see below, may be roughly divided into classes, including terms connected with the sea, and with the wool trade, general trade terms, a few art terms, introduced comparatively late, some military terms, many of which were brought back by English adventurers who fought against Spain in the Low Countries, and a number of general terms, but they have one feature in common, a feature which they share also with loan-words from Scandinavian, another closely-related Germanic language, in that they are not learned or bookish words, but rather are they homely words which one might expect to be adopted quickly in everyday speech. Also, like other loan-words accepted into everyday speech, and, indeed, as may be expected from their Germanic origin, they are short, simple words.

Among early loans, recorded in the Middle English period and up to the end of the fifteenth century, we find *bowsprit, luff* and *skipper*, and a little later *buoy, freight, keel* and *lighter*, all before the end of the fifteenth century, among the nautical terms, *pack* (*package* and *packet* are later derivatives), a word borrowed from the wool trade in early Middle English, and *selvedge* from the weaving trade, general trade terms such as *excise, guilder, huckster, mart*, general terms such as *drivel, groove, loiter, poll,* and *spool*, and two words connected with drinking – *hops*, for the Dutch apparently taught the English the advantages of including hops when brewing, and *booze* – to drink deeply, one of the homely words already mentioned. Two other words connected with the cloth trade, *stripe* and *scour*, are also early loans. All these words are still in common use.

In the sixteenth and seventeenth centuries we find military words, such as *furlough, knapsack, onslaught*, probably introduced by English mercenaries on their return from the Low Countries. *Tattoo*, originally confined to military contexts, developed from Du. *taptoe* – the tap (or tavern) is closed; it was originally the signal, beaten on the drums, to close the taverns, but the meaning has since been extended. There are also terms connected with the sea and warfare, as might be expected from the powerful position of the Dutch at sea and the long struggle in the seventeenth century: these latter include *dock, cruise, jib, reef, sloop, smack, yacht,* and *yawl. Cambric*, from the town Cambrai, occurs in the sixteenth century, and among general and commercial terms we find *brandy, hawker, isinglass, decoy, domineer, hustle, ravel, smuggle, snuff* (first as the verb), and *stoker*. We are inclined to think the majority of our art terms are from Italian, but the influence of the Dutch School of painters is seen in a few loan-words, such as *easel, etching, landscape, maul-stick, sketch,* and *stipple*.

Among other loans from this source are to be noted *duck* and *nap*, both from the cloth trade, such nautical terms as *belay, boom, commodore, schooner*, two words probably introduced first in the brewing-trade, *scum* and *tub*, commercial words such as *dollar* and *groat*, and *wagon*.

Geneva, later shortened to *gin*, is from the Dutch form of the Latin loan word *juniperus*. *Forlorn hope*, introduced during the sixteenth century is from Dutch *verloren hoop*, literally 'lost troop', (Dutch *hoop* being cognate with NE *heap*), a body of men specially selected for a hazardous military task, and, as the Dutch form clearly shows, the English phonetic confusion of 'hoop' and 'hope' has tragically little connection in fact.

The Dutch words adopted later, in the nineteenth century, through contact with the Boers, are discussed below.

The next important influence to be noted in this group is that of Spanish and, closely related to it, Portuguese. Here we shall find words reflecting the adventurous nature of the Spaniards in crossing uncharted seas, the most important result of this being, from the point of view of English vocabulary, the Spanish colonization of the New World, and the later contact of Englishmen with the products of those colonies, and with the people themselves and their customs. Some words had come into our language in Middle English, through French, chiefly words of a scientific nature adopted from the Moors, but the majority of words to be put down to Spanish influence are connected with trade or travel. England was brought into close contact with Spain, through the marriage of Mary Tudor to Philip of Spain, at a time when that country was one of the great powers of Europe, and the undoubted leader in colonization, for Spanish seamen had been probing westwards since the late fifteenth century, and many settlements had been established by the middle of the sixteenth century in Central and South America, but the contact later was rather of bitter enmity in war and keen competition for the benefits to be derived from the settlements in the New World. Words were adopted in the sixteenth, seventeenth and eighteenth centuries from Spanish itself, but comparatively few Spanish words have been adopted, and the greater number were Spanish forms of native American words, or direct adoption of the words from the native languages. As a result of the contacts with the New World, first made through the knowledge of the riches being obtained by Spain and Portugal from the new possessions, and a desire to share in those riches, our language has itself been enriched with words from Mexico, Peru, Brazil, and other Central and South American countries. This is the really important influence of both Spanish and Portuguese. A fair number of words have been adopted in the ordinary way from both languages, chiefly connected with exploration and commerce, but the direct influence is not so important as that exerted indirectly; the efforts of Spain in the west and the Portuguese in the east led eventually to the establishment of our own overseas settlements, for their success tempted our own adventurers. Therefore we are indebted to them, indirectly, for many of the native words from our own Empire in areas which they first opened up.

The words from or through Spanish appear chiefly in the many travel books of the sixteenth and seventeenth centuries, and the reason for their appearance is clear; the writers had no English words available to express the new ideas introduced through contact with these strange countries.

We may note in passing that American English contains many more words of Spanish origin than does British English, because of the closer contact with Spanish-speaking America, and indeed Spanish was once the language of some areas in the southern United States. Many of these words have made their way from the United States to Britain in recent years.

In the sixteenth century we find *sherry, rusk, renegade, tornado*, and *bravado*. *Galleon* and *armada* reflect sea contacts, and *grenade* is a military word. *Breeze* occurs at this time, an adaptation of Spanish *briza* – the north-east trade wind in the Spanish Main. Of words connected with the American colonies, either Spanish words used to describe objects found there, as *alligator*, or Spanish forms of native words adopted, we may note *cannibal*, a Caribbean word, *negro, mulatto, armadillo, mosquito, potato*, a South American word adopted, and *cochineal*.

The seventeenth century yields *cargo, embargo, desperado*, and *esplanade*, all in common use. *Siesta, guitar, castanet* – really the Spanish word for 'chestnut', and so named either from a fancied resemblance to the nuts, or because they were made of chestnut wood – and *toreador* and *matador* are frequent in English, but usually with a Spanish flavour. Also to be noted are *llama, chinchilla, vanilla*, and *cockroach* (Spanish *cucaracha*, and nothing to do with 'cock').

Among eighteenth-century loans we may note *flotilla, stevedore, jade* and *cigar*, and some names of animals and plants, such as *cinchona* and *alpaca*, the latter having as its second element the Spanish form of a Peruvian word.

The later Spanish loan-words are derived from America rather than directly from Spain, and most of those in common use are words adopted in agricultural and ranching areas; noteworthy among them are *silo, lasso, stampede, lariat*, and *bronco. Vamoose* is a Spanish word adopted into American slang, and used on the same level in England, and *cafeteria* is a very recent loan, again adopted from the United States.

There are, of course, many other Spanish words used in English, such as names of dances, and of plants and animals, but the above list has been limited to words in common use, and not found only in specifically Spanish contexts.

Before discussing in more detail native American words which have been introduced through Spanish we may first turn to the influence of Portuguese, for it will be convenient to deal with the native American loan-words adopted through both Spanish and Portuguese at the same time. Like the Spaniards, the Portuguese were also intrepid navigators and explorers, and they had followed the western coast of Africa southwards, rounded the Cape, and reached India during the fifteenth century. By the middle of the sixteenth century they had established settlements on the Guinea Coast, in East Africa, in India, and, in the New World, in Brazil and Guiana. We see, therefore, that while the Spaniards had turned their faces westwards the Portuguese had gone chiefly to the east; it was in these two widely-separated areas that the English came into contact with them, and the division is clearly indicated in the loan-words adopted; our borrowings from the Portuguese have been chiefly the result of our contact with their colonial empire, particularly in Asia and Africa.

Two of the earliest loans are connected with new objects seen first in these strange territories. Both *flamingo* and *coco* (nut) are recorded in the sixteenth century; the latter is an interesting word, being derived from *coco* – a bogey, an obvious reference to the appearance of the nut, which resembles a grotesque human or monkeyish face. *Molasses* is also recorded about the same time. These three are probably due to western exploration; from Africa and the east in the sixteenth century we have *buffalo*, *madeira*, and *yam* and *mandarin; yam* is probably a native word adopted by the Portuguese, and *mandarin* is an eastern word borrowed by them from Malay.

The best-known of Portuguese loan-words – *port*, the name of the wine – is not recorded until near the end of the seventeenth century. As most people know, the word has its origin in the place-name *Oporto*. Also in the seventeenth century we find *dodo*, really the Portuguese word for 'stupid', and at first an epithet applied to the bird, a native of Mauritius. *Peccary* and *macaw* come from the west, the former perhaps a Portuguese form of a native word. *Guinea* is also recorded in the same century, first as the name of the *guinea-fowl*, and later as the name of the coin, one made from Guinea gold.

It was through Portuguese that many early words denoting Indian objects came to us. The Portuguese had already established settlements in India before, in 1600, Queen Elizabeth granted a charter to the group of merchants who were later to become the famous East India Company. One of the best-known general words arising from this contact is *caste*, from a Portuguese word denoting pure race or descent. *Padre* is a Portuguese word, adopted in a religious sense in the east, and then

Turning again to the old world we find one or two words introduced from African languages, including perhaps *yam*, through Portuguese, though the etymology is not certain, and *banana*, through Spanish.

Through Portuguese a few Dravidian words, from the original languages of the Indian sub-continent, have made their way into English. They appear chiefly in the sixteenth, seventeenth, and eighteenth centuries, when the East India Company was in contact with the Portuguese settlements established earlier. *Mango* has made its way to us through Portuguese, from Tamil, as may also have *curry*, though this may represent a later borrowing direct from Tamil. These words appeared in the sixteenth century, and in the following century we find recorded *teak*, which reached us from Malayalam, again through Portuguese.

Some of the earlier loan-words from Malay-Polynesian have also come to us through Portuguese, for they established settlements in the East Indies at an early period. The words begin to appear in the sixteenth century, and some have passed into common use. Of words which have passed to us through Portuguese we may note *gong*, from Malayan, through either Portuguese or Spanish, recorded at the very beginning of the seventeenth century, though from the reference to it in *The Antiquary* its use as a signal for meals was still 'new fangled and heathenish' in the nineteenth century. Other nations were also establishing settlements in the Pacific, notably the French and the Dutch, and words have come to us through those languages also in the seventeenth and eighteenth centuries. *Bamboo* and *cockatoo* came to us from Malay through Dutch, and through French we have *junk* – a ship, and *gingham*. *Launch* is another word Malay in origin, which reached us through Spanish in the seventeenth century.

It may be convenient here to complete our study of words adopted from Malay-Polynesian by noting the commonest and most important of the words which have reached us direct from those languages. *Sago* is recorded, apparently as a direct loan, midway through the sixteenth century; *paddy* and *rattan* also seem to have been adopted direct, both in the seventeenth century, as was also the most characteristic of the Malay loans, *orang-outang* – lit. man of the woods. *Amuk, amok* was borrowed from the same source in the seventeenth century but it has perhaps not become quite so much a part of our vocabulary as other words already mentioned; it still retains something of its foreign flavour. *Caddy*, from a Malay word meaning 'weight', was adopted, apparently direct, in the eighteenth century. *Bantam, kapok,* and *ketchup* are other Malay words first recorded in the eighteenth century. *Sarong* and *gutta-percha* appear in the nineteenth century from Malay, as does also *raffia*, this time a Malagasy word. Malagasy, the language of Madagascar, is a member of the Malay-Polynesian group of languages, in spite of its geographical position. A few Malagasy words had made their way into English in the eighteenth century through French.

From the Polynesian Islands, further south and east, we have *taboo* and *tattoo;* words from this area came into English in the late eighteenth century, following Captain Cook's journeys of exploration in the Pacific, and he himself used both these words in his *Journals. Ukulele,* from the same area, is a recent loan.

The number of words which have filtered into the English language from the Malay-Polynesian languages is surprisingly large, but not many form part of our everyday vocabulary.[4]

One fact which has already been touched upon in general terms may be noted here. English, French, Spanish, Dutch, and Portuguese alike felt themselves to be the superior race in their dealings with the natives of these areas, whether in the eastern or western hemispheres, the new areas had nothing culturally superior to offer, and, as we may expect, the linguistic result is that only words denoting indigenous phenomena, names of animals, plants, trees, products, and customs, have been adopted. We may note further that in very few cases have the settlers taken the trouble to use their own languages – in a few cases the Spaniards did so – but instead they have taken the easy way and adopted the native name; for example, *orang-outang* is found in English, French, Spanish, Portuguese, Italian, Dutch, German, Russian, and the Scandinavian languages.

From this discussion of words which have come into our language through early exploration and the Elizabethan spirit of adventure, and the later developments of contacts made then, we pass to an examination of the way in which our vocabulary has been enriched from many areas as the British Empire has gradually evolved. Not all territories have contributed equally, however, and some have provided few or no additions to our vocabulary.

We shall, of course, examine native words from various territories which have made their way into our language, but this will not be the only line of study open to us. We must, however, try to get rid of our insular view of English. Some Englishmen would be inclined to the view that the language spoken in Scotland, Wales and Ireland is hardly to be considered English. The matter goes deeper than that, however, and we must realise that British English, as the Americans have called our language since the day of Webster, is not the only kind of English. The English language taken to the British possessions originally was, of course, the language spoken in these islands at the time, allowing for any differences of class or regional dialects according to the origin of the settlers, but from that time the two languages developed in conditions of at least partial linguistic isolation, and naturally the languages have diverged. We must also bear in mind what we may call linguistic nationalist movements, deliberate attempts to set up a standard language for a dominion or colony independent of the standards applicable in the British Isles. Such a movement took place in America in the eighteenth century, and is to be seen today to some extent in Australia and Canada. In South Africa it is so strong as to threaten to oust English in favour of Afrikaans. With the justifications for these movements we are not concerned here, but we do need to take into account differentiations which might arise as a result, particularly if some of these differences are eventually carried back to the homeland and influence the mother-tongue – using that expression now in the sense of British English – as has happened in recent times, particularly in the case of American English.

There are also other reasons to account for differences between British English on the one hand and American and Commonwealth English on the other. The settlers came face to face with new races, with new customs, clothes, tools, and weapons; birds, animals, and plants were all strange; there were new geographical and topographical features. Morris, writing of the conditions in Australia says: 'It is probably not too much to say that there never was an instance in history when so many new words were needed, and that there never will be again, for never did settlers come, nor can they ever come again, upon Flora and Fauna so completely different from anything seen by them before'.[5] In other words, new objects, new ideas, new activities, all requiring to be talked about in everyday speech, called for a wide extension of vocabulary. This need could be met, as indeed it was, in two ways, by accepting the native name for the new feature, which seems to have been by far the commonest way, accustomed as Englishmen were by this time to pick up their vocabulary from every language with which they came into contact, or they could adapt English words to meet the new needs, or form new compounds. This has been done, particularly in Australia, but not very widely or very frequently. We are not concerned here primarily with the differences between the English spoken in the British Isles and that spoken in America and the Commonwealth, but only with specific words from these latter areas which have become accepted as part of the standard English vocabulary, but we may perhaps note just a few differences, in order to make clear the point that the languages are not identical, and to do this we cann͠ perhaps do better than quote a passage referring to another domini͠ the Dominion of South Africa, of whose language Pettman says: 'In South Africa a *mason* is not one who dresses stone or builds with it, he is simply a bricklayer; a *camp* is part of a farm which is wired or fenced in; a *boy*, if he happens to be a native, may be, and sometimes is, a grey-headed grandfather . . . *lands* in South Africa are not the broad acres of an estate, but just those portions of a farm that can be used for cultivation of crops; a *canteen* is a low-class drinking place. . . .'[6]

Some of the Commonwealth territories have been discussed already in this chapter, and we shall now confine ourselves to North America, India, Australia and New Zealand, and South Africa.[7] Perhaps a few historical details may serve as an introduction, and also to indicate chronologically the break-away from the language spoken in the British Isles. The English settlements at Jamestown in 1607 and Plymouth in 1620 – the latter by the famous *Mayflower* expedition – were the first in a series of settlements which soon established the Atlantic sea-board of North America as an English possession. In Canada French, English, Spanish, and Portuguese fishermen had established temporary quarters in the early sixteenth century, but colonization really began in 1608, when the French established themselves at Quebec. From there, Montreal, and the St Lawrence basin they spread west and south, taking over great expanses of the Middle West and what is now the United States. French influence in America began to wane with Wolfe's victory over Montcalm at Quebec in 1759, and eventually they were driven from Canada, although there is still much linguistic evidence of their stay, and finally they ceded their territories in the United States. As we have already seen, the Portuguese had first established themselves in India in the sixteenth century. The Dutch, and later the French, soon began to compete for the riches to be gained from trade with the east. Englishmen also began to get a foothold in India, and in 1600 the East India Company received its charter. By the middle of the eighteenth century the position had resolved itself into a struggle between England and France, and the victories of Clive eventually settled the issue. Dutch navigators had made contact with Australia in the early seventeenth century, and Tasman and Cook later penetrated to New Zealand, the former in the middle of the seventeenth century, and Cook more than a century later. In this case no wars were needed to establish sovereignty, and soon a͏ͭer Cook's exploratory voyages, sponsored first by the Royal S͏o͏c͏iety for astronomical purposes, and continued purely as exploration after that object had been achieved, settlements were established, New South Wales, Tasmania, Western Australia, Queensland, and South Australia being settled in that order between ..35, and five years later settlements were made in New

Zealand. The Portuguese, through the adventurous voyages of Vasco da Gama, had been first to make contact with South Africa, in 1497, and in the middle of the seventeenth century, settlements were made by the Dutch in the Cape of Good Hope region. When, during the Napoleonic wars, Holland came under French domination, the English seized these settlements, in 1795, and thus the Dominion of South Africa had its beginning. Some forty years later came the Boer migration to the Transvaal, and then followed the gradual extension of British control further and further north, resulting eventually in a large part of South and East Africa being added to the Empire, and contact finally being made with the Mediterranean by way of the Sudan and Egypt. This is the historical background for our study of the extension of the English language over the two hemispheres, and the effect of this upon the language spoken in the mother country.

Apart from American influence, which is so extensive as to merit a complete book of this size, and even then much would be left unexamined, the Indian languages provide us with most words.[8] Indeed, India is the only Asiatic country to provide a considerable number of words to enrich our vocabulary. As may be expected, the majority are native names for animals, plants, foods, occupations, the type of word that would be adopted during three hundred and fifty years of close commercial contact. Words have also been adopted as a result of our administration of the country, and many, particularly slang words, have been introduced by soldiers returned from Indian service.

Some words have been adopted from the classical language of India, Sanskrit, particularly in the early period and again recently. As we have already seen, a few words had made their way into our language in the Old and Middle English periods, as, for example, OE *meregrota*, the common mediaeval word for 'pearl'; *ginger*, *pepper*, and *sandalwood* recall the atmosphere of the east, as does *sendal*, a rich fabric, mentioned by Chaucer, and *panther* occurs in Old English. All these words are recorded before the end of the Middle English period. In the nineteenth century much attention was paid to Indian philosophy, and although the study can hardly be said to be widespread it did result in the introduction of a few Sanskrit words which are frequently used, and are certainly understood by many more people than use them; among these we may include *avatar*, *karma*, *nirvana*, literally 'a blowing-out', and used to denote the state of supreme good or blessedness, *swastika*, from a word indicating well-being or good-luck, and hence used as a symbol of good luck, and *yoga*. Apart from this type of word, most loan-words from Indian languages refer to material things.

Most of the words have, however, come to us through the common colloquial language of India, Hindustani, itself a development of the original Indo-Aryan speech, as was Sanskrit, and therefore, being a member of the Indo-European family of languages, distantly related to English, as we saw in an earlier chapter. But this Hindustani is much contaminated with Arabic and Persian, as a result of the Mohammedan conquest of India, and therefore words introduced through this medium may contain not only the original Hindi words, but also Arabic and Persian words introduced into Hindi, and finally producing the composite Hindustani. A few words are recorded in the sixteenth century, in travel books, of which only *lac*, a type of resin, and *raj* have survived, and even these to a very limited extent, the former being purely a commercial term, and the latter confined to politics. These words probably passed to us through other languages, Portuguese being the most likely. After the establishment of the East India Company in 1600 there was direct contact, and from that time onwards there has been a steady stream of loan-words, resulting in a considerable addition to our vocabulary, though most have a distinctively eastern connotation, and few are really popular words. For example, the use of *sahib*, *nabob*, *rajah*, *rupee*, *sepoy*, *coolie*, and *durbar* would immediately give an eastern flavour to a piece of writing, as would perhaps the Dravidian loan *curry*, and perhaps *cheroot*, but *bangle*, *bungalow*, *cot*, and *shampoo* are all in fairly common use.

The words cover a wide field, including clothing and textiles, food and drink, plants and animals, and official words, including military terms and titles and names of people and occupations, and we have *calico* (perhaps Dravidian, but of course introduced through trade contact with India), *cashmere*, *chintz*, *jute*, *nainsook* and *tussore*, all names of materials; foodstuffs include *chutney*, *curry* (Dravidian), and the drink *punch*, from a word meaning 'five', because there were originally five ingredients; and there are many general words, such as *bangle*, *bungalow*, *cot*, *dinghy*, and some names of animals, such as *cheetah* and *mongoose*.

It may be of interest to note chronologically the appearance of some of the commoner words. In the seventeenth century we find *bungalow*, *chintz*, *cot*, *dungaree* (though not used in its present sense of 'trousers' until the late nineteenth century), *durbar*, *kedgeree*, *lascar* (Persian, but borrowed in India), *mongoose*, *nabob*, *punch*, *sahib*, and *tussore*. This is a mere selection from a much longer list. Dr Serjeantson has recorded fifty-one words in the seventeenth century, and thirty-five in the eighteenth, noting that most are introduced in the second half of the century; she comments: 'There seems to be a slackening of interest in Eastern travel, and the East India Company was apparently carrying on much the same kind of trade as in the previous century. But in the middle of the century India and the Company were disturbed by the French bid for power, and after Clive's successful campaigns before, and after the beginning of the Seven Years' War (1756), a renewed interest in, and growing knowledge of, India is reflected in a new peo d of borrowing. Now we have again a number of words denoting persons and rank, some of them military, rather fewer concerned with textiles and clothes, a fair number of plants and animals, etc'.[9] Among common words we may note *bandana*, *bangle*, *cheetah*, *gunny*, *jungle*, *jute*, *nawab*, *seersucker* (originally Persian, borrowed in India, and meaning literally 'milk and sugar'), a word which has become quite common in recent years, and *shampoo*. In the nineteenth century the number of words adopted is considerably larger, and again the loan-words cover a wide field, names of textiles, plants, and animals, and words descriptive of Indian life, the latter found particularly in the many books, fiction, biography, and travel, which appeared during the century. Among these are to be found *cashmere*, *chutney*, *dacoit*, *dinghy*, *gymkhana*, *khaki* (a Persian word originally, meaning 'dusty', and used to describe military uniforms), *loot*, *nainsook*, *polo*, *puttee*, *pyjamas*, *thug*, and *topi*.

We turn now to Australia,[10] and here a difference is to be noted. When Englishmen made contact with India they seem to have been content in practically every case to adopt the native word. In Australia a number of words were adopted from the aborigines, but the settlers also made considerable use of their own language in naming the new objects and ideas with which they came into contact. This is a rather surprising feature, but it may perhaps be explained by the type of person first coming into contact with Australian conditions. The earliest British people to inhabit Australia were either convicts sent to the penal settlements, speaking Cockney or some regional dialect, soldiers, who would probably speak a similar dialect, and a few officials who may have spoken standard English but were hardly numerous enough to be effective from a linguistic point of view. Moreover, with settlers speaking almost every regional dialect to be found in England, Scotland, Ireland, and Wales, and with the class dialects representative of the lower rather than the upper classes, there would be little inherent respect for the standard language, and even today Australia is note-worthy among the members of the Commonwealth for a powerful nationalist movement so far as language is concerned. The position which resulted has been well described by Jespersen, who, speaking of the use made by these early settlers of material from their own lan-guages, refers to 'the ease with which new terms actually *are* framed whenever the need of them is really felt, especially by uneducated people who are not tempted to go outside their own language to express their thoughts'.

There were two processes open to the settlers when faced by the need to find names for the amazing variety of new ideas and objects confronting them. They could do as the settlers in India did, and as we frequently find newcomers do when faced by strange phenomena in a foreign country, that is, they could adopt the native word along with the object or idea. But we find that the language of the Aborigines has not influenced English to any great extent, the chief examples being, as we should expect, names of animals, birds, and plants, and some place-names, which are hardly part of popular vocabulary. The second process open to them, one which was extensively followed, was to rely on their own language, by using English words for objects which seemed to them to resemble objects known to them in England, or to form new compounds.

. We may take first words borrowed from the languages of the Aborigines. One of the first words which comes to mind in thinking of Australia is the name of the animal which for most people is the symbol of the continent; *kangaroo* was recorded by Captain Cook in the late eighteenth century. *Corroboree* and *wombat*, both adopted in the same century, may be called Australian words rather than part of the standard vocabulary of English, as may also *koala*, the Australian bear, and *paramatta*, or *parramatta*, a lightweight fabric, both recorded first in the nineteenth century, but another word adopted about the same time, *boomerang*, has found a permanent place in our language, where it has developed a wider use in a figurative sense than as the name of the article itself. *Budgerigar* (literally 'good cockatoo') is now in common use, as the bird is very popular as a pet, and the names of two Australian trees, *jarrah* and *karri*, are also often used.

The English words used by the settlers to describe new phenomena concern us here only in so far as there may be a change of meaning; for example, *robin* is used to describe birds which do not resemble our own robin, a *jackass* (shortened from 'laughing jackass') is a bird, so named because its harsh call resembled the bray of a donkey, and the Australian oak is not the same tree as the English oak. Words such as those quoted by Jespersen, selected from Morris' *Austral English*, 'names of birds like *friar-bird, frogsmouth, honey-eater, ground-lark, forty-spot*, of fishes like *long-fin, trumpeter*, of plants like *sugar-grass, hedge-laurel, iron-heart, thousand-jacket*',[11] do not really concern us, for they again are rather Australian words than part of the common vocabulary, but we must agree with Morris when he says of such formations 'the settler must have had an imagination. Whip-bird, or Coach-bird, from the sound of the note, Lyre-bird from the appearance of the outspread tail, are admirable names', and also with Jespersen's comment: 'It certainly seems a pity that book-learned people when wanting to enrich their mother-tongue have not, as a rule, drawn from the same source or shown the same talent for picturesque and "telling" designations'.

New Zealand has contributed little to our vocabulary. It is perhaps the most English of all members of the Commonwealth, and has preserved a speech nearest, apart from pronunciation, to the speech of the motherland. A few words borrowed from the Maori languages, such as *kauri* and *kiwi*, have made their way into the general vocabulary of English, but on the whole the influence is slight.[12]

A different state of affairs is to be found in South Africa,[13] where conditions have at times been far from peaceful, and where the English language has had to contend with a strong rival, the original Dutch language as it developed in South Africa into Afrikaans. English is now the language of a minority of white people in South Africa, and whereas up to 1900 the English language was important in the Dominion, its influence has steadily decreased in the last fifty years, for in that period the Boers, the upholders of Afrikaans, have gradually evolved from a defeated people to the governing race, represented by a strongly Nationalist government elected by democratic and constitutional means. It is not surprising, therefore, to find a very strong nationalist linguistic movement.

Contributions to our vocabulary from South Africa may conveniently be discussed under two heads, words from the native African languages, and words from Afrikaans, and here an important difference is to be noted in the attitude of the two groups of settlers, the Dutch and the English. The Dutch, confronted by new natural objects, met the need for new words in the same way as their near neighbours and linguistic cousins, the Germans, do; they used the resources of their own language, either modifying the meaning of existing Dutch words or coining new words, usually compounds. For example, they did not enquire after the native name for the wide, open plains, but used their own word *veldt* (or perhaps preferably *veld*) – a field. Another well-known word so used is *kopje* – a little head or cup, to denote the low, flat hills, and similarly many animals, birds, and plants were given Dutch names. The English, on the other hand, followed their usual practice, bۛ ̄ ̄ ̄ ing words indiscriminately to name the new features, and adopting both native-African and Dutch words impartially.

Many of the words adopted, such as *veldt*, *kloof*, and *kopje*, are found only in South African contexts, and others, such as *spoor* and *trek*, have both a limited and what we may term a colonial connotation.

The words which have been adopted from the native African languages are of the type usually borrowed from a subject or culturally-inferior race, words descriptive of local flora and fauna, natural features, social customs and classes. The African languages, as we saw in an earlier chapter, are exceedingly numerous, the inter-relationship is far from clear, and they extend from the Hottentot and Bushman languages in the south to the Hamitic languages on the Mediterranean coast. Therefore, although in the beginning this part of our survey was confined to South Africa, it will be convenient, when dealing with the native-African words, to consider all the dialects, from all the areas. Some of the Mediterranean words had already made their way into our language by the Old English period, the most remarkable being perhaps *elpend* – elephant, from Egyptian, which was later superseded by a French form of a Latin form of the same word. OE *nǣp*, found in modern English as the second element in *parsnip* and *turnip*, is also probably an Egyptian word borrowed by the Greeks and adopted by us in its Latin form; the full form *turnip* is not recorded until the sixteenth century. Two other Egyptian words remain to be noted, both adopted indirectly, *ebon*, *ebony*, through Latin in the Middle English period, and from which *ebonite* is a modern scientific coining, and *oasis*, through Greek and Latin in turn, in the seventeenth century.

Englishmen, following the example of the Portuguese, settled on the Guinea Coast in the sixteenth and seventeenth centuries, competing with the Portuguese for the native trade, and some words have been adopted from the native languages of that area, either direct or through Portuguese. We have already noted *yam*, through Portuguese, and *banana*, through Spanish. In the seventeenth century the word *drill*, the name of a kind of baboon, is recorded, the animal being a native of Guinea, and the name apparently the native word. Also from Guinea, in the eighteenth century, we have *chimpanzee*. The word *gorilla*, found much earlier in Greek, appears for the first time in English in the nineteenth century; it also is an African word, as is *voodoo*, also recorded first in the nineteenth century. Direct loan-words from Bantu are all comparatively late, though *zebra* occurs as early as 1600, having reached us, probably through Portuguese, from a dialect of the Congo basin. None of the direct loans have been established more than a hundred years, and only one, *tsetse*, may be said to be at all common; there are others, chiefly of a military or administrative type, but they rarely occur outside African contexts; for example, *impi* would immediately suggest the background of a work in which it appeared. A few words, chiefly names of animals and natural features, have been adopted from Hottentot within the last hundred years or so, but of these only *gnu* and *karoo* are common, and even then in limited contexts.

Of the words taken over from Dutch, none are recorded before the eighteenth century; the words introduced from then onwards are from two sources, from accounts of voyages, travellers' memoirs, and so forth, and military and political contact. Many of the words borrowed are Dutch words which the Boers preferred to the native term: for example, *kaama*, from the Hottentot language, appears in English early in the nineteenth century, but the Dutch had given their own name to the animal a century earlier, and the Dutch word, *hartebeeste*, is recorded in English before the end of the eighteenth century. Other Dutch words which have come to us in this way include *eland*, *kloof* and *springbok*, recorded in the eighteenth century, and in the nineteenth *commando*, which achieved a sudden popularity in the last war, *kopje*, *sjambok*, which has a curious history, being a Persian word which found its way into Malay-Polynesian and was brought back from their East Indian settlements to Africa by the Dutch, *spoor*, and *veldt*, though it must be admitted that all these, except *commando*, are very limited in use, and hardly part of our general vocabulary. *Kraal* has come to us through South African Dutch, but has its origin in Portuguese *curral* – a pen for cattle, and is therefore to be connected with *corral*, a word which has come to us, by way of North America, from Spanish.

We come finally to the influence of the North American continent, a tremendous subject, particularly in the last fifty years or so, and one which can be no more than touched upon in the space at our disposal here.[14] Fortunately we are not concerned here with differences between British and American English, but only with vocabulary, and not even then with the many differences in meaning of the same words on the two sides of the Atlantic – *The Historical Dictionary of American English* will provide the material for answers to those problems – but only with specifically American words, either from Amerindian sources, or from other sources which have developed on individual lines in America, which have passed from American English, considered as one dialect of English, just as British English, Australian English, Canadian English, and all the others are sister-dialects, and have become part of the general vocabulary of English. We may note here, as particularly pertinent, the remark made by Horwill: 'Certain uses of familiar words, which at the beginning of the century (or, at the outside, fifty years ago) were peculiar to the United States, are now either completely naturalized in this country or evidently on the way to naturalization. Numerous examples will be found by noting the words to which daggers are prefixed in my Dictionary' (Horwill found it necessary to

K

indicate changes taking place at the present time by using a single
dagger to indicate American words he considered 'on the way towards
being naturalized in England', and a double dagger for 'those whose
naturalization here is by this time complete'). He further adds: 'Many
words and locutions invented in America find their way, sooner or
later, into everyday speech and writing in England. This is by no means
a recent phenomenon. Generation after generation, English purists have
protested against the admission of these aliens, but their demands for
the enforcement of an embargo on them have usually been in vain.
Today many of these importations have become so thoroughly incorporated in the language that few of us are aware that they are actually
American coinages. Everyone recognizes, of course, that such terms as
banjo, blizzard, bogus, bunkum, and *lynch law* came to us from across the
Atlantic, but it would surprise most Englishmen to be told that they
owe to America *belittle, boarding-house, businessman, governmental, graveyard, hurricane deck, law-abiding, lengthy, overcoat, telegram,* and *whole-
souled*'.[15] Less than a century ago *bogus* was apparently considered rather
American than English, for in the *Cornhill Magazine* (1866) we find: 'A
mere juggle, or, as the Americans would say, a bogus parliament'. It
is with such words, coined in America, or words which have changed
their meaning in America and then been accepted here with the changed
meaning, that we shall be concerned.

The chief differences between American and British English lie in
pronunciation, spelling, and vocabulary. With the first we are not
concerned here, with the second only in so far as it alters the form of
the words, and the last is often exaggerated. The differences are to be
found rather in colloquial and easy language than in the literary language: there is no difficulty for an American in reading an English
book, or for an Englishman in reading an American book, unless a
great deal of use is made of colloquial language, or of words denoting
native features. Indeed it is almost true to say that differences of spelling
may be as disturbing as differences in vocabulary. On the other hand,
many magazines and newspapers make use of language on a different
level, and these are often influential. Weekley has illustrated the
difference by a quotation from Bretherton's *Midas:* 'The American
speaks American – a crisp, virile, colourful language, full of copious
possibilities – and writes English which he really does not really
understand'.[16]

There are two aspects of American influence on our vocabulary, and
these arise from the way in which the need for new words has been
met. One obvious way was to borrow words used by the native
inhabitants; words were also borrowed from French settlers, and later,

though this influence is unimportant in American English, from the languages of other nations some of whose people settled in the United States. Finally there is the adaptation of English material to meet new needs, and the coining of new words and compounds. We shall examine here the first and the last of these.

Borrowing from the Amerindian languages took place as soon as the settlements were established, and were, as might be expected, the names of new plants and animals, food, products, customs, and so forth. In the seventeenth century we find several names of animals, including *moose*, *musquash* (now common chiefly as the name of the fur), *opossum*, *racoon*, and *skunk*, two names of trees, *persimmon* and *hickory*, and several typically Indian words, such as *hominy*, *moccasin*, *squaw*, *tomahawk*, and *wigwam*. In the eighteenth century among others we may note *caribou* and *totem*, and in the nineteenth *apache*, *tepee*, and *toboggan*, and the common slang-word *mugwump*.

We turn now to the use of English material. Although the settlers did use some Indian words for the unfamiliar plants and animals they met with, they also used English words, as we have seen the Australian settlers did, when the object seemed to them to resemble something with which they had been familiar at home. As a result of this very different animals, birds, trees, and plants share the same name in England and America.

The language they used at the outset was Elizabethan or Stuart English, and there are survivals in American English of meanings and usage found in that period which have not survived in standard English. On the whole – and we find evidence for this in Commonwealth English too – the language of emigrants tends to change less than that of the people in the homeland. On the other hand, too much can be made of this so-called 'archaic' character of American English. The pronunciation may often be archaic, for many so-called American peculiarities are survivals of earlier English; intonation differs, and may represent an earlier stage, but for intonation we have no historical evidence; spelling is certainly not archaic, and American forms go back no further than Webster. Moreover, the extreme examples are often limited to particular areas, and it is not only in America that we find such survivals; there are as many, and often the identical survivals, in our own regional dialects. We may think the past participle *gotten* typically American, but it is common in our northern dialects, and the American use of *mad* in the sense of 'angry' is widespread throughout the midlands and north. Admittedly conservatism has preserved six-teenth- and seventeenth-century meanings and usages in American – and in some cases they may have been reintroduced here, though this is not always easy to establish – but this trait should not be over-emphasized, for the American language has changed considerably in three hundred and fifty years, just as the language in the British Isles has also changed, and this change in the American language, causing it to diverge from British English, is to be expected, for not only were the settlers faced with new natural phenomena, but also in the course of time the population has changed, a large non-British element having been absorbed, and the whole environment – social, educational, economic, and political – has changed.

The transfer of vocabulary was in one direction only until the early nineteenth century; until then words were travelling westwards only, but by the middle of the century the current was already flowing strongly in the opposite direction, though the early newcomers were not usually welcomed. Southey said of prairie: 'If this word be merely a French synonime for savannah, which has long been naturalized, the Americans display little taste in preferring it'; indeed, there was a tendency to label as 'Americanisms' – the word dates from 1784 – many words felt to be unacceptable, and as late as 1890 *scientist* was described as 'an ignoble Americanism', though it had been coined by an English-man many years earlier. Such has been the movement eastwards in recent times that, if we were to treat the subject historically, it would be necessary to differentiate, as Horwill has done, between those Americanisms peculiar to America and those which have made their way into British English.

But, speaking generally, we may say that specifically American words, like words from any other language, have been accepted when-ever they were really needed, and Weekley has well said, 'It is difficult now to imagine how we got on so long without the word *stunt*, how we expressed the characteristics so conveniently summed up in *dope-fiend* or *high-brow*, or any other possible way of describing that mixture of the cheap pathetic and the ludicrous which is now universally labelled *sob-stuff*'.[17]

In most cases the words which have come to us from America differ from those we have adopted from other countries. These American words are our own words; in some cases they have been lost in England and then reintroduced from America; others are our old words given new meanings, or new compounds, derivations, or uses of the old words.

They are, too, words from the living language, for most of them have come through colloquial speech rather than from the literary language. Because class distinctions are so much less rigid in America than in Britain it is easier for a word to rise from what we may call the lower levels of language and achieve the respectability of the literary language.

It is in the lower levels that the differences between American and British English are most marked, and it is perhaps because most of the Americanisms that the average Englishman hears are really slang or vulgarisms that the impression has been formed in England – a purely false impression – that American English is more vulgar than British English.

These American words have been introduced chiefly in two ways, through American speech in sound-films, and through magazines and newspapers. The influence of the former is often exaggerated, and it is largely ephemeral: one may be sure that much of the 'low-life' slang now so quickly picked up will last no longer than our words of the same class, for neither satisfies a real need in language. The influence of the latter is stronger, and it is often reinforced by the presence on English newspaper-staffs of Americans, or Englishmen who have worked on American papers; and it is in magazines and newspapers, and not in more serious literary work, that these words first appear.

It is hardly possible to make a representative selection of words which, originally American, have established themselves in the general vocabulary. A complete list has never been compiled, though there are a large number in R. H. Thornton's *An American Glossary*, which contains several thousand dated quotations of Americanisms, yet is far from complete. Purely as illustration we may note a few words denoting natural features and new conditions encountered, such as *backwoods, blizzard, bluff, canyon, clearing, lumber, prairie, prospect* (as a verb), *shanty, squatter, swamp*, some political words, such as *bunkum, carpet-bagger, caucus, wire-pulling*, commercial terms such as *appreciate* – rise in value, *balance* – remainder, *boom* (noun and verb), *corner* (noun and verb), *dry-goods*, and general words such as *belittle, cloud-burst, daily* (a newspaper), *doughnut, elevator, graveyard, half-breed, lengthy, loafer*, and *snow-plough*.

The Americans have been compared with the Elizabethans in their striving after novelty and vividness, and their delight in playing with words and testing their capacities, and just as the Elizabethans extended our vocabulary by extending the function of words, so the Americans have been responsible for much functional change. To them we owe the use of many original nouns in verb function, as, for example, *list, sense, voice – progress* is only a revival, for it was a verb in Elizabethan times – but we have also resisted a great many of their uglier types. Horwill notes: 'It would scarcely be an exaggeration to say that an American writer never hesitates to turn a noun into a verb if it will serve his purpose. In various American books and periodicals I have come across the verbs anguish, antidote, archipelago, bill of sale, candidate, climax, commentary, convenience, culture, detour, fellow-ship, grit, hothouse, language, lesson, message, metre, pedestal, suicide, suspicion, ultimate, and wharve'.[18] The Americans have also extended the use of nouns as adjectives, and among other examples Horwill quotes *Hoover agitation, employer responsibility,* and *vessel excellence.* It is much to be doubted if the type exemplified in these last two lists will ever find a permanent place in the language, important though functional change has been in the history of our language.

Once all the historical material is available to us it will be interesting to see how long it took for a word to be established in American standard, and then how long before it was accepted generally, and if it was first slang and colloquial before being fully accepted.

Finally a word about the future: there are differences between British and American English, and also between these and Australian, Indian, Canadian, South African, and all the other types of English, but, ignoring the possibility of extreme nationalist linguistic movements, these differences must decrease, for intercommunication is becoming progressively easier, and the linguistic isolation needed to create and preserve dialects is not so easy under present-day conditions, especially among such a highly-civilized and progressive group of nations as the English-speaking peoples.

CHAPTER NINE

★

THE SEVENTEENTH CENTURY
AND AFTER

The title of this chapter is obviously a misnomer, for parts of the ground have already been covered. Our study of classical influence in the later period, extending through the formation of a new scientific vocabulary, carried us right through this period in one aspect of vocabulary, as did also our study in the last chapter of words connected with exploration, colonization, and trade, and the influence of Commonwealth and American English. But in some ways the title is a good one, for we shall here take the opportunity of considering the various influences which have affected the development of vocabulary in the last three centuries, not only the adoption of foreign words, but also the use for new purposes of native material, and the consolidation or adaptation of the existing vocabulary.

It is fitting to start with an influence which is generally admitted to have been one of the strongest on our vocabulary and diction in the last few centuries, that of the English translations of the Bible, and in particular the Authorized Version of 1611, but to appreciate this influence fully we need to go back well beyond the seventeenth century, at least to the translations of Tindale and Coverdale in the early sixteenth century, and perhaps even to the still earlier Wyclifite versions. The main purpose in providing a Bible in the vernacular was to bring the Scriptures within the reach of the ordinary people. It would have been purposeless to use a learned vocabulary, full of Latinized words and the language of theology and philosophy. Words were needed which the people themselves would use to describe objects and emotions with which they were familiar. As Cook has said: 'It will abound in concrete expressions, and need but few learned or recondite terms. The words should, if possible, exhibit their primitive meaning on their face, or, at least, suggest immediately a single central meaning which can be accepted as radical and primary. They must, in general, while racy and vernacular, be free from degrading or belittling associations, so that they may be equally suitable for the middle or ordinary style and for passages of any degree of elevation up to the highest'.[1]

It is, therefore, obvious, that we shall not look here for the introduction of long learned words, though, of course, translation from another language is an obvious channel for introducing such words, and, as we shall see, some have been so used; it is rather in the preservation of old words which might otherwise have been lost that we are to look for the influence of the Bible on our vocabulary. Words such as *apparel* and *raiment* for clothes, *damsel*, *quick*, in the sense of 'living', and *travail* all probably owe their survival to the Bible. It must be remembered that until comparatively recently all classes of our people were accustomed either to read or hear the words of the Bible very frequently – under the Commonwealth, laws were passed compelling its public reading – and the words so heard would not easily be lost from our vocabulary. Words read or heard thus regularly, whether loan-words or native terms, become so familiar that they are unlikely to be lost. But there are many words in the Bible used in an archaic sense; these words have been kept alive, sometimes, admittedly, only in a limited context, but if the present decline in Bible-reading continues it seems certain that such words will be largely lost to many people, for they will cease to be living vocabulary.

The vocabulary of the Bible is surprisingly small. According to Marsh there are about six thousand different words in the complete Bible, Old and New Testament. Marsh has also examined the proportion of native words, and, counting all the words and repetitions of the same word, he estimates that ninety-three per cent of the words in the Bible are from native sources.

The influence of the Bible may be more easily demonstrated by the use of phrases and turns of expression than in single words, but even in the latter it is not lacking. The main influence is of a conservative nature, tending towards the retention of words familiar in earlier times, and perhaps retained now only through the influence of the Bible. It has also encouraged the use of concrete rather than abstract terms, and simple words rather than long learned words.

Even as early as the Old English period the influence of Biblical diction may be seen, but our real study of its influence may perhaps begin with Tindale. It has been said by many competent to judge that the Authorized Version is, in the main, Tindale, and we may therefore spend a little time examining this early translation, and later pass on to Coverdale's translation. With Tindale, who was to some extent indebted to the earlier Wyclifite translations, Puritan prose begins. Tindale first used *elder* instead of the Catholic term *priest*,[2] and he also introduced *congregation* in preference to *church*. Our modern sense of *godly* is also due to Tindale's use of the word. The Prayer-book version of the Lord's Prayer, 'Forgive us our *trespasses*', used the word from the

Tindale New Testament, where the Authorized Version has *debts*. He also seems to have given us *peace-maker*, *long-suffering*, *stumbling-block*, and one exceedingly good word – *scapegoat* – as the result of a mistranslation. He first used *shew-bread* and *mercy-seat* in English, but perhaps here merely translated Luther's forms. Both More and Bishop Gardner objected to Tindale's translation, the former because he felt that it lacked the dignity and reverence needed for such a subject, the latter because Tindale aimed at clarity in his translation, but Tindale, in his effort to ensure that 'a boy that draweth the plowe shall know more of the scriptures' than one of his opponents, also made certain of the purity of our Biblical language, and saved it from being swamped by learned words. In his effort to make himself easily understood he also established the custom of using concrete rather than abstract terms. Coverdale, who followed Tindale, has been described as writing in a feminine style, as distinct from Tindale's strongly-masculine idiom; he has given us *loving-kindness*, *noonday*, *morning-star*, and *blood-guiltiness*. To these two we are indebted for a pair of words which seem so obvious that we can hardly imagine how the language carried on before without them; Tindale gave us *broken-hearted*, and Coverdale *kind-hearted*. The Authorized Version of 1611 does not give us many new words, preferring to use the best of all the earlier versions rather than give a completely new translation, but its influence on vocabulary may be clearly seen in the language of many of the Puritan pamphlets, and, in particular, the works of such men as Bunyan and Fox.

Next we may consider political vocabulary, which really had its origin in the sixteenth century, alongside, and perhaps as a result of, the development, particularly under Elizabeth, of a feeling of national unity, and the growth of ideas on political unity and independence, the new conception of nationality, and the equally new conception of patriotism to one's native country. These ideas were able to develop only after the earlier over-riding loyalty, to the Roman Catholic Church, had broken down as a result of the Reformation and also, so far as England is concerned, the later developments under the Tudors.

At this time *nation* changed its meaning, which had previously suggested only difference of race, or type of people, and took on its present sense. The adjective *national* followed shortly after, and in the sixteenth and seventeenth centuries this new ideal of patriotism, of loyalty to one's own country, is suggested by the appearance of such words as *fatherland* and *mother-country*, *compatriot*, and *fellow-countryman*. *Patriot* and *patriotic* occur also in the seventeenth century, but not with their present meaning; that was reached only in the eighteenth century, when we find also *patriotism*.

As may be expected, side by side with this new nationalist spirit there developed political consciousness, in our own sense of the word. In the sixteenth century we find *politics, political*, and *politician; parliamentary* is recorded about the same time. There is a significant development in the meaning of the first group; at first *politician* had the sense of 'statesman', but in the seventeenth century it almost always suggested intrigue and underhand scheming, and only gradually did it develop to its present meaning. *Legislator*, a loan from Latin, is also found in the seventeenth century. Our modern *Cabinet* is foreshadowed in the *Cabinet Council* of the early years of the reign of Charles I, and the *Cabinet* is mentioned as such before the end of the reign. *Cabal*, still in use in a political sense, is really a Hebrew word, reinforced by the coincidence that the names of five of Charles II's ministers could be so arranged that the initials made up the word, though it had been used earlier for the select committee of the Privy Council which later became the Cabinet. *Privy Councillor* belongs to the same period, and *the Army*, in its modern sense of a standing army, came into use with the Commonwealth. *Cavalier* and *Roundhead* belong now only to our history books. *Whig* and *Tory* both appear towards the end of the seventeenth century, and, like the last two examples, were originally terms of abuse. *Tory*, a Celtic word, was first used for the Irish Catholics outlawed by Cromwell, then generally with the same sense of 'plundering outlaw', and eventually it was applied to those who supported the claim to the throne of James, Duke of York, a Roman Catholic. On the accession of William of Orange the term was applied generally to members of one of the two opposing parties, the members of the other being called *Whigs*, an abbreviation of a Scots word *whiggamore*, first used politically to refer to the Scottish Covenanters, then to the opponents of James, Duke of York, and finally to all the members of the party who opposed the Stuarts and supported the Hanoverian succession. *Whig* developed in the nineteenth century to include the Liberal Party, which had evolved from the old Whigs, and *Tory* naturally described the members of the Conservative Party, though today Whig has almost disappeared, and Tory is used chiefly now as a term of abuse by opponents of the Conservatives, its present sense being one of extreme Conservatism. *Ministry* dates from the time of Queen Anne, *Premier* from George I's time, and *Prime Minister* immediately recalls for us Sir Robert Walpole, to whom it was first applied in a derogatory sense; only in the nineteenth century did it become generally accepted with its present dignified meaning, and as an official title it goes back only to the early years of the present century.

With the end of the eighteenth century we are in the period of the

French Revolution; it is not surprising that such an important political event, taking place on our very doorstep, should make its influence felt in our vocabulary. *Aristocrat* and *democrat*, recorded first in 1789 and 1790 respectively, came into our language as a result of the Revolution, and they are still used by some people in a sense suggestive of the violent class-hatred then evident in France. *Liberal* and *Conservative*, which have replaced Whig and Tory except as terms of abuse, have their origin in the Revolution, though they were slow in making their way into English. At this time *despot* came to have its present sense, and *conscription* has its present meaning from the conscriptions of the Republic. One of the features of the Revolution was the preoccupation of some of the leaders with abstract political theories, and their attempt to put them into practice – a thing not unknown today – and one of the results of this was the appearance of a crop of abstract nouns ending in *-ism*, such as *despotism*, *royalism*, *terrorism*. Since then we have had a steady succession of such forms, including *nihilism*, *socialism*, *communism*, all first recorded in the first half of the nineteenth century, *collectivism*, *militarism*, *opportunism*, *pacifism* by the end of the century, and very many more in our own century.

We can hardly leave the political vocabulary of the eighteenth century without at least a glance at Burke, who has added quite a number of words and phrases of this type to the language. *Chivalry*, in our modern sense of the word, the ideal attitude and character of the perfect knight, is first used by him, as are also *Jacobin*, *diplomacy*, in its modern sense, and, characteristic of his love of order and reason, and hatred for anarchy, his use of *disorganize*, in the sense of upsetting the established customs and ideas of a country. Among other words of a political or administrative nature which seem to have been used first by him we may note *colonial* and *colonization*, *electioneering*, *expenditure*, *federalism*, *financial*, *municipality*, *representation* (in its modern sense), and *resources* (also in the modern sense).

Next we may consider the development of commerce from the seventeenth century to our own times as reflected in vocabulary. We have already examined one aspect of this influence, the introduction of foreign words for new objects and ideas encountered as a result of overseas trade: now we shall investigate the growth of what we may call a purely commercial vocabulary, the abstract terms connected with financial operations and the less picturesque side of trading. The establishment at that time of commerce as we know it today is clearly shown by the first appearance, in the seventeenth century, of many of the basic terms, and many more were added in the eighteenth century. In the seventeenth century we find recorded for the first time, in our modern sense, *bank*, adopted from Italian, though it had been originally a Germanic word, the same word as developed into NE *bench*. In Italy it seems to have developed a special sense of 'moneychangers' bench, or table', and in that sense it was carried by the Lombards into the languages of many European countries. Such basic terms as *capital* (a Latin form, being a later borrowing direct from Latin of a word which, borrowed twice through French, gave, as we have already seen, *cattle* and *chattels*), *commercial, discount, dividend, insurance,* and *investment* were first used at this time. *Machine* and *manufacture* also begin in this century to develop their modern meaning. Almost at the end of the century we hear of the *Bank of England*, an association formed to lend money to the king, and the result of this, the *National Debt*, is mentioned early in the next century. In the eighteenth century we find *bankruptcy, banking, currency,* and *remittance* in the first half, *business* is used in its modern commercial sense, and the familiar Stock Exchange *bulls* and *bears* also appear. Later in the century we have *bonus, capitalist, consols* (an abbreviation of Consolidated Annuities, and therefore originally a slang term used on the Stock Exchange), and *finance. Speculation* seems to have been first used in its modern commercial sense by Horace Walpole in this century. In the same century we have the combination of politics and finance on its present scale foreshadowed in *budget* and *estimates.*

Next we may consider the effect on our vocabulary of the Restoration, in 1660, when the Stuarts returned from their exile at the French court. One of the obvious effects of the Restoration, indeed the one most to be expected, was the reaction to the atmosphere established by the Puritans during the Commonwealth. Perhaps it is because of the mocking attitude of the returned Royalists to the discomfited Puritans that we find, used either for the first time, or suddenly becoming popular, so many words indicating scornful jesting and derision, such as *badinage, banter, burlesque, raillery, ridicule,* and *travesty.*

This is a revival of French influence on our language, for the returned exiles brought back with them ideas and customs from France, and used French words to describe them. Many of the plays of the period hold up to ridicule the court set who revelled in the imitation of everything French; perhaps the best example is Dryden's *Marriage à la Mode,* in which some of Melantha's favourite French expressions, such as *repartee, devoir, foible, ridicule,* and *embarrass,* are held up to scorn. Among words introduced at this time we may note *apartment, brunette, cajole, chagrin, champagne, muslin, soup,* and quite a number which, although they have come into fairly general use, seem never to have acquired an Anglicized pronunciation: among these are *ballet, contretemps, cortège, décor, démarche, métier, penchant* and *tableau,* all recognizably French words, in both form and pronunciation, but to be found in most of our English dictionaries. In some, too, we may note the retention of French accentuation, the words not having been sufficiently Anglicized to have the stress changed according to the Germanic system: examples are *bagatelle, barricade, cadet, caprice,* all with stress on the final syllable.

Dr Serjeantson[3] has pointed out the difference between the first half of the seventeenth century and the period after the Restoration, so far as French loans are concerned. She notes that there are comparatively few between 1600 and 1640, and that they are chiefly naval, military, and diplomatic; among common ones still in use today are *brigade, dragoon, fanfare, parole,* and *stockade.* A few terms connected with art, literature, and the social side of life are also found. In the second half of the century there are also naval and military terms, among which we may note *carbine* and *commandant,* but there is a much larger number connected with more pleasant aspects of life; Dr Serjeantson quotes, among terms connected with games and dancing, *ballet* and *pool,* among words of art and literature, *crayon, burlesque, memoirs, tableau;* fashion is also well represented, in both dress and materials, as *cravat, shagreen, moire, denim,* and *batiste.* Among what are classified as 'fashionable social terms' we find listed *complaisance, contretemps, façade, invalid, liaison, nonchalance, penchant, repartee, reservoir, reverie,* and *routine,* among words still in common use, and many which have never really become English, but still retain their French flavour. All these words are of the type which one might expect to find adopted from a highly-cultured, highly-civilized people, with a great regard for the social graces.

French loans continue to enrich our vocabulary in the eighteenth and nineteenth centuries, and we find the same type of loan-word adopted. Among terms connected with the arts we find *belles-lettres, connoisseur, coterie, critique, nuance, salon, savant;* among words denoting aspects of fashion and personal adornment are *chenille, corduroy, moquette,* and *rouge.* Words connected with food and drink are numerous, and include *cuisine, liqueur, meringue,* and *rissole.* We have noted the form *blankmanger,* used by Chaucer; the later borrowing, *blomange,* on which the present-day English pronunciation is based, is also recorded at this time. Among other words recorded in the eighteenth century, selecting only from words in common use today, are *brochure, bureau, canteen, devoir, encore, ennui, etiquette, hors d'œuvre, police, route,* and *souvenir. Persiflage, debut,* and *sang-froid* seem to have been introduced by Lord Chesterfield, and *fête, vignette, chef d'oeuvre* by Walpole, who also used *douceur* (bribe).

After the Middle English period the nineteenth century was richest in French loan-words, and, as we may expect from the type of word already noted as being borrowed in the modern period, the words are connected chiefly with the arts, with food and drink, with fashion, including also many terms connected with the adornment of the home, and, of course, many words which denote social graces and the refinements of life. It would be impossible, in the space at our disposal here, to present even a representative selection, but, from among a very large number of French words adopted in this century, the following may be noted. Words connected with the arts include *baroque, baton, cliché, foyer, matinée, nocturne, première, renaissance, repertoire, resumé;* with fashion, dress, and materials, *beret, blouse, chiffon, corsage, crêpe, cretonne, crinoline, crochet, fichu, layette, négligé, picot, piqué, tricot, rosette, suède, voile;* with ornaments, personal and for the house, *cheval* (glass), *parquet, reticule, secretaire;* with food, *bonbon, café, chef, fondant, gourmet, mayonnaise, menu, mousse, restaurant, sauté, soufflé;* among social terms we find *aplomb, blasé, chauffeur, débutante, fiancée, flair, prestige* (in the modern sense), *raconteur.* Since French has long been one of the acknowledged languages of international diplomacy we may expect to find terms of this kind also, and in the nineteenth century are recorded *attaché, chargé d'affaires, communism, dossier, entente, laissez-faire, rapprochement,* and *secretariat.*

Ever since the Norman Conquest we have borrowed military terms from the French; the early loans have already been noticed, and we may now complete the picture by surveying the loans from the sixteenth century to the present day, choosing only a few in each century from the many words adopted, and again limiting our choice to words in common use today. In the sixteenth century we have *cartridge, colonel, trophy, volley,* and others, such as *pioneer* and *rendezvous,* originally in this class but now used much more generally. In the seventeenth century are recorded *brigade, dragoon, fanfare, platoon, stockade,* in the eighteenth century *bivouac, corps, depot, espionage, fusillade, manœuvre, ricochet,* in the nineteenth century *barrage* and *chassis* (of a gun-carriage; its use applied to a motor-car dates only from the early years of the twentieth century).

Words are still being borrowed, and among common words adopted in the present century are *camouflage, fuselage, garage, georgette, hangar, limousine, rayon, revue,* and every year adds more to the list.

It will be noticed that these words differ in two respects from those borrowed earlier; there are comparatively few of the homely words which seem to be almost as much at home in our language as the native words themselves. This may perhaps be due to the fact that they have not been so long in the language, though some words borrowed in this century seem more familiar to us than words which were borrowed three or four hundred years ago. We note also that many of these words look strangers, although they are in frequent use; this is probably due to our having made little change in the form of the word in the more recent borrowings; for example, *café*, *élite*, *epaulette*, *etiquette*, *genre*, *lorgnette*, *mayonnaise*, *meringue*, *passe-partout*, and *roué* would never, in their present forms, be taken for English words, as *button*, *chair*, *coat*, *dinner*, *face*, *feast*, *peace*, *pity*, *prison* and *river* would, in spite of their French ancestry.

One influence which might have been dealt with in both the preceding chapters is that of Italian, for we have Italian influence on our vocabulary as a result of the Renaissance, and also as a result of mercantile contacts. If we are merely to count examples, the influence of Italian is very important,[4] for numerically it ranks after Latin, French, Greek and Scandinavian, but three points must be remembered: the influence has been exerted over a comparatively short period, there being few loans before the sixteenth century, many of the words, particularly in art, architecture, and music, form part of what we may call the common European vocabulary of technical terms, and, lastly, it is probably not an exaggeration to say that at least half of these Italian loan-words have reached us through French. Here we shall make no distinction between direct loans and those adopted through French, our test being the actual origin of the word.

There was contact with Italy through trade and banking as early as the fourteenth century, and we know of literary contact from Chaucer's works – It. *pellegrino* (Lat. *peregrinus*), which developed to *pilgrim*, is very early – but early loans are few, and almost always through French; some scholars consider that *pilgrim* reached us through French. In the fourteenth century we find *alarm*, *ducat*, *florin*, and *million*, and the early use of *Lombard* – preserved for us today in Lombard Street, one of the centres of London banking – gives direct proof of the early connection through banking. *Brigand* and *bark* are two early sea-terms. Trade terms came in during the fifteenth and sixteenth centuries, when there was direct contact through the Flemish galleys, which regularly called at English ports on their way to and from Venice. In the sixteenth century we find *bankrupt*, *contraband*, *frigate*, *milliner*, and *traffic*, and, among the merchandise carried, *artichoke*, *citron*, and *porcelain*. With the opening up of new sea-routes Italy's position in the middle of the Mediterranean became less and less important from a maritime point of view, and trade with Italy declined steadily from the latter part of the sixteenth century, there being few new words of a commercial nature introduced in the later centuries, though we may note one important word, *mercantile*, in the seventeenth century.

But, although commercial influence declined, there was an amazing increase in cultural influence from the time of the Tudors, and, although we have a few words of a warlike type, such as *bandit, battalion, citadel, duel,* and *squadron,* most of the Italian influence on our vocabulary has been exerted through gentler, more peaceful channels, as, for example, music, art and architecture, and social terms. A mere glance at our vocabulary is sufficient to show that the Italians have been our teachers in music and the fine arts, and, much as the 'Italianate Englishman' was derided by his stay-at-home fellow-countrymen, there can be no doubt that we have benefited much from contact with the Italian people. Travel in Italy became popular in the sixteenth century, and the attraction for Englishmen of Italian scenes, life, and customs which began then has declined little in the last four hundred years. As a result of this travel we note one difference in the loan-words: previously they had been borrowed through French, but, although some later loans do come through French, the majority have been adopted direct from the Italian, and this has usually meant a difference in form.

It will perhaps give us a better picture of the scope of Italian influence if we allow the chronological aspect to take secondary place in our examination, and place the chief emphasis on the aspects of life involved. The influence of Italy on our musical life has continued unbroken from the sixteenth century, reaching its peak in the eighteenth century, when Italian music was introduced into and was very popular in England. In the sixteenth century we find *fugue, madrigal,* and *viola da gamba,* in the seventeenth century *opera, serenade, sonata, spinet,* in the eighteenth century *aria, arpeggio, cantata, concerto, finale, mandolin, oratorio, pianoforte* (the abbreviation, *piano,* is later), *rondo, soprano, trombone,* and *violoncello,* to choose only a few from many examples, and in the nineteenth century *cadenza, intermezzo, piccolo, sestet.*

In spite of an attempt in the nineteenth century to make use of German expressions the directions on musical scores have remained in Italian, and these terms have been introduced into our vocabulary continuously since the sixteenth century. Although they are hardly part of our everyday vocabulary they are used frequently enough to merit attention, and, choosing only those in very common use and familiar to most people, we may note *adagio, andante, crescendo, largo, legato, staccato,* and *tremolo.*

Next we may turn to the fine arts, including architecture in this group, and dealing with it first. In the sixteenth century are recorded *cornice, cupola, frieze, pedestal, piazza,* and *stucco;* in the seventeenth century, when Italian influence on English architecture was strong, we find *balcony, catacomb, corridor, dado, grotto, pergola, portico,* and *villa* (perhaps direct from Latin); in the eighteenth century are to be noted *arcade*, *colonnade*, and *loggia*.

Words connected with painting and sculpture have been borrowed from Italian regularly since the sixteenth century. In that century we find *cameo*, *fresco*, *miniature*, and *pastel*, in the seventeenth century *cartoon*, *chiaroscuro*, *filigree*, *mezzotint*, *relief* or *relievo*, in the eighteenth century *costume*, *picturesque*, *terra cotta*, and *torso*, and in the nineteenth century *baroque*, *replica*, *studio*, and *tempera*.

Italian influence in literature may be traced as early as the time of Chaucer, but it is only with the Renaissance that it becomes really important, and many words connected with literature and criticism have been borrowed since that time. Translations from Italian were numerous in the sixteenth century, and Wyatt, Surrey, and Spenser owe much to Italian models. Milton also was affected by this influence in the next century. Italian themes were popular in the drama of the sixteenth and seventeenth centuries. In the sixteenth century we have *canto*, *stanza*, and *sonnet*, in the seventeenth century words from Italian, such as *burlesque*, were introduced after the Restoration alongside the French words already noticed, and Italian terms have also been introduced in the eighteenth and nineteenth centuries, though these have not become so popular as the earlier loans.

There are not very many Italian words connected with food, drink, and cooking, but we may note *macaroni*, in the sixteenth century, *macaroon* and *vermicelli* in the seventeenth, *semolina* in the eighteenth, and *spaghetti* in the nineteenth, along with a few natural products such as *artichoke* and *broccoli*. *Cantaloup* and *gorgonzola*, both introduced in the nineteenth century, are from place-names, and were originally purely adjectival, but are now used regularly as common nouns.

As our last classified list we may take words connected with Italian life, customs, dress, and social habits. In the sixteenth century we may note *carnival*, *gambol*, *gondola*, and *pall-mall* (a once-popular game, but the word survives now only as the name of a famous street in London; the connection here seems to be that the word was also used for the alley in which the game was played). *Cozen* – to cheat, frequent in Elizabethan English, is early, and may have developed from *cozzone* – a horse-dealer. In the seventeenth century are recorded *caprice*, *cortège* (through French), *gala*, *gazette*, *incognito*, *parasol*, *regatta*, and *umbrella*, in the eighteenth century we have *casino*, *cicerone*, *conversazione*, and in the nineteenth *vendetta* (cf. the Latin form, *vindicta*, in the sixteenth century).

There are also many general words, or words from groups too small to classify individually here, which have become common in English.

Many of these were originally technical terms which came later to be used more generally, as, for example, *manage*, originally a term of horsemanship, in the sense of controlling a horse, or *escort*, used at first as a military term. From a long list we may note the following, again choosing only words which have survived in common use: in the sixteenth century *ballot, cavalcade, disgrace, lottery, model, pedant, scope*, in the seventeenth century *balloon, bulletin, lagoon, muslin, valise, volcano*, in the eighteenth century *bronze, firm* (a commercial concern), *influenza, lava, malaria, poplin*, and in the nineteenth century *gelatine, inferno*, and *tirade*.

One final point must be made about the form of these loans. Many have become fully anglicized and naturalized, so that it is difficult to recognize them as foreign loans; for example, *race*, borrowed in the fifteenth century, might be accepted as a native word. Others have come in through French, as *bagatelle* and *cortège*, and this has affected their form in English. Still others have been adopted entirely or almost entirely unchanged; such words as *conversazione, intermezzo, maraschino, mezzotint*, and *extravaganza* could never succeed in looking English, and we have no doubt of the country of origin of *gorgonzola, macaroni, spaghetti*, and *vermicelli*.

The language of the eighteenth century deserves more attention than it has had so far. This century has been called the Age of Reason, and there can be no doubt that one of its chief characteristics was a strong tendency towards order and regulation, and a healthy respect for authority. Indeed it is true to say of this period, if we look at it purely from a linguistic point of view, that most of the grammarians and orthoepists spent their time searching for and attempting to establish some final authority by which the language might be fixed. The adventurous spirit of the sixteenth and seventeenth century, the cavalier treatment of language, lack of respect for earlier custom, the delight of twisting words, playing with them so as to find out how much could be done with them, had its inevitable reaction in the eighteenth century, when the cry was for a regularized system. This naturally led to what has been called the eighteenth-century 'doctrine of correctness', the worshipping of correctness for its own sake, and the making of standards by which this correctness might be measured. In their search for such a standard, eighteenth-century grammarians were attracted by the classical languages, and they saw their ideal in Latin, a language perfectly regular in its grammatical rules, unchanging in its vocabulary. The inevitable result of this was the attempt to make the English language as perfect as Latin. On comparing English grammar with Latin grammar, the scholars soon discovered a complete lack of order; there was no definite rule or authority to which one might turn to establish the correctness of an English form. The writers of the previous century and a half had made so free with the language, turning nouns into verbs, adjectives into nouns, making their own grammatical rules, that there was naturally a good deal of uncertainty about what could or could not be done, and this, of course, was in complete contrast to the desire for regularity, reason, and authority of the eighteenth century. Dryden confesses that at times he was compelled to put his thoughts first into Latin in order to express them correctly in English. This desire to give English a polished, rational, and authoritative form, similar to that of Latin, led to the attempt to settle all disputed points either by appeal to authority, which at first meant Latin authority, or by reasoned argument, and eventually to the demand for a law-giving body, an Academy which should have authority first to purify the language, and then fix it in its final perfect form.

We are not concerned here with all the aspects of this attempt to regularize the language, refine it, and fix it permanently, but only with its effect on vocabulary. Most of the people who concerned themselves with the language in the eighteenth century felt that it was degenerating. They had before them the degeneration of Latin from its 'golden age', and they wished to prevent that happening to English. Swift thought that the golden age of the English language began with Elizabeth's reign, and ended with the outbreak of the Civil War. He says: 'From the civil war to this present time, I am apt to doubt whether the corruptions in our language have not at least equalled the refinements of it; and these corruptions very few of the best authors have escaped'; he thought language had been debased in the Restoration period through 'ignorance and caprice', and considered Court influence to be bad. Johnson agrees with him: 'I have studiously endeavoured to collect examples and authorities from the writers before the restoration, whose works I regard as the wells of English undefiled, as the pure sources of genuine diction'. Others, such as Buchanan, Sheridan, Monboddo and Webster, place the Golden Age of English in the Restoration and Queen Anne periods, and Priestley calls it the 'classical period' of the language. On the whole, the favourite theory in the eighteenth century was that the best had been passed, and it was ideas such as these which led to the attempt to purify the language, to rid it of imperfections; one result of this was a tendency on the part of almost everyone concerned with the language at the time to set himself up as an authority, and pass judgement on the suitability of words, idioms, and grammatical constructions. The result of all this pedantic sifting of archaic, 'low', and dialect forms was to impoverish the language, temporarily at least, for the authorities tried to ban many vigorous words and expressions.

One aspect of this critical attitude to language was the examination of some of the Latin words introduced into the language since the Renaissance. We have already noticed the tendency towards a highly-Latinized vocabulary in the sixteenth and seventeenth centuries, and by the time we come to writers such as Burton and Browne we realise that the English language had taken in more Latin than it could comfortably assimilate. Browne, particularly in his *Pseudodoxia Epidemica*, or *Vulgar Errors*, as the work is often called, makes use of a great number of new Latin and Greek constructions: in *Vulgar Errors* he writes: 'That which is concreted by exsiccation or expression of humidity, will be resolved by humectation, as Earth, Dirt, and Clay; that which is coagulated by a fiery siccity, will suffer colliquation from an aqueous humidity, as Salt and Sugar'. Passages such as this, and the use by Browne and his contemporaries of such words as *aberrancy*, *areopagy*, *australise*, *clancularly*, *congelation*, *deturpated*, *digladiation*, *discruciatingly*, *dissentaneous*, *effluency*, *exenteration*, *favaginous*, *fictile*, *immorigerous*, *improperations*, *incrassated*, *intenerate*, *prescious*, *quodlibetically*, *sollicitudinous*, *stillicidious*, and *vadimonial* leave us in no doubt that the language needed to be purged, although other words used by these writers have resisted all attacks and, fortunately for us, found a permanent place in the language, for we could ill do without such words as *ascetic*, *carnivorous*, *deleterious*, *electricity*, *hallucination*, *insecurity*, *incontrovertible*, *literary*, *medical*, *precarious*, and *retrogression*. We are not surprised to read, in the *Tatler*,[5] a suggestion that the paper should set itself up as a judge of the vocabulary 'and by an annual index expurgatorius expunge all words and phrases that are offensive to good sense', and in the *Spectator*[6] about the same time, that 'certain men might be set apart as superintendents of our language, to hinder any words of a foreign coin passing among us'. Well might Campbell say, towards the end of the century, 'our language is in greater danger of being overwhelmed by an inundation of foreign words, than of any other species of destruction'. We must, indeed, be grateful to those purists who, misguided as they often were in their choice of words they considered unsuitable, yet by their efforts freed us of some of the worst of the unnecessary Latinisms such as are quoted above.

That this highly-Latinized style was neither necessary nor universal may be seen by comparing the first sentences of Browne's *Religio Medici*, in which almost all the important words are of Latin origin, with the opening paragraph of Bunyan's *Pilgrim's Progress*, in which the foreign words can be counted on the fingers of both hands, and even then they are the type of loan-word which had been so thoroughly assimilated that it was hardly felt to be foreign.

Religio Medici

For my Religion, though there be several Circumstances that might perswade the World I have none at all, (as the general scandal of my Profession, the natural course of my Studies, the indifferency of my Behaviour and Discourse in matters of Religion, neither violently Defending one, nor with that common ardour and contention Opposing another;) yet, in despight hereof, I dare without usurpation assume the honourable Stile of a Christian.

Pilgrim's Progress

As I walk'd through the wilderness of this world, I lighted on a certain place, where was a Den; and I laid me down in that place to sleep; and as I slept I dreamed a Dream. I dreamed, and behold *I saw a man cloathed with Rags, standing in a certain place, with his face from his own House, a Book in his hand, and a great burden upon his back.* I looked, and I saw him open the Book, and read therein; and as he read, he wept and trembled: and not being able longer to contain, he broke out with a lamentable cry; saying, *what shall I do?*

It should be borne in mind that it was not only the use of Latin words that was being attacked, when the purists spoke of foreign languages; Dryden says, 'I can not approve of their way of refining, who corrupt our English idiom by mixing it too much with French', and in the *Spectator* we find expressed the desire to 'prohibit any French phrases from becoming current in this kingdom, when those of our own stamp are altogether as valuable'.

Moreover, the attempts to refine and purify the language were not confined to foreign words. In an earlier chapter we have seen how new words have been introduced into our vocabulary by the abbreviation of established longer words, but many of these shortened forms did not come in without opposition. At the beginning of the century Swift had protested against such forms, produced, as he says, by 'pronouncing the first syllable in a word that has many, and dismissing the rest; such as *phizz*, *hipps* (for *hypochondriacs*), *mobb*, *pozz* (for *positive*), *rep* (for *reputation*) and many more, when we are already overloaded with monosyllables, which are the disgrace of our language'. Almost at the end of the century Campbell was still writing in condemnation of this practice, which he calls a barbarism, 'the abbreviation of polysyllables, by lopping off all the syllables except the first, or the first and second'.

He quotes seven examples, *hyp, rep, ult, penult, incog, hyper* (hypercritic), and *extra* (extraordinary), but notes 'all these affected terms have been denied the public suffrage'. It is worthy of note, however, that he is compelled to admit *mob*, against which Swift had fought so hard, because by his time it has been established by usage. Harris, Buchan, Withers, and Hornsey also wrote against abbreviations. These abbreviations have already been discussed, in the chapter on word-formation, and little need be added here, except to note the conservative attitude to a practice which can, if not used to excess, be a convenience to language. Admittedly, many of the abbreviations were ugly, and often failed to justify themselves on the score of convenience, for some of the words so shortened were not in frequent use, yet this attitude, if persisted in logically, and accepted as a rule of our language, would have denied us such useful and everyday abbreviations as *bus, phone, taxi,* and others mentioned above.

Before leaving the eighteenth century we may note the appearance, or difference in usage, of a few words which illustrate some of the characteristics of the period, an age of order, reason, commonsense, and good society. We find Shaftesbury using *self-control* and *well-regulated* early in the century, and the atmosphere of the age is foreshadowed in the use of *sense*, for *commonsense*, and *good sense* late in the seventeenth century. It is interesting to note that the opposite of commonsense was *romantic*, in the eighteenth-century sense of the words. *Respectable* and *disreputable* developed their modern sense during the century. Elegance and refinement is shown by words suggesting a distaste for the cheap and gaudy, as *over-dressed, showy, vulgarity, vulgarism,* as Chesterfield's 'vulgarism in language is a certain characteristic of bad company and a bad education'. There was a revulsion from everything *low-bred*, another new formation, as we remember from the conversation in 'The Three Pigeons' in *She Stoops to Conquer*, when one of Tony's fellows exclaims, 'O d—— anything that's low, I cannot bear it', to which another replies, 'The genteel thing is the genteel thing at any time'. This naturally led to a rejection of certain words considered indelicate, an attitude which reappears in the Victorian Age; in the Preface to *The Goodnatured Man* Goldsmith refers to 'the public taste, grown of late, perhaps, too delicate', and 'hopes that too much refinement will not banish humour and character from ours, as it has already done from the French theatre'. Among purely social words, Pearsall Smith points out, '*polite* and *club* take on new meanings, we hear of *callers* and *small talk;* and the immense number of compounds formed from the word "tea" (*tea-room, tea-party, tea-drinker,* etc.) would afford much material for the student of social customs'.[7]

The rise of the present custom of holidays at the seaside is reflected in the appearance of such words as *watering-place* and the many compounds of *sea*, such as *seaside, sea-bathing, sea-view, sea-beach,* and others, all showing, as Pearsall Smith has put it, 'the discovery of the sea as a source of pleasure and well-being which we also owe to this period'.

We may conclude this study of the attempt to purify the language by noting some of the words which might have been lost if the purists had had their way and removed from the language the words they considered to be archaic, words, as Campbell says, 'no longer understood by any but critics and antiquaries', and others which 'though not unintelligible, all writers of any name have now ceased to use'. By this test *behest, fantasy,* and *tribulation* would have been lost to us. Writers such as Milton and Dryden were held to have used words no longer acceptable; among Milton's words to which exception was taken are *bland, carol, chaunt, fervid, hostile, jubilant, minstrelsy, murky, ornate* and *reluctant;* Dryden's *array, beverage, mood,* and *smouldering* were also considered unsuitable for the language of the eighteenth century, and towards the end of the century Beattie considered *bridal, gleam, hurl, plod, ruthless,* and *wail* no longer current vocabulary, except for poetry.

Just as this desire to purify the language had been a reaction from Elizabethan excess, so over-refinement and the proscribing of many useful native words produced another reaction, the deliberate re-introduction of old words, noticeable in the Romantic Revival at the end of the eighteenth century, continued in the work of some nineteenth-century writers, and no doubt aided by the increased interest in the past which came from a wider understanding of history. Writers such as Wordsworth, Coleridge, De Quincey, Hazlitt, Lamb, and Scott went back beyond the vocabulary of Johnson's Dictionary for the words they needed, and in so doing gave new life to old words rejected in the eighteenth century, and often also gave them a romantic charm and glamour not attached to the words in earlier times. Pearsall Smith notes: '*chivalry, chivalrous, minstrel, bard,* etc., have now taken on a romantic glamour they by no means originally possessed. *Minstrel* was a name for a buffoon or juggler, as well as a musician in early times; while *bard,* as a name for a Gaelic singer, was often used, with "beggar" and "vagabond", as a term of contempt, until it became associated with the classical use of the same word, and was idealized by Sir Walter Scott'.[8]

A final point to be noticed from the eighteenth century is the emergence of a way in which the vocabulary might be fixed. The efforts of the lexicographers, who become increasingly important during the century, paralleled those of the purists in refining and fixing the language. English dictionaries begin in the early seventeenth century, with the lists of hard words, provided to meet the needs of the ordinary reader who could not understand the many words derived from Latin introduced after the Renaissance. Not until well into the eighteenth did the change take place from a collection of difficult words to a list containing English words in general, and not until Johnson's Dictionary, published in 1755 in two volumes, and containing between forty and fifty thousand words, was there anything approaching an authoritative collection of all the words in the language. This is not the place to trace the development of English lexicography in the eighteenth century, or to weigh up the merits and demerits of Johnson's Dictionary. We are concerned merely with any effect the evolution of the dictionary may have had on the development of vocabulary. The influence of an authoritative dictionary on orthography is obvious, but this touches only the form of words, whereas we are concerned with creation and adoption, and the life and death of words. The eighteenth century was concerned with fixing the language, the main fear of the reformers arising from what they considered to be the instability of the vernacular. Johnson says in his Preface: 'Those who have been persuaded to think well of my design, require that it should fix our language, and put a stop to those alterations which time and chance have hitherto been suffered to make in it without opposition'. This was at first Johnson's aim, but he soon came to realize that a living language can never be static, that changes must take place, gains be made and losses suffered. He writes, following immediately on the last quotation: 'With this consequence I will confess that I flattered myself for a while; but now begin to fear that I have indulged expectation which neither reason nor experience can justify. When we see men grow old and die at a certain time one after another, from century to century, we laugh at the elixir that promises to prolong life to a thousand years; and with equal justice may the lexicographer be derided, who being able to produce no example of a nation that has preserved their words and phrases from mutability, shall imagine that his dictionary can embalm his language, and secure it from corruption and decay, that it is in his power to change sublunary nature, or clear the world at once from folly, vanity, and affectation. With this hope, however, academies have been instituted, to guard the avenues of their languages, to retain fugitives, and repulse intruders; but their vigilance and activity have hitherto been vain; sounds are too volatile and subtile for legal restraints; to enchain syllables, and to lash the wind, are equally the undertakings of pride, unwilling to measure its desires by its strength. The French language has visibly changed under the inspection of the academy. . . .' This is a long quotation, but it merits inclusion for two reasons: not only does it reveal one aspect of the eighteenth-century attitude to language, but it is also a valuable comment, from one of the greatest of our early lexicographers, upon the development of a nation's vocabulary. In spite of Johnson's admission on the instability of vocabulary three important results emerged from the publication of his dictionary: words were established in usage by the authority of his great work, the forms of the words were fixed, and, although other lexicographers had done this before, an attempt was made to establish levels of language by the exclusion of 'low words'.

These 'low words' are obviously our next subject for examination, for we can imagine how the eighteenth-century purist would regard them. Withers expresses his determination to write only of words such as 'people in decent life inadvertantly adopt', and says such 'purity and politeness of expression' is 'the only external distinction which remains between a gentleman and a valet, a lady and a mantu-maker'. Johnson excluded words of this kind from his dictionary, though not thoroughly enough for some of the purists, for one of the grounds of criticism of his dictionary was that he had admitted this type of word; among words condemned by Johnson as 'low' are *banter, coax, dodge, flippant, fop, frisky, fun, fuss, simpleton*. Campbell condemns 'words of low or dubious extraction; such, for instance, as have arisen, nobody knows how, like *fig, banter, bigot, fop, flippant*, among the rabble, or, like *flimsy*, sprung from the cant of manufacturers'. But in modern times, with much intercommunication between all classes of speakers, words cannot be confined to certain levels of language. Even before the eighteenth century words had been making their way upwards from slang and cant languages into the standard language. This movement of words upwards and downwards is a study in itself; fashion in words is often as short-lived as fashion in women's clothes, and often depends on the party in power at the time. Words have been fashionable in polite society at one period, then degenerated, and been finally lost, and conversely, words once used only among the lower classes have made their way into the accepted language of polite society. The movement upwards of such words has been rendered easier in the modern period by the steady rise of people from the lower to the upper ranks of society. Here we can merely touch upon the subject, but it is interesting to consider even a short selection of words considered by eighteenth-century purists to be slang or cant or 'low' words, and unworthy of inclusion in a refined, regularized vocabulary, noting in passing that Withers, in his *Aristarchus*, has no fewer than eighty pages on vulgar usage; among these words we may note *banter, bigot, budge, dumbfound, enthusiasm, extra, flimsy, flippant, flirtation, fop, fun, gambling, hanker, humbug, jilt, mob, nervous, prig, quandary, shabby, sham, shuffle, snob, squabble, stingy, tiff, topsy-turvy, touchy* – all words in common use in the ordinary spoken language today, and most of them accepted in the literary language too.

The purists also objected to words being transferred from the regional dialects into the standard language, a movement similar, in their opinion, to that of slang or cant words into literary English. The main objections in the eighteenth century were to Scoticisms and Irishisms, probably because so many men of these two races came to London to 'set up schoolmaster'. Kenrick writes: 'There seems indeed a most ridiculous absurdity in the pretensions of a native of Aberdeen or Tipperary to teach the natives of London to speak and read'. Even in Shakespeare's time the old regional dialects were still in use among the country gentry who had little contact with the court, and even among some of those who had, for we have evidence that Ralegh spoke a broad Devon dialect to the day of his death, and words from the regional dialects were introduced into literature, not only, as in the case of south-western dialects, for the speech of clowns and rustics in drama, but also in serious usage, as, for example, by Spenser in his *Shepheardes Calender*. Ever since the establishment of a standard language there has been a tendency for words from regional dialect to be introduced; Shakespeare used many words which suggest his knowledge of Warwickshire dialect, Johnson has introduced words from Midland dialects into his dictionary, Scott's use of the Scottish dialect is too well known to need more than mention, George Eliot used midland dialect for her rustic characters, and more recently Hardy has made much use of the Wessex dialect, and Miss Sheila Kaye-Smith of Kentish and Sussex dialects. Such words are introduced first often to provide local colour, as in the case of Scott, and Spenser's use of northern words, but often they meet a need and so find a permanent place in the language.

There are three distinct types of dialect spoken in the British Isles today alongside Standard English and Modified Standard; they are regional, occupational, and class dialects. Modified Standard will not concern us in our study of vocabulary, for it is what we may call a 'half-way stage', being the language spoken by people who spoke at first a regional or occupational dialect, and then have modified this, perhaps at school or in college, or by their own efforts later in life if they have managed to move from their original surroundings, but have not quite attained to the Standard English at which they have aimed. Obviously, such a dialect could not influence Standard English except by introducing into it words carried over from the original regional or occupational dialect, and so it is these, and not Modified Standard, which would be influencing Standard English. Moreover, these speakers would in most cases be extremely careful not to make conscious use of the old forms. Natural speakers of regional dialects – and to a less extent of occupational dialects – have little contact with Standard English, written or spoken, and therefore words from these dialects are introduced through the written language rather than directly through the speech of natural dialect-speakers.

The words introduced fall into three classes: words which are falling out of use in the standard language, and are strengthened by their use in regional contexts; words which were never in the standard language, or have long ago been lost, and are introduced from the dialects; new coinings in the dialects, to meet new conditions which, from being local, became general throughout the country.

Compared with the freshness and vigour of dialects, our standard speech is faded, and it is a good thing that men of letters should take words from the rustic and unlettered speech of their neighbours in areas where regional dialect is strong, and with them regenerate the tired and overworked standard vocabulary. The regional dialects have been hard-pressed since the passing of the Education Act of 1870, and many teachers have fought hard to eradicate dialect, though they have succeeded only in making the children bilingual. Radio and the 'talkies' also bring a new speech to the dialect-speaker, and all are having their influence, but the loss of dialects would also be a serious loss to the literary language, for many of our most picturesque and romantic words have fought their way up from the dialects.

Most of the words which have found a place in our standard vocabulary seem to have come from northern dialects, including Scottish, and Sir William Craigie[9] has listed more than a hundred northern words, adopted chiefly in the last two hundred years, and he divides them into three main groups, those dealing with natural features, those describing northern life and customs, and supernatural words. Among them we may note the following words, all now familiar in the standard language: *beck, fell, force, gill* or *ghyll, glen, tarn; bracken, heather, ling, rowan; bothy, shiel* or *shieling; cairn, reel; kilt, plaid, tartan; claymore; bard, clan, cateran, slogan; kipper, scone; bogle, brownie, eerie, warlock, weird, wraith;* and *whisky, wee, canny,* and *bonny.*

Words have, of course, come into the vocabulary from other areas; *clever* is usually considered to have been first an East Anglian word, and *trolley* was adopted in the nineteenth century from the Suffolk dialect. Shakespeare used words apparently from his own Warwickshire dialect, some of which have found their way into the standard vocabulary, and last century Barnes made an attempt to introduce Dorset words. Many of our writers have used regional dialect words, generally for the sake of atmosphere, but to attempt a list of such introductions is outside the scope of the present book. The enrichment of vocabulary by this means is, of course, still going on, and not many years ago Bridges examined dialect words introduced into the poems of Edmund Blunden. There are still many dialect words one would wish to see in more general use, such as *bairn*, *fain*, and *speer*, and Pearsall Smith made a plea some years ago for the introduction of such words; 'There are many excellent words spoken in uneducated speech and dialect all about us, which would be valuable additions to our standard vocabulary if they could be given currency in it. Many of these are dying words like *bide*, *dight*, *blithe*, *malison*, *vengeance*, and since these are still spoken in other classes, it might be less difficult to restore them to educated speech. Others are old words like *thole* and *nesh* and *lew* and *mense* and *foison* and *fash* and *douce*, which have never been accepted into the standard English, or have long since vanished from it, in spite of their excellence and ancient history, and in spite of the fact that they have long been in current use in various districts. Others are new formations, coined in the ever-active mint of uneducated speech, and many of these, coming as they do full of freshness and vigour out of the vivid popular imagination – words like *harum-scarum*, *gallivant*, *cantankerous* and *pernickety* – or useful monosyllables and penny pieces of popular speech like *blight* and *nag* and *fun* – have already found their way into standard English'.[10]

The purist attitude towards vocabulary that we have noted in the eighteenth century continued into the following century. An anonymous book, *The Vulgarities of Speech Corrected*, which appeared in 1826, contained several lists of words which the author considered should be avoided. Included among these is a list of commercial terms such as we might find held up in modern books as examples to be avoided. Landor was one of the leading spirits of purism: some of his objections, such as to the use of *execute* in the sense of 'put to death', were based on etymology and the original sense of the word, and he paid little attention to established usage. Macaulay also objected to several words in common use, including *gentlemanly*, *influential*, and *talented*, all of which have survived his attack. Indeed, at this time, so strong was the feeling in certain quarters that any new word was sure to be carefully scrutinized before being accepted, and very many words, both new and well-established, which we have in common use, were subject to fierce criticism.

Two minor points of interest in connection with the development of vocabulary in the nineteenth century may be noted, both unimportant in their effects, but worthy of attention in that they show some of the tendencies of the time, the reflection of Victorian prudery, and the cult of Anglo-Saxon diction. One word may aptly serve as an introduction to the first topic, the adjective *improper*, as applied to people, and a certain aspect of their behaviour. Euphemisms were used for any word thought to be at all improper or suggestive; *leg* was too natural, and *limb* was preferred, and *nude* or *undraped* somehow seemed less suggestive than *naked*. A striking feature of twentieth-century English, however, is an almost complete absence of this attitude to language. Perhaps the spread of scientific knowledge has introduced an air of realism rather than romance or mystery. Physical facts are no longer avoided, and the euphemisms formerly used to avoid direct mention of such things have given way to a stark realism in language which can sometimes pull us up with a jerk, since we have again turned to words once rejected because they were coarse or brutal. We have an apt comment on this present-day tendency in the story told by J. W. Clark to illustrate this point, referring specifically to the fact that *bitch* 'is today pretty generally inoffensive'; he adds: 'This is true despite the young woman, or, as she would say, lady, that I heard of not long ago, who blushed on a distinguished professor's uttering the word to her of the mother of some pups they were looking at, and then said she didn't really mind at all – it was only that she had never before heard the word applied to a dog'.[11]

The second, the craze for replacing foreign words by native terms, and even coining new words from native elements when the words did not already exist, is connected at least in part with the Romantic Revival at the beginning of the nineteenth century, and the consequent interest in the language of the mediaeval past. Scott preferred *leechcraft* to *medicine*, as the art of healing, going right back to the Anglo-Saxon for his word, for the same compound is recorded in that period, and Morris also used the word. *Preface* was well established in the language, but an attempt was made to replace it by *foreword*, and later Belloc writes 'what Anglo-Saxons call a foreword, but gentlemen a preface'. *Folk-lore* was used to replace *mythology*, and Barnes named his English grammar *Speechcraft of the English Tongue;* in this work he achieves the extreme in *markward of suchness* for 'adjective'; yet one cannot but feel that *folkwain* is more expressive than *omnibus*, if we allow for the familiarity of the latter. But the feeling of the language was now against this type of formation, for since the influence of French and Latin had been so strong English had lost its old facility for coining, compounding, and the use of native material to meet new conditions, and such words were looked upon as the foibles of cranks. Jespersen describes at some length the difficulty experienced in the nineteenth century in

reintroducing OE *handbōc*, after it had been replaced in Middle English
by the French or Latin loan which yields NE *manual*, citing Rogers,
who 'speaks of the word as a tasteless innovation', and quoting Trench:
'we might have been satisfied with "manual", and not put together
that very ugly and very unnecessary word "handbook", which is
scarcely, I should suppose, ten or fifteen years old'. Jespersen notes that
handbook has become more popular in recent years, but concludes, 'I
cannot help thinking that state of language a very unnatural one where
such a very simple, intelligible, and expressive word has to fight its
way instead of being at once admitted to the very best society'.[12] Here,
then, we have the two aspects of Anglo-Saxon diction, a subject to
which we shall return in the next chapter, but Jespersen sees the heart
of the matter, surely, in his 'simple, intelligible, and expressive': *folkwain*
meets all these conditions, and is self-explanatory, which *bus* certainly
is not, *handbook* must mean more than *manual* to the non-Latinist, and
even for the Latinist 'book' is merely implied, but one can hardly argue
for *markward of suchness;* it may be easily intelligible, though that can
be questioned, it is certainly not simple, or expressive, and, moreover,
fails on the score of convenience.

     We may conclude this chapter with a brief investigation of some of
the most recent trends. It is not proposed to deal with modern innova-
tions at great length, for it has been the purpose of our study to confine
our attention to words which have been accepted in the standard
vocabulary. Thousands of words have made their way into our language
in the present century, but we can not be sure how many of these will
find a permanent home. Yet we can hardly conclude our study of the
development of vocabulary in the Victorian period. All too often the
charge is made that the teaching of the history of the English language
usually finishes with Chaucer. That charge has become less and less
based on fact in recent years, when the development of our language
after the fifteenth century has received great attention, and, although we
may perhaps stand too close to twentieth-century English to pass judgement upon it, we may at least examine some of its tendencies, if only
briefly, in the very limited space here left to us.

     An outstanding feature of the last fifty or hundred years has been the
rapid expansion of vocabulary, paralleled in our language only in the
period following the Renaissance. Kipling has commented on this
similarity: 'The Elizabethans stood on the edge of a new and wonderful
world filled with happy possibilities. Their descendants, three hundred
and fifty years later, have been shot into a world as new and as wonderful, but not as happy; and, in both ages, you can see writers raking the
dumps of the English language for words that shall range further, hit

harder, and explode over a greater area than the service-pattern words in common use'[13]. There are points of resemblance between the two periods. In both cases the expansion of vocabulary followed a great expansion in knowledge, of classical knowledge and knowledge of new countries and peoples in the earlier period, and in our own times of scientific knowledge, using the word in its widest sense.

One of the most important aspects of twentieth-century vocabulary – the rapid extension of scientific vocabulary in recent times – has already been dealt with, but a feature of this has been the spread of what we may call semi-scientific words to general aspects of life, usually abstract conceptions; this is particularly noticeable in a group of words all of which end in -ize, and many of which have also a secondary form, generally with change of meaning, beginning with de-; there are usually two forms at least, the verb in -ize and the corresponding abstract noun in -ization. Forms of this kind are not all very recent; Bentham, for example, used minimize, but there is a great increase in such forms in the nineteenth century, and the process continues today. The forms are often deceptive; actualize might strike a reader as being very recent, but it was used by Coleridge a hundred and fifty years ago. Among examples we may note scientific words, which are to be expected, as carbonize, a term in the woollen trade, and decarbonize, recognizable chiefly as a motoring term, decolourize, dehydrogenize, dehypnotize, demagnetize, deoxidize, and depolarize; demonetize still belongs only to the world of economics; deodorize and devitalize have spread from science to a more general application; among more general terms we have decentralize, decivilize, dehumanize, demobilize, denationalize, denaturalize; some forms seem unnecessary, and some are ugly, as dechristianize, depauperize, and desynonymize, though this last example will be used in the next chapter. The only argument in favour of some of these forms is that they allow us to do in one word what would otherwise require three or four, and that seems to be a great virtue in the modern world.

Two other groups of words, originally scientific, but which have spread into the common vocabulary, both show developments of modern science. One of the recent aims of the scientist has been to replace human labour by the efforts of the machine, and this is reflected in our vocabulary by a number of recent words with the prefix auto-, and of newly-formed compounds with the first element automatic. In the latter case the word has even changed its function, for we now rarely speak of an automatic-pistol, but merely of an automatic. One of the latest examples, a trade name, reverses the process, for Agamatic is presumably Aga automatic; but one must admit the un-English position of the adjective has produced a better compound. Similarly, man's conquest of space, and his ability to perform certain actions over long distances, is shown in the large number of words containing the prefix *tele-*.

We have not concerned ourselves much here with semantic change, but have been content to record the mere presence or appearance of words. The change in meaning of a word is obviously of great importance, and has sometimes been touched upon here, but a subject so wide and important as this deserves to be examined on its own, and not dealt with briefly, which is all that would be possible here. One aspect, however, has become increasingly important in recent times, and deserves mention. The development may be partly due to one type of journalism, and the desire for emphasis and sensation, though examples are to be found long before the days of the popular press. In the search for emphasis words are dragged into contexts for which they are really far too powerful, and, as a result of over-use to describe unimportant affairs, they soon lose much of their original force and tend to become mere intensives, later losing all their original meaning. The once-powerful words *awful* and *appalling* had already lost much of their original meaning early in the nineteenth century, and were on the way to being used as mere intensives. Before the end of the century *astounding*, *dreadful*, *ghastly*, and *tremendous* had followed in the same path. Today *terrible* and *horrible* can be applied to the most trivial objects or ideas, and *sensation* and *crisis* have been so overworked by the press that they have lost all their meaning for us. So strong has been the tendency to use violent imagery to excite sensation that the very power of these images to effect this has gradually been lost. Every minor misfortune is a *tragedy*, *epic* is used in contexts undeserving of the original meaning of the adjective, and anything at all out of the common is *dramatic*. We often hear today of the difficulty of making the average man understand the gravity of a situation, but that is only to be expected when all the words which could be used to put over the idea have been used for minor incidents; one wonders what word the popular press would require now in place of *crisis* if they were really compelled to bring out the difference between their earlier 'crises' and a life-and-death matter.[14] Our only consolation is that this is not new, for Chesterfield, two hundred years ago, wrote: 'Not content with enriching our language by words absolutely new, my fair country-women have gone still further, and improved it by the application and extension of old ones to various and very different significations. They take a word and change it, like a guinea into shillings for pocket-money, to be employed in the several occasional purposes of the day. For instance, the adjective *vast*, and its adverb *vastly*, mean anything, and are the fashionable words of the most fashionable people. A fine woman, under this head I comprehend all fine gentlemen too, not knowing in truth where to place them properly, is *vastly* obliged, or *vastly* offended, *vastly* glad, or *vastly* sorry. Large objects are *vastly* great, small ones are *vastly* little; and I had lately the pleasure to hear a fine woman pronounce, by a happy metonymy, a very small gold snuff-box that was produced in company to be *vastly* pretty, because it was *vastly* little'.[15] The difference today is that the habit has passed from a small class of people to a powerful force for good or evil in our language.

In other ways, too, journalism is a much more powerful force now than it was earlier. Its power becomes apparent with the rise of the popular press in the nineteenth century. In the effort to be interesting, newspaper-writers make use of colloquial expressions, and so present to a wide public words and phrases which otherwise would have been limited in use. Thus they bring slang and colloquial expressions into regular use, for to many people the authority of the popular press equals that of any dictionary or academy. Further, not only do they pass on such forms, but many of their writers, especially the slick columnists of American papers and magazines – and we have already seen how that influence spreads to English publications – are extremely clever at coining new words; many of these, such as *newshawk*, *pulp magazine*, and *tabloid magazine*, are unlikely to find a permanent place in the language, but there can be no doubt that we owe a great deal of our colloquial vocabulary to journalism.

In an earlier chapter we considered the development of scientific language chiefly as a technical vocabulary, but we may here take note of the increasing tendency for many of these words to pass from the vocabulary of the specialist into our common vocabulary as science becomes more and more popularized, and its achievements more and more familiar. In psychology far too many people speak regularly of *complexes* and *fixations* without understanding the words,[16] but technical words of some of the sciences touching life more nearly are both used and understood. *Vaccination* has long been in common use, and the modern mother is equally familiar with *immunization;* we speak frequently now of our *glands*, and their purposes; *iodine* and *aspirin* have long been household words, and, thanks to increasing knowledge of the work of doctors, the names of such drugs as 'M and B' and *phenobarbitone* are increasingly becoming part of our normal vocabulary. There are few people nowadays who have not some idea of *vitamins*, and many more use the word frequently, *calories* have made their way from the physics laboratory to the kitchen, and, while the adjective *allergic* is not always understood, it is certainly widely used. The housewife and the motorist are equally familiar with *benzine*, most

L

of us use *creosote* for one purpose or another, the *dynamo*, being no longer a mystery to the layman, has also enriched his vocabulary, sometimes figuratively, as at Dunkirk, and the motorist both understands and uses *magneto*. *Radio*, as a name for the wireless set and the broadcasting service generally, is on everybody's lips, and, as a prefix, in ordinary speech, trade names, and advertisements, is extremely popular, though in some contexts it is perhaps now yielding to the later development; certainly *atomic* seems to be applied to many things with which the nuclear physicist would not connect the word.

Popular adaptations of science tend to gather around themselves their own particular vocabulary, sometimes scientific words pure and simple, sometimes ordinary words adapted to special uses, but, as with other scientific vocabulary, usage will vary. The enthusiastic short-wave amateur will use many more words connected with radio than will the ordinary listener, but we all of us use such words as *aerial, condenser, earth, frequency, lead-in, microphone, oscillate, output, speaker, 'super-het,' transformer, valve, wave-length* as part of our normal vocabulary, and quite naturally give a specialized meaning to some of the common words according to the context. A similar state of affairs is to be found among motorists, and one point to be noticed here is the number of words in everyday use which have come to be used with a restricted meaning; most of us today, even if not motorists, if asked by a motorist where the nearest *park* was, would certainly not send him anywhere but to a place where he could leave his car for an hour or two, and all of us are familiar with the special sense of *bumper, choke, clutch, knock, plug, radiator*, though some may use the words more frequently than others. The use of so many words already established in the language may be due to the fact that motoring has been popular from the beginning, for only in the earliest years was it confined to the specialist. Under such conditions we might expect the adaptation of existing words, where any likeness or connection could be perceived, as these would already be familiar to the wide range of people taking up motoring. The same state of affairs seems to have produced a similar result in the case of another popular amusement, the cinema, where *cartoon, film, reel*, and *screen* have acquired specialized meanings, but here there has also grown up a collection of new words, such as *close-up, fade-out, newsreel*, and many others, familiar to the majority of people, even if some make little use of them, for few people today are unaffected by the cinema.

Two world-wide wars, with the throwing together of English-speaking people from many parts of the world, and the introduction of many objects and ideas hitherto unfamiliar, have naturally affected our vocabulary in the last forty years. The influence has been exerted in two ways, by the adoption of words on the literary level, and also of words from soldiers' slang. Many of the former are words already established which came to have a specialized or restricted meaning. People in England automatically connect *raid* – the original *air-raid* soon came to be less and less used – with enemy aeroplanes, and the original sense of the word, and its connection with *ride*, fell into the background. (Those who write letters to the newspapers deploring the loose use of *ride* and *drive* today will see the point of a recent development of this word to criminal raids carried out in stolen motor-cars.) *Aeroplane* had usually the sense of military aircraft, fighters or bombers, and only slowly is the civilian *air-liner* restoring the old position. *Underground* developed a new sense in the occupied countries, as did the related French word, *maquis*, frequent in English in the last war. *Sector* was used in a limited military context, and *barrage* came to have a new meaning; originally it had the sense of an artificial obstruction placed to direct the course of a river, but in the 1914–18 war it was used to describe a curtain of artillery-fire to protect advancing troops on one's own side, or to prevent the advance of enemy troops. *Fraternize* developed a new sense in the last war, and there even arose from it the new forms *fratter* and *fratting*, though these have remained slang. A curious development was the use of *ace* to describe an airman who had proved consistently successful in single-handed fights with the enemy. Other words such as *gas-mask*, *war-bride*, and the later *G.I. bride*, were new formations called into being by new conditions, as is also *gremlin*, perhaps, though this is rather a slang term.

Two German words, *kultur* and *strafe*, adopted in the 1914–18 war, had a very short life afterwards, and such forms as *blitzkrieg* – and the new verb *to blitz* – and *ersatz*, adopted in the last war, may not last much longer, though some signs of longer life are perhaps to be seen in the case of the verb *to blitz*, which has recently been used in other contexts. *Ersatz*, with the same basic sense of 'substitute, temporary', was adopted in the 1914–18 war, but used of different objects and ideas, but it fell completely out of use between the wars, only to be revived by the German use of substitutes for important articles of food in the last war. *Lebensraum* and *Weltpolitik* came into English for a time, but seem as little likely to survive as the German form *Kamerad*, popular in the first war, and such coinages as the verb *to coventrate* will obviously not last. *Fifth-columnist* has already penetrated into some dictionaries, and this word, and the closely-related *quisling*, may survive, as they are convenient, expressive, and meet a need, and similarly *camouflage*, adopted with an extension of meaning in the 1914–18 war, has developed so many secondary and figurative senses that it seems likely to survive.

CHAPTER TEN

★

PROFIT AND LOSS

What of the position of the English vocabulary today? In the sixteenth century Cheke wrote of the English language and its tendency to borrow words from other languages: 'if we take not heed by tijm, ever borowing and never paying, she shall be fain to keep her house as a bankrupt'. We have certainly continued to borrow; is English richer or poorer as a result?

The survey we have just completed brings out one undeniable fact, the enormous increase in the vocabulary of English in the last fifteen hundred years. Our vocabulary is much richer than the vocabulary of, for example, two other leading languages, French and German, and this has arisen chiefly because English has been prepared to accept words from almost every language with which her people have come into contact, whereas French has been restricted by the regulations of the Académie Française, and German by the tendency of the people to rely on native material rather than on loan-words, a tendency inherited from the time of common Germanic. The attitude of English is well summed up by Dryden: 'I trade both with the living and the dead for the enrichment of our native language'. Yet, although these loan-words have been the chief factor in the enrichment of our vocabulary, it would be a mistake to consider them as the only factor. Admittedly, the language lost much of its old power to create new words from native material after the Norman Conquest, yet the power was never completely lost, and, as we saw in the chapter on Word-Formation, compounding and derivation are still active processes, and from time to time there have been movements which sought deliberately to reduce the number of loan-words by replacing them by native material.

Yet, in comparing English, French, and German, we may indeed ask if mere number of words is in itself an advantage. Johnson referred to the 'copious vagueness' of English, a point to which we shall return, and Selden comments, 'we have more words than notions, half a dozen words for the same thing'. It is not merely the number of words in a language which gives that language a rich vocabulary, but rather the ability of that wealth of words to express a wealth of ideas. Words are useful only in so far as they can be used efficiently to express ideas. Our final task here is to see if, alongside the development in vocabulary, there has also been a development of the power of expression.

The question we must ask ourselves, then, is whether English is a better instrument for the expression of ideas now, as a composite language, than it would have been had it been content to rely on native material, as it did so largely in the Old English period, and as some Germanic languages have done consistently since. This question may lead us to a discussion on purity in language, and perhaps to the further question of whether or not Pure English is a worthwhile ideal, even if it could be achieved. We shall not concern ourselves with the long-drawn-out discussion of the abstract principles of linguistic purity further than to note some of the main arguments which have been put forward. The purists claim that there is in native words a tradition which can not be found in foreign words, that the tendency to borrow is merely a sign of decadence and mental laziness, and shows a lack of imagination, that very often the words are used only through a feeling of superiority in being acquainted with another language, and, perhaps most important, there is a serious objection to such borrowing in that many people are unable to understand the new words. Against that we may set the very cogent argument that no great languages are absolutely pure, and one can hardly imagine a perfectly pure language under modern conditions. It has also been pointed out that the demand for linguistic purity is often allied to a belief in racial purity, although there are today probably no pure races, and that it is strongest among certain people who wish to remove the taint of political domination; in other words, that linguistic independence often arises from a desire for political independence, or a desire to forget earlier political dependence. Finally, since civilization is international, even supranational, it is felt that there should be free exchange of words used to denote the major benefits of civilization, according to the language of their country of origin. This is, of course, the first step towards an international language, which could be the final result of large-scale mixing of national languages.

As we have seen, there have been periods in the history of English when the feeling for purity of language has been strong. The Anglo-Saxons showed a strong preference for the native word, and, although Middle English preferred to borrow, there was a strong reaction to this attitude in the Renaissance period, when the purists opposed the introduction of 'inkhorn' terms. The linguistic licence of Elizabethan times was followed by a further reaction in favour of purity in the eighteenth century. There was a cult of Anglo-Saxon diction in the nineteenth century, and its followers tried to replace loan-words by native forms.

The movement is not dead even today, for there are still teachers who drill their pupils in a blind preference for the Anglo-Saxon word, no matter how expressive its foreign synonym may be, or, more moderately, to prefer the native word, other things being equal. But other things rarely are absolutely equal, and the advice of Hazlitt, 'the best word in common use', irrespective of origin, should be preferred. The native word is often shorter, pithier, more expressive, but to follow blindly the dictates of the purists is as bad as to go to the other extreme and write an artificial, Latinized language such as we find in the seventeenth and eighteenth centuries.

The general opinion is that English is better for all this borrowing, but whether this is so or not is difficult to determine. The answer can be found, if at all, only by an analysis of the powers of the language at different periods, in order to show whether or not there has been a gain in convenience, whether or not the language is better able to express new ideas as they arise. The starting-point of such an analysis must obviously be Old English. One of the main purposes of the chapter on the language of the Anglo-Saxons was to show that their language was fully equal to all the demands they could reasonably make upon it. The vocabulary was sufficient for all the activities of life for which we have evidence, their love of fighting, admiration for personal bravery and prowess in battle, the simple emotions of a primitive people, the virtues and ideals of such a people, their social life, centred chiefly around the comitatus and fellowship in the hall. They were also well supplied with words describing the natural features of their country, and for the organization of the land on the simple lines which sufficed for them. If that were all it would perhaps be sufficient, yet we have already seen that when these people came into contact with quite unfamiliar ideas, as a result of the impact of Christianity and Mediterranean civilization upon a race hitherto heathen and barbarian, they were able to adapt their own language to express most of these ideas. We may, therefore, go a long way towards agreeing with Jespersen's opinion that, left to its own devices, the language might well have been able to cope with the new ideas as they presented themselves, just as German has done. The remarkable capacity of early English for compounding and derivation might indeed have sufficed for all the demands which were later to be made upon the language; yet we must bear in mind one point already raised, the desirability of separating scientific and technical vocabulary from that in everyday use. If, however, we admit that this is a specialized vocabulary, we may still think that the native material might perhaps have sufficed for all ordinary purposes. If it be argued that to remove all loan-words from our present vocabulary would leave wide gaps, and

that therefore many ideas could not be expressed because we should
have no words for them, the answer is obvious: those gaps were filled,
as they arose, with foreign borrowings only because, as a result of
French influence on our language after the Norman Conquest, we had
lost much of the old facility to form new words, and this tendency to
borrow was reinforced later by the wide knowledge of Latin and the
universal use of that language for scholarship. It is by no means certain
that the gaps would not have been filled by native words had this
power not been lost by disuse.

Before discussing the question further, however, we ought to examine
these loan-words to see if we can differentiate between them. In an
early chapter it was emphasized that all words of foreign origin were to
be regarded as loans, no matter how well they might be established in
the language, but now that we are considering the question from the
point of view of improvement of the language, and as the question of
the type of word will arise, and the difference between native and
foreign words, we should bear in mind that the earliest Latin, Scandinavian, and French words have been so well assimilated that they seem
to be almost as English as the native words – for the ordinary man there
is a great deal of difference between such words as *mile*, *ounce*, *law*, *face*,
and *beef* on the one hand, and *hypochondriac*, *orthodontics*, and *schizo-
phrenia* on the other – and often the early loans are as short, expressive,
and convenient as the native words. There is, then, a difference between
the two types of loan-words, and the position of the former group lies
perhaps midway between that of the original native word and the easily-
recognized loan-word of later times, so that there is perhaps not the
wide gulf between native word and loan-word, the hard and fast
division into two sharply-differentiated types, that might be expected.
We have indeed, in the ultimate analysis, native words and borrowed
words, but it would seem that, apart from actual origin, there is a good
deal in common between some of the loan-words and our native words.
This has been recognized from the very beginning of the purist reaction
against loan-words, for very rarely has there been objection raised to
these earlier, well-assimilated loan-words, especially from Scandinavian
and French, but only to the later, longer, usually learned borrowings.

Another point must also be borne in mind in discussing the effect of
all this borrowing on our language. If we are to base our reasoning on a
study of the forms recorded in the dictionary it is very easy to overestimate the effect of the foreign words. The actual number of native
words in any of our large standard dictionaries is extremely small compared with the number of foreign borrowings recorded, and even if we
were to confine our examination to those words in common use we

should still find the native material outnumbered by about four to one. On the other hand, if we were to take a piece of English written on the popular level, or, better still, a passage of familiar conversation, we should find the proportions about reversed. It has been estimated that less than fifty words, all of them native words, suffice for more than half our needs, if we count every word used, including repetitions. The proportion of native words to foreign will naturally vary with the subject-matter, and a present-day article on some aspect of scientific knowledge would naturally contain a higher proportion of loan-words than, say, a simple essay on a walk through the countryside, yet even in the scientific article the native words would probably outnumber the borrowings, if each word is counted every time it is used. Emerson, quoting from George P. Marsh's *Lectures on the English Poets*, notes that, on such a count, Shakespeare has only ten per cent of borrowed words, Milton nineteen per cent, Johnson twenty-eight per cent, Gibbon thirty per cent, Tennyson twelve per cent, and the Bible (basing the count on three Gospels only) has no more than six per cent.[1] We see, therefore, how important for all purposes is the comparatively small nucleus of native words.

Since the general opinion is that English has, in the main, benefited from the adoption of so many foreign loan-words, the advantages which have accrued from the use of these borrowings may be taken first, and the obvious one is the wealth of synonyms which have been created by the adoption of a foreign word – in some cases, words, from more than one foreign language – to express an idea for which English already had a word. Some of these are what we may call perfect synonyms, those in which it is very difficult to detect any difference at all in the meaning; others are not quite so exact, and there is some differentiation, though perhaps only in usage; a third group shows marked differences within the same basic idea, differences which arise from desynonymization, a process which we might expect to take place in any language which possesses several words for the same idea. It may be useful for the writer concerned with style to have available a number of synonyms or approximate synonyms, but a multiplicity of such words might even become inconvenient in ordinary language, since it will call for a careful choice between words where none need be made if the language were not so rich. Under these conditions we find that there is a tendency for the words to diverge somewhat in meaning, while still retaining the original basic idea, and the result of this is extremely advantageous, for the language is thereby enabled to express subtle differences in the same thought. Sometimes the differentiation may go no further than the use of a particular word in one context and its approximate synonym in another; there is really no difference in the ideas expressed by *begin*, *commence* and *start*, and yet the practised writer feels instinctively that one of these words 'belongs' in a particular passage, and that the other two could not be used there. Other pairs of this type, where the differentiation is one of usage rather than actual meaning, are *bloom* and *flower*, *buy* and *purchase*, *luck* and *fortune*, *work* and *labour*, the native word being here placed first in each case.

Sometimes the difference may be an emotional one, perhaps because the native word is closer to the spirit and tradition of the language. As a result of this the associations are deeper, simpler, and the word is more expressive, more powerful emotionally. There is often a coldness and aloofness about the borrowed word, even when it is used to express a feeling in which we might expect such qualities to be lacking. *Charity* is a fine word, and can be used with great effect, as in the famous passage in St Paul's Epistle to the Corinthians, but it does not possess for us the warmth and friendliness of *love*, and in more recent times the meaning of *charity* has moved even further from that of *love*, so that it has become somewhat impersonal, and not far removed from what we now call Public Assistance; indeed, in the later nineteenth and early twentieth centuries, as regard for the welfare of the poor passed from the individual to the Board of Guardians, the word *charity* was used for the help dispensed by the Relieving Officer, as in the expression 'living on charity'. We can be quite sure that *love* could never have been used in that context. Emotional difference is to be seen also in *happiness* and *felicity*, *friendly* and *amicable*, *lonely* and *solitary*, perhaps in *wretched* and *miserable*, *fellow-feeling* has not the same sense as the Latin loan *compassion* or the Greek loan *sympathy*, and the simplicity attached to the native word may be seen in *house* and *mansion*, and even more particularly in *stool* and *throne*, where there has been a remarkable divergence. In Old English the symbol of kingly authority was *cyne-stōl*, literally the king-stool, but a *stool* is now a very humble seat, far removed from the king's *throne* (this latter word being a loan from Greek, through Latin), and not even to be compared with the French loan, *chair*.

We may now consider examples, again confining ourselves to pairs comprising a native word and a loan-word, in which there has been an appreciable divergence of meaning. If we use the adjective *boyish* of some action it implies rather approval, in a friendly manner, than condemnation, as when we refer to 'a boyish escapade', something mischievous, but no more than that. If, however, we describe an action as *puerile* the attitude we have adopted towards it is a very different one. Although we shall, for the time being, confine ourselves to pairs of words, it may be noted here in passing that a third word, also a native

L*

word, *childish*, belongs in this group, again with a difference of meaning, and occupying a position midway between the others, not so
derogatory as puerile, not so tolerant as boyish, and yet not having
quite the sense of either. It would be a mere waste of time to give here
a lengthy list of such pairs, for they spring at once to the mind, yet a
few may be quoted to illustrate the point: among pairs in very common
use we may note *brotherly* and *fraternal, fatherly* and *paternal, hearty* and
cordial, heavenly and *celestial, lively* and *vivacious, motherly* and *maternal,
murder* and *homicide, shepherd* and *pastor, timely* and *temporal.* Sometimes
we may extend the differentiation so as to include three or more words,
such as *kingly, royal,* and *regal,* all expressing one basic idea, but each
also expressing a different aspect of it. Among groups of four we may
note *earthen, earthly,* and *earthy,* all from the native word, and all with
different meanings, and also the loan-word *terrestrial,* or we may compare the different senses of *male, manly, mannish,* and *masculine,* or
female, feminine, womanish, and *womanly;* here we may note particularly
the wide difference in meaning between the native words *manly* and
mannish, womanly and *womanish.*

We have already noted that differentiation is not only between
native word and loan-word; different senses, as we saw, developed
from one root in *earthen, earthly,* and *earthy,* to take a native example,
or *royal* and *regal,* to take loan-words. The last pair shows us another
type of synonym, where the form of one word borrowed from a particular language may differ from that borrowed from the same root in the
same language at a different time. *Ward* and *guard* are obviously connected in sense, though their meanings are not identical today, and the
difference in form arises from the fact that the words were borrowed
from different French dialects at different times. *Warden* and *guardian*
provide another example, but in the case of *warranty* and *guarantee* the
divergence in meaning has not been so pronounced. French, as we have
seen, is developed from Latin, so that if we borrow from both these
languages we are in effect borrowing from one language at different
periods; from the same root we have *royal,* adopted through French,
and *regal,* borrowed directly from Latin, with a difference in form
arising from borrowing at different periods, and also a distinct difference
in meaning. In a similar case we may note three forms, *legal,* direct from
Latin, *loyal,* through French, and the archaic and dialectal *leal,* also
through French. Or we may note *dish,* borrowed from Latin in the
Old English period, *desk,* borrowed in the Middle English period from
a Low Latin form, a later borrowing direct from Latin to give *disc,*
without the fronting of the final consonant which had taken place in
Old English, a straight-forward adoption of the Latin word itself, as a

technical term, *discus*, and an indirect borrowing, through Old French, represented in *dais;* there is an identity of meaning in all these forms, from the shape of the object represented by the original Latin form, though the individual meanings have diverged, particularly in the case of *desk* and *dais*. *Captive* has come to us direct from Latin, and *caitiff,* now archaic, is derived from the same word, but borrowed this time through French.

There can be little doubt that the ability to express such fine shades of meaning is a distinct advantage, for the English writer who really knows his own language need never be at a loss for a word to express exactly what he means; *le mot juste* is, in most cases, available to him, and his thoughts can be expressed with the greatest precision. But there is a pitfall in this very advantage; the clear and accurate thinker will use his words well, but few attain to a complete control over both thought and language, and any loose and inaccurate thinking will inevitably be revealed by a faulty choice from the wealth of words available; either the clear distinctions will be lost in the writings of such a man, careless choice tending to blur the sharp lines dividing one sense from another, or the words may even be used inaccurately, with a meaning or in a context not applicable to that particular word. There is, therefore, a disadvantage in the very richness of the vocabulary, for the greater the choice the greater the risk of error.

The claim is also made that Greek and Latin words and elements are so well known throughout the civilized world that they constitute almost an international language – the point has already been made in connection with the vocabulary of science – and that English must therefore have gained by the adoption of so much material understood in many other countries. In these modern times, when the world-wide dissemination of ideas is so easy, this is an advantage not to be taken lightly, but against that we must set the question of national convenience. After all, the main purpose of our language is to enable English-speaking people to express their thoughts to each other as accurately and conveniently as possible, not to make themselves understood by people who speak another language. If we wish to do that we must learn that language, or persuade all peoples to adopt an international language. Therefore, if it proves that the use of these internationally-understood words makes for less convenience in the use of English among English-speaking peoples, or increases the possibility of ambiguity or misunderstanding among them, it is by no means certain that the adoption of such words is an unmixed blessing. This statement, of course, applies only to the language of everyday life; technical language is, for our purpose here, a thing apart.

Against this question of universal intelligibility may be set that of the value of a Latinized vocabulary today. There is no doubt that the possession of such a vocabulary may be a great advantage to a man well grounded in the classical languages, but the study of these languages has shown a marked decline this century, and to a man who knows little or no Latin this type of vocabulary, far from being an advantage in expressing his thoughts clearly among his own people and making himself more easily understood abroad, may lead to the loose or even inaccurate use of words only half understood. Most people would perhaps like to command, at need, a Latinized style similar to that of Johnson and Gibbon, but we must be warned by the many examples in English literature of the person who uses long words without understanding them; with our wealth of Latin words it is all too easy for a person who knows little or no Latin to resemble Dogberry, Mistress Quickly, or Mrs Malaprop, rather than the great writers just mentioned.

One of the complaints of the purists has always been that the tendency towards borrowing developed after the Norman Conquest has had the effect of diminishing the capacity to make use of the native material to hand. The truth of this cannot be denied, for the decline in compounding and derivation has been marked since the Middle English period, yet the power has not been completely lost, as we have already seen.

A further point arises here from the mention of purism and derivation. Not only must we consider native words on the one hand, and loan-words on the other, but we must also take into account the multitude of hybrids which have been formed, both from native root and foreign affix, and foreign root and native affix. There can be no question but that the formation of such hybrids has added tremendously to our stock of words. The attitude of the purist towards such formations, and the question of whether or not the language would have been as efficient, convenient, and (which perhaps counts for all too little these days) as beautiful in sound and form, has already been discussed in an earlier chapter, and the argument need not be repeated here.

A much more serious objection is that, as a result of the borrowing of learned words, there is often no visible and obvious connection between pairs of related words. This is particularly noticeable in the case of adjectives, for we have far more adjectives derived from loan-words than from native words. As a result of this it frequently happens that we have kept the native word as a noun, but used the foreign form for the adjective, and as a result there may be no similarity in either sound or form; as examples we may note *eye* and *ocular*, *mind* and *mental*, *moon* and *lunar*, *mouth* and *oral*, *sea* and *marine*, *son* and *filial*, *town* and *urban*, to choose only words in common use. There can be little doubt that such a wide difference between forms expressing related ideas is a source of difficulty to one unfamiliar with Latin.

It seems, then, that this very wealth of vocabulary may make English difficult. It is hardly an advantage that there is always present the danger of using words carelessly or inaccurately, of dignity or even pretentiousness when the subject does not call for it. Yet this can hardly be described as a fault if, as a result of the enrichment of the vocabulary, the language is really better in the hands of one who has taken the trouble to master it. Here we are not concerned with the question of the difficulty of English for foreigners, but rather with its use by English-speaking people. Convenience is obviously a factor in language at which we ought to aim, and if English can be made simpler without losing its powers of expression we should welcome such a change, but ease of usage is not the only consideration, otherwise we should be satisfied with monosyllabic forms and an almost complete absence of syntax.

To conclude, we may say that, in spite of Gill's statement in his *Logonomia Anglica* (1621) that English had been harmed more by the classical languages than by the ravages of either the Danes or the Normans, there can be little doubt that our vocabulary has been enriched, and that, in the hands of the master, the language is now a better instrument than it was fifteen hundred years ago, though it also presents more difficulties to the careless writer or speaker. Variety and precision are both available to us, but greater skill is required if they are to be achieved.

There is, perhaps, no better way of concluding this short discussion of the advantages and disadvantages which have resulted from this enrichment of the vocabulary from outside sources than by quoting what two eminent scholars, looking at the question from different viewpoints, have said. Pearsall Smith's opinion is as follows: 'These, then, are the two opposing ideals – nationalism in language, as against borrowing; a pure, as opposed to a mixed, language. To those for whom nationalism is the important thing in modern life, and who could wish that their own race should derive its language and thought from native sources, a "pure" language is the ideal form of speech; while those who regard the great inheritance of European culture as the element of most importance in civilization, will not regret the composite character of the English language, the happy marriage which it shows of North and South, or wish to deprive it of those foreign elements which go to make up its unparalleled richness and variety'.[2] Henry Bradley, after discussing what English owes to foreign tongues, concludes his chapter as follows: 'Against the sentimental purism that regards mixture in language as a sin which no gain in expressive power can atone for, it would be vain to attempt to argue. But if we are content to estimate the worth of a language by its efficiency in fulfilling the purposes for which language exists, we cannot reasonably deny that English has been immeasurably improved by its incorporation of alien elements. The slender vocabulary of Old English might, no doubt, have attained a great degree of copiousness purely by development of its native resources, without foreign aid; but, so far as we can see, the subtlety and varied force characteristic of modern English could never have been acquired by this means. It is true that our language is a difficult instrument to use with full effect, on account of its richness in those seeming synonyms which ignorant or careless writers employ without discrimination; but in skilled hands it is capable of a degree of precision and energy which can be equalled in few languages either ancient or modern'.[3]

With those words we may leave our study of the development of our vocabulary, confident that the story has been one of steady advance from its earliest days right up to the present time, when English yields pride of place to no other language in both the wealth and power of its vocabulary.

SELECT READING-LIST AND NOTES

A. GENERAL READING-LIST

The list which follows has been compiled for the benefit of the general reader and non-specialist. It consists of works which deal in whole or in part with the vocabulary of English. Many of the standard works of reference on the English Language are written in languages other than English, and these have not been included, since the ordinary reader will probably not wish to consult them. These standard works, and specialized studies of particular aspects of the subject, are, however, mentioned in the Notes which follow.

References will be made in the Notes to the works listed below by quoting the author's name, followed by initials, in parenthesis, indicating the title of the work.

(HEW)	BARFIELD, O.	*History in English Words*. Methuen, London.
(HEL)	BAUGH, A. C.	*A History of the English Language*. N.Y. and Routledge, London.
(ME)	BRADLEY, H.	*The Making of English*. Macmillan, London.
(HEL)	CLASSEN, E.	*Outlines of the History of the English language*. Macmillan, London.
(HEL)	EMERSON, O. F.	*The History of the English Language*. Macmillan, N.Y.
(WW)	GREENOUGH, J. B., and KITTREDGE, G. L.	*Words and their Ways in English Speech*. Macmillan, London.
(HEW)	GROOM, B.	*A Short History of English Words*. Macmillan, London.
(GS)	JESPERSEN, O.	*Growth and Structure of the English Language*. Blackwell, Oxford.
(MEM)	McKNIGHT, G. H.	*Modern English in the Making*. Appleton-Century, N.Y.
(WW)	PARTRIDGE, E.	*The World of Words*. Hamish Hamilton, London.
(BAE)	PARTRIDGE, E., and CLARK, J. W.	*British and American English since 1900*. Dakers London.
(OL)	POTTER, S.	*Our Language*. Penguin Books, London.
(DME)	ROBERTSON, S.	*The Development of Modern English*. Prentice-Hall, N.Y.
(GT)	SCHLAUCH, M.	*The Gift of Tongues*. Allen and Unwin, London.
(HFW)	SERJEANTSON, M. S.	*A History of Foreign Words in English*. Routledge and Kegan Paul, London.

(EL)	Sмiтн, L. P.	*The English Language.* O.U.P.
(HEL)	Toller, T. N.	*Outlines of the History of the English Language.* C.U.P.
(EL)	Weekley, E.	*The English Language.* Deutsch, London.
(EL)	Wrenn, C. L.	*The English Language.* Methuen, London.
(MMW)	Vallins, G. H.	*The Making and Meaning of Words.* A. and C. Black, London.

B. Notes and Special References

PREFACE

1. Partridge and Clark (BAE), p. 203.
2. Emerson (HEL), p. vii.

CHAPTER ONE

1. Jespersen (GS), §37.
2. Serjeantson (HFW), p. 6.
3. Bloomfield, L., *Language* (Allen and Unwin, London), p. 494.

CHAPTER TWO

1. Jespersen, O., *Language, Its Nature, Development and Origin* (Allen and Unwin), p. 374. This work will be referred to below as (Lang).
2. Jespersen (Lang), p. 375.
3. Jespersen (Lang), p. 379.
4. Jespersen (Lang), p. 367.
5. For discussions of Echoism and Sound Symbolism see Jespersen (Lang), Chapter XX, Bradley (ME), pp. 156–9, and Smith (EL), pp. 64–6. Some of the examples used in this section have been taken from these sources.
6. Jespersen (Lang), p. 396.
7. For a readable account of this process, with many illustrations, see Bradley (ME), pp. 128 ff. In Sweet, H., *New English Grammar* (O.U.P.), pp. 450–499 there is a full treatment of many native and foreign affixes.
8. Bradley (ME), p. 136.
9. Robertson (DME), p. 380.
10. Potter (OL), p. 88.
11. H. W. and F. G. Fowler, *The King's English* (O.U.P.), p. 32.
12. Fowler, *loc. cit.*, p. 51.
13. See the excellent discussion in Bradley (ME), pp. 111–128.
14. Sweet, *loc. cit.*, §68.
15. Bradley (ME), p. 115.
16. Sweet, *loc. cit.*, §440.
17. Sweet, *loc. cit.*, §1546.

18 Bradley (ME), p. 113.
19. Jespersen (GS), §157.
20. H. W. Fowler, *A Dictionary of Modern English Usage* (O.U.P.), p. 243; also *The King's English*, p. 284.
21. See Sweet, *loc. cit.*, §§889 ff.
22. See also the following: Louise Pound, *Blends, their Relation to English Word Formation* (*Anglistische Forschungen Heft* 42); Bergstrom, C. A., *On Blending of Synonymous or Cognate Expressions in English* (Lund, 1906); Wentworth, H., *Blend Words in English* (Ithaca, 1933).
23. Nonesuch edition (London, 1939), p. 678.
24. Jespersen (Lang), p. 312.
25. *American Speech VI* and subsequent lists in later numbers of this periodical.
26. See K. Senden, *Contribution to the Study of Elliptical Words in Modern English* (Upsala, 1904).
27. Jespersen (Lang), p. 169.
28. Schlauch (GT), p. 102.
29. Jespersen (Lang), p. 173. See also C. P. G. Scott, *English Words which have gained or lost an Initial Consonant by Attraction* (Trans. Amer. Phil. Assn. XXIII, pp. 179–305), and Partridge, E., *Articled Nouns* in *From Sanskrit to Brazil* (Hamish Hamilton, 1952), to whom I am indebted for some of the examples which follow.
30. Partridge, *loc. cit.*, p. 126.
31. *Englische Studien*, LXX, p. 117.
32. See Bradley (ME), p. 144 for a full discussion of this word.
33. For this example I am indebted to Robertson (DME), p. 382.
34. See Partridge, E., *Name into Word* (a dictionary), Greenough and Kittredge (WW), Chapter XXVI, and also Weekley, E., *Words and Names* (a study).
35. Greenough and Kittredge (WW), p. 288.
36. Schlauch (GT), p. 102.
37. A colleague notes: 'The worst offenders in the U.S.A. are -*burger* and -*teria*. I have seen *fishburger*, *cheeseburger*, and many others. I have also eaten at a coin-in-slot chop-suey place called a *chinamat* and could if I wished have washed my shirts in a *laundramat*.'

CHAPTER THREE

1. For an account of the chief families of languages see Bloomfield, L., *Language* (N.Y., 1933), Graff, W. L., *Language and Languages* (Appleton-Century, N.Y., 1932), Meillet, A., and Cohen, M., *Les Langues du Monde* (Paris, 1924), Partridge (WW), and Pei, M., *The World's Chief Languages* (N.Y. and London, 1949). The standard works on the Indo-European and Germanic languages are: Brugmann, K., and Delbruck, B., *Grundriss der*

11. Jespersen (GS), §138.
12. Savory, *loc. cit.* p. 47.
13. Savory, *loc. cit.* p. 52.
14. Savory, *loc. cit.* pp. 33 ff.
15. Savory, *loc. cit.* p. 72.
16. Savory, *loc. cit.* p. 75.
17. See, for further reference, Darwin, C. G., *Terminology in Physics* (S.P.E. Tract XLVIII), and Morton, W. C., *The Language of Anatomy* (S.P.E. Tract IX).

CHAPTER EIGHT

 1. Jespersen (GS), §152.
 2. See Bense, J. F., *A Dictionary of the Low-Dutch Element in the English Vocabulary* (The Hague), and Llewellyn, E. C., *The Influence of Low Dutch on the English Vocabulary* (*Publications of the Philological Society*, 1935).
 3. See also *The Debt of English to South America* in Partridge, E., *Here, There, and Everywhere* (Hamish Hamilton, 1950).
 4. Scott, C. P. G., *Malayan Words in English* (American Oriental Society, 1897).
 5. Morris, E. E., *Austral English: A Dictionary of Australian Words, Phrases, and Usages* (London, 1898), p. xii.
 6. Pettmann, C., *Africanderisms: A Glossary of South African Colloquial Words and Phrases and Other Names* (London, 1913), p. 15.
 7. The most recent general account of Commonwealth and American English is Partridge and Clark (BAE). This work contains a number of essays, each contributed by a scholar living in the particular country and therefore familiar with the most recent linguistic developments. These will be referred to individually below.
 8. See Sir Henry Yule and A. C. Burnell, *Hobson-Jobson* (Murray, London, 1903), S. Mathai, *The Position of English in India* (Partridge and Clark [BAE], p. 96), and R. C. Goffin, *Some Notes on Indian English* (S.P.E. Tract XLI).
 9. Serjeantson (HFW), p. 223.
10. The best and most up-to-date work on Australian English is Baker, S. J., *The Australian Language* (Sydney and London, 1945). See also Partridge, E., *Australian English* (BAE, p. 85), and Thomson, A. K., *A Supplementary Article upon Australian English* (BAE, p. 332).
11. Jespersen (GS), §157.
12. See Wall, A., *New Zealand English* (BAE, p. 90), and Orsman, H., *New Zealand English* (BAE, p. 93).
13. See Hooper, A. G., *English in South Africa* (BAE, p. 80).

14. The following authoritative works on American English should be consulted: Mencken, H. L., *The American Language* (N.Y., 1923 and supplements), and Krapp, G. P., *The English Language in America* (N.Y., 1936). See also Clark, J. W., *American English* (BAE, p. 203), and, for Canada, Priestley, F. E. L., *Canadian English* (BAE, p. 72).
15. Horwill, H. W., *A Dictionary of Modern American Usage* (O.U.P.), p. xxix. The Introduction to this work is recommended as a general survey of the field.
16. Weekley, E., *Adjectives – and Other Words* (Murray, London), p. 166.
17. Weekley, *loc. cit.*, p. 182.
18. Horwill, *loc. cit.*, p. xxi.

CHAPTER NINE

1. Cook, A. S., in *The Authorised Version and Its Influence* (CHEL, Vol. iv, p. 36).
2. See Bradley (ME), p. 221, for a full discussion of this point.
3. Serjeantson (HFW), p. 161.
4. See Mario Praz, *The Italian Element in English* (*Essays and Studies*, xv, p. 20).
5. *Tatler*, 28th September, 1710.
6. *Spectator*, 8th September, 1711.
7. Pearsall Smith (EL), p. 139.
8. Pearsall Smith (EL), p. 151.
9. S.P.E. Tract L, Northern Words in Modern English.
10. S.P.E. Tract III, A Few Practical Suggestions.
11. Partridge and Clark (BAE), p. 241.
12. Jespersen (GS), §47.
13. Weekley (EL), p. 109.
14. See also Ivor Brown, *A Word in Your Ear*, p. 17.
15. *The World*, No. 101, 5th December, 1754.
16. Ivor Brown, *loc. cit.*, p. 19.
17. See Partridge, E., in *War as a Word-Maker* [*Words at War: Words at Peace* (Muller)], p. 115.

CHAPTER TEN

1. Emerson (HEL), p. 126.
2. Pearsall Smith (EL), p. 37.
3. Bradley (ME), p. 110.